Perspectives in Sociology

FOURTH EDITION

From its first edition in 1979, *Perspectives in Sociology* has provided generations of undergraduates with a clear, reassuring introduction to the complications of sociological theory. This fourth edition has been wholly rewritten and restructured. While retaining its wealth of information about the founding figures of sociology, it also includes much new material on contemporary social theory and particularly the challenge of sociology posed by the rise of poststructuralism with its questioning of the whole Enlightenment project.

New features include:

*   a concise introduction to the major debates of the twentieth century
*   information on thinkers of the nineteenth and early twentieth centuries whose relevance to modern social thought is only now being recognised, e.g. Nietzsche, Saussure and Freud
*   key debates placed in historical and philosophical context
*   connections drawn between poststructuralist thinkers like Foucault and Derrida and the founding figures of sociology: Marx, Weber and Durkheim
*   four wholly new chapters tracing developments in social theory from structuralism to postmodernism
*   new, easy to read format.

E.C. Cuff was formerly Head of the Department of Educational Studies at the Didsbury School of Education, Manchester Polytechnic; **W.W. Sharrock** is Professor of Sociology at Manchester University; **D.W. Francis** is Senior Lecturer in Sociology at Manchester Metropolitan University.

Perspectives in Sociology

FOURTH EDITION

■ E.C. Cuff, W.W. Sharrock
and D.W. Francis

LONDON AND NEW YORK

First edition published 1979
by Unwin Hyman Ltd
Third edition published in 1990

Fourth edition published
by Routledge
11 New Fetter Lane, London EC4P 4EE

Simultaneously published in the USA and
Canada
by Routledge
29 West 35th Street, New York, NY 10001

© 1998 E.C. Cuff, W.W. Sharrock and D.W.
Francis

Typeset in Janson and Futura by Keystroke,
Jacaranda Lodge, Wolverhampton
Printed and bound in Great Britain by
TJ International Ltd., Padstow, Cornwall

British Library Cataloguing in Publication Data
A catalogue record for this book is available
from the British Library

*Library of Congress Cataloging in Publication
Data*
Cuff, E.C.
   Perspectives in Sociology / E.C. Cuff,
   W.W. Sharrock, and D.W. Francis. — 4th
edn
      p. cm.
   Includes bibliographical references and
index.
   1. Sociology. 2. Sociology—History.
I. Sharrock, W.W. (Wes W.) II. Francis,
D.W. III. Title.
HM66.C84   1998
301—dc21   97–30113
                             CIP

ISBN 0–415–17371–X (hbk)
ISBN 0–415–15979–2 (pbk)

Contents

CONTENTS

Chapter 1

Introduction:
rethinking sociology

Once again, there is a sense of crisis in sociology, and realisation of the grand ambition that it should contribute to (if not play the key role in) a rational reconstruction of society for the benefit of all humanity now seems further away than ever. At the present time, there are even suspicions that the discipline has virtually put itself into liquidation.

Since we wrote the first edition of *Perspectives in Sociology* in 1979 there have been considerable changes in the nature of what goes on under the title 'sociology'. If sociology has not perhaps lost all point, then it has lost much of its distinctiveness. Indeed, within a number of different academic disciplines – including (to name but a few) linguistics, psychology, history, media, literary and cultural studies, and even archaeology – there is a pursuit of issues which would, once upon a time, have been dubbed 'socio-logical'. The substitution of the terms 'social theory' or 'cultural theory' for 'sociological theory' often marks the fact that discussion of things in terms of their social nature now goes on across many disciplines, and not just the academic branch called sociology. A better title for this fourth edition might, then, be *Perspectives in Social Theory*, for certainly some of the recent work we will review is done by philosophers rather than sociologists; this work has been intensely influential on sociology itself.

Many of the tendencies which have given rise to current developments were already present – at least in nascent form – when the first edition came out. At that time they were only marginal; now they have risen to a predominant status and have immense international and interdisciplinary influence. In order to give a proper account of these tendencies and some understanding of the philosophical and theoretical reasons for their significance, we need to recast the entire form of the book. The 'perspectives' described in the first and subsequent editions have by no means disappeared entirely from the sociological (or even wider intellectual) scene, but their importance in defining the issues at the forefront of contemporary debate has much diminished. They are still present in this book, but their place in the story is very different, and the manner in which they are presented has altered considerably. The need now is to give much greater presence to positions – particularly critical theory, structuralism and poststructuralism – which, though mentioned, were comparatively marginalised in earlier editions.

The current predominance of Continental or European social theory is the first main change which needs to be registered. During the immediate post-war period, up to the mid-1960s, Anglo-American sociological theory was confident that it was in the vanguard of social theory, and making large strides towards making sociology the rigorous science that it had long hoped to become. Though ready to acknowledge roots in European social thought – especially in the work of the great French theorist Emile Durkheim and the German Max Weber – the conviction was that Anglo-American theory was building upon these predecessors' thought and moving ahead.

The 1960s is notorious as a fateful decade. The outbreak of student dissidence in the USA as a reaction against the Vietnam war and the associated student disturbances in Europe, which reached their peak in the 'events' of May 1968 in Paris, changed things substantially in sociology. The mainstream of Anglo-American sociology was accused of intellectual complacency and political dishonesty in presenting as science what seemed in fact to be more of an ideological justification of business, the military and the state. There was a strong reaction against the idea that sociology should try to be a science. Accordingly, positions which advocated sociology as a soft rather than a scientifically hard discipline became temporarily popular, e.g. symbolic interaction and ethnomethodology.

The developments, resulting from the 1960s' reaction that were more decisive in bringing Anglo-American sociology to its present condition, however, were the attempts to *politicise* the discipline, to build up its capacity to criticise modern society. They involved the revaluation of, first of all, Marxism and, second, Continental social thought, especially the Marxist-influenced variety.

Marx is now routinely numbered amongst the three crucial founders of contemporary sociology, along with Durkheim and Weber, though earlier we did not mention his name together with the other two. By the early 1960's, it was widely argued that Marx's mode of analysis had become thoroughly outdated. Whatever merit there might have been in his teaching – and many held that there was not much – then his main doctrines (prophesying working-class revolution in the advanced industrial countries) had been falsified by the rise of the prosperous and politically quiescent societies of the Western post-war world. The disappointment with the sociological establishment led to a re-examination of Marx, who came to be seen as much more sophisticated and continuingly relevant than had hitherto been portrayed. Furthermore, outside the mainstream of sociology Marx's ideas had been elaborated and developed into a tradition of Western Marxism, which was based either in Europe or in the work of European thinkers exiled to the USA during the Nazi period.

The extent to which Marx's work implied criticism of science as a means of oppressive political and administrative power was one point which had been especially developed by the Western Marxist tradition. It gave that tradition special appeal to the new, critically minded generation of sociologists. The growing prestige of Western Marxism meant that European social thought began to be considered much more respectfully in Anglo-American sociology. Previously, it had been regarded with indifference, if not contempt.

The work of French Marxist philosopher Louis Althusser was particularly crucial in massively boosting the influence of European social thought in the UK and USA. Under the name of structuralism, the development of a new, apparently radically different conception of the human and social sciences was taking place in French, especially Parisian, thinking in the 1960s. This approach seemed to offer the prospect of a successfully scientific sociology, albeit in ways which no one would have expected. Althusser's work, identified as structural Marxism, seemed to combine very attractive features: (1) the prospect of an authentically scientific sociology, which (2) took an up-to-date Marxist form and (3) had strong political implications. The ensuing immense enthusiasm for, and controversy over, Althusser's work ensured that the exciting, fashionable, much-discussed work in sociology was increasingly of European origin.

Alongside enthusiasm for Althusser's 'structural Marxism' there developed a renewed concern with a number of Marxist thinkers of the inter-war period. This new interest in Western Marxism, whose history goes back to about the time of World War I and the Russian Revolution, heralded a profound shift towards the politicisation of sociology. Outright dismissals of Marx's work were based on an understanding of it as little more than a critique of the injustice of economic inequality in capitalist society. Yet the modern Western economies were no longer so nakedly exploitative as they were in the late nineteenth century, and the working class was not the militantly revolutionary force that Marx's theory required it to be. Western Marxism acknowledged and sought to come to terms with these facts. It argued that Marx's basic way of thought was not invalidated by these developments. Rethinking Marx's *method* would give tools for analysing the condition of contemporary society. Many different attempts at such rethinking were made in the years between the two great wars of 1914–18 and 1939–45, and most of them emphasised the need to develop Marx's theory more in the direction of the criticism of the *culture* of capitalist society. Capitalist society dominated and pacified the working class as much through control of the cultural sector as through its direct economic and political power. It was through ideological manipulation, by the shaping of the desires and beliefs of its members, that capitalism was able to persuade the vast mass of the population that they were happy and content, even though (in fact) the pleasures and rewards which life brought were shallow and inauthentic in comparison with those which might be had under an arrangement of life different to that allowed by capitalism.

Since this particular strand in Western Marxism has been most influential upon developments of sociology in the post-1960s period, we have therefore focused our treatment of the various approaches we consider below with respect to their implications for cultural analysis and critique. Thus we emphasise as a strong influence upon sociology the move from critique of economic inequality to that of cultural domination.

Even as Althusser's Marxism was enjoying its heyday in Anglo-American sociology, deep opposition to it was developing in its home base of Paris, where many young intellectuals were disillusioned by the political ineffectiveness of the Marxist intellectuals, including Althusser himself. This opposition was to embrace not merely Althusser, but also the entire school of structuralism with which he had been associated. This generation of thinkers – prominent amongst whom were Michel Foucault and Jacques Derrida – were just as critical of Western society and its traditions of social thought, but wanted to make their case without reliance upon Marx's doctrines. They were impressed by some aspects of structuralist thinking, but doubtful about other main parts of the approach; this mixture of acceptance and criticism of structuralism earned them the title of poststructuralists.

The manner of their reaction against, first, structuralism and, then, the idea of social *science* comprises the second main development which contributes to the reshaping of our book. The Western Marxist tradition and associated efforts at politicising sociology had led to a mode of thought wherein Western society was to be criticised predominantly for its ideological domination. The basic idea had been that social science was necessary to reveal the truth about society and to expose its ideological falsifications. This seemed wrong to the poststructuralists. The idea that knowledge is the basis for achieving freedom through the rational, science-based reorganisation of society seemed, itself, a particularly *ideological* conception. It had been bequeathed to the modern age from a previous period in Western thought, the so-called Enlightenment (usually dated to the eighteenth century), which thought that the vital thing was to free the capacities of human reason from the domination of authority (as wielded by the church and the state). Thus liberated reason could be used to obtain a true understanding of society in the same way as reason had gained understanding of nature, and could then be turned against traditional authority, using its knowledge to reorganise society in a way which would increase human freedom generally. The advocacy of the powers of reason owed much to a founding figure of modern philosophy, René Descartes (1596–1650; see Chapters 6 and 7), who also bequeathed to subsequent thought two other conceptions: (1) of the sharp separation of body and mind, of reason as a purely mental activity, and (2) of the immediate self-knowledge of mind and reason, i.e. that our mind consists of consciousness, which means that we are aware of, and therefore know, the contents of our own minds and understand the workings of Reason. Though mightily influential, these two notions have often been questioned, and severe attack upon them has been intensified in recent arguments.

This Enlightenment idea came to be seen as just part of the ideological structure of modern society, and the need to reveal this fact became the leading imperative: the critique of 'the Enlightenment project' (of bringing about universal human freedom through scientific knowledge) became the focus of attack, rather than capitalist society as such. Thus Marx's legacy to sociology has been reviewed a second time. He is nowadays seen by poststructuralists as *part* of the Enlightenment project, along with Durkheim. With poststructuralism the moment had arrived for sociology (along with science more generally) to have its technique of criticising ideology in the name of science turned upon itself. Sociology (and science more generally) were to be criticised as being, themselves, merely ideological. The idea of the social and human studies as science had been called into doubt previously, but in this latest phase it was to be treated to much greater and more intensive questioning than ever before. So much so, in fact, that the examination was often accused of offering only a kind of nihilism, i.e. a thoroughly negative rejection of current beliefs, making any kind of knowledge impossible and eliminating all hope for the use of theoretical knowledge for alleviating the human condition. The degree to which these poststructuralist conceptions seem to deny all possibility of genuine knowledge and, therefore, of science prefigures references to the uselessness and dissolution of sociology, thereby precipitating the recent talk of crisis. Our second main objective is to show how these profound doubts about the possibility of sociology in fact represent a continuation of sociology as it has been all along; they very much involve a turning of the long-established techniques of sociology for the criticism of ideology against sociology itself.

From everything we have said so far, it is clear that the story we have to tell can be told in a broadly chronological way. This is another significant difference between this book and previous editions, in which we interpreted the idea of sociological perspectives in an *atemporal* fashion. Of course, the chronological links between the ideas and approaches we now go on to discuss are complex and multi-faceted. Nevertheless, it is essentially correct to say that the shifts in theoretical thinking in sociology over the past thirty or so years have followed a definite, albeit loose, pattern.

Accordingly, this book is divided into four parts. In Part One we examine the classical nineteenth-century theorists, Marx, Weber and Durkheim. Part Two takes up the story early in the twentieth century and carries it through to the perspectives which became influential in Anglo-American sociology during the 1950s and 1960s. In Part Three we consider the thinking which inspired a new interest in European social theory, originating as early as the 1940s, but having its first main effects on Anglo-American sociology in the 1960s. Part Four deals with the more recent movements in European theory and some reactions against them. That this version of sociology's history is a reconstruction on our part goes without saying. It is a 'story'. But then, contemporary wisdom emphasises that *everything* is in the end just stories.

Part one

Chapter 2

Karl Marx

Introduction

The formative, decisively influential figures affecting, first, sociological theory and, now, social theory remain the trio of Karl Marx (1818–83), Max Weber (1864–1920) and Emile Durkheim (1858–1917). Though the first of these three has now – again – apparently fallen into eclipse, none the less Marx has had a decisive and continuing influence upon the development of sociological thought. Moreover his *method*, partly derived from G.W.F Hegel, continues to exercise extensive influence. So does the *problematic* which he played a main role in forming. Durkheim and Weber also, to different degrees, for different reasons and in varying ways, contribute key ideas to the contemporary configuration of social thought.

We begin with Marx, whose 'humanism' has provided, over the past three decades, such a bone of contention.

Was Marx a humanist?

The influence of Marx's ideas within social theory over the past thirty or so years has been enormous – not just upon avowed Marxists, but much more generally. It has shaped social thinking about fundamental issues to such an extent that the defining issues of contemporary theory are largely of Marxian origin. For example, a common central theme of recent theoretical discussion, which transcends a range of perspectives and approaches, concerns the role of cultural institutions in the analysis of contemporary industrial societies. While concepts and assumptions differ across the theoretical spectrum, there is broad consensus around the idea that cultural institutions – however conceived – have taken over the dominant position in society formerly occupied by strictly economic ones. Loosely speaking, then, the issue concerns the relationship between – using Marx's terms – the *base* and the *superstructure*. While we might now reverse the relationship between them which Marx posited and recognise cultural institutions as being far more significant and powerful in shaping social life than they were in Marx's day, the fact remains that the problem continues to be defined in its most basic terms by reference to a model of society which originates in Marx, and which is explained below. In this sense, the spectre of Marx continues to haunt social thought, even among those who explicitly reject his theories and claim to have outstripped his influence. Indeed, the base–superstructure model as a *method of analysis* is as popular and widespread among contemporary social theorists as it has ever been.

For our purposes, a central question has dominated debates about and interpretations of Marx's thought over the past thirty years: 'what does it mean to say that Marx was a humanist?'

Humanism

The concept of humanism refers to the extent to which social theories account for the organised character of social life in terms of the individual: is social order conceived as constructed out of action? How far is structure explained by reference to the creative powers of a society's members? In this sense, humanism is a theoretical assumption, or, better perhaps, a *meta-theoretical stance*, i.e. a stance looking at theory from outside.

The question we are posing, therefore, is whether this stance is correctly attributable to Marx, and if so, what follows from reading him in this way.

In developing this question, we need to begin not with Marx himself, but with G.W.F. Hegel (1770–1831).

Hegel: the dialectic of history

Hegel was the most influential thinker of the first half of the nineteenth century, in Germany and, arguably, in Europe as a whole. Hegel's philosophy aimed to give an account of history-as-a-whole. The history of all humanity can, he argued, be grasped as a single, unified, organised and *rational* progress. History might look like a mere accidental succession, one thing after another in a rather disorganised, chaotic sequence, but that impression is only superficial. Seen in the right way, history can be recognised as making up a coherent story about development and progress. Progress is not smooth, continuous and cumulative, but rather comes through struggle, conflict and discontinuity, which none the less is of an essentially logical kind.

How was Hegel able to make such a counter-intuitive proposal plausible? Surely struggle, conflict and change are inimical to order and logic? Grasping how these apparent opposites are reconciled is the key to Hegel's thought. The crucial idea is that conflict is itself an *orderly* process, consisting in the creation and overcoming of oppositions. Compare the history of human beings to the growth of a plant from a seed. The seed contains the plant, and out of the seed grows the plant, destroying the seed. Thus the life of the plant is the development of the seed into what it has the potential to become: first, the shoot, eventually the fully grown plant. In the same way, consider history as the life of humanity, and see, therefore, that history is merely the unfolding of the potential which was present at the earliest stage of its being. History is the natural expression of the essential nature of human beings, just as the plant is the natural expression of the essential nature of the seed. Humanity *must* itself develop into what it has the potential to become. Note that Hegel takes it for granted that his history is a *collective* one, i.e. it is a history of humanity as a whole, or of large groups of people, not of particular individuals.

Just as the seed is destined to turn into a plant of a specific kind, human beings – Hegel argues – are destined to develop towards complete freedom. What human beings essentially are will never be fully expressed if their capacity for development is restricted, inhibited by circumstances; the potential of humanity will only be fully developed when they are truly free, which means free of *all* circumstantial inhibition. Over the course of history, human beings necessarily represent something less than the true or full nature of humanity. For just as the full potential of the seed is only realised when the plant is fully matured, so the full potential of human beings will only be realised after the period of growth – i.e. history – is over. The achievement of complete freedom will be the 'finished growth' of human beings., Consequently, there will be an end to history. Since history is a process of change through which humanity develops its full potential, then when that has been realised there can be no further development and therefore no further history. History is directed towards an end in two senses: (1) in the form of a particular result; (2) in being directed towards a literal end or finish.

Teleological conception

The notion that something is driven or striving towards a particular end is called a teleological conception; therefore Hegel presents a teleological account of human history.

'The spirit of the age'

In what sense does humanity develop? For Hegel, the *primary* manifestation of development was the development of the intellectual life, of the *mind* or *spirit*; the German term used by Hegel is *Zeitgeist* (i.e. 'spirit' of the age'). He held it to be plain, if one studied the history of a given people, that their art, religion and philosophy would at any given time have a certain uniformity, a common cast of mind, a shared outlook. This concept reaffirms Hegel's *collectivist* aspect, for it was his firm conviction that the commonality across many different thinkers was not a matter of mere coincidence; individuals were driven by larger, widespread influences affecting them all in similar ways. In short, the mind or the spirit that drives the historical process is the mind of humanity, as manifested in particular peoples and periods, not the mind of individual thinkers.

Idealism

In actuality, Hegel's study of the mind was the study of the development of ideas, so naturally he concentrated upon those areas of society which were creative or expressive of ideas: art, abstract thought (particularly philosophy) and religion. Hence Hegel is termed an *idealist*: he thought that the true nature of history and human existence was to be understood in terms of the development of thought, of *ideas*.

The purpose and logic of history

Since the purpose of thought is to achieve knowledge, then the progress of history must be towards knowledge, and the end of history will therefore come with the achievement of full knowledge and full understanding. In other words, history is completed when humanity finally comes fully to understand its own nature. The development of history is humanity's continuing struggle to understand itself, and Hegel's philosophy was meant to provide an understanding of humanity's true nature as a historically, progressively developed thing which consists in self-understanding. Hegel's philosophy amounts to the self-understanding of humanity. It should, therefore, expose the complete understanding of history and humanity's nature – they are, after all, the same thing – and therefore comprise the finale to history. History has completed itself when it arrives at Hegel's conclusions.

What of the nature and role of logic in this process? Since the development of history is a development of thought and the essential process of thought *is* logic, it follows, then, that the development of history must be an essentially *logical* process. If so, Hegel's initial claim that history-as-a-whole was amenable to rational understanding would be vindicated at this point. For him history effectively *consists in* thought and its logical operations, and these are, of course, our very means of understanding. Thus to see history as a rational process is nothing other than to grasp its underlying logic. This, approach, however, required Hegel to reform logic; he maintained that the logical process is more complex and roundabout than it is presumed to be in classical logic. What was needed, he argued, was a *dialectical* logic.

Philosophy was, in Hegel's view, the crucial vehicle for the development of thought, since it purported to be the apogee of rational, logical thought. Yet a survey of the logic of Hegel's time, shows a preoccupation, as throughout its history, with absolute distinctions between irreconcilable opposites, e.g. truth and falsehood, being and non-being, the animate and the inanimate, and the mortal and the immortal. The distinctions were absolute in the sense that things were immutably of one kind or the other. Thus if something was false then it could not become true, could not change into its opposite. From Hegel's standpoint, this was a false conception of the nature of things. It did not recognise the fact that things could change; the flatly oppositional thinking of philosophy was too simplified.

Dialectical logic

Classically, truth is often sought in discussion – in dialogue, or *dialectic*. Hegel bases his logic on the model of discussion exemplified by Socrates in classical times. Discussion originates in disagreement, the conflict of oppositions, which spurs debate. The argument proceeds by the putting of one position and the countering of it by another opposed position. The search for truth is not about standing pat on one's own position, but about attempting to reach agreement with one's opponent, to arrive at a conclusion both can accept. It incorporates elements of each of the two previous, opposed positions, but now combines them in a third, new position, an improved, superior one which overcomes the opposition between the preceding two.

In grossly simplified terms, we may glimpse Hegel's dialectical logic as an exposition of the way in which seeming opposites can be reconciled and combined in a new unity. Of course, arriving at an agreed position might end that discussion, but it does not end all discussion, for this newly agreed position will be put in some other conversation, will provoke a counter-statement, initiate a new debate and a search for yet another more inclusive, mutually acceptable conclusion, and so on.

This logical progression is the very stuff of history. Hegel is saying that history arises from *conflict*. Far from conflict being an undesirable and unnecessary blemish upon the face of human existence, it is the driver of history, the essential motor of progress. Conflict engenders new and better ideas and pushes towards a more comprehensive understanding. Conflict is not only necessary, it is also productive, for conflicts are eventually resolved and result in improved outcomes, before yet further conflicts are initiated.

We must emphasise, also, that though the development of philosophy is crucial to Hegel's understanding, his history is a general history of civilisations and their activities, including their wars and other social struggles. At any point in history, the mind or spirit of a people and their civilisation are dominated by oppositions, or *contradictions* (the logical term for opposition between propositions stating conflicting positions). Although philosophy has always concerned itself with oppositions, in fact, the whole civilisation is affected by them; people act out oppositions in their social, political and economic affairs as much as in their intellectual culture. Thus conflict, and development through conflict, are an integral part of social existence, involving, in Hegel's rendition, the working through and working out of these contradictions.

For example, the military conquests of Napoleon were just as much part of the logical pattern as the philosophical arguments of René Descartes or John

Locke (1632–1704); the history of society, of its intellectual culture, and of philosophy itself were all part of one and the same enterprise. Of course, Napoleon, Descartes and all the other individuals who have contributed significantly to human history were not aware that they were playing a part in this pattern; Hegel spoke of the 'cunning of reason' to refer to the way in which this logical patterning worked itself out in history through the activities of individuals without their awareness of the part they were playing. Only someone equipped with Hegel's philosophy could know about this inherent logic of history.

Marx's reformation of Hegel

Hegel's philosophy was humanist in treating humanity as occupying a special, central place in the whole historical process and seeing that the very point of history was to improve and fulfil the human spirit. His ideas certainly had immense impact; he dominated German intellectual life and influenced most young German philosophers of the time. One of these was Marx, who appropriated much of Hegel's scheme, certainly in his early writings. He was, however, sceptical of Hegel's significance as a political thinker. Marx could not accept Hegel's contention that the key to human emancipation lay in the development of philosophy, carrying people to the level of complete understanding of their own nature and thus to complete freedom through his, Hegel's, own philosophical works. After all, this supposed final enlightenment and full elaboration of humanity's progress co-existed with jails filled with political prisoners. Freedom in philosophy, freedom only in the mind, obviously was not the same as real political freedom. Therefore Hegel's idea of history could not offer an account of progression of history to a *real*, i.e. practical, political freedom if it only resulted in freedom in theory. For Marx, the real history of human development could not be a history solely of thought or ideas; it would have to be a history of human life in the real world, i.e. the world of economic and political being.

Despite this important reservation, Marx initially adopted much of the *form* of Hegel's argument, i.e. the idea of a scheme for history-as-a-whole, and of history as a progressive development of the true character of human nature that could only be fully realised when history reaches its final stage. These ideas were taken over. So was the idea that the driving force of historical change was conflict. Change was structured in the dialectical pattern of conflict, resolution, further conflict and higher, more advanced resolution. It went through a succession of ever higher stages of development, with increasing degrees of freedom, eventually resulting in a final, full enlightenment and emancipation of humankind.

Production and human essence

Of course, Marx's reservation referred to the *inequality* of the then existing society. At that stage only a very few individuals had participated in the development of human thought, or spirit, in the sense of its intellectual expression; the vast majority were excluded from the process of creating these purported expressions of human essence. This majority had been engaged in producing human history all right, but not by way of intellectual creation and discussion. Rather, it had produced human history through physical, not mental effort, creating through its *labour* the actual conditions of human existence, and the material conditions under which thinking, for example philosophy, might be done. Marx denied Hegel's view that the human essence was to be found in thinking; he favoured the view that the human essence is to *work*.

Work

Work, involving as it does the physical transformation of the world around us, literally changes our world, whereas thinking makes no physical difference to anything. Work also provides the most basic means to freedom, to liberation from necessity. For, of course, our labour provides us with food, shelter, and clothing, giving us some freedom from the challenges and pressures of nature. Further, progress in labour sets us free from the necessity for labour itself by giving us time and resources to do other things than labour, including the opportunity to engage in intellectual thought.

This is not to say that *thinking* does not matter at all, for, of course, thinking is part of labour, part of what Marx calls 'practical consciousness', i.e. the thinking involved in and for the purposes of carrying out labour. Indeed, for Marx as for his predecessors, Aristotle and Hegel, the capacity for thought marks out human beings as distinctive; the capacity to think about things and to imagine them being otherwise enables human beings to envisage new (improved) ways of making the physical world meet their needs, bringing about changes in the physical environment itself. In this capacity they differ from animals, whose ability to alter the physical world is fixed in instinct-given ways; animals have no capacity for reflection and foresight.

It is important to recognise that Marx's contempt was reserved for *speculative thinking*. The kind of theorising that Hegel had engaged in had, for Marx, a fundamentally self-deluding character.

The fundamental division

If labour is the essence of humanity, then special attention needs to be paid to the phenomenon of the *division of labour*.

The division of labour

The division of labour has both a positive and a negative aspect. On the one hand, it is an enormously powerful device for harnessing and maximising the creative potential of human labour; by dividing work, immensely more can be produced than is possible if all the members of a group pursue the same task. However, such division can – invariably does – lead to separation of human beings into different categories, with some having power over others.

Thus the existence of the division of labour means the dislocation of the human essence, the division of humanity against itself. It also means a division between thought, i.e. between speculative thinking, and practical, physical, world-transforming activity – because some specialise in the former activity, some in the latter. The division of labour's fateful moment is not when it produces people who specialise in different aspects of a work task, but when it produces a division between those who do the physical work and those who do not. Some are now supported by the products of other people's physical labour, to which they do not contribute themselves. Those who do not engage in physical labour often occupy themselves with thinking, but their thinking is now freed from a crucial constraint to reality, i.e. from the crucial connection with physical labour and its patent reminder that human existence owes everything to the capacity for labour, that everything of real value in human life is made possible by someone's physical production.

As a consequence thought can begin to *misrepresent* reality by presenting thought itself as the source and embodiment of everything valuable, as something more important to human existence than 'mere' physical labour. This misrepresentation of reality not only denies the true facts, but it also serves a social use: by elevating thought above physical labour, thinkers also elevate themselves above those who do physical work, thereby justifying their entitlement to the material necessities which they have not produced themselves. Further, they often claim a disproportionately large share. This is the source of an idea which is fundamental to *all* of Marx's work.

The fundamental idea

The progress of history and the organisation of society are to be understood as being decisively shaped by the division between those who do and those who do not engage in physical production, those who produce and those who consume a portion of what is produced even though they have not produced it.

The fact that humanity is divided within itself in this way means, of course, that actual human beings cannot be full and proper expressions of the human essence. The human essence is prevented from achieving its full development by two things:

1   Those who engage in physical labour, which is purportedly the fulfilment of their human essence, do not engage in this freely: they are, in one way or another, unfree. The stark example is, of course, the slave, but the medieval peasant and the industrial worker are also unfree in important ways. The industrial worker differs from the slave and peasant in being *legally* free, but this is not the same as being truly free – i.e. free of all external limitation.
2   Those who do not labour are in that way cut off from their true species nature, their human essence. They may believe that they are living the highest form of human life possible and feel entirely happy, without realising that they are only very partially fulfilling human potentiality, since their own achievements and privileges are acquired at the expense of other human beings. The vast majority pay the price in deprivation and suffering; the cultural achievements of the few cannot be considered the fulfilment of the potential of humankind *as a whole*.

In such circumstances – which are only too familiar – there is, then, a basis for the criticism of society and the formation of proposals for its reorganisation. Society can be criticised for the way in which it distorts the human essence by limiting freedom, and a case can be made as to what needs to be done to move the development of that essence further forward. Hegel himself had used his philosophy in a conservative way, to justify the rule of a tyrannical king, but Marx saw in his method the basis of a programme for *revolutionary* change.

Alienation

Given his borrowing from Hegel, it is not surprising that Marx's criticism of his contemporary society was initially cast in terms of one of Hegel's key concepts, *alienation*.

Alienation

This concept refers precisely to the separation of human beings from their very essence. Engagement in productive work *should be* the expression of human essence, thereby fulfilling the rich potential of human energy, imagination and creativity. It was clear to Marx that work in the developing industrial societies of the nineteenth century was very different. Far from being the fulfilment of their very being, work for industrial workers was experienced as, at best, a necessary evil and undertaken out of the need for survival. For the overwhelming majority it was a deadening experience – physically unpleasant, mentally unrewarding and spiritually numbing.

Further, the members of industrial society are alienated not just as a collection of individuals but as a *population*. Human essence is not the possession of individual beings, but of the species as a whole, and will be fully realised only when human beings have developed their full potential. The industrial society, however, was divided within itself between those who could enjoy physical comfort and intellectual stimulation, engaging in freely creative activity, e.g. of a cultural and artistic kind, and those who were reduced to being near sub-humans in the foul and brutal conditions of the factory system.

Another aspect of alienation involves the misrepresentation of reality in the form of the *self-denial* of human essence when people misapprehend their own true nature. In their thinking, people come to underestimate their own powers, failing to realise that certain things are actually the product of their own, human effort and not of some other source. A leading example is religion, where people often take a fatalistic line towards what occurs because they believe God determines what happens to them and that they can have no control over their own fate. But, Marx, the atheist, following another critic of Hegel, Ludwig Feuerbach, maintains that there is no God. God is just an idea made up by human beings, partly to muddle up and mislead people, partly to express unsatisfied human longings. By accepting the idea of God and taking such a fatalistic line, people are resigning their own capacity to control their own destiny, are wrongly thinking of themselves as subordinate to great, super-natural forces over which they can have no control. In fact there are no occult beings or forces, so that everything that human beings can possibly be is within their own (collective) control.

A further example of this kind of alienation is Hegel's own philosophy, where the human spirit, made up of ideas, achieves an almost occult existence of its own. This strange, superhuman force directs history from behind people's backs, making use of them as unwitting pawns to carry out its plans. It is human beings, however, who produce ideas, including 'the human spirit', not the other way around, and it is human beings, not quasi-supernatural ideas, which make history. In so far as things are done behind people's backs, then, it is not 'ideas' which are doing these things, but only other people.

For Marx, another most important kind of alienation is the way in which people accept their economic situation, e.g. unemployment or badly paid labour, because they suppose that their fate is decided by economic laws over which they can have no control. The recent tendency of many governments to insist that the market is a near-infallible mechanism for regulating all activities, the possessor of greater wisdom than individuals or their governments are capable of, might show the persistence of this kind of conception. For Marx, the market cannot be some super-human, super-wise entity but only a set of relationships between human beings, something which human beings have created (albeit not by any conscious intention) and something which they potentially can control. He maintained that there is no need to accept that we are assigned a miserable fate by the nature of things, and that we simply have to resign ourselves to it. Human beings make themselves through their labour, they develop their own nature through changing the world about them, and they have (collectively) the capacity to *reshape themselves* through further reshaping their physical, economic and social world.

The remainder of Marx's intellectual career, in which his writings principally were concerned with economic ideas, was devoted to exposing illusions of this kind. They are self-limiting misconceptions of human destiny which must be removed.

The real basis of society

For Marx, it was not enough to liberate people from a set of illusions; human progress involved liberating them from real social, political and economic conditions. The objective must be to determine within reality itself the way the human essence was developing through the formation and reformation of social, political and economic conditions. He wanted to discover how the movement towards emancipation could be assisted and expedited. In short, the potential for emancipation has to exist in the real conditions of life themselves, and not in the logical potential of ideas alone. For this reason, Marx's attention turned to the analysis of economic and political arrangements, considered as socially organised complexes.

Marx replaced Hegel's history of ideas by analysis of socio-economic conditions, but he remained attached – at least arguably so – to his conception of an underlying logic, a *dialectical* structure, to history.

Dialectical structure

In Marx's version, the conflict was not between contradictory ideas, expressed first in thought and subsequently also in social relations. The reverse applied. The root historical conflict was between opposed *social groups*. Their conflicts would sometimes find their expression in thought, in the realm of ideas, but they originated in differences of *economic interest*. The key to understanding a society was to begin by understanding the way in which it organised its economic activity, the arrangements through which it carried out its physical production.

The question of the relationship between economic interests and ideas will recur on several occasions below, for central to the subsequent decisive shifts in Marxism has been an ongoing dispute over the way in which Marx is to be understood as intending this procedure. In crude terms, the issue concerns whether or not Marx can be fairly considered to be an economic – even a technological – determinist.

At this point, we simply recapitulate the shift from Hegel's idealism to Marx's materialism:

Materialism

The human essence is the capacity to labour, to work upon and modify the world about it, to shape it better in accord with human needs, thereby enhancing human existence and potential. In short, labour is human nature – human essence itself. The capacity of labour has a cumulative character, since human beings can contrive new and improved ways of carrying out their work on the world given their capacity for practical thought; e.g. the creation of tools increases human powers.

Change: quantity and quality

The cumulative character of labour, however, is not smooth and continuous. Here another Hegelian notion informs Marx's analysis: quantity into quality. Hegel had noted that many changes are continuous up to a point, and then they involve a drastic, discontinuous alteration. For example, if we heat or cool water for a time we get a continuous cumulative change, and the water just gets hotter or colder, but if we continue then, at a certain point, there is a change not just of quantity – so many more degrees – but in nature or quality. The water starts to boil and turn into a gas, or freeze and turn into ice. This quantity-into-quality change is characteristic of historical processes, where a society changes in a cumulative way. For example, an agricultural society might expand the area of land under cultivation but, at a certain point, further changes are not possible except through a change in the whole nature of the society, and an agricultural becomes an industrial society.

Human beings develop tools – technology – to enhance their labour power, and in a given period of history a certain level of technology prevails. This prevailing technology is amenable to continuing improvement, but at a certain point a new, different kind of technology is created which is superior. This emphasis upon the development of technology invites the view that Marx is a *technological determinist*, i.e. he sees the development of new technologies of production as giving rise to historical change. However, Marx was precisely concerned to oppose this kind of idea of technology as an independent force, since technology in itself is inert. Instead, the social relations between human beings make a technology conceivable and practical. Economic, productive activity is a *social*, a *collective* affair. The prevailing form of technology might be among the forces of production, but the social relations of production are most critical.

The social relations of production

A technology implies, so to speak, certain kinds of relations amongst people. For example, a horse-drawn plough can be operated by one person, but an industrial plant obviously requires the complex organisation of a team of individuals, involving, among other things, an elaborate division of labour into specialist tasks.

Economic change is never just a change in technology; it also requires a set of changes in *social relations*; and not just in the social relations involved in production itself. For example, the horse-drawn plough can be operated by an individual alone, someone living in isolation, remote from any neighbour, but an industrial plant cannot be operated by members of a population that is as thinly scattered across a landscape as prairie farmers. People have to be resident near to the plant if they are to work there. Obviously, there is much more to this idea that economic relations require social relations of specific kinds, but this example indicates its force.

In summary, Marx's idea that economic production is *basic* to the life of a society has at least a threefold justification:

1   Productive activity is definitive of human nature.
2   Productive activity is logically prior to other activities, in the sense that we cannot do anything else until we have met the conditions of our physical existence, i.e. we cannot theorise or paint or play sport until we have provided food, protection from the environment and so forth.
3   The structure of productive activity has causal consequences for the form taken by other social activities. For example, an aristocrat and a peasant lived completely differently, i.e. the aristocrat could have a leisure-filled existence, but the overwhelming bulk of the peasant's time was consumed in producing what was needed for his or her own (and, ultimately, the aristocrat's) existence.

The economic foundations of power

One other element vital to these considerations was the fact that some people *controlled* and directed the activities of others.

Ownership of the means of production

In production, there was often the difference between those who did the physical work, and those who supplied them with the means to do that work – access to land, or raw materials or technology – but did not themselves do it. The aristocrat controlled land and granted the peasant permission to work it, the industrial employer controls the physical plant and machinery and pays workers wages to use them. The one who possesses 'the means of production', therefore, has power over the one who makes use of them.

Hence for Marx the crucial division in society became not just that between those who worked and those who did not work in physical production, but more specifically one based on the existence of private property, i.e. between those who possessed – who owned – the means of production and those who did not. In production, the latter controlled (and *exploited*) the former. The exploitation consisted, in crudest terms, in the fact that those who did not work were able to have at least a portion of the product physically created in work handed over to them, though they had contributed nothing to its actual creation.

The relationship of power, of control, which was found in economic relations based on private property was, Marx conceived, reproduced in the wider society. Those who dominated within the process of economic production ruled the society; for example, the aristocrats who controlled the land also made up the ruling group within pre-industrial society. The key positions and relationships in society were those of class.

Class

Under any particular regime of production, there are many people who would stand in the same relationship to one another; in the productive process, as we have said, people either work or own the means of production. Those people in the same position on one side of this divide were in the same class.

The pattern of this divide not only exists in the economic sphere, but obtains across all areas of life. Life in society, even in those areas most remote from physical production, is class-divided, class-based. Hence, the concept of class is wider than the analysis of economic relations alone; it involves the analysis of the structure of society as a whole. This is another respect in which economic structures are 'basic' to society for Marx, for it is in terms of the relationships established around a given form of economic production that social class is formed, which, in its turn, becomes the fundamental relation around which all other social activities are structured.

Classes and class conflict

The idea of society as composed of classes is the key to the materialist implementation of Hegel's dialectical concept. To reiterate: by 'materialist' we here mean nothing more than a view of history as the product of real, striving human beings, rather than of any occult or supra-individual forces such as God or the human spirit.

Classes are *relational* entities: one class can exist only if other classes do; a 'one-class' society must be a no-class society, since to speak of a class is to speak of a collection of people who are differentiated from one or more other collections of people. The relationships between such classes are those of *opposition*.

Class interest

The two classes of owners and workers have opposed *interests*, for the owning class can only meet the conditions of its physical survival – or, indeed, of its much more luxuriant style of existence – if it takes the means from those who create the things that can be consumed.

In Marx's view, someone who does not take part in physical production is not entitled to a share of its product, and thus those who do not work exploit those who do.

This conception of the fundamental organising character of class has implications for the way in which the structure of *society as a whole* is to be understood. The class nature of ownership and exploitation have consequences within the economic structure and also carry implications for the organisation of the rest of the society. Since the inequality between the owning class and the labouring class is not simply an economic one, narrowly defined, but involves a social relationship of *power and control*, the difference of interest between these classes refers to *freedom*. The capacity of the owning class to deprive the physical producers of their physical product is a difference in power, a manifestation of the fact that the owners can restrict the access of labourers to the means of economic activity. When they do grant them access to these, e.g. renting them land to farm, or hiring them for industrial work, they have the capacity to direct what they will do. In other words, those who labour are not free, a fact most starkly apparent in the case of the slave and also, albeit less starkly, in the cases of the peasant legally bound in service to the lord, and of the industrial worker hired for a wage to work under the control and direction of plant management.

Class conflict

The conflict of interest between owning and labouring classes is, then, a conflict over power and freedom. It must pervade the rest of society's organisation because the owners wish to protect and preserve their position. For them to realise their own interest requires control not only over the immediate circumstances of economic production, but also over the way the rest of the society is arranged.

This broader dimension of power and control is necessary to ensure that the position of the owning class within the economic structure is sustained. If the conflict of interest between the owning and the labouring classes becomes an open and direct confrontation, then the interests of the owning class require that their position within the economy be recognised in the society as legitimate and defensible, for which they are entitled to call on the use of whatever force – police, army – is available. In this way the economic and the political dimensions of society are interrelated; the owning class have *an interest* in the nature of the law and in the disposition of political power, in their need to be assured of support in any challenge to their ownership and control.

Class, economic order and social institutions

This need entails more than simply containing direct challenges to ownership and control, since the requirements of the arrangement of production must also be reproduced. A given way of organising production depends upon the availability of a sufficiently numerous and suitable labour force available and able to do the kind of labour involved in the work of the economy. The economy itself does not provide this labour force, which, rather, derives from the way the rest of the society is organised. For example, family arrangements must produce enough individuals to fill the places for labour. These family arrangements (perhaps in conjunction with other institutions and organisations) have to ensure that the individuals are healthy enough and suitably educated to be able to do the available work. The owning class has *an interest* in the ways the family, health provision, education and training are organised in the society, for these provide preconditions for the continuation of its own position.

There is one further element. To be suitable, a labour force have to possess not merely the capacity to do the work available, but also the outlook and motivation to do it. Crucial here is the outlook which will lead it to accept its position within the productive process, to be docile and co-operative in the system. This is not to be taken for granted it has to be produced and reproduced, for the kind of outlook on life people have depends upon their social background, experience and learning. Thus the owning class has *an interest* in the intellectual culture of a society, in the nature of the ideas that are being circulated, and in the ways they are being disseminated. If ideas challenge the right of ownership or encourage a dissident and uncooperative attitude to work within the prevailing arrangements, then they are not *in the interest* of the owning class.

The owning class, therefore, has an interest in the way the general affairs of society are organised. In fact, it is *in the interest* of that class either to control the society as a whole, or to have that society controlled on its behalf. In short, the interest of the owning class entails a direct concern with the politics of its society. Of course, such control of the whole society is the very focus of politics. Hence the economically dominant class wishes to be also the socially and politically dominant one, the owning class aspires to be a *ruling* class. This class might rule directly, as in a feudal society, where the rulers are the landowning aristocrats, or relatively indirectly, as in industrial societies. Here the owners of economic production in the form of companies do not themselves operate as the political, i.e. parliamentary, rulers, yet, according to Marxist interpretations, they none the less get their way in matters of politics, exercising sufficient control over parliamentary representatives to ensure that their interests are advanced in law and statute.

As well as political dominance, the owning class also seeks *intellectual* control, which came to be called *hegemony* in the later Marxist tradition (see Chapter 8). Marx himself explicitly pointed out that the ruling class in society controls the channels through which ideas can be created and circulated, and we have indicated its reasons for having an interest in the kinds of ideas that are circulated, i.e. to inculcate in workers an outlook which makes them tractable and compliant. We have also mentioned Marx's view about the way the division of labour produces a separation of physical and mental labour, and how the liberation of thinkers from the practical demands of productive work exposes thought to the risk of self-delusion.

The nature and functions of ideology

In combination, these views of Marx contribute to the notion of *ideology*. This notion of ideology has been a particularly key one in shaping the subsequent impact of Marx's thought upon sociology. Though the appeal of Marx's ideas within sociology is at its lowest point for some time, and though Marx's teachings have been largely repudiated by contemporary poststructuralist thinkers, none the less he continues to be hailed as one of the three thinkers – along with Friedrich Nietzsche (see Chapter 10) and Sigmund Freud (see Chapter 9) – who created the idea that individuals' actions are shaped by forces of which they are not conscious. The idea of unconscious determinants of conduct is a vital, indispensable element to both structuralist and poststructuralist thought. Nietzsche, Marx and Freud have been jointly nominated as 'the masters of suspicion' for the collective suggestion of their contributions to the notion of unconscious determinants of action, i.e. the actual determinants of conduct are much more base and unattractive, much more unacceptable, than those which we consciously believe to be governing what we do. In both Nietzsche and Freud, the idea is more of unconscious *psychological* determinants of thought, which originate in the individual's own mind, while Marx's ideas are more about the *social* origins of distorted thinking: the socio-political necessity to keep the real causes of people's actions inaccessible to their conscious thought.

Ideology

An ideology is a system of ideas which *systematically* misrepresents reality. It does so in ways which serve the interests of social groups, particularly the ruling strata. Ideologies misrepresent reality in various ways: they conceal unacceptable aspects of it; they glorify things which are of themselves less than glorious; they make out things which are neither natural nor necessary as though they were both.

To give a simple and crude example, many theories of human nature created in capitalist societies treat human beings as though they are naturally selfish and unrelentingly competitive, as though it is in their nature to look out only for themselves and to seek every degree of advantage over others that they can find. This kind of idea today comes over as 'scientific', through interpretations of Darwin's evolutionary, biological theories as about 'the selfish gene'. It is presented in popular form in Richard Dawkins's (1976) book of the same name. The idea here is that selfishness is in the nature of all living things (as a result of the imperative of our genes to survive) and that existence is a matter of competing for the marginal advantages that will ensure the survival of our genetic matter into future generations.

Such a view has two features which are common among ideologies: the suggestion that it is simply in our nature to be selfish and self-interested; and the implication that there is nothing we can do to change it because it is built into our natures. From the Marxist point of view, we are not innately competitive in this way. To talk about the natural, immutable competitiveness of the human species offers a false picture of our human natures. Such theories serve to justify a socio-economic system – competitive capitalism – which *is* based upon unrelenting individual competition. These ideas justify that system by suggesting that, first, it gives full rein to our fundamental human natures and is therefore best suited to us and, second, there is little point in disapproving of or attempting to moderate the competitiveness of the system since it is our nature to be competitive. In being 'natural', no alternative seems possible and therefore competitive capitalism seems to be unchangeable. In one way or another, systems of ideas play this ideological role of convincing people that they cannot change their society, or that it is not worth their effort to try changing it; one of the purposes of Marx's analysis is to expose these ideas' ideological character as a means of encouraging the view that change is conceivable, possible and necessary.

The point about such ideologies is that they are instilled into the thought of individuals and become the basis upon which those individuals act. The individuals may think they are freely choosing to do the things they do, but they are, rather, acting in ways which are in the interest of the ruling class only, and in which the system needs them to act if it is to survive and prosper. The systems of thought which exist in society are not shaped by the freely operating minds of thinkers, but are decisively influenced by the needs and structures of the society itself. On examination, these systems will be seen not to be objective and general, but to be specific and partial, developed not because they show how things are in themselves, but because such ways of thinking are necessary to the particular form of society in which they grow up. The individuals subject to these systems of belief are not, therefore, aware of the true reasons for their holding these beliefs and, from a Marxist point of view, are misguided about what it would be in their own interests to do. As mentioned, the ideological distortion of thought is an indispensable notion for many current forms of social theory.

The base–superstructure model of society

We now are well on the way to setting in place two central pillars of Marx's thinking:

* the base–superstructure metaphor, with the concept of ideology;
* the idea of history as a progression through class conflict.

The debate over whether or not Marx was a humanist thinker turns on what interpretation is given to these elements. To set up this issue clearly, it is necessary to say a little more about the base–superstructure model.

The account we have given has set out the general lines of Marx's thinking. At the centre is a model of society which provides one of the main bones of contention about the actual nature of his theories, namely, the model of an economic *base* and an institutional and intellectual *superstructure*. It has been implicit in our discussion above, i.e. in suggesting that the other institutions and the culture of a society are to be understood in terms of the needs of its economic arrangements. We have just been saying that organising and perpetuating a given form of economic organisation requires the whole of the society to be appropriately structured; the economy could not function or persist if, for example, the legal system, the educational arrangements and even the religious beliefs of people were not of a suitably supportive kind. For example, religious beliefs can contribute to economic docility if they teach the importance of accepting authority in all its forms and the spiritual merit of hard work.

The base–superstructure model

The idea is of the economic structure being the *foundation* upon which the rest of the social edifice is raised. It fits with Marx's conception that productive activity is *logically* prior to other things; only after the requirements for survival and sustenance have been satisfied is it possible for human beings to do other things, to engage in leisure and creativity. Consequently the nature of and the extent to which productive activity meets these basic human needs sets limits to the things which people can otherwise do.

Two readings of Marx

Marx was thus proposing that the form which social institutions and the intellectual life of a society takes is decisively shaped by its economic institutions, a proposal which was – at the time he was making it – extraordinarily radical and drastic. A century and a half later it has become commonplace and very widely assumed, usually without any recognition of its affiliation with Marx. The proposal, however, remains controversial, and only comparatively recently has been the focus of heated contention. Is Marx an *economic determinist?* In other words, is Marx saying rather more than that productive and non-productive activities presuppose one another, and that a given form of economic activity has certain preconditions to its existence and operations which must be met by other institutions in the society? Is he going on to say that the economic base of society *dictates* the shape of all the other institutions in society and thereby *drives* the whole history of the society? If the economic base dictates – or *determines* – how the family, legal, religious and intellectual arrangements of the society must be, then the economic base drives the history of the society as a whole.

Economic determinism

If the economy changes its fundamental character, then the preconditions for its operation and persistence will also change, and will causally necessitate suitably adaptive modifications in the rest of the society. The form of the economy will then dictate the form that will be taken by the family, the political system, religious practices and the rest.

Though many have extracted such a picture from Marx's work, it is often disapproved as 'vulgar materialism', the idea that the superstructure is a simple and direct function of the base, changing at the behest and in the manner dictated by the base. For many, this view may have a considerable element of truth, but it cannot be entirely true; they cannot seriously hold that *all* aspects of life and thought are straightforwardly dictated by the requirements of productive organisation. After Marx's death, his friend and close, long-time collaborator, Friedrich Engels, keen to dissociate the pair of them from any such implication, suggested that the relationship between base and super-structure was more complex and mutually affecting than this 'vulgar Marxist', one-way, rigid determinism.

Dissent importantly focuses upon the issue of *voluntarism*. The strongly 'economic determinist' reading suggests that human individuals are mere play-things of economic forces; whatever they attempt to do makes no difference to anything. This, many feel, either makes Marx's theories entirely unattractive, or would do so if this determinist reading were accepted. Of course, some may find this idea of total determination an attractive one. However, one can read Marx as precisely seeking to distance himself from any such determinist conception; after all, it is one of the main themes of his life's work to demystify economic relations, to dispel any suggestion that they are super-human, quasi-supernatural forces which have human lives at their mercy. He favoured the view that economic relations are *social*; they are relations between human beings whose true nature has been obscured behind clouds of ideological falsification. One can read as the message of Marx's work that it is necessary for people to realise that their economic systems and their social institutions are their own creations; if they have created them, then they can recreate them in a new and improved form. Only by the realisation that they are not puppets of supra-individual forces – such as God or the market – can people take proper control of their own destiny.

On this reading, Marx does not deny that *individuals collectively* can make a difference; he does deny that *isolated* ones can. Marx finds laughable the idea that Hegel, just by working out a philosophical system, can bring the whole of humanity to complete freedom. The absurdity of this supposition is manifest in the fact that next to nothing in the real world of social, political and economic injustice was altered by the arrival of Hegel's theory. It is entirely unrealistic to think that one individual, just by writing a book, can get armies to disband, prisons to close and the owners to surrender their property. Hegel's underlying idea that history and social change are collective phenomena is correct, but Hegel himself failed to apply it properly. A given historical, socio-economic system can be changed, but to turn such a system upside down requires consid-erable, collective, concerted effort. In short, only the might of a large and well-organised social group (properly directed by the right understanding of social reality) can bring about full human freedom.

Indeed, organised social groups (not technology or economic systems) have been the driving force of social change; and they will bring the process of change – history itself – to completion. It is the process of *class conflict* which makes up the story of change.

Change and conflict

A Hegelian logic can be seen in Marx's treatment of the pattern of social change. If we treat an actual society as built around a central conflict of interest, i.e. an irreconcilable (or seemingly irreconcilable) opposition, then, after the fashion of Hegel's dialectic, we should expect this situation to be unstable. There are pressures to change, to escape from and to overcome this conflict. Also from Hegel can be taken the idea of conflict as a productive, creative force, i.e. the attempt to overcome a conflict will result in a more developed situation, in which the initial conflict will be resolved, but within which a new opposition can be expected to arise. At the heart of any given society then, we should expect to find a central opposition, which defines the whole character of the society, and, on Marx's reinterpretation of Hegel, we should expect to find that opposition will take the form of class conflict. The system of economic organisation gives rise to two classes, those who own and control and those who labour, and their opposed interests will place them in mutual struggle, with the ruling group seeking to establish its pre-eminence within the whole society.

The decisive moment for change will not come, however, from this confrontation of ruling class with labouring class – at least, not until the final stage of the historical process with the full development and final overthrow of the capitalist system. In the first instance, the capacity of human beings to envisage and create new and improved ways of production will provide the impetus to ensure that, within a society dominated by a given economic system and a property-owning class, a new way of organising economic affairs will begin to develop, and new ways of organising relations between owners and producers will begin to form. Since the new means of organising production are an improvement, they will have the potential to replace the existing system, thereby providing a threat to the existing system and the class whose ruling power is based upon that existing system. The system as it stands will not favour the development of the full potential of the new ways, but those new ways will continue to develop, and those who own and control the new economic forces will have the characteristic desire to have things arranged to maximise the realisation of these forces. In so doing, they will want to control the whole society. Those who dominate within the newly emerging system will find themselves in conflict with the existing ruling class, and will begin to see that they will need to replace that ruling class if they are to realise their own objectives.

Consequently, a struggle will develop over the question of who is to be the ruling class. For example, the Marxist version of the history of Western Europe was the struggle between the aristocrats, who dominated within the agricultural system that prevailed across the whole of Europe for such a long time, and the bourgeoisie, the city-based businessmen who controlled the emerging industrial plants. The latter system eventually became the prevailing mode of production throughout Western Europe and the USA; its powers, needs and products enabled these societies to dominate and to make use of the rest of the world that had not developed such production. With the shift towards industrial production as the dominant system, the owners of industrial property became the true powers in society, influential enough to reshape the law in the interests of their type of property, and decisively to direct political policy, even though they did not hold political positions themselves. But trouble was storing up in such societies.

As we have seen, on the Hegelian, dialectical model, the progression from one stage of history to the next involves the development of something which is already present in the current stage beyond the point at which it can continue to exist within the confines of this current state; the transformation which Hegel referred to as 'quantity into quality' is involved. Applying this logic to capitalism, the system, like other forms of society before it, ought to contain the seeds of its own destruction, to be producing something which will eventually, for its realisation, have to carry development beyond the capitalist stage. The relevant development within capitalism is the *proletariat*.

The proletariat

This is the force of urbanised industrial workers, whose ranks were relentlessly expanded as all kinds of other individuals (farmers, shop-keepers, etc.) found their livelihoods destroyed by the superior productive power of capitalist production; they had no choice but to seek work in the expanding industrial plants.

At the same time, of course, capitalism was expanding the working class *across* societies, as well as within them, as its system continued relentlessly to expand internationally.

The logic of capitalist expansion

This expansion was 'driven' by competition: the system is such that every member of the bourgeoisie is in competition with others. The capitalists have no choice; they have to expand their industrial capacity for economic survival. As the logic of competition brings a relentless drive for efficiency and, as the potential for efficient production is greater the larger the productive unit, there is a continuing drive towards bigger industrial plants. An inevitable consequence is the continuing expansion of the industrial working classes; the process of expansion serves not only to increase their numbers, but also to provide the basis for their *unification*.

Workers' unification

Industrial expansion concentrates the working classes in urban areas, and provides them, through the wonders of capitalism's products, with an increasing capacity to communicate with one another and, therefore, to organise.

At the same time, the expansion of the system also provides them with the motivation to organise and to oppose the capitalist system itself, for, in Marx's most simplified model, the development of capitalism involves (1) the *simplification* of social relations, the concentration of the overwhelming mass of the population into two sharply divided social classes – those who own, and those who do not own property; and (2) *intensification* of the exploitative relationship that obtains between the two. It results in (3) the *immiserisation* (i.e. impoverishment) of those who are exploited. These developments, together with improvements in communication, meant that it becomes increasingly apparent to the proletariat – especially if aided by Marx's theory – that their miseries are the result of the system, and that all their important interests starkly oppose them to the ruling class of capitalist entrepreneurs. In brief, here is a very promising basis for the revolutionary uprising of a working class who could destroy capitalist society.

Viewed from a historical perspective, the destruction of capitalism is not a negative but a positive change, albeit not, of course, from the standpoint of the bourgeoisie, whose domination of society would be terminated. It would remove the causes of massive human misery and, even more importantly, would involve making the productive power created by capitalism into a *collective* possession, thereby releasing its tremendous powers and the benefits to serve the needs of all, not just a few.

Conclusion

On the reading we have given, Marx is a humanist because he is understood as having inherited Hegelian ideas that human beings are the centre of history, and that history is the story of the development of their essential nature (i.e. the mind in Hegel's case, the capacity for creative labour in Marx's). In both accounts, the whole of history is seen to be centred on a particular, unifying theme. This theme, to be seen in each phase of history, is that society embodies a dominant contradiction: it is formed around a central opposition which determines all other aspects of its existence. Such a contradiction can be found in the succession of each stage of history, as one society takes up the further development of the unfolding nature of the human species.

Yet to come

We have said little in this exposition of Marx's thought about his last writings, especially his largest work, *Capital*, which consisted much more in technical economics than his previous works. This is not to say that the underlying logic of those writings could not be absorbed to the above scheme, for the Hegelian reading of Marx can encompass writings from all phases of his career. However, the inclination to read Marx in this way has been contested fiercely, with great consequences for contemporary considerations, by the French Marxist Louis Althusser. He insisted that while Marx, in his early work, had indeed been a humanist under Hegel's influence, he had later come to see that such a way of thinking was not truly scientific. Marx saw that essentialism is unscientific, being in reality, ideological, and purged *all* Hegelianism from his thought. He moved from ideology to science, and stated the scientific position in *Capital*. Accordingly we continue the story of Marx's thought and a consideration of *Capital* at the later point when we encounter Althusser's structural Marxism (see Chapter 9). Before that, we will continue the account of the Hegelian reading of Marx in our remarks on Western Marxism, particularly with respect to the writings of the Frankfurt School, which were the epitome of everything that Althusser condemned (see Chapter 8).

Questions

1   What is a humanist? What implications are there in defining Marx as a humanist?

2   What is alienation? How does Marx show that the division of labour produces alienation?

3   Why is it important for the development of historical materialism to argue that the essence of human beings is work?

4   Show how Marx relates class, power and social institutions in (a) feudal societies and (b) nineteenth-century capitalist societies.

5   What is ideology? How can Marx claim that it misrepresents reality?

6   Outline Marx's base–superstructure model of society. What major problems does it have?

7   What place has the individual in Marx's thinking about society?

Further reading

Bottomore T. and **Rubel, M.**, 1965, *Karl Marx: Selected Writings in Sociology and Social Philosophy*. Penguin. Still a useful selection of original texts.

Carver, T., 1980, *Marxist Social Theory*. Oxford University Press. A useful introduction to Marx's thought.

Hughes, J.A., Martin, P. and **Sharrock W.W.**, 1995, *Understanding Classical Sociology*. Sage. Chapter on Marx.

Kitching, G., 1988, *Karl Marx and the Philosophy of Praxis*. Routledge. Modern study which argues for a humanist reading of Marx.

Kolakowski, L., 1981, *Main Currents in Marxism. Vol. 1: The Founders*. Oxford University Press. A comprehensive survey of the origins of Marxism, the first part of Kolakowski's definitive three-volume history.

Marx, K. and **Engels, F.**, 1967, *The Communist Manifesto*. Penguin. A classic, brief statement of historical materialism by the originators.

—— 1977, *The German Ideology*. Lawrence and Wishart. For Marx's classic statement of the concept of ideology and its role in society.

Singer, P., 1983, *Hegel*. (Oxford University Press). An accessible, short introduction.

Taylor, C., 1979, *Hegel and Modern Society*. Cambridge University Press. Slightly more advanced but clear, well-written introduction to Hegel's social thought.

■ ■ ■

Chapter 3

Max Weber

Introduction: methodological commitments and substantive themes

Weber's sociology is much closer to Marx than Durkheim's, comprising a critique of so-called vulgar Marxism, i.e. the idea that social life, including culture, is a simple function of the economic structure. Weber took Marx for a vulgar Marxist – understandably, given the unavailability to him of Marx's early writings, which quite unequivocally contradict such vulgar readings. Coming from a very different philosophical background to Marx, Weber was allied to the Neo-Kantian rather than Hegelian tradition in German thought. Neo-Kantians were philosophers of the late nineteenth and early twentieth centuries who followed the teachings of Immanuel Kant (1724–1804). Kant saw human beings as existing only partly in the world of natural causality, and partly in a realm of freedom, governed by moral rules rather than causes. This meant that human beings could not be understood entirely by natural science and that the study of their moral and spiritual life would have to be pursued by other means. Nevertheless, Weber shared some of Marx's key assumptions and also his core concern with the nature of capitalism. However, he held very different conceptions of the nature of history, and of the methodology of historical and sociological studies.

One legacy of Immanuel Kant's philosophy is a sharp distinction between the realm of physical nature and that of human mental life. Physical nature is a realm of rigid, mechanical determination, whilst human mental life is one of freedom and the absence of causality. At the end of the nineteenth century, this distinction gave rise in German culture to a hot debate over the limits to scientific inquiry: were cultural phenomena, the topics of history, by their very nature precluded from the kind of scientific study applied to natural phenomena? This debate framed Weber's own preoccupations. For him, the difference between natural science and history was not basically a result of the different natures of natural and social phenomena; rather, it came out of our relationship to them, out of the interests that we take in them. With respect to nature, we have, on the whole, an interest in understanding its general patterns; the difference between one rock and another hardly matters at all to us and certainly does not matter for its own sake. Rather, we are interested in the way in which rocks in general behave; we can therefore be satisfied with an understanding of them which is abstract and generalised. However, when it comes to human beings, their *individuality* captivates us. For example, our interest in Adolf Hitler derives not from the characteristics he had in common with other human beings, but from his distinctiveness, the extent to which he was quite unlike other politicians. Similarly, in England we are interested in the study of English society because, for us, England holds a different place in our lives to that of other societies; after all, it is our home. Thus we are not satisfied by studies which take out all that is distinctive about the historical figures that have affected us and shaped our lives, i.e. by studies of our society which give a highly generalized account of people and societies. Weber did not conclude that there is no room for generalities in the social sciences; rather, they are not the be-all and end-all of such sciences in the way they are within the natural sciences. Generalities can be useful in the study of history and society as means to another end in so far as they help us to understand better the individual case.

Individuality

For Weber sociology as a generalising approach was subordinate to history; it provided abstract concepts, which could be useful in understanding concrete, complex, *individual* historical cases. Such concepts were created not for their own sake but precisely for their usefulness in informing historical studies.

Weber's own studies were wide ranging, geographically and historically; they encompassed the civilizations of the West from the time of the Greeks, and Asiatic societies such as India and China over thousands of years, and were meant to include the world of Islam also (though the study of Islam was barely launched, and most of the other studies unfinished). Their purpose was to tackle questions about the role of religion in social and economic change, and about the relationship between ideas and economic conditions of the sort posed by Marx. Nevertheless, understanding of the general issues and of the other societies was not sought for its own sake, but gathered with respect to its relevance to the situation at home, i.e. understanding the individuality of the Western European and North American capitalist civilizations (especially Germany, for Weber was strongly nationalist in sentiments) in the nineteenth and early twentieth centuries. The 'individuals' with whom history was concerned could be quite large complexes, such as 'Western civilisation in the modern world', and not just individual human beings. Further, historical/scientific knowledge had only a relatively subordinate role in relationship to politics. Weber wrote two major essays on politics and science as vocations, putting views which provoke controversy to this day.

Objectivity and value freedom

Most contentious is the idea that science should be 'value free'. A major political concern of Weber's was to ensure civic responsibility within modern society, where technical and scientific expertise was assuming ever-increasing importance. Weber worried about the blurring of the roles of scientist and citizen, and the prestige of science being used to bolster the claims of demagogues. He feared that those who occupied the role of scientist would often be irresponsible enough to take advantage of the prestige given them by their position of scientific eminence, and of the authority deriving from their expertise in order to advocate political policies, which can have no scientific basis or authority. He believed that in the universities of his time the professors were exceeding the bounds of their scholarly competence in the lecture hall by delivering impassioned speeches about political issues in the guise of scholarly disquisitions. Academics and scientists are no less entitled to the right to present their political viewpoints than anyone else, but they are no more privileged in the political arena than anyone else and should therefore confine their political persuasion to the public, political arena. There the greatest historian, physicist or sociologist is just one more citizen, one more voice. The responsible discharge of scientific obligations requires sober compliance with the usual rules of scholarly investigation and evidential proof, and abstinence from political polemics in the classroom.

Facts and values

The distinction between the scientific and the political was, for Weber, the recognition of a longstanding philosophical distinction between *facts* and *values*. A very standard position, which Weber shared, is that values cannot logically be deduced from facts. Scientists can only report upon what happens, upon how things are, but they cannot tell us how they should be, how we should live, or what we should do. The provision of research and evidence cannot relieve us of the necessity to make choices at the level of values.

This was a key to Weber's conception of human existence as well as sociological method: there is an irreducible variety of incompatible human values; and there is no possibility of a scientific or rational basis upon which to choose between them. We cannot excuse ourselves from the need to make a choice by arguing that science shows one value to be preferable to another, for science cannot do this. We have to make up our own minds: with which 'Gods or Demons', as Weber put it, to affiliate ourselves; which gods to worship; which leaders to follow; which causes to fight for. Such choice is a tragic aspect of human existence and surely a source of terrible conflicts within and between individuals. Consequently, Weber is sometimes spoken of as a *decisionist*; i.e. we have to choose our values, the things we treasure and strive for, from a range of possible and irreconcilable values, and must therefore make a decision to go one way rather than another and, having made it, live with its consequences.

Therefore, science can never displace politics, and the scientist can never, acting purely as scientist, be a political leader. The (legitimate) role of science in politics can only ever be advisory. Scientists understands what happens and how things work causally. They can, therefore, give good advice on how to make a certain thing happen. They can tell us, on the basis of their expertise, that certain ways of attempting to make something happen are more likely to bring about the desired result, but they cannot, from that same expertise, tell us whether we should desire that result or a different one. The question as to whether we want X or Y is a *political decision*, a matter for the political leadership to deal with. Scientific knowledge can be of great value to politics, but it cannot displace or substitute for politics. It is an illusion to think that politics can be made scientific, for politics entails struggle between values, not empirical knowledge.

Weber never sought to keep the social scientist out of politics but merely to keep distinct the two roles a scientist might play, as disciplined inquirer and as active citizen. Within the sphere of scholarship, the scientist can be objective, since objectivity requires only sober compliance with the obligations of the scientific role to proceed according to the standard rules of evidence and proof. Within politics, the danger is that the difference between the scientific and political roles is obscured, giving a false authority to someone who just happens to be a scientist. In the administration of politics, those serving as scientific advisers to politicians might exceed their role, might begin to usurp the decision-making prerogative of the legitimate political leader through attempting to reduce real issues of value decision to matters of mere technical choice or by obscuring the political issues in talk that sounds like science. Science itself, as Weber recognised, also rests upon values. For example, if we do not value knowledge for its own sake, then what would be the point of pursuing scholarship? 'Value freedom' as Weber understood it operates within the framework of accepted scientific values. He himself was not abashed in being politically active or in seeking to use scientific knowledge in the formation of social policy. He was concerned about the absence of decisive, heroic political leadership, leading some critics to see in his ideals a prefiguration of the kind of leadership Hitler would shortly offer the German people.

The particularity of Western capitalism

The 'individual' which captured Weber's scientific interest was the capitalist civilisation of the West. It was unique and unprecedented. It had arisen only in Western Europe and the USA, and had not developed in other societies. What was special about it? Why did Western civilisation have this individuality? What had given rise to it?

Weber certainly rejected all-embracing historical schemes of the sort both Hegel and Marx had employed, and decried any suggestion that capitalism was 'one stage' which *all* societies must go through in their progression from the most primitive to the most developed. The idea that there is anything supra-individual, anything super-human about history was anathema to him: history and society consists of human individuals and nothing more. Abstract sociological statements and laws are, in the end, statements about the activities of those individuals and nothing else. Talk about the actions of a social class, such as the working class, makes assertions about the behaviour of the typical or average individual in a certain socio-economic position; and ideas of the Marxian type about the members of a social class having the interests of the class to which they belong but of which they are unaware is just a nonsense in this context. Since history consists only in the decisions and actions of individuals, then any idea of history itself having an overall purpose or direction is also a nonsense. Thus Weber's inquiries into the origins of modern, Western, capitalist society were into a *specific* set of conditions, and not directed towards identifying any necessary, general tendencies of that history.

Weber's fame rests upon his account of *The Protestant Ethic and the Spirit of Capitalism* (1985). Marx was certainly right that the modern, Western societies were capitalist. Yet, though it might be their dominating feature, it was not, of itself, their distinctive one. Capitalism – the organised pursuit of profit – had taken many forms in different societies across history (including, for example, the pirate ship). What was distinctive – not to say peculiar – about the capitalism in the West was its highly *organised* character and, even more, the highly *moralised* tone of profit seeking. Thus Weber's account was not of capitalism in general, but of one of its forms, the *rational* form found in the modern West, i.e. Europe and the United States. For Weber, the capitalist business in this period had two crucial characteristics: (1) capitalist business was kept in continuous existence and operation; (2) this ceaseless operation was in the service of the relentless accumulation of profit. Throughout history, capitalist business was a sporadic venture, undertaken in pursuit of sufficient profit for purposes of utility and consumption. On completion the venture would be placed in abeyance until another foray for profit became opportune. The modern Western capitalist business was organised on the basis of a continuing operation, utilising the most advanced calculative knowledge of how to link means to ends in both delivering its products and also structuring its own internal financial and organisational affairs.

Rational capitalism

This unrelenting commitment to means–ends efficiency makes rational capitalism what it is. The capitalist business continues to accumulate profit even though there is no practical need for it, even though the level of profits exceeds what its recipients can ever spend. Rather than being acquired for use, seemingly wealth is sought for its own sake and the aim of business is the ceaseless expansion of profits. This pursuit of ever-greater profit is not, however, driven by greed or grandiosity of ambition. Instead, it is seen as morally righteous, with the resulting profit being the just deserts of the capitalists for their industry.

Indeed, capitalists share with their workforce and the population at large the conviction that a life of dedicated toil is the good life; this conviction that provides the true distinctiveness of modern, Western, rational capitalism. In most civilisations, work has not been so regarded; rather it is seen as a necessary evil, endured only when unavoidable. In the capitalist West, however, 'lazy' is a term of severe disapproval and those who are without a job may well be regarded, and may even regard themselves, as 'worthless'.

Linking the capitalist spirit with Protestantism

Weber's view is that this kind of remorselessly hard-working, endlessly productive society, i.e. the capitalism we know, could not exist without this attitude to work (or 'spirit', as he terms it). What needs explaining is the origin of this vital element. Whence could 'the spirit of capitalism' develop? Weber looked for any precedents for such a spirit in the part of the world where this capitalism developed. He located an attitude which was very similar to the spirit of capitalism, in regarding work in one's business or occupation as morally worthy. It differed in one important respect: it was religious, held by Protestants, particularly those influenced by the teachings of John Calvin. For Weber, the spirit of capitalism looked very like a secularised form of 'the Protestant ethic', as he called it. That the similarity may not be wholly coincidental is indicated by the spirit of capitalism developing in the same regions of Europe as those in which the Protestant ethic had earlier formed. Furthermore, in the historical evidence available to Weber – though subsequently questioned – Protestants were disproportionately successful in business.

The Protestant ethic was itself distinctive in the context of religious attitudes to the world of daily life. It is commonplace for religions to deny value to the world by contrasting mundane, everyday existence with the truly religious life; they insist that daily life is meaningless in itself and is of importance only relative to the life in the next world. From this viewpoint, the affairs of daily life should not matter much to the individual, who should, ideally, withdraw from them. Indeed the medieval Catholic church was one of a number commending the ascetic life as the ideal existence, supporting a monastic existence, cut off from the secular world. One of Weber's essays focused on such religious rejections of the world. By contrast, the Protestant sects of the European Reformation entirely rejected monasticism and embraced the world of daily life, commending the vigorous fulfilment of obligations within mundane society as serving God's greater glory. This sense of living vigorously, fully and unrelentingly up to the responsibilities of one's secular role at God's behest shows the same energy which those in capitalist society invest in their work and the righteousness they also bring to it.

Capitalism and Protestantism

The spirit of capitalism and the Protestant ethic are much alike, except that one is commended by God, and the other is a free-standing, secular morality, held for its own sake. The one could, then, easily be the predecessor of the other: the spirit of capitalism could have grown out of the Protestant ethic.

Weber's views of sociological method are again relevant here. The broad methods of science apply to sociology as to natural sciences, but the subject matters are rather different. Since human beings are not inanimate objects there is the possibility of *understanding* them, whereas there is no possibility of doing so with natural phenomena. We can ask questions of human beings and otherwise attempt to get into their minds in order to see things from their point of view and to grasp the framework of assumptions in terms of which they live. Weber's approach to sociology is often known as the *verstehen* (German for 'understanding') approach. He certainly thought a most important element in studying what people did was to seek such an understanding. This kind of understanding was just what he attempted in making a meaningful connection between the Protestant ethic, the spirit of capitalism, and capitalism.

How could the teachings of the Protestant sects, which condemned materialism and the accumulation of wealth, give rise to the spirit of capitalism and the valorisation of industrial work? Weber's argument employs a two-step process.

The first established the radical orientation of the Protestant mentality. Martin Luther had certainly made a major change in people's attitudes towards the mundane world, when he had introduced the notion of 'the calling', i.e. one had been called to one's earthly position by God, and it was, therefore, God's will that one should conscientiously fulfil the duties of that trust. For Weber this move, though in the right direction, was not assertive enough to be sufficient of itself to inspire something like the spirit of capitalism. Luther's notion called upon the individual conscientiously to fulfil the duties of a position that had been traditionally defined, but that would not be enough to account for the genesis of an attitude which – for Weber, as for Marx's characterisation of capitalism – disdained and usurped all tradition. If the first step was taken by Luther, the decisive moves were made in John Calvin's teachings, albeit largely as an unintended result. Calvin's teachings put the believer in a difficult position in having a psychologically, not a logically, contradictory character. Calvin taught predestination. In his wisdom at the beginning of all things, God had chosen only certain individuals for salvation. This decision was fixed for all time so that amongst the living only a few were of God's elect. God's decision of salvation had been settled in advance, and could not be altered, but it was not one which God had made known to mortals. As a consequence, Calvin taught that one's conduct in this life was no means to salvation, that one's actions here on earth could not alter one's ultimate fate. But he offered no licence to live howsoever one chose. Instead Calvin commanded that whatever God's decision, be it 'saved' or 'eternally damned', one was none the less called upon to live for God's greater glory and to abide rigorously by his commandments. The psychological contradiction results from the tension between the doctrine of predestination, on the one hand, and the intense seriousness of the question of salvation of the immortal soul for the true believer. How to cope with an existence in which one's fate was settled yet unknowable? How to live a religious life faced with the knowledge of the ultimate irrelevance of one's conduct for standing in the eyes of God, a standing which is not even known?

Here again is a point of contrast with Marx, who regarded religion as a form of ideology, referring to it contemptuously as 'an opium of the people', which simply justifies and props up earthly arrangements. For him religious beliefs concern illusory matters and were to be derogated – at least in vulgar Marxism – relative to 'real', economic, i.e. material interests. For Weber, by contrast, people's religious interest is not to be gauged against the sociologist's idea of what is really important to them; for him, it is simply an observable fact that, for many people, religious concerns and interests, such as the fate of their soul after death, are just as real and at least as important as any material interest. Indeed, people's religious interest in salvation is often greater than their material interests, in that they would put the former far ahead of the latter, to the extent of sacrificing their lives for it. So, for a religion as spiritually demanding as Calvinism, believers must have been intensely concerned about religious matters, above all in the fate of their soul. Yet they were told that their actions could not influence the fate of their soul, which mattered more than anything else to them; and also they were told that they could not even know what that fate was.

On Weber's reading, this element is the key to the situation which led to the faithful adapting Calvin's teachings, albeit quite against the grain of their meaning. If God had indeed discriminated between the elect and the condemned, would he truly have made it so that those who were saved could have no inkling of his choice? Would it indeed be the case that God would have given salvation to those who would flout his commandments, and was it not more likely that those whom God had saved would live in accord with his law? Might not one's conduct be a *sign* of one's salvation? Not a means to salvation, of course, but a manifestation of one's inclusion in the elect? Since this notion of ascertaining one's own salvational status through one's own conduct was against the tenor of the teachings, any conclusion about salvation would be fragile. If one's conduct *was* such a sign, then it would only be so if it were flawless, if there were not the slightest hint of deviation from God's law. Even the faintest such failing might indicate against one's salvation. Thus the closest self-monitoring and control of one's entire conduct was introduced into the life of the religious lay person.

Self-discipline and rational capitalism

Religions often demand rigorous self-control, but normally only on the part of their most advanced practitioners, not of the mass of believers. It was the introduction of such thorough and stringent self-discipline into the activities of daily life which struck Weber as providing another parallel with secular – especially business – conduct under capitalism, namely, its extensively *rationalised* (i.e. worked out and consciously controlled) nature.

One further element of Calvinism was noted: the teachings of Calvin emphasised that opportunities within the world were gifts from God; it would be sinful to refuse such opportunities, which should be seized and exploited as the opportunities to magnify God's earthly glory.

Going beyond tradition

Here was the crucial step beyond Luther; Calvinist doctrine, rather than teaching resolute fulfilment of obligations within the bonds of tradition, recommends the taking of all opportunities, even if they go beyond the bounds of tradition.

This amended teaching resolved the psychological tension within Calvinism. Weber argued that the immediate consequence of the creating a conviction that one could at least know if one was saved would be the introduction of a rigorous, systematic self-control into the conduct of everyday affairs, including economic activities. Economic success and expansion would be the almost inevitable consequence of such dedicated application. Since the official Calvinist teachings railed against the dangers of earthly wealth, it could certainly not be used for consumption. Successful Calvinists could do nothing with their wealth apart from reinvesting it, for to leave wealth idle and not increasing itself was, in this new, activist climate, also sinful. Reinvestment would of course only ensure even greater wealth, and so on.

Ideas as causes

Weber had taken a first step and made a connection at the level of meaning: he had tried to show how in the minds of Calvinist believers the official teachings provided an unresolved problem of their own salvation, and how its resolution led them to impose iron self-control over their everyday affairs, resulting in them coming to look upon economic affairs as righteous activity, to be conducted in a way which did not respect tradition. This attitude has clear parallels with the spirit of capitalism. In Weber's method, success at the level of meaning establishes a possibility; that is, he claimed to have shown what he calls 'an elective affinity' between the Protestant ethic and the spirit of capitalism, i.e. to have shown they were naturally drawn to each other.

But a second step was needed. He had gone far in establishing a case for the Protestant ethic actually giving rise to the spirit of capitalism, and thus to capitalism itself, at 'the level of causality'. Weber had made an *intelligible* connection between the two crucial elements, the ethic and the spirit; we can see (i.e. understand) how the one could have given rise to the other. But the causal question remains: *did* the Protestant ethic actually create the spirit of capitalism? Did the Protestant ethic actually play a part in making capitalism happen? The study of the Calvinist outlook added one element: the compulsion to reinvest made a strong contribution to capital accumulation as a necessary precondition to the rise of capitalism. Nevertheless, Weber was far from claiming that the case at the level of causality was conclusive.

Weber was raising the general issue of the causal role of ideas, of which religious ideas were one kind, albeit in his judgement they were historically very important. Weber was consciously arguing against Marx, but how much he disagrees crucially depends upon how one interprets Marx. If Marx is interpreted as holding that ideas are *epiphenomena* of society, i.e. phenomena without real substance or causal force which operate at best as mere rationalisations for things that they misrepresent and cannot control, then Weber is completely opposed on this point. If, however, Marx criticises Hegel for overestimating the power of the ideas of the individual thinker and for not realising that ideas can only matter in history when they are associated with collective movements, then he and Weber are not very far apart on this point, since both agree that ideas can have causal force in history. It is not the teachings of Calvin himself which matter in the above account, but the way his ideas are taken up by the mass of believers.

Marx and Weber on ideas

If Marx is construed as supposing that only economic interests are real interests, and that other interests such as political, national and religious ones are mere smokescreens for economic interests, then Weber is adamantly opposed. For him, arguments of this kind err towards what we should nowadays call *reductionism*, i.e. seeking to reduce every kind of phenomenon to just one, here the economic.

The Protestant Ethic is about the way a religious interest can lead to decisively influential historical activity, which is indispensable to the creation of capitalism as we know it.

So does Weber become an idealist in reacting against Marx's materialism? No! Weber is as much a materialist as the early Marx in recognising that, of course, the substance of history is the existence of real, material human beings (and not occult forces of any kind). Weber is certainly opposed to a materialism giving the most prominent place in understanding history to economic relations. For Weber, economics are vitally important to sociological understanding, as shown by his main, extended theoretical statement which comprises a very large (characteristically incomplete) work translated under the title *Economy and Society*. Yet not everything in social life boils down to economics. The interplay between economy and society is complex, two-way and many-sided. In summary, his overall judgement on Marx might be that Marx (as Weber encountered him) provided altogether too schematic an account of things, attempting to tie up in rigidly formulaic ways relationships which were more open-ended and variable.

It should be clear, then, that Weber was certainly not saying that the Protestant ethic, alone, created capitalism; the Protestant ethic was capable of bringing capitalism about, regardless of material conditions. Weber's argument about capitalism was that the truly distinctive feature of modern, Western capitalism is an attitude, a particular moral outlook, which he dubs 'the spirit of capitalism'. Without this outlook, it would not and could not be the same, for part of its nature as a system resides in its capacity for disciplined, systematically organised work. The motivation for such work is now mostly built into the system, and its whole organisation reproduces the attitude of diligence in its members, but this could not have been true of the *origins* of modern capitalism. This necessary attitude could not have been conjured from nowhere; it must have had roots. Since these roots would have had to have grown up with capitalism itself, they could not have originated in capitalism, but must have first developed elsewhere. The Reformation provides a likely historical location.

Of course, the attitude is only part of the story. In many respects, Weber accepts that other parts of the story have been told by Marx and others concerning the rise of a whole range of material conditions for the development of modern capitalism, e.g. the productive conditions, the rise of urban areas, the development of urban-based business and trading classes, the freedom of labour from agricultural work, and the development of a money economy. Far from giving importance to only one element, Weber emphasises the large plurality of elements involved. The development of a certain attitude, the spirit of capitalism, was essential to the formation of capitalism only in this sense: that the existence of a set of material preconditions for a social development will not, of themselves, bring about this development. The mere fact that there were suitable technology, currency, property laws and so forth would not have given rise to the capitalism that we know without the *motivation to exploit the opportunities* that those conditions presented. A given state of economic development presents many different possibilities; which ones are realised depends on other aspects of the situation. Thus the economic preconditions of capitalism could have been developed in very different ways or perhaps not at all: they would not have been developed in the direction they have gone were it not for the motivations provided by the 'Protestant ethic', with its associated spirit of capitalism.

The contingency of history

Historical events

In Weber's eyes historical events are a matter of the coming together of independent causal chains, which have previously developed without connection or direct import for one another.

There is nothing remotely predestined about the rise of modern, Western, rational capitalism. At the time of the Reformation the economic situation could well have turned out otherwise. The rise of the Protestant sects did not happen 'in response' to those conditions, and its effect on them was purely fortuitous. The development of the Protestant ethic mainly arose out of matters internal to religious life and thought, and just happened to occur at the same time as changes in manufacturing technology, etc., were beginning to develop; it was simply the way things worked out that the two developments – coincident in time – became interwoven into the origins of modern, Western, rational capitalism. In reality the spirit of capitalism is only one contributory cause amongst many; it is no more significant a cause than the others. Weber gives it such prominence to ensure its recognition as one indispensable cause of the specific complex of modern, Western, rational capitalism along with the numerous – even uncountably many – other indispensable causes. Giving it such prominence acts as a corrective to those who, as a matter of policy, deny to the ethic and spirit (and ideas generally) any causal role in such developments. To make out that the ethic/spirit had either more or less of a role than that of one cause amongst many others would be to misrepresent the complexity of causal situations.

It follows from the logic of Weber's argument that an explanation at the level of causality can be tested if he can find a parallel case of *embryonic capitalism*, which differs in only one vital respect, i.e. the absence of a Protestant ethic. In his view such a situation had (virtually) existed in traditional China. It had had the material capability for the same kind of dynamic economic expansionism as Western Europe, but this capability had not been taken up because there was a quite different 'economic ethic' attached to its religions. The development of such a case dominated the remainder of Weber's life-work, especially in the form of his comparative study of the world religions. He managed to complete substantial work on the religions of India and China, and on ancient Judaism, as well as to write a book-length account of the general evolution of religious practice and thought, and several other related essays. Weber's interests were wider than the study of the world religions, though everything had some connection with the core issue of the origins and distinctive character of the modern, Western civilisation. For example, his work on the development of music was designed to show that even the form of Western music was shaped in relation to the rationalising tendencies of the civilisation.

Power and the forms of social inequality

Weber also provided some general concepts for sociological analysis, which shaped the form taken by his descriptions of the world religions. Most basically, Weber looked upon the organisation of society as involving struggles for power. For Weber no less than for Marx, social life is about inequality, which can take many forms. In a given situation, inequality is not necessarily economic. Economic inequality is important and frequently plays a leading part, but it is only *one form* taken by inequality. Inequalities are the basis for the organisation of groups, and the struggle over inequalities is most commonly between groups. Therefore the key element in Weber's account of society is his account of stratification.

Stratification

Inequalities are arranged on three dimensions, but all are forms of power. In Weber's terminology, power is the capacity to get done what you want despite resistance from others. For example, economic wealth is a form of power, giving the capacity to get what one desires. All forms of inequality are inequalities in power. The three dimensions of power are (1) economic, (2) prestige and (3) pure power. They are the basis for three characteristically different forms of grouping: the class, the status group and the party. It is among and between these three kinds of groups that the historically decisive struggles over power are apt to take place.

Weber's conception of social *class* is much akin to Marx's. Class is defined in terms of position in the process of economic production, and specifically in terms of one's relationship to a market: what does one have to sell on the market? Labour power, or does one have products, or what? Weber does not think of classes as real groups, i.e. persons self-consciously interacting with one another; rather they are a product of a sociological analyst's definitions.

Classes

A class is more a category than a group, i.e. a collection of people identified together on the basis of some common characteristic. We can have as many or as few classes as we like depending on how grossly or finely we draw the criteria.

We can reduce the number of classes basically to two, by making the distinction between those who sell labour power on the market and those who buy it, i.e. Marx's proletariat and bourgeoisie. Within just the one category, e.g. of those (workers) who sell labour power, we can increase the number of categories by distinguishing the broad kinds of labour power sold; e.g. is it skilled or unskilled, manual or non-manual? We can multiply it up to an enormous number of classes by making the criterion of common position the specific kind of labour power being disposed of; e.g. is it the capacity to fix plumbing, to repair electronic wiring, to lay bricks, or to dig ditches? Contrary to Marx's assumption, there is nothing *naturally* unified about a class, and the social conditions which cause classes to act as co-ordinated social units in the struggle for power only rarely arise. The members of a class often react to situations in the same way – what Weber termed 'mass action' – because, of course, they share a similar background and experience, but they are not aware of one another's response, and are certainly not acting out of any sense of a joint venture in so responding.

The second form Weber describes is the *status group*. Status groups are real groups: the very specification of such a group involves and is dependent upon mutual recognition by its members. The inequality which separates classes is economic, the kind of returns which can be expected from the market relative to the things to be sold there, but status groups are differentiated by *prestige*, i.e. the level of esteem in which people hold themselves and are held by others.

Status groups

A status group is a collection of people who recognise themselves as equals, who look upon one another as equally worthy, and who look up to and down on other social groups. A status group involves shared understandings, mutual recognition amongst its members and, of course, acknowledgement from its superiors and inferiors of its standing in the general scale of social position.

Thus there is mutual awareness and some – at least diffusely – co-ordinated action integral to the very existence of a status group. The mechanism of such a group's existence is *closure*. It includes some, excludes others, and takes steps to ensure that those who are not equals are kept out.

From an economic point of view, a status group is defined in terms of consumption, not production. What makes someone an equal is how they live, their *life style*, as Weber termed it. For example, to lead the life of an educated, cultured and leisured person might be the basis for mutual acknowledgement. In the end the status group is dependent upon economic inequality because someone's capacity to lead a certain kind of life presupposes the wealth to fund it. It is not the wealth as such, however, that is decisive. Further, the status group's attempt to preserve its existence and identity through closure characteristically involves economic intervention in attempts to restrain the operation of the market, to prevent the hallmarks of a life style becoming available to mere purchase (which would directly link them to wealth). The extreme case of a status group system is that of the Indian caste system, where the operation of the market has been restricted to such an extent that even jobs are not available on it, but are retained within the various caste groups through inheritance. Inevitably class and status are mutually inimical forms of social organisation, since the existence of one – status group – involves reduction in the operation of the conditions – the market – conducive to the formation of class. The conditions under which the status group can thrive, Weber held, are those of long-term social stability – which is why they occupy such prominence in his discussion of traditional China and India. In situations of rapid social and economic change, social class possesses greater prominence.

The *party* is the third element in Weber's scheme. Whereas the status group has a diffuse sense of solidarity and common interest, providing a more promising basis for the organisation of co-ordinated collective action than that available to the class, this capacity for collective action is not easily going to amount to the focused, carefully calculated pursuit of common interest, which is what the party is all about.

Parties

The party is a self-conscious organisation for the pursuit of power. As a body created specifically for the purpose of struggling for power, it therefore works out its objectives and organisation to maximise its chances of attaining power.

The party, as Weber intends this term, is an analytical notion and does not just refer to formal political parties. It includes any and all associations developed purely for the sake of winning power. For example, it can include factions in business, leisure and religious organisations as well as large-scale political power. Such a group has self-awareness, mutual recognition amongst its members of shared specific purposes, and the capacity for closely concerted action in pursuit of them. It is the most effective vehicle in the struggle for power in society. Parties can, of course, attempt to base themselves in specific social groups; they can set out the goal of winning power in society for a specific group, e.g. a socialist party might aim to take political power for the working class, setting out to recruit from amongst that group and therefore actively seek working-class membership. However, they need not do so, and may seek power for goals and interests which are not those of one, or any specific, class, and may draw their membership from different social groups.

The forms of authority

Despite this view of society as a struggle for power, Weber is not offering a general model of all social relations in terms of conflict being pervasive of all aspects of social life. His emphasis on the role that conflict plays is far from suggesting that all relations between people are a struggle for advantage akin to Thomas Hobbes's (1588–1679) idea of a 'war of all against all'. On the contrary, the passivity of the great mass of people is most striking. The characteristic of power is in achieving results even over resistance, but the fact is that for those who hold power there is often comparatively little resistance. The behest of the powerful is often readily obeyed. Power is often legitimate, i.e. some people are recognised as leaders or commanders and so are recognised to have the right to command obedience from others. Such relations of legitimate domination are broadly of three kinds, each differing, in terms of the bases for obedience: charismatic, traditional and rational-legal domination.

The three kinds of authority

Charismatic domination is based upon the power of the leader's personality; traditional domination depends on the existence of traditional entitlement to position and to compliance; rational-legal domination derives from occupation of a position in accord with the proper requirements, such as the satisfaction of legal conditions. The charismatic comes to power by self-assertion, his or her power over others deriving from the strength of his or her personality and will. The traditional ruler has power very typically by inheritance (or similar mechanism, e.g. the selection of the Dalai Lama). In the rational-legal case, power comes from holding an office by formal appointment, paradigmatically through an electoral process.

The *charismatic* can take many forms: as the leader of a religious cult or a military group, or as a political demagogue. Such leaders claim to be special persons either because they have powers specially granted to them by greater forces, as with religious leaders (e.g. Jesus claiming to be God himself come to earth), or by virtue of some special mission they alone can realise (e.g. Adolph Hitler leading Germany towards its national destiny). In this way they assert themselves over their followers by personal power. Loyalty is entirely personal, and all members of the group are loyal to the leader, who, being an individual of 'inspiration', is very often apt to be lax about matters of organisation and regularity of arrangements. Taking care of these matters has to be done, but it is a secondary consideration and delegated to particular followers not because they are best at it, but because they are the favourites of the leader. The leader's own capacity to lead will be under constant test, for it exists only by continual proof in action. The leader can make things happen, and *must* therefore make things happen, and continue to do so; failure will be a massive setback to the leader's claims and, thus, authority. And, of course, the leader will most probably eventually fail, for the likelihood of endless dramatic success is small, and sooner or later even the most successful charismatic will certainly die.

Thus true charismatic authority lasts less than a lifespan and, upon the death, if not the previous discrediting, of the leader, results in either the end of the movement or its transformation into a more routinised form. The basis of authority changes either into tradition, where the new leader has power by dint of holding the position that the original leader held (e.g. the Pope holds power by holding the office that is the surrogate position of Jesus), or into the rational-legal type, where the leader's powers derive from formal appointment. While it exists, however, charisma is irruptive power. By virtue of the intense loyalty and emotional identification which members have towards the leader, the charismatic movement can create vital and dynamic impetus for change, impetus that can suddenly and unpredictably challenge and break up established structures of power. Typically, this dynamic is short-lived and inherently unstable, being moved by the leader's whims. It lacks any solid administrative structure.

The authority of *tradition* comes from time immemorial. Things are done this way because they have always been done so. The authority of the traditional ruler resides, characteristically, in the fact that the ruler's family have always held power. The classic form of traditional authority is the royal court, which is attached to the ruler, and made up of the ruler's friends and family. The court is also the pool from which the principal administrators are drawn, and their selection depends upon the trust the ruler has in them. The extent to which the ruler might be interested in administration varies from one to another, and so does the interest and capacity for administration of those whom the ruler appoints to office. As with charisma, traditional administration is founded on personalised, particularised relationships, and appointment to administrative positions has nothing necessarily to do with proven competence in the work.

Rational-legal authority is founded upon some formalised code of law, and awards position on the basis of formal appointment consistent with impersonal principles explicitly laid down. Such principles typically require – for positions of leadership – the holding of elections, or – for those in administrative positions – appointment on the basis of attested competence. Rational-legal authority is associated with what Weber regards as the most efficient form of large-scale administrative structure: the *bureaucracy*. This identification of bureaucracy was made with an awareness that bureaucracies are not perfect organisations, that they have their own inefficiencies and deficiencies. The relevant comparison, however, is with the two identified alternative kinds, charisma and tradition.

Bureacracy

The bureaucracy is an administrative system built – at least in principle – on the appointment to administrative posts of specialists in such work. It is organised in ways meant to ensure the impartial devotion of their expertise to the organisation and management of administrative affairs.

The bureaucracy is a system of administrative positions, of offices (or bureaux) in a hierarchy, itself involving increasing levels of administrative competence. The activities of the incumbents of these offices are governed by written rules; the authority of the senior over the subordinate figure derives from having greater expertise. Appointments are made on the basis of competence as assessed through formal examinations. The office-holder's loyalty to the bureaucracy is ensured, ideally, by that person's exclusive dependence for live-lihood upon the employing organisation. Thus the 'ideal' bureaucracy, i.e. in the ideal case when all these criteria are satisfied, involves the concentration of administrative expertise within the structure. The organisation of relations and distribution of work within the structure optimise the way expertise is focused upon administrative problems in as objective and dispassionate a way as (humanly) possible. For this reason, administrative decision-making in the bureaucracy (whatever its actual shortcomings) should ideally be superior, since charismatic and traditional administrations are, in the end, at the arbitrary mercy of the leader's whim.

If anything, with bureaucracy the situation is reversed; the political leader is at the mercy of the administration. The leader may have the formal political control over the bureaucracy, but may not have the administrative competence to keep it under control. Weber certainly thought that there was a need for strong, determined and visionary leaders in democratic society who could counter the strength of the bureaucracy. Such leaders must keep an eye on the main issues rather than being persuaded into looking at all decisions (including the important ones) as if they were mere matters of administrative technicality. The Civil Service, as caricatured in the *Yes Minister!* television comedies, is exactly what Weber had in mind as threatening the role of the political leader, who is the person entitled to be making the decisions and exercising leadership.

Weber's comparative sociology

We now, return to Weber's comparative studies of the world religions, which are centrally concerned with the *economic ethics* of these various religions. They extend to providing broad analyses of the structure and dynamics of the civilisations where these religions developed, in order to highlight the situations within which the social groups acting as bearers of these economic ethics were situated and influential. In other words, the comparative studies of world religions were also studies of the cultural dominance of specific status groups.

The Protestant ethic is a case study of the economic ethic of the Protestant sects, of the attitude which they formed towards economic conduct. They viewed it as a morally worthy pursuit within which proof of salvation could be sought. In contrast we noted the Roman Catholic conception that it is inferior to a truly religious life.

Economic ethics

Weber held that all religions develop such an economic ethic, but it is seldom so favourable to economic activity as Calvinism. Some religions come to dominate whole civilisations, and their attitudes set the tone for the whole culture. If such religions have an economic ethic unfavourable to economic activity then economic development is inhibited, preventing the growth of anything like Western capitalism despite otherwise favourable material conditions.

Weber thought that this analysis was particularly true of traditional China, which had developed science and technology as well as socio-economic conditions comparable to those of the Reformation.

Weber was particularly interested in a status group which occupied a key position within the social structure of traditional China. It was the collection of officials who administered the state's business, the mandarins, who were not the ruling economic or political group who yet had a powerful influence on the culture at large. Although the mandarins were as worldly and economically acquisitive as any modern capitalist, their Confucian religion took a completely disdainful view of industry and trade. It encouraged an exclusive concern with personal development, i.e. turning oneself into a cultured and aesthetically sensitive individual through literary and artistic concerns. It also encouraged practical indifference to the existing order of things. Piety towards elders and superiors was required, and life had to be conducted in accord with the conventions in order to prevent disturbance to the harmony and well-being of the entire cosmos, of which human existence was seen as a small and orderly part. There was no obligation for the believer to proselytise these beliefs;

Confucian beliefs owed their cultural dominance to the strategic position of their *bearers*, i.e. those who held and perpetuated the beliefs within the stratification system of the society. Within the population at large, however, other religions and magic held sway, and Weber maintained that the inward-looking nature of their religion prevented the mandarins from making any assault upon magic in society. By contrast, a feature of the Christian tradition was opposition to magic, which came to the fore most decisively in the Protestant phase. Indeed, Weber thought that the elimination of magic was a precondition for the development of thoroughly rational organisation of economic activity.

The religions of India presented a very different situation from the worldliness of the mandarins. They were predominantly other worldly, such as Hinduism and Bhuddism, and greatly disvalued earthly involvements, extolling a contemplative religious existence. Weber was again much interested in the position within the caste system of a patticular status group, the Brahmins. Though only teachers and preachers without economic or political power, they were also culturally dominant, being the group which provided the yardstick for the measure of the proper life.

In summary, these two great oriental cultures had dominant, religiously inspired economic ethics which would discourage economic activity of the kind favourable to the development of capitalism; their religious outlooks inhibited the development of the rational approach so prevalent within the West.

The rationalisation of social life

On several occasions we have used the term *rational*, persistently mentioning it as a leading feature of modern, Western capitalism.

The rational

In Weber's usage 'rational' refers to the attempt to work out means to ends, and to the attempt to develop a systematic understanding of things so that ends can also be worked out systematically and can even be ranked by calculation.

Weber thought that all actions could take only a few basic forms. Many actions are traditional or habitual in character, i.e. they are done without thought or calculation. There were two kinds of action worthy of the title 'rational'. One type he called *value rational* actions, where the means had no practical relationship to the end, but were simply a way of acting out, of realising, a value the actor held. His own example was the captain who goes down with the ship; his action does not achieve anything practical, but it does continue the commitment to dignity, integrity and honour which the captain may have made the hallmark of a whole life. The other kind of rationality is the *practical*: the working out of the best, most effective means of getting towards the end that one desires. It is most prevalently exhibited in our economic affairs and our civilisation, drawing extensively and dependently upon scientific understanding. Because we have such a worked-out understanding of the natural world, we are able to calculate with great effect and in very fine detail the best technical solution to any practical business, administrative or other problem.

In the West there has been a progressive process of *rationalisation*, i.e. of the extension of this practical kind of action, thereby giving a systematic understanding and calculability of practical means–ends relationships through-out the whole of society. This development has been massively accelerated under capitalism and has been especially associated with the rise of science. Though distinctive in its particular character and in the sheer extent of its development in the modern Western world, the process has very deep roots in Western culture. Weber traced its origins both to early Greek civilisation – with its scientific mentality – and, as part of the comparative studies of world religions, to the traditions of ancient Judaism, which were formatively influen-tial upon Christianity. For example, he argued that Judaism was notably hostile to magic, a hostility which it bequeathed to Christianity. In itself, magic is intensely traditionalising in binding people to the repetitive performances of prescribed actions; to be effective, the magical action must be done in the same way on every occasion. Consequently, the possibility of attempting to think out the conditions of effective action, of envisaging how the action might be made more effective by being reorganised, is inhibited. Thus, the rationalising process has remote roots in Western civilisation and a long history of development. Its apotheosis came with the capitalist phase, when we have not only rationalised our understanding of nature and our mastery of practical actions, we have also rationalised our human relations in the form of bureaucracy. For bureaucracy is nothing other than an attempt to rationalise, i.e. to make calculable, pre-dictable and controllable our own relations and activities. For Weber, it was the one of most inimical features of life today.

We have discussed religion in relation to its economic ethic, which was, indeed, the aspect on which Weber's studies were centred. Yet religion is certainly something more in Weber's eyes. It is a major source of meaning, of significance, in human lives; it gives people a sense that their lives are more than mere reactions to situations, that their activities are part of a greater order of things, and that their fates are connected to some greater purpose. Weber noted the role of religion in giving sense to otherwise meaningless suffering; it gave those who suffered the idea that the suffering was *for something*, and that there might be compensation in another life. The development of rationalisation has given us an immense understanding of the world and nature, but at a considerable price, namely the *disenchantment of the world*.

The disenchantment of the world

Our capacity to see meaning in the world and to understand our relationship to it have diminished. Paradoxically, the capitalist West has given people conditions of hitherto unmatched material satisfaction, but a civilisation of happy people has not emerged. Rather, people complain about the emptiness and spiritual barrenness of their lives.

The future, as Weber could see it, would be grim, with rationalisation and bureaucratisation expanding unchecked, and becoming more and more oppressive upon the citizenry, until the sense of life would not be of prosperity and freedom, but of containment within an iron cage.

Conclusion

In recent years, there have been arguments about whether Weber's life-work was indeed a unified whole and, if so, what the unifying theme might be. Rationalisation has been nominated, and we can see how such a case could be made. We suggest that it does not really contradict the claim that his central concern was with the individuality of modern, Western, rational capitalism, since rationalisation is such a distinctive and integral feature of capitalism as a social system.

It will become clear just how much influence Weber has had, even on Marxists. Weber's emphasis upon the necessarily irrational sources of seemingly rational phenomena, such as administrative structures and procedures, and his bleak view of life in a society subject to bureaucratic domination, were strongly endorsed by the Frankfurt School (see Chapter 8). Similarly, Michel Foucault (perhaps the most widely acknowledged and influential of recent thinkers, and not a Marxist: see Chapter 11) gives a critical account of the rise of modern society and of the pervasive spread of administrative control which, though formulated in an utterly different fashion to Weber's, is none the less very close to Weber in the characterisation of the structure of modern society.

With the decline of class as the most prominent social division, and the loss of Marx's direct influence, Weber's approach to the analysis of inequality, with its emphasis upon the heterogeneity of status groups, has been seen as a more suitable strategy for the analysis of social stratification in a world in which nationality, ethnicity, gender and religion are more prominent bases of division (and the source of dissident social movements).

Questions

1 To what extent does Weber bring individuals back into sociological analysis?

2 How does Weber's analysis modify Marx's view of capitalism?

3 'People are not just things – they answer back!' Discuss in relation to Weber's recommendation on how to study society.

4 Compare and contrast Marx and Weber's views on the part played by religion in society. How much have they in common?

5 By focusing on the motivations induced by the Protestant ethic, is Weber abandoning a search for the social causes of capitalism in favour of a psychological approach?

6 In what ways is Weber's approach scientific?

7 Does Weber's analysis of social inequality complement or undercut Marx's theory of class?

8 Outline Weber's concepts of power and authority. Are they related to Marx's concept of ideology?

9 Discuss the main differences between charismatic and rational-legal authority. Illustrate these differences with empirical examples of both types.

10 'In his criticism of the rationalisation of modern life, Weber is in effect wanting to turn the clock back.' Discuss.

Further reading

Brubaker, R., 1989, *The Limits of Rationality: An Essay on the Social and Moral Thought of Max Weber*. Allen and Unwin. Excellent short study of Weber's account of rationalisation in modern society.

Collins, R., 1986, *Max Weber: A Skeleton Key*. Sage. Useful overview of Weber's thought.

Crompton, R., 1993, *Class and Stratification*. Polity Press. Chapter 3, 'Class analysis: the classic inheritance and its development', presents a useful comparison of the Marxian and Weberian traditions of class analysis.

Gerth, H.H. and **Mills, C.W.**, 1948, *From Max Weber: Essays in Sociology*. Routledge. For Weber's essays on 'Bureaucracy', 'Class, status, party' and 'The social psychology of the world religions'.

Marshall, G., 1982, *In Search of the Spirit of Capitalism*. Hutchinson. An excellent critical survey of the debate over Weber's thesis.

Parkin, F., 1982, *Max Weber*. Tavistock. A useful, brief introduction.

Weber, M., 1985, *The Protestant Ethic and the Spirit of Capitalism*. Unwin.

Chapter 4

Emile Durkheim

Introduction: the denigration of Durkheim

We have noted that the reputation and influence of Marx within sociology have recently waned. Durkheim's reputation too has undergone travails, though in his case the decline came a good deal earlier, and there are now signs of recovery. With the rising popularity of poststructuralism there are moves to revisit his thought. Even so, Durkheim's influence in contemporary sociology is much less than forty years ago. In the immediate post-World War II period it seemed that Durkheim's influence was to be greater and more sustained in sociology than Marx's or Weber's. A main reason was the pre-eminence within Anglo-American sociology then of Talcott Parsons's theoretical scheme (see Chapter 5), understood to be a consensus theory and, therefore, owing more to Durkheim than the other two great founders. Another source of Durkheim's reputation was his methodological writings exemplified in his study of *Suicide* (1951), which was widely regarded as his most significant work. If Durkheim's concern with social solidarity rather than conflict was dominant at the theoretical level, then his manipulation of suicide statistics in *Suicide* made him for a time the very model for sociological method. He had given a decisive lead to the development of more sophisticated statistical techniques, which were seen as the key to scientific progress in the discipline.

The turning of the tide against Durkheim involved a reaction against both elements of his reputation. He was condemned on two main grounds: his conservatism, and his positivism.

The accusation of *conservatism* took its force from Durkheim's emphasis upon society as a moral unity. His concern with social solidarity and the containment of damage to it were understood by his critics to mean that the application and development of his approach would necessarily serve the existing social order. This interpretation downplayed – in fact, wholly neglected – the social criticism in Durkheim's writings, together with his reputation in his own time as a socialist and a radical. The charge of *positivism* was more justifiable.

Durkheim and positivism

Durkheim argued for his own methods on the grounds that they were essential to the development of a 'positive science', i.e. an approach

---

seeking to find law-like relations amongst phenomena and modelled on the physical sciences. In this respect Durkheim was an inheritor of the legacy of his French predecessor, Auguste Comte (1798–1857), a founder both of positivism and of sociology in the mid-nineteenth century.

In *Suicide*, Durkheim subjected official figures on suicide to statistical analysis, indicating how sociology might be taken in a *quantitative* direction. For a time in the 1950s and early 1960s, this approach had ensured Durkheim much attention from methodologically minded social scientists. The idea that sociology could and should be a science was very strong; so was the notion that science required the discipline to be quantitative. However, with the *interpretative turn*, which began in the mid-1960s, talk about sociology as a positive science, and about quantification became hallmarks of the *positivist* outlook, by then anathema to many in sociology. Indeed Durkheim came to emblematise all that was politically and epistemologically unacceptable in sociology.

To dismiss Durkheim from serious consideration on such grounds would unjustly diminish his stature and would overlook other aspects of his work which continue to influence sociological thought and social theory today. Camille Paglia (1993: 223–6) has observed, for example, that if Americans were aware of the debt that the (currently) immensely fashionable work of Michel Foucault owes to Durkheim, they would be much less impressed by the former's apparent originality. She is not alone in noting the links between Durkheim's thought and current concerns; several eminent writers have asserted the contemporary relevance of his ideas.

Against individualism

In line with our earlier consideration of the theme of humanism in Marx, we begin with Durkheim predominantly as a critic of individualism. His critique has two main strands:

- It is a fundamental misconception to suppose that society is (only) an aggregate of individuals, i.e. he opposed the view that the properties of society are merely the properties of individuals writ large.
- Individuals cannot pre-exist society, i.e. individualism as a doctrine is only conceivable in a certain kind of society; individuals, as represented by this idea of individualism, are only possible in the same kind of society.

Durkheim's major target, then, is the idea, the doctrine of 'individualism', which he seeks to expose as an ideology, to use Marxist terms.

Individualism

In this sense, individualism prizes unconditionally the distinctness and independence of individual human beings, who are to be treated as inviolable in their freedom and autonomy. The idea that individuals should be subordinate to any collective authority is to be borne, if at all, only in the most limited and necessary circumstances.

Thus the doctrine of individualism is in many respects a *political* doctrine (its classical statements remain the political theories of Thomas Hobbes and John Locke) about the relationship of the individual to the rest of society and, in particular, to the putative representative of that society, the state. However, individualism also has a potentially *scientific, methodological* aspect to it, proposing that the constituents of social reality are only and exclusively individual human beings.

According to this view, 'society' is merely a name for the other individuals in relationship with whom a given individual co-exists. The only way to understand society, then, is to understand the general nature of all those individuals as an aggregate. To take a simple example of the kind against which Marx railed, the competitive nature of capitalist society is understood as a result of the natural competitiveness and acquisitiveness of human beings generally. Indeed, individualism often conceives of human nature as essentially anti-social, for the individual is conceived as being motivated only by self-interest. In a picture explicitly painted in Hobbes's *Leviathan* (see Chapter 5) individuals lack all concern for others; they exist in society most reluctantly, conceding to the collective some of their freedoms and rights only for the sake of the benefits to be derived. Durkheim maintained that such conceptions were quite false; to attempt to apply them was entirely the wrong method for a genuine science of society. Nevertheless, Durkheim was unswervingly confident that society could be studied scientifically.

How is a science of society possible? Durkheim assumed that for there to be a science it has to have a subject matter. On the face of it, the appropriate science of society is psychology, the science of the individual mind. After all, if we can understand the mind, we shall understand why individuals behave as they do, and will have no need of an additional science, sociology. Durkheim was eager to dismiss this assumption, but was aware, also, that it has a natural appeal; individual human creatures are tangible, we can encounter and observe them in the flesh, whereas society seems to be no more than an abstraction from their behaviour. We do not meet society in the street, exchange words with it, watch it going about its activities. It would seem that individuals are real but society is not. However intuitively true this view may seem, Durkheim insists it is false. True, society is not directly observable perhaps, but it is observable *in its effects*. It does exist; it may not be detected by the conscious awareness of those individuals, yet it causally affects their actions.

Thus Durkheim argues that sociology can be a science which treats of a genuine subject matter because society exists as an authentic natural reality. It is as much a reality as physical nature, though different in character. Early on, in the way he set out *The Rules of Sociological Method* (1966), he tried to lay out the lineaments of his general strategy. There he argued that the way to establish, in principle, the reality of society was to reveal the criteria which define something as a reality. They are general criteria, of which the instance of physical reality is a special case.

Criteria for reality

To say something is a reality is to say two main things:

- It is *external*, i.e. exists outside our individual consciousness.
- It is *constraining* i.e. that its existence sets limits to our actions.

For example, a brick wall is patently a reality, because it exists in the world out there and it resists our actions if we try to walk through it. If these are the criteria of *facts*, i.e. of real things, then society satisfies them.

How can this assertion be justified? It cannot sensibly be disputed, of course, that the patterns of life in our society are not simply individual inventions. The law is not something which I or any other individual has invented. The law is something which has been developed *collectively*, built up over a long time by many individuals. It now confronts me as a thing which exists in the world, whether I will it to do so or not. One test for reality is satisfied, such social facts are external. Further, if I try to act in the world the law will offer me resistance. I cannot do just anything that I want to do. Yet the law is not necessarily constraining from a subjective point of view, even though objectively this is the case. For many of my actions, I take account of the law in a way which affects those actions, but I do not perhaps experience it as resistance to my individual will. I have simply become accustomed to doing things in ways which comply with the law. For example, when I decide to get some cash, I go into the bank, present a cheque and am given the cash in return. Consequently, it may seem that I freely do what I want. However, I am doing it in a way which conforms with the law, the way I have to do it if I want my actions to be unimpeded. Suppose I decide to do otherwise, by entering the bank armed with a pistol. In that case I will meet 'resistance', people will try to refuse to give me the money; they will try to capture me and, eventually, to incarcerate me in prison. The law exists then as something which, in designing my actions, I must take into account as a real consideration, just as much as I take into account the brick wall adjoining the door which I use to pass through to the next room. Consequently, the second test of a social fact is demonstrated, i.e. it constrains actions.

The nature of social solidarity

By such arguments, Durkheim proposes the reality of society and the existence of a phenomenon for sociology to study. It cannot be appropriated by psychology, for that is the study of the content of individual minds. In many ways the law may be the product of individual minds, yet it exists outside them. Just as there are natural facts, so too are there social facts. Having established this point, Durkheim is left with two questions:

1   What kind of existence does this external reality have?
2   On what aspect of this reality is social science to focus its attention?

Throughout the rest of his life he was concerned with answering them in terms of the relationship of society to the individual, and the *solidarity* or *cohesion* of society.

Durkheim's concern with the second of these questions legitimately categorizes him as a *functionalist* sociologist, thereby earning him much criticism as a conservative. We noted that Durkheim insists on the moral unity of society. To speak about 'a society' is to speak of some kind of unit. If we are to talk about English society as opposed to French society, then there must be some sense in which each is a self-subsistent unit, distinct and distinguishable from the other. In that sense, English society must hold together and have some persistent identity as a single whole, however much, and in whatever ways, it is otherwise internally differentiated. Obviously societies have *boundaries*, and in respect of the society's existence as a bounded, unified entity Durkheim sets in train a very consequential line of thought.

Social unity

If a society is to be said to exist, then it must satisfy certain conditions for unity (otherwise, as a matter of simple tautology, it would not exist, and we could not say that it did).

Durkheim's functionalism originates in the notion that for a society to exist it must be ordered in such a way as to meet these conditions.

If a society exists, and is bounded, in what way is it bounded? It must have an inside and an outside, but what does the line between the two differentiate? A tempting idea might be geography, for, of course, societies are often identified with territories. In Durkheim's view, this cannot be an answer, not least because of the methodological rule which he has laid down that a social fact cannot be explained by any other kind of fact, physical, biological, geographical, climatological or psychological, but only by other social facts. The boundary which demarcates a society must be social: it must relate to *membership*, which includes or excludes people. For example, French persons visiting England do not, thereby, become part of English society; although they are present on English territory, they do not have the relevant membership. Further, the boundary is *moral* in nature. The line of demarcation runs between acceptable and unacceptable conduct; those who transgress basic rules – criminals, the mentally ill – are outside the society. That the very existence of society presupposes such a demarcation Durkheim illustrates with an ingenious account of the nature of crime.

Crime

Crime exists even in societies which do not have laws, courts and the police. Durkheim asserts that *all* societies have crime, since all societies involve a differentiation between two kinds of actions, those that are allowed and those that are forbidden. He calls the latter type *criminal*.

Theories of crime – of which there are many – comprise attempts to understand the basis for this distinction. In seeking a rational basis for determining the nature of the contrast between the criminal and non-criminal, something about the nature and consequences of criminal acts as such is often assumed, e.g. they are harmful to society. Also, attempts to understand the punitive reactions to criminal actions are often regarded as a rational kind of response, with the punishment fitting the crime, or deterring it.

However, these rationalist conceptions do not really fit the facts about the relation between the crime and the reaction it gets. First, if punishment were a rationally worked-out form of response, then we would expect a proportionate relationship between the extent of harm caused to society by the act and the punishment inflicted. In fact, actions which do not harm society, e.g. many 'crimes without victims', such as prostitution, receive punishments, whilst actions which *do* harm society, such as spreading pollutants, often do not. Second, the punitive reaction to crime is not rational and calculative, but intensely emotional; the sense of outrage (fuelling the desire to exact punishment) is often a substantial component. Having established that this rationalist line of thought does not capture the nature of the response to crime, Durkheim's next move is to say that the intrinsic nature of the action involved is essentially irrelevant to the matter. It is not the specific nature or result of the offending action as such which matter, but the fact that action transgresses widely shared and strongly held sentiments, whatever these might be in any particular case. The reaction to crime is not reparative, it is punitive; an expression of the outrage and anger against the offender is precipitated when strongly held convictions are transgressed. Reaction against criminals makes of them social outcasts and sometimes literal outcasts. The offender is regarded as falling outside normal society, and the punishment provides a display of the fact that some individuals are being set apart from everyone else, at least symbolically. Often they are excluded from the rest of society by denial of full membership rights or by physical separation, i.e. being locked in prisons or put to death.

Thus there is a boundary drawn between those who are proper members of society, and those who engage in improper actions and so are not true members of society. The boundary is, therefore, moral. In a way, then, the reaction against crime is a *community* reaction which both vents and creates feelings of mutual solidarity amongst those who react against the criminal. Being together on the right side of the line gathers in 'the decent people' and sets them against those whose conduct is unacceptable. The reality of society consists, then, very much in moral phenomena, in conceptions of right and wrong and, therefore, of what conduct is permissible.

For Durkheim society must be something more than a collection of individuals and in many ways, he twisted and turned to say what that 'more' might be. In *The Rules of Sociological Method* he was really arguing that the 'something more' is the *product of association*, which can only exist in relationships. For example, to disagree we need others; disagreement is a relationship between two or more individuals. For Durkheim the 'something more' is not mysterious. It is what is shared between individuals, primarily the *conscience collective* (i.e. the beliefs and sentiments shared within the community) and the *representations collective* (i.e. shared ways, such as language, of expressing thoughts and representing things); they have been learned from others and depend for their operation on being held in common. Here we note in passing the germ of Parsons's idea that ends or goals are not random but shared, an idea that he expanded on greatly (see Chapter 5).

Durkheim's opposition to individualism was spelt out in his first book, *The Division of Labour in Society* (1984). He aimed to prove that the very idea of the individual, and the realization of that idea, are only possible in a certain sort of society. Durkheim was developing a line which was to come to full fruition in his later work, namely that it is only possible to think certain sorts of thoughts under specific social conditions. Far from its being self-evident that society acquires its characteristics from its component individuals, Durkheim argues, on the contrary, that individuals acquire their characteristics from society itself.

The foundations of society

Durkheim's rejection of individualism takes the form of a thoroughgoing critique of the *utilitarian* school of thought. Some thinkers have argued that the ways and practices of society are made up by individuals on the basis of their practical usefulness to them. For example, Thomas Hobbes (1588–1679) offers the picture of individuals setting up a sovereign authority as a means of regulating their relationship between themselves and restricting the mutually destructive tendencies which unregulated competition would produce. Herbert Spencer (1820–1903) had the idea of society consisting in individuals devising contractual relationships as a way of facilitating their transactions with one another. This explanation does not work. It might seem that a contract is created purely by the individuals who are party to it, but this is something of an illusion. Certainly, any one specific contract is made by the individual parties to it, but these parties expect this particular contract to be like all contracts in general, i.e. to be created within a pre-established *moral framework*. After all, if contracts were merely a matter of individual-to-individual agreement, then what would be the point of creating them? If individuals did not trust one another to do as they say, then there would be no point in attempting to improve one's position towards the other by getting him or her to make an explicit, formal agreement obliging the required actions. If one's word were not to be trusted, then why would a mere signature on an agreement be any more reliable? The value of a contract resides in its being made against the background of institutional arrangements. It does not simply bind the actual parties, but also involves obligations on others who are not party to the contractual agreement. The forces of law and order will support the claims of someone who has made a contract if that contract is validly made. Furthermore, society lays down what a contract can validly be; it is defined in terms of understandings in the society at large so that, for example, in our society one cannot make a contract to sell oneself into slavery.

Non-contractual elements in contract

A framework of moral understandings and of social arrangements of enforcement is presupposed in the making of a contract. This framework is not established by the parties to the contract, but it is necessary if their action of making a contract is to have any sense.

Consequently, the idea of society being *founded* in some sort of contractual arrangement between individuals – invoked by Jean Jacques Rousseau (1712–78) as well as Hobbes and Spencer – is a non-starter. Thus Durkheim's argument about non-contractual elements in contract opposes the idea that the actions of individuals can ante-date the existence of society, since the capacity to perform actions, and not just those of contract making, extensively presupposes the existence of a social framework, i.e. shared rules and forms of social organisation.

The idea of the individual – which we described above as 'political' – is essentially one of distinctiveness and autonomy, of someone entirely independent of others; individuals should, ideally, be left free to do whatsoever they want (within distinct but very broad limits). This idea is not a conception of human nature, though it offers itself as such. Rather, it is only thinkable in a certain kind of society, namely, the complex, modern society we now inhabit. The individual, in this sense, cannot exist in the simplest, most basic form of society – one which Durkheim's terms 'mechanical'.

In the very simplest societies (as Durkheim conceived them) there is little specialization; the individual human beings engage in similar activities on a self-sufficient basis. Self-sufficiency means that there is little interdependence within the society: any single part of the society – an individual or family group – is not significant to or essential for the group's continued existence. The solidarity of such a group derives from *likeness*, not interdependence; the members feel bonds of unity because they are much alike in their pattern of life and also in outlook. Under such basic conditions, life is homogeneous, and the space for the development of distinctive patterns of thought or outlook is severely restricted. Individuals learn their convictions from others and have little or no reason to challenge or depart from them. Since the variety of their own experience is so limited, it serves only to confirm those same, shared beliefs in the eyes of each individual.

The analogy underpinning this notion of *mechanical solidarity* comes from the conception in physics of the mechanical structure of a gas which is made up of identical, individual and independent atomic units. Of course, in line with Durkheim's argument about crime, it follows that if a mechanical society ensures such standard existence and uniformity of belief, then there will be strong, widely shared sentiments and, therefore, intense, punitive reaction against crime, i.e. against anyone who might become different.

Under pressure of population growth, such a society will begin to change its nature, for it cannot simply continue to expand whilst remaining the same. Here Durkheim is echoing Hegel's idea of quantity into quality. The need for a society to cope with increasing numbers gives rise to the development of specialisation, i.e. a division of labour.

Effects of the division of labour

Here the analogy changes to one borrowed from evolutionary theory: the capacity of an area of territory to support life is greater if the inhabitants are diversified. If they all have the same needs, they will all be competing for the same scarce resources relevant to that need, but if they are different species, with different needs, then they will not be in such direct competition for resources. Thus the pressure of population leads to increasing diversity within the population through specialization in the parts people play in society. With specialisation the basis of social solidarity, shifts from mechanical into *organic*, i.e. from likeness to *interdependence*.

'Organic' draws on a biological rather than a physical metaphor. The living organism is a composite of differentiated structures; metaphorically there is a division of labour amongst its parts. For example, the heart functions to pump blood, the lungs function to transfer oxygen to the blood, the eyes function as instruments of sight. Clearly, the parts are different, but interdependent – the loss of one has consequences for the rest, e.g. if the heart stops, then everything stops. Comparably, in a complex society with much specialisation there is interdependence; an individual's capacity to specialise in doing just one thing depends upon others doing the complementary things that the first requires for his or her survival. For example, someone practising medicine requires that someone else be producing food; someone producing food depends on others for clothes. Here specialisation is not just in economic activity, but in all areas of life, for Durkheim has in mind a *social* and not just an economic division of labour. Consequently, the members of such a society are held together by their need for one another. Hence with specialisation evaporates the basis for likeness, which derived, of course, from the commonality of experience. Increasing specialisation in society brings on complexity, making for a vastly wider range of possibilities of experience out of which are formed very different conceptions and convictions. Under such circumstances, one individual's life can be very different from another's. Thus the idea of individuals *as* individual, i.e. as distinct and different, can gain a hold and seem convincing. Only in such a context is there any real individuality to be prized and any toleration for autonomy of outlook and sentiment. Under such conditions there cannot be uniformity of sentiment throughout the population; there will be fewer widely shared and strongly held sentiments, so that for anyone to offend by mere difference from the prevailing pattern will no longer comprise crime. Durkheim contends that the role of law in organic society is not so much to repress differences as to reconcile the results of differences. The law has to settle damage to the society resulting from dispute and disagreement arising from the different needs, interests and outlooks of different kinds of persons.

The individual is, then, a creation of organic solidarity in the sense that a creature with individuality is only truly conceivable and possible within a certain kind of society. The very characteristics of the individual derive from the kind of society in which he or she is involved. Thus society creates 'the individual' and not the other way about.

Diagnosing social pathology: suicide

The attachment of previous social theorists to individualism is, for Durkheim, symptomatic of the fact that the idea of the autonomous individual has such a powerful hold on modern society that it bids to become ever more extreme, threatening the well-being of society itself and, thereby, the individuals living in it. With mechanical solidarity, the society overwhelms individuality; with organic conditions, it seemed to Durkheim that the opposite threatens. Much of Durkheim's later work was motivated by his concern with the appropriate balance between individual and society, trying to identify the threats to it and to theorise solutions.

In arguing the social foundations of individualism, Durkheim recognised that a degree of individualism was 'natural' to modern societies. He was not against individualism as such, but opposed its rampant, *pathological* forms. The issue, therefore, was how to strike a balance between independence and individual freedom, on the one hand, and subordination to the collective, on the other. He thought individualist doctrines were partial and one-sided; they put absolute priority on the individual's freedom over any restraint by the collective. He felt that such doctrines did not express the true desires of individuals, but only one aspect of the ambivalence which is characteristic of the modern mind. Part of it revolts against all restraint by the collective, but another part clings to and yearns for such restraint. Durkheim aimed to specify this requirement by formulating a conception of the correct proportions of individual autonomy from and individual dependence on the collective. What was the proportion required for general social and individual well-being?

Durkheim's study of suicide needs to be set against this background.

Suicide

For Durkheim, suicide was a result of imbalance in the independence/autonomy relationship. In brief summary, suicides occur amongst those subject to too much or too little social solidarity.

Suicide is notable in taking what appears to be the most individual of acts, and therefore least likely to exhibit any regularities of a social kind, and then going on to demonstrate that suicide varies *according to social ties*, to their presence or absence, their strength or weakness. We noted earlier that *Suicide* had a considerable methodological impact through its manipulation of statistics to reveal the interconnection of various facts about suicide rates. It is important to remember that it is differential rates between social groups that Durkheim sought to explain, e.g. Protestants commit suicide proportionately more frequently than Catholics and Jews, single men more frequently than married ones, urban dwellers more than rural, etc. Durkheim argues, of course, that these differentials reflect differences between the social groups, i.e. the different ways individuals are connected to society, and the kind of social support that results.

Durkheim proposed four basic types of suicide: the egoistic and anomic reflect social ties that are too weak; the altruistic and fatalistic types arise from connections that are too strong, so that the group suppresses individuality.

Egoistic suicide results from the social isolation of the individual. It occurs amongst those who have fewer and less social ties, such as those who live alone in rooming houses rather than with a family, or those burdened with an intense spiritual loneliness. For example, Protestants have a higher suicide rate than Catholics since Protestant teachings emphasise that one is face to face alone with God, that one's relationship is entirely direct, and that one must, therefore, carry the entire burden of effort essential to one's salvation. This contrasts with Roman Catholic teachings which make the church and its practices the basis for one's relationship with God, providing mechanisms (such as the confessional) to share the burden and so giving support in life.

By contrast, *anomic* suicide was occasioned by insufficient social regulation of the individual. In effect, the moral code of society failed to maintain its hold over the individual. The seemingly paradoxical feature of suicide was that although suicide rates rose during times of economic recession, as we might expect, they also rose during times of economic boom and prosperity, when we might expect them to decline. The superficial element of the explanation is that both situations of boom and bust occasion dislocation between the individual's social position and the socially prescribed morals which relate to them. Within a socially stratified society there are different norms (moral standards) for the different social classes, and they specify different tastes and aspirations for the members of the respective groups. For example, middle-class people may expect to go to university, whilst lower-class people may not expect or even aspire to do so. Such norms develop on a collective scale and over time; as they arise from the real situations of the group, they have a realistic character. Even if lower-class people aspire to university attendance, they are less likely to succeed. However, economic bust and boom both result in abrupt movement of people up and also down the social scale. Middle-class people find themselves in greatly reduced circumstance in crashes, whilst lower-class people can be rendered enormously prosperous by economic booms. In other words, the standards to which they have become accustomed become inapplicable, precipitating suicide. How so?

We noted above that Durkheim's ideas principally have been understood through the writings of Talcott Parsons. The significance of the anomic form of suicide is a case in point. Mainly due to Parsons's influential interpretation of Durkheim, anomic suicide has been held to be a particularly notable category in Durkheim's typology. The idea of anomie, Parsons argued, represented a shift in a key feature of Durkheim's concerns. Previously he had talked about the constraining nature of social facts, identifying them as *moral* facts, which set requirements on how people should act. In his earlier work, however, Durkheim had emphasised the external nature of those constraints, as though society's moral rules were simply a fact in our environment (in the way that a brick wall is) of which we have to take practical account. Therefore, our compliance with society's rules seems a rather *instrumental* matter, i.e. we obey because we fear the disapproval and punishment that would follow any infraction. Durkheim's development of the concept of anomie is very different. For him, the standards of life become part of the individual's personality; the requirements of society's moral order become – to use a post-Durkheimian vocabulary – *internalised*. In short, we do not refrain from doing things which society forbids just because we fear the consequences, but because, very often, we do not want to do those things; we feel that it would be wrong to do them.

If unrestrained by social upbringing, the individual personality would, Durkheim says, be insatiable. It would have endless wants and, furthermore, would have no realistic basis for working out which of them could be realised.

Individuals simply cannot work out the practical possibilities of life for themselves; to have any realistic sense of them, they must pick them up from other people, from their social setting, where cumulative, collective experience has provided the requisite exploration by trial and error. Individuals with insatiable and unrealistic wants would lead utterly frustrating and, eventually, unbearable existences; this fate is prevented only by the learning of the appropriate social standards. Rapid and extreme movement up and down the social scale disrupts this social learning, putting individuals in a situation in which there is no realistic guide on how to live, allowing them to develop unrealistic expectations and inevitable frustrations which may finally become unbearable and self-destructive. For Parsons the importance of this argument in Durkheim is in conceiving social restraint as internal and not purely external. We will return to this point and develop it further when we come to discuss Parsons (see Chapter 5). The more immediate import of the anomic case is Durkheim's suggestion that an element of socially imposed discipline is essential to individual well-being, that socially prescribed limitations on otherwise natural human appetites is an essential for sheer survival.

Altruism and fatalism are at the other extreme. Altruism involves individuals seeing the pre-eminence of the group over themselves to the extent that the group's needs seem greater than theirs. In fatalism, individuals are dominated by the group so intensely and oppressively that they are rendered entirely powerless over their fate. *Altruistic* suicide is instanced by cases such as the suicide of military officers for the honour of the regiment, or the self-sacrifice of a leader's family and retinue on the leader's death. In such cases the bonds within the social group are so strong and intense that they create amongst the members a powerful sense of group identity, with individuals being dependent upon the group for their sense of identity; so much so, in fact, that the individuals think themselves less important than the group and are willing to give up their lives for it in order to respect and preserve it. The *fatalistic* form, which receives barely a mention from Durkheim (one brief footnote), occurs when individuals in a group are placed in a position of such restriction that they feel nothing can be done to control their own life save to exit from it, e.g. suicides amongst slaves.

This argument for a balance between social regulation and individual autonomy concludes that the problem in modern, i.e. organic, society is that the balance has swung too much towards freedom from social regulation. Durkheim's concern was with understanding the mechanisms which structured relations between the individual and society, with a view to working out how to readjust those mechanisms in the desirable direction.

As for making out a case for a science of sociology, in the analysis presented in *Suicide* Durkheim felt he had succeeded in demonstrating the existence of supra-individual patterns in terms of which individual fates were decided. In any given society the rates of suicide did not vary much over time, and Durkheim wrote of society as 'demanding a certain rate' of individual deaths. This kind of remark might seem to justify the impression, which alienated many from Durkheim, that he was giving far too great a reality to society. He seemed to treat it as something not only arising from association amongst human beings, but also as having a life of its own. Arguably, however, Durkheim did not intend any such suggestion. After all, he did point to *collective* phenomena to justify his talk about the reality of society's existence and did seek to avoid conveying the impression that society was something utterly dissociated from its members. From this point of view, his remark about society 'demanding' a certain rate of suicides was really only a way of saying, admittedly loosely, that the conditions which exposed people to the risk of suicide remained constant for comparatively long periods of time. Rather than unjustifiably *reifying* society (see Chapter 8), Durkheim can be read as emphasising the fact that our membership of society is neither of our choosing, nor something we can cast off at will.

The social foundations of religion

The topic of religion provided Durkheim with a further opportunity to examine the relationship between the individual and the society and to investigate what he perceived to be a major mechanism of social solidarity. As an atheist Durkheim could not accept that the ostensible point of religion – to worship a god – could be its real explanation. Here he was not alone, as numerous anthropologists and sociologists before him had sought to explain what religion was 'really' about. Many of these explanations were of an individualist and psychological sort, seeking to understand religion as the product of properties of the individual mind, e.g. as a result of mistaken apprehensions of natural phenomena. Durkheim, entirely in accord with his own past practice, wanted to demonstrate that religion was a collective, and not an individual phenomenon.

He reasoned that since religion was such a widespread phenomenon, it cannot simply be dismissed as entirely false. If it were, then surely people would see through it, and not so many would be in its sway. There must be something to it – but what?

It was characteristic of Durkheim's approach to empirical analysis to take his point of departure from a general definition of the relevant phenomenon, be it suicide or religion. Thus the first task was to develop a definition of religion which would include all its diverse forms across the span of humanity that we would count as religions. He rejects the most obvious answer as too narrow, i.e. that the notion of a god or of supernatural beings is a universal feature of religions. For example, Confucianism involves no belief in deities. The essential feature of religion is its association with the notion of *the sacred*, that is of something quite special to be treated with exceptional levels of awe and respect. The sacred can include things which are in one sense secular, such as the national flag; for many, it would be *profaned* by being treated as just an ordinary thing.

Sacred and profane

Durkheim says that religion divides the world into two spheres, the sacred and the profane. On the one hand, there is the ordinary, everyday world of practical, material and other concerns: on the other is the world of the special and ritualised which must be sharply separated. For example, changes in dress, attitude and manner can be required of people when what they are doing involves them in contact with the sacred. This distinction is also connected with collective existence, since a church is an organised group, a collectivity of believers. The church requires of its members certain beliefs and, above all, the performance of certain sorts of actions, namely, *rites*.

In *The Elementary Forms of Religious Life* (1976), Durkheim worked on a now outmoded, evolutionist conception of society's development. To examine the essential forms of religion he felt it necessary to study what were then seen as the simplest, least developed societies, here those of the Australian aboriginal peoples. If religion has an essence, then it must be present in all cases and will be easiest to detect in the most basic, simple ones. Aboriginal religion, 'totemism', had been closely studied and was subject to much controversy before Durkheim took up the topic.

Totemism

Totemism involves the worship of specific things in the environment – animals, plants, particular places or objects – and the making of representations of these things in the form of symbols (called *churinga* and usually carved on wood) which are used in religious rituals.

Durkheim drew upon other people's studies of the totemic system to argue that it is misguided to look at the totemic object, the item worshipped by a particular group, in order to find a solution to the question of what totemism was really about. The totemic object, which seemingly could be almost anything, was certainly sacred. For example, if it were an animal it could not be killed or eaten. Yet why should these ordinary objects be the recipients of such exceptional treatment? There seemed to be nothing about them which distinguished them from other, quite ordinary, objects, but surely there must be something.

Durkheim held that imagining ways these ordinary objects could acquire such special status cannot work. It is not the objects themselves but what they stand for that is the key. These objects derive their exceptional character from that with which they are associated. Vitally, Durkheim recognised their symbolic dimension; totemic items are, in fact, *symbols*, and their symbolic meaning is the source of their power. This finding is indicated by the fact that the prohibitions relating to the items themselves – the animal or plant – could be lifted under certain exceptional circumstances, yet the symbolic representations used in the ceremonies are still accorded special status and strictly governed by the prohibitions. What is it, then, that is symbolised? What is there in the environment of the aborigines that can have such respect-inspiring status? Given Durkheim's proclivities, there can be only one thing: society. The above analogy with the national flag is apposite: in representing the social group, the totem is very like the national flag, for it was an emblem of a social group: those whose totem was the kangaroo would call themselves 'the kangaroos', and they would differ from 'the emus' and so on.

The role of the totem symbolises something not explicitly, intellectually understood by the aborigines: their dependence as human individuals upon their society. The totem expresses things which people know in their experience, but cannot comprehend or express in an overt, intellectual way. Thus religion is a symbolic, rather than a discursive, activity; we know but cannot say in so many words. We know through our practical lives the extent to which society is some- thing greater than each of us individually. The life we lead is dependent upon other people and the support of our social group. Moreover, the society of which we are a member is much mightier than any one or even a group of us. In comparison with us, society is immortal, as it continues to exist though we individuals pass away. Given Durkheim's initial assumption that religion must have some essential truth to explain its widespread acceptance and persistence, then religious beliefs must be about something *real*. Religions assign to the sacred immense power and eternal persistence. These must be the properties of something in the world. In aboriginal life there is only one such thing: their society itself. Thus the attitude towards the sacred, the posture of worship, is a posture towards society, an obeisance before the power that truly gives us purpose and rules our lives.

In Durkheim's account, then, the totem is connected with a worshipping group for which it functions as an emblem. The totem involves various beliefs about its special nature, which are symbolic expressions of the nature of society. Only the rites remain to be considered.

The aboriginals' way of life involved a cycle of dispersion and reassembly. The occasions of reassembly were those of rituals, called corroboree, in which those involved would get themselves into an emotionally intoxicated state. Here, Durkheim saw further testimony to the power of society; the association between human beings has potent effects upon the feeling states of individuals.

Collective effervescence

Involvement in the group activity created *collective effervescence*, an unusual state of shared excitement, involving exceptionally intense feelings. The shared expression of these emotions served to heighten them still further.

More mundanely, the effect is akin to the feeling of being at a good party: one feels different and better because of the occasion. The exceptional states of the corroboree, however, are not attributed to the persons present as such, but rather understood as expressions of the totem's power. To the aboriginal peoples, the totemic animal or plant had the capacity to induce exceptional states in people, e.g. enabling men to mutilate their bodies without feeling any pain. For Durkheim, the individual's participation in such a common occasion explains such things. Collective involvement renews and strengthens the feelings towards the totem, and the benign and intense character of the emotions created extends to others present in the same situation. The feeling of commonality with them is intensified by the fact that they share the same exceptional experiences. Thus the rites reinforce the solidarity of aboriginal society in two ways: through the symbolic relationship to the totem; and through the relationship of shared experience between the individuals who make up the group.

Thus Durkheim's contention that religion is 'society worshipping itself' becomes somewhat plainer. The members of society collectively give symbolic expression (through ceremony and ritual) to their sense of membership of the large, less transient collective within which they live and upon which they depend. Durkheim supposed that people's reactions are subject to attrition and that over the course of daily life capacities for certain kinds of feeling will diminish if they are not periodically stimulated. It is the role of both the criminal offence and the ritualised religious life to provide periodic stimulation to feelings, to keep them alive, to restore them to their prior strength. Thus the criminal stimulates feelings of outrage in connection with society's rules, and reinforces our sense of what we have in common with others who endorse those rules, whilst the religious rite revitalises the senses of attachment and solidarity which we have with others who belong to our group.

Durkheim on knowledge

Finally, there is one, slightly discontinuous, aspect of *The Elementary Forms of the Religious Life* which served to sustain Durkheim's influence when the conception of him as a positivist and a functionalist cast his ideas into disrepute in many circles. Toward the end of the book he offered the view that the categories of thought have a social origin. The philosopher Kant had maintained that the fundamental categories of thought are innate in the human mind, e.g. thinking of things being distributed in space and time, or as standing in causal relationships to one another. Durkheim's study of the anthropological material on the aborigines and his collaboration with his colleague, Marcel Mauss, in a study of *Primitive Classification* (1973) convinced him that conceptions of space and time vary from society to society. In short, not all humanity shares our conception of space as something that extends out evenly in all directions. (Indeed, after Einstein we no longer hold such a view, either, for space now 'curves'. Some other people think of space as, for example, circular.) Of course, we all have the capacity to apprehend space; it is an innate part of our capacity to see that the chair is across the room, or that the ball is off the ground and moving through the air. What Durkheim has in mind, however, is not our subjective experience of space, but the conception of space as an objective environment within which we are located. For example, we do not think of ourselves as dwelling at the centre of all things as once we used to; we do not think of ourselves as specially located in a space which radiates out from us. Such conceptions of space could not be figured out from our individual experience of space, but must be acquired collectively. Thus the concept of space as something possessed of an overall order must have a social origin.

Durkheim reasoned that human beings cannot truly originate conceptions out of nothing; we can only contrive things on the basis of some given model. He held, therefore, not only that concepts of space (and, on the basis of comparable arguments, time) were social in the sense that they are collectively created, but they are also social in respect of their content. Again, as far as Durkheim could see the only things on which the comprehensive schemes of space and time could be modelled are *social arrangements*.

The social construction of knowledge

The concept of space held by a group is modelled on the spatial arrangements of the group's social life; for example, the layout of its camps or the routes of its travels, in that a group with a concept of space as circular derives it from the circular layout of its huts. Similarly, temporal concepts are based upon the rhythms of the group's collective life, just as the Western year is still structured around feasts and holidays like Christmas, Easter and the New Year. A notion of time as having a structure, a rhythmic pattern, is stimulated by such facts about our social life.

Though much criticised in its specifics, this idea of Durkheim's has been enormously influential upon the sociology of knowledge. The idea of knowledge as socially shaped and socially constructed has become central to many recent strands of sociological thought, structuralist and poststructuralist included, as we will see in chapters 9 and 10. Consequently, far from being simply an outmoded positivist and functionalist, Durkheim is now once again coming to be regarded as a major thinker whose work is a source of profound sociological insights.

Durkheim the radical reformer

We remarked earlier in the chapter that Durkheim was regarded in his own time as a socialist and a radical and not as a conservative. For example, he played an active role in the 'Dreyfus affair', started by the false imprisonment for treason of a French Jewish army officer, which so divided French society in the final years of the nineteenth century. Durkheim's activities as a 'Dreyfusard' were hardly those of someone entirely anxious to defend the social and political status quo. In his sociological writings, he also allied his interest in social reform to his critique of individualism and his theme of the need for collective identity and social integration. For him, the purpose of a scientific sociology was very much to guide social reform along effective lines, based on an objective under-standing of society and its problems. His basic diagnosis of modern society as subject to an increasing lack of integration, with the relationship between the individual and society becoming increasingly attenuated, led him to focus upon ways in which this situation might be reversed. The conditions of organic society meant that there was great diversity in outlooks, including moral ones, but Durkheim thought that there was a need to strengthen attachment to shared morals, and also to provide better support for the individual's connection to society.

Since what we earlier referred to as 'internalisation' (using a Parsonian term) of society's moral code occurs in childhood and largely through the process of education, Durkheim was profoundly interested in education and educational reform. Indeed he has a strong claim to being the originator of the sociology of education. He was more interested in education's role in the trans-mission of a shared moral sensibility than in issues around the relationship between education and social inequality. This role might serve to reunify an increasingly divided society. In *Moral Education* (1961) he argued for the idea that the fundamental purpose of education is the inculcation of moral values and a 'spirit of discipline'. This idea might now sound rather right-wing in tone, but to jump to this conclusion would again miss the point. Durkheim was pointing out something more fundamental: a complex and differentiated society places demands upon its members to be able to co-ordinate their activities with others, thereby requiring individuals to be capable of controlling their conduct in specific ways in order to align it closely with other people's. Furthermore, such control has to be second nature, not something which requires individuals to stop and think and consciously plan how to fit their conduct to that of others. Consequently, the general moral attitudes of individuals not only have to be similar, but also require each person to be able routinely to monitor her or his own and others' conduct with respect to these moral assumptions. In modern society, the child first becomes involved in complex, collective activities in the school classroom; therefore the 'spirit of discipline' is acquired in school.

The classroom as a moral order

Durkheim was pointing to something that has only became fully appre-ciated by sociologists of education in recent years: underlying the content of schooling, e.g. the teaching of subjects by teachers and the taking and passing or failing of examinations by students, is a more fundamental social reality, the classroom as a *moral order*.

Long before the concept of the 'hidden curriculum' had been coined, Durkheim was arguing that the *social form* of the teacher–student and student–student relationships is what above all shapes the educational experience. These relationships are infused with values, and the role of the teacher in relation to the student is to exemplify society's values.

Durkheim was also led into the field we now call 'industrial relations' by his concern at the breakdown of order and loss of collective morality in modern society. Like Marx, Durkheim believed that the direction in which industrial societies were moving, with ever bigger enterprises and ever greater competition, meant the destruction of any sense of morality guiding economic activities. Economic life was becoming dangerously amoral: the expansion of capitalism was accompanied by polarisation and atomisation; i.e. workers were increasingly isolated from their employers and from one another. The result was the rapid increase in social conflict and more individualised forms of pathology, while civic morals were in decline. Given his methodological view that social facts can only be explained by other social facts, Durkheim believed that social solutions had to be sought, since the causes of these problems were social. New social structures were required to counter these trends. He believed one such structure was the professional association.

Professional associations

Since workers in the same or similar occupations experienced the same treatment, economically and socially, Durkheim, like Marx, saw a basis for collective action around common interests. Forming occupational groupings such as trade unions or professional associations to pursue these common interests on the basis of shared values would not only tie individuals more strongly to one another, but would also provide society with an intermediary form of collective existence between the individual and the nation state.

In arguing for the need for such organisations, Durkheim anticipated much of the subsequent debate about *mass society*, the dangers of which so exercised later thinkers, e.g. those in the Frankfurt School (see Chapter 8). These 'moderate-sized' bodies would bridge the gap between the massive edifices of the state and the capitalist enterprise on the one hand, and the individual on the other. Paradoxically, though Durkheim was himself somewhat leftward-leaning in his politics, this idea of a set of corporate groupings between the individual and the state seem close to the kind of ideas that the Fascists were subsequently to develop.

Conclusion

Durkheim's influence on Anglo-American sociology (and British social anthropology) was considerable. He was one of the key figures that Talcott Parsons (see Chapter 5) identified as making a decisive break with the limitations of nineteenth-century thought. Important parts of Parsons's theory derived directly from Durkheim, and it was through them that he figured as a major influence on mid-century sociological theory. However, the reaction against Parsons on the grounds of the conservatism of 'functionalist' and 'consensus' views (which allegedly emphasise agreement and harmony in society, and downplay conflict) meant that Durkheim too came to be reviled for the conservatism of his outlook. At the same time, there was also a strong reaction against methodological views, which held up Durkheim as a heroic precursor on the grounds that he had attempted to make sociology scientific by making it quantitative, through the sophisticated use of statistics in *Suicide*. In this connection Durkheim was attacked as a positivist, which became a term of abuse applied to all those holding that sociology might be scientific. At present these harsh and dismissive judgements are being reconsidered and the radical implications of his thought are being stressed. His consideration of the social basis of ideas has also been influential on what are currently considered radical ideas, such as those of contemporary French theory and the Anglo-American sociology of science.

Questions

1   What is positivism? Does Durkheim's *Suicide* illustrate it?

2   What place has the individual in Durkheim's thought?

3   Why does Durkheim put so much emphasis on the non-contractual elements of contract?

4   How does Durkheim's treatment of the division of labour differ from Marx's?

5   Has Durkheim's *Suicide* any modern relevance?

6   What is the function of religion in society for Durkheim? How does his view compare with those of (a) Marx and (b) Weber?

7   Does Durkheim's theory of ritual as marking the distinction between the sacred and the profane have application beyond the bounds of religion? If so, to what?

Further reading

Alexander, J. (ed.), 1988, *Durkheimian Sociology: Cultural Studies*. Cambridge University Press. A collection of studies in the Durkheimian tradition to demonstrate its continuing, up-to-date relevance.

Douglas, J., 1967, *The Social Meanings of Suicide*. Princeton University Press. Part III remains the definitive interpretivist critique of the use of statistics in suicide research.

Durkheim, E., 1951, *Suicide*. Routledge.

—— 1966, *The Rules of Sociological Method*. Free Press. Especially Chapter 1, 'What is a social fact?'.

—— 1976, *The Elementary Forms of the Religious Life*. Allen and Unwin.

Giddens, A., 1978, *Durkheim*. Fontana. A useful, short introduction.

Hughes, J.A., Martin P. and **Sharrock W.W.,** 1995, *Understanding Classical Sociology*. Sage. Chapter on Durkheim.

Lukes, S., 1975, *Emile Durkheim: His Life and Work*. Penguin. A major critical study.

■   ■   ■

Part two

Chapter 5

Consensus and conflict

Introduction: Parsons – the project for a systematic sociology

The impact of 'the classics' on Anglo-American sociology was, in the first instance, very much the achievement of Talcott Parsons (1902–79), whose graduate studies in the UK and Europe in the 1920s had familiarised him with the work of, among others, the trio of Marx, Weber and Durkheim (see Chapters 1–3). In the 1930s Parsons set out to construct a major work of theoretical synthesis, drawing especially upon the work of Weber and Durkheim. The result of his efforts, *The Structure of Social Action*, appeared in 1937. The work consisted in large part in the presentation of four thinkers, two of whom – Alfred Marshall, the economist, and Vilfredo Pareto, the economist/sociologist – have not enjoyed such continuing significance for sociology. This book provided the world of English-speaking sociology with its first significant and systematic presentation of the ideas of Weber and Durkheim.

Parsons was also familiar with Marx's work and on p. 119 of *The Structure of Social Action* is his sympathetic summary of some of Marx's views. None the less, Marx was deliberately excluded from Parsons's grand synthesis. Parsons acknowledged Marx to be a great thinker, but argued that he remained firmly within the prevailing nineteenth-century way of thinking in the social sciences, while Weber and Durkheim had, by contrast, contributed to breaking it down.

One of the main targets of Parsons's criticism was utilitarianism, which, as we saw in our discussion of Durkheim (see Chapter 4), involves the idea that people's actions follow fundamentally practical objectives, and that the human mind is essentially a mechanism for calculating the most effective way to get the most rewarding results. This picture captures the very essence of economics, where 'the economic human' (*Homo oeconomicus*) is an individual with a clear set of wants and the economic capacity to fulfil some of them; he or she then sets out to figure out a way to get the most rewarding assortment of goods in terms of the resources available. In constructing its theories upon the assumption of such a rational, *maximising* individual, economics is building upon the model which was very widespread in pre-twentieth-century social thought. This model, as previously noted, found its most explicit and, in some ways, most crucial expression back in the seventeenth century, in Thomas Hobbes's *Leviathan* (1994).

Very briefly, Hobbes's argument was that human beings are selfish creatures living in a world of scarce satisfactions. Each individual has wants, and seeks to satisfy as many of them as possible. Working out the most efficient way of getting what they want, individuals realise that they are in competition with one another, that one person can only gain at another's expense. Thus individuals are by nature truly selfish and see others only as obstacles or possible resources in their own pursuit of maximum satisfaction. The most logical way to achieve one's ends, then, is either to eliminate the competition – remove others by killing them – or to turn them towards the service of one's own ends, by forcing or deceiving others into compliance with one's will. However, if every individual is conceived as a rational (i.e. logically operating) being, then each will reach the same inevitable conclusion, making social life into a state of perpetual struggle. Hobbes called it a 'war of all against all', colourfully characterising it in a justly famous passage as 'solitary, poor, nasty, brutish and short'. Of course, for most of us human life is not that bad, as Hobbes himself explained: valuing their own lives above all else, these rational individuals can perceive the slippery slope to mutual misery and destruction down which they would slide if they did not accept some restrictions on their freedom of competition. These restrictions are in the form of society, as represented by the sovereign ruler to whom individuals effectively cede their autonomy.

Hobbes's idea of society

This expressed two ideas that were immensely influential over the next three hundred years:

- Society is to be understood in terms of the characteristics of its individual members, as an association of individuals.
- Those individuals have the kind of self-interested, calculating character that the utilitarian model supposes.

Hobbes thus held the basic *individualistic* conceptions of human beings, drew out its strict logical implications, but then backed away from them: the invocation of 'the sovereign' was, for Parsons, a theoretical cheat.

Similarly, it was Parsons's view that Marx, for all his emphasis upon social classes, i.e. *social groups*, nevertheless remains within this individualist tradition by virtue of conceiving social life in terms of struggles over material interests. This reading of Marx is not unique to Parsons, as recent commentators such as Jon Elster (1985) argue a similar view.

Parsons was interested in Durkheim, Weber, Pareto and Marshall because they were all, in their different ways, concerned to think their way out of the framework of utilitarian assumptions. The key move which they all made was to reject the utilitarian assumption that people's ends are random. In a scheme like Hobbes's, it does not matter what kinds of things people want, only that they have plenty of wants, more than can collectively be satisfied by the finite resources of the world, and it is this simple fact which makes them competitors. In such reasoning, the way people come by their wants, or what wants they have, is essentially irrelevant and, viewed as a theoretical system, those ends might as well be random. Durkheim, Weber and the others had perceived, however, that people's ends are not random; they are *socially* acquired and, in consequence, are *related* to one another in systematic ways. For example, Durkheim examines the notion of anomic suicide in terms of the way people's wants are patterned; they are shaped by social arrangements which accord with the hierarchy of stratification and embody normative requirements which prescribe proper and acceptable wants.

Hobbes's thought had bequeathed the problem of social order: how is it possible for people to go about pursuing their individual ends without falling into the state of war of all against all? He had provided an answer, but it was unprincipled. Parsons's four theorists had begun to offer a principled solution, which rejected the individualistic picture of human beings and recognised that they develop and form their wants within a social context. Furthermore, the very acquisition of these wants is made possible *by* the social order, by what Durkheim calls society's 'moral order' and its systems of 'collective sentiments' and 'collective representations', i.e. what we would nowadays call *culture*. Wants are formed through this social order; far from being random, individual wants are often common and shared. Moreover, in being shared they are viewed as right and proper wants for anyone to possess. In other words, they have a moral character. It was in this way that Weber, for example, provided a very different conception of capitalism to Marx's in so far as he brought out the moral nature of the emphasis upon disciplined hard work in capitalism; this emphasis had its origins in religion and the desire for salvation rather than in the calculation of material benefit.

The project takes shape

On this basis, Parsons thought that a start could be made on developing a general scientific scheme for understanding human life. Between his first major work and his next there was a fourteen-year break – though Parsons did publish many essays in that time. Then in 1951 Parsons published two books, one self-authored, *The Social System*, the other a collaborative work, *Toward a General Theory of Action*. In a way, Parsons had retreated from the ambitions he held in 1937, but the plan laid out in these two books was none the less grandiose. *Toward a General Theory* drew its contributors from across several disciplines; necessarily so, for Parsons sought to lay out a groundplan for a large range of the social sciences – or 'sciences of action', as he called them. Thus psychology, sociology, economics, political science and other disciplines were all to be unified within a single theoretical framework, which was basically devised by Parsons. *The Social System* was the sociological element in the project, showing how this general scheme, this general theory of action, would be developed in sociology.

Parsons drew from the work of his four theorists a picture of social life involving *motivated compliance*.

Motivated compliance

Social life does work rather than disintegrating into Hobbes's war of all against all. It works because people go about their activities in ways which are not only socially prescribed for them, but also because these are ways they believe to be right and therefore actually want to follow.

He proposed that the actual operating life of a society is made up of the following elements:

1   the abstract *patterns* of behaviour which prescribe what individuals should properly or appropriately do in particular cases. For example, the highway code prescribes how fast drivers should drive under what conditions and how they should co-ordinate with fellow motorists;

2   the pattern of ongoing activity, i.e. how actual people in actual situations behave in ways which (roughly, more or less) accord with the abstract patterns. For example, in traffic on the road, drivers are busy looking out for what others are doing, and tactically adjusting their driving to accommodate and avoid one another, such action depending in various ways upon the conventions of the highway code being respected by most, if not all, drivers;

3   the personalities or characteristic patterns of preference, of reaction and so forth that the individuals carrying out these patterns have. For example, in traffic they act as drivers, and they interact with one another in terms of their characters: some drive much more quickly than others, some are more respectful of others' rights on the road, some get angry with traffic conditions, others remain calm, etc. However, the great majority of these drivers abide broadly by the rules of the road and do so not merely from prudence, for safety's sake, or from nicely calculated considerations as to just how much adherence to the rules would maximise their self-interest, but because they think this is the right thing to do. They regard these rules as binding on themselves and on others. They can become indignant with other drivers just because those drivers show disregard for the rules of the road, even though the infraction of these rules may cause them no danger or harm them in any way.

'Motivated compliance' means no more than the drivers being motivated to abide by the rules of the highway code, but this illustration of the idea draws attention to the way actual situations in society are made up of three elements:

•   *culture* – the pattern of ideas, principles, etc., which abstractly specifies how people should behave;

- *social system* – the ordered patterns of activity and relationship amongst individuals as they go about their affairs in conjunction, even collaboration, with one another;
- *personalities* – the psychic make-up of individuals which affects how they behave in such actual situations, how they go about doing things and how they react to other people.

Parsons argues that any actual society has to provide somehow for the *integration* of these three elements.

Integrating culture, social system and personalities

Somehow, things will have to work out so that:

- Culture will prescribe what people should do in ways which will prove practically effective, relative to what people want to do
- The pattern of activities and relationships in which people engage will prove capable of allowing the prescriptions of the culture to be effectively followed out (a good deal of the time)
- The parties to social life will have personality structures that will enable them to associate with others, to participate in conjoint, collective ventures, and to accept and comply with the demands that the culture lays on them.

The key word here is the first, 'somehow'. Parsons made the examination of this 'somehow' the focal concern of the remainder of his long career.

Cultures, social systems and personalities have themselves to interact in integrated ways if there is to be any social order. Cultures have to be organised in ways in which their prescriptions will be viable in actual activities, and social activities themselves have to be organised in ways that will offer sufficient reward to the personality types who will participate in them; if people are utterly frustrated and completely alienated, they will withdraw. Parsons insists that these are the *minimal condition* for social order. Without sufficient integration, social relationships cannot be organised and carried on. Of course, 'sufficient' is far from being a precise notion.

In view of the hostile response which Parsons's work eventually met, we should draw attention here to the fact that he does not see the integration of culture, social system and personality as either automatic or complete: far from it. In dealing with something as complex as the order of a society, its pattern of institutions and relationships, its culture built up over its history, and the varied personalities of its numerous members, we should recognise that integration is *highly problematic*. In any ongoing society which is not collapsing into internecine strife, it must be the case that there is a level of integration, since things are getting done, people are acting broadly in line with their cultural prescriptions, and many individuals are engaged in and committed to activities. The perceptible stability of society indicates that its members (or the great majority of them, for most of the time) are not alienated, in the sense of 'turned off'. However, there may not be thoroughgoing integration, since some aspects of the culture may conflict with the way the social system is organised, and the way both of these are organised may impose deprivations on participants' personalities. In any real society, many people may not be so disenchanted with their jobs that they would rather give them up, so opposed to authority that they would rather fight their supervisor than do what he or she says, or so contemptuous of the law that they will happily violate it. Nevertheless, those same people may be unhappy in their work, reluctant to comply with their supervisor and so uncommitted to a law-abiding existence that they may not pass up every temptation to transgress. Parsons recognises just such possibilities. They are partly what we mean by the integration of culture, social system and personality being problematic, i.e. the working out of the interconnections between them is something which is neither automatic nor guaranteed. Although any real society must have exceeded the 'minimal' requirements of integration – as testified to by the sheer fact of its existence – none the less it is an empirical question as to how far beyond this minimum the integration extends.

In talking about the achievement and surpassing of this 'minimal' level, Parsons is not discussing the ways the members of the society, through conscious, deliberative processes, 'work out' solutions to the problem of integration between these three aspects of social reality. Such matters do not exercise the members. The terms in which these issues are formulated are analytical and sociological; Parsons is talking from a sociological standpoint about the way things work themselves out; how the social order through the interaction and mutual effects of the culture, social system and personality becomes at least minimally integrated.

It is important to note that the three elements Parsons identifies are 'integrated', in the minimal sense that any concrete social situation is made up of all three of them. These three elements are all mixed up in actual situations. In fact, says Parsons, they *interpenetrate* one another. People in social relations do not just stand in purely personal relationships, but relate to one another on the basis of social positions (the status, or status roles) they occupy. Thus two individuals in a workplace stand not just as 'Joe' and 'Jim' but as, say, a worker and his supervisor. Their respective positions are not just a matter of what they are doing, but of rights and entitlements, e.g. Jim may be entitled to give Joe orders, and Joe required to do as Jim tells him. In other words, a work relationship, like any other, is a matter of rights and responsibilities, i.e. of cultural elements, and so cultural elements go to make up the social system. In its turn, the social system becomes part of the personality of its participants; the position that one holds, the job one occupies, is not merely a matter of external requirements, but is, obviously, something which is bound into and constitutive of the way one thinks of oneself. As the kind of position one occupies is contributory to one's self esteem these, too, interpenetrate. Further, in so far as one identifies with one's job, then of course one comes to regard the things one is entitled to do and to be responsible for not simply as things to be done because they are formally required of one, but as things one would want to do even if one was not required to do them. In this way, the cultural requirements and responsibilities of a job become part of one's personality.

In Parsons's terms, the social system is made up of cultural elements and of personalities. The social system and the culture interpenetrate because the latter is *institutionalised* in the former. In one sense, a social system is a pattern of institutionalised culture, i.e. a set of rules and requirements which have become accepted as defining how people should act and relate to one another, just as the highway code is ubiquitously accepted as saying how drivers should handle their vehicles and communicate with and respect the drivers of other vehicles. The connection between the social system and the personality is through *internalisation*.

Internalisation

This concept refers to the ways the members of society come to make the requirements of their various positions an integral part of their personality, 'taking over' these requirements and building them into their own convictions about how and what they should do.

For example, when we see other persons breaking a rule of the road we may become indignant because we feel that we personally have been affronted by what was done. Since a social system is itself significantly institutionalised culture, when people internalise the social system – identify with their position in it – they also internalise culture (since their position in the social system is made up of institutionalised culture).

Parsons's functionalism

'Functionalism' is often a bogy word: to characterise an argument as functionalist is enough, in some circles, to condemn it. Parsons's work gave the debate over functionalism prominence. His work developed from earlier thinkers: Durkheim, Bronislaw Malinowski and A.R. Radcliffe Brown in social anthropology (both also influenced by Durkheim) as well as Parsons's contemporary, Robert K. Merton.

Parsons proposed, as a kind of theoretical half-way house and not as an ultimate objective of sociology, the adoption of *structural functionalism*. His original idea had been to approach society from the bottom up, analysing it as a complex composite of *unit acts*, i.e. actions performed by individuals. Moreover, he had imagined representing the relations between actions as a set of mathematical equations, rather in the way the behaviour of a gas can be expressed in equations capturing the behaviour of its constituent molecules. However, he had realised that such an objective was, at least in the short term, quite un-realistic and so, to work towards it, he would adopt a different, top-down, conception of society, i.e. one taking the viewpoint of the society-as-a-whole in order to look down upon the behaviour of individuals. From this point of view, sociological knowledge was equated more readily with biology than chemistry, since the elements of the whole are understood in terms of their relations to the whole. The emphasis is on the functions of the elements, i.e. the contributions they make to the continuing operation of the whole, such as the part played by – the function of – the kidney in eliminating noxious elements from the circulatory systems of the body.

Remember that Parsons's problem was to understand how the integration of culture, structure and personality was achieved. This tripartite scheme was the basis of his structural functionalism. He had a very simple but crucial assumption: human beings are sensitive to one another and they treat one another's reactions as meaningful, as either rewarding or punishing. It is not just materially rewarding satisfactions which gratify people; they are pleased and pleasured by the approval and affection of others, are hurt by others' disapproval and rejection, and treat one another's reactions as expressions of feelings of liking, approval, distaste and so on.

Socialisation

Sensitivity is the lever of *socialisation*. Socialisation is simply learning to be social, and works through the giving and withholding of affection and approval in the relation between parents and children. Con-sequently, children come to adopt the parents' attitudes and standards as their own. Internalisation goes together with *identification*: children do not behave in certain ways simply to produce parental approval; in addition they want to become like the parents, to identify with them. They do so by taking on the parental attitudes as their own, wanting and approving the same things themselves.

On the basis of favourable and negative reactions, then, people can build up patterns of stable interaction. Each knows what the other wants, and each wants the other's approval, so each will act in ways which are expected to win the other's approval and solicit an approving, rewarding response. On the basis of this simple, uncomplicated case, Parsons developed the notions of *expectation* and *role* as key elements of social order. Strictly, Parsons's notion was of the *status role*, since it involves a position (the 'status' element) and an associated pattern of approved or expected behaviour (the 'role' part).

Status roles

To know that persons occupy certain status roles is to know what they *should* do, to have some *expectations* as to how they will behave and, in relationship to them, how one should behave oneself.

In this way one can imagine two individuals working out a balanced pattern of expectations about each other's behaviour until they arrive at a stable arrangement, so that each acts in ways which he or she knows the other will approve of and avoids acts he or she knows the other will not like.

Parsons asks us to imagine such a process working out across society as a whole so that the expectations that people attach to particular statuses are *standard* throughout the society. Then, of course, a high level of social order is possible; people who have never met before can immediately enter into a co-ordinated transaction if they know what roles they respectively occupy, since they will have mutual expectations about appropriate, matched behaviour. For example, if we see someone sitting in a vehicle recognised as a cab, we identify him or her as the cab driver and feel entitled to climb in the vehicle, to give some address, and to be driven to that place. Social life would not be possible on any scale of complexity if we had to work out our social relations from scratch each time. Parsons holds that we do not have to do so, for we acquire through socialisation these cultural elements, these expectations, about one another's appropriate conduct, to which we attach *moral* force: we not only expect but demand this behaviour. If it does not result we have punitive reactions to the other person.

Furthermore, the patterns of expectations – the *norms*, as he often called them – that pertain to different roles cannot be altogether dissimilar. A moderately complex society requires persons to be involved in many different kinds of status roles and in many different activities, e.g. as manager and secretary might be involved in office life, and pupil and teacher in education. It is not possible, Parsons argues, for the expectations attached to one relationship to be utterly incongruous to those attached to another; it would be neither practically nor psychologically tolerable for the kinds of things expected/allowed in one context to be utterly at odds with those in another. There must be some broad consistency across the range of status roles in respect of the kinds of things they allow.

Values

This consistency derives from the *values* which persons hold and which a society centrally institutionalises. Somehow, a society develops a set of cultural elements, beliefs about how things are, about how things should be, and what people should do; these are installed in its main parts and regulate the broad pattern of its arrangements.

For example, US society has been heavily influenced by its Protestant heritage; the idea of success through hard work has been powerfully impressed upon its members' lives. Most spheres of US life are pervaded by this idea, and hard work is everywhere recommended as the ideal for conduct: in the workplace, in the school classroom and so on. That people are commonly attached to such a shared ideal, such a value, makes for a measure of compatibility between the ways in which activities are conducted in different spheres of life. Here we recall the notion that Parsons found in Durkheim and Weber: ends are not merely random but are held in common.

Parsons is not by any means suggesting that everyone shares the same ideas or does so in the same degree, nor is he suggesting that there is nothing but thorough and detailed compatibilities between patterns of expectation in one area of life and another. Hence our frequent use of the term 'broadly', since Parsons is well aware that social life is complex, varied and subject to exigent circumstances. His project was to explore how a complex social unit, a *social system* – to use the abstract general term used to capture anything from a two-person conversation to the international system of nation states – could be organised so that at least the minimal requirements for its survival could be satisfied. He wanted to know how it could so organise itself as to interrelate the perpetuation and dissemination of its shared culture with the socialisation of incomers into the system. Further, how can both of these requirements be related to whatever business the system is supposed to do – whether that is to educate small children in the school classroom, to produce goods for sale in a commercial business, to prepare for battle in a military platoon, or to witness to God's glory in a religious occasion?

Systems theory

In Parsons's usage, the idea of *system* is important.

Systems

A system has persistent identity in an environment, it is distinct from its environment, but must transact with it so it is, in the jargon, an *open* system. For example, a mouse as a living creature is an open system; the mouse is not the same as its environment, but it must take in necessities (air, food) from the environment and must release waste products into it. The overriding task of the system to maintain its own identity in the face of that environment involves two main aspects:

- the regulation of transactions with the environment;
- the maintenance of effectively operating relations inside the system itself.

On the basis of these very simple assumptions, Parsons attempted to provide a completely general analysis of the way social systems operate.

After the books of 1951 Parsons saw a new way to develop his analysis, largely (or so he claimed) as a result of an association with Robert F. Bales, a social psychologist who had been trying to develop a general model to describe the behaviour of task-oriented small groups. Bales saw such groups as going through four *phases*: (1) they gather together the things they need to do a task; (2) then they organise themselves into carrying out the task; and, in doing so, (3) manage their own internal relations, e.g. stifling quarrels and keeping people interested; and when they have successfully completed their task (4) they relax for a while into task-unrelated activities before gathering themselves for the next task. Parsons adapted these four phases into the *four-phase model of system exchanges*. The elaboration of this model and its application to various situations was the abiding focus of his subsequent work.

A system must, then, transform its environment: the motor of activity is the gap between the way that the world is now and the way that the system (be it an organism, a small group or a large society) requires it to be for the satisfaction of its needs. Systems are 'goal oriented' in that there are ends they must achieve, situations they must bring about, if they are to survive and operate; and the realisation of the goal orientation involves activity to transform the environment. The pattern of activity in the system will vary over the course of the attempt to realise this goal, much of this activity being involved in goal attainment, i.e. whatever is necessary to deliver the desired end state – see (2) above. The pursuit of such an activity often begins with preparing the conditions for the activity of goal attainment, for the acquisition and assembly of the means necessary to the pursuit and realisation of the goal – a phase (see [1] above) which Parsons terms *adaptation*, involving extraction from the environment (be it the physical or social environment) of the means towards the goal (which includes, of course, people capable, suitable and willing to do the work to get to the goal). The pursuit of the goal will, of course, involve problems and troubles, and stresses and strains in the relations of those involved in the group (see [3]). There will, therefore, have to be things done to maintain working relationships or to restore fractured ones – this is what Parsons terms the 'integrative' phase (see [4]). Systems do not remain permanently in activity; people are members of many different systems and, after a group has attained a goal, a system will often dissolve as people go about other activities, and contribute to the goal attainment of other groups. The group continues to exist: the fact that all one's family is out of the house, at school or at work or whatever, does not mean the family ceases to exist, only that it is in a 'latent' state, i.e. not currently active as a unit. After goal attainment, the group can enter the 'latency' phase. During this phase, however, things have to happen to ensure that the system's capacity for collective action is kept up, that people will be able to recuperate their energies and commitment for another phase of activity.

The AGIL system

Thus the sequence of phases can run (1) adaptation, (2) goal attainment, (3) integration, (4) latency (or *pattern maintenance and tension management*, as Parsons terms the keeping up of attachment to the system's objectives). This four-phase system is often known as the AGIL system.

Of course, within a complex system not all parties will be involved to the same extent in all phases, and different parts of the system will specialise predominantly in one or other of these activities for the rest of the system. We can structurally dismember a system in terms of the priorities given by its different parts in respect to the functional phases of the system as a whole.

It is important to note that for Parsons it is systems all the way down, i.e. the question of 'what the system is' is relative, depending upon the purposes of analysis. For example, the family can be treated as a part, a sub-system, of the society's social system; or it can be treated as the system itself, so that the relation of husband and wife, of father to daughters, of mother to daughters, and so on, are seen as sub-systems of the family system. Thus Parsons's categories apply to systems and their sub-systems. Of course, any sub-system will not engage purely in one of the four functions, for each sub-system will have to satisfy its own functional requirements. For example, within the society's four phases, the family can be allocated to the latency phase, for people at home with their families are often taking time out from other social commitments, are relaxing, engaging in leisure pursuits and building up their capacity to face another day at the office or whatever. However, if we decide to analyse the family as a system in its own right, then its activities will also have to go through the AGIL cycle, and we might find that within the family some members specialise in one or other of these functions. For example, in the traditional nuclear family, the wife/mother specialised rather more in integrative activities than other members; she was held responsible for smoothing relations between the others, providing comfort and support for those in distress or under pressure.

In the AGIL model the issue of internal relations within the system came to dominate the latter phase of Parsons work. He sought to understand the *interchanges* between the functionally differentiated phases. For example, the adaptive phase (A) involves the accumulation of the means for transforming the environment for the system, but if they are to be put to use in goal attainment (G), then they have to be handed over to those engaged in these goal-attaining activities. There has to be some incentive, some return, if those involved in the A phase are to make resources – or *facilities*, as Parsons often talks of them – available to the G phase. If people keep on handing over things without any reward or return, they are likely to feel resentful and, eventually, will become fully alienated. For any system to work there has to be some (at least minimally) balanced exchanges between the various phases.

For an overly simple example, the government fulfils the goal-attainment function for the society, seeking to direct the society as a whole towards its objectives (such as economic growth or national glory, or some combination of both). The economy is the adaptive component of the society, i.e. producing resources out of the society's natural and social environment. Obviously, the running of government consumes resources, both to support its existence as an organised structure and to pursue its policies, so the adaptive system must hand over some of its product to government. Equally clearly, the government has to deliver something to the economy, and we can see that some of its policies sustain, enhance and gratify those who work in business. Parsons's scheme is intended to be used in more subtle, delicate ways, but it should be possible to see how it can be elaborated. One way is with reference to the patterns of interface and exchange between the different phases (for example, the I and L phases also need facilities). Another is the way that these exchange patterns are nested inside each other, as we uncover by investigating the hierarchy of sub-systems, their interrelations with the system in which they are included, and their own internal exchanges. Since the AGIL model applies to a two-person situation as well as to the level of the total society, and to everything in between, the pattern will need to be complex and sophisticated.

Parsons and his critics

Parsons was much criticised, more so than any other figure in modern sociology, even his inability to write plain, concise English being held against him. Much of this criticism is superficial as well as repetitive and can be placed aside without too much difficulty. Three initial points of criticism need to be dealt with:

- Society is portrayed as a perfect harmony, devoid of conflict.
- This portrayal partly derives from Parsons's neglect of the source of social conflict, namely, the unequal distribution of power.
- By emphasising harmony and excluding conflict, Parsons's theory cannot explain social change.

All three of these criticisms are false. That Parsons did not consider change, conflict and power in the same way as his critics is not to say that his theory could not deal with them. In fact, in his later writings Parsons went out of his way to deal with just these issues.

From the start, the assumption behind Parsons's theorising is that the functional organisation and integration of the society are problematic; the integration of such complex arrangements involved in a whole society must take place in an intricate and thorough way, with difficulties and failures. Any real society has to be less than exhaustively integrated, and it is only to be expected that there are many discontinuities and incongruities in society between its different spheres and their organisation. Such discontinuities and incongruities show up as tensions, if not outright conflicts. Further, Parsons does not assume that a highly (though not perfectly) integrated society would not and could not change. After all, to assume in biology that a living organism must be meeting its functional requisites for survival does not translate into the assumption that the organism is immortal (will continue interminably to fulfil its functional requirements), or that whilst surviving it will remain unchanged (will not age, develop illnesses, etc.).

An idea of a functional system attaining an internal balancing between its parts introduces an idea of equilibrium, of things developing to a stable point and then remaining unchanged, and Parsons's model might suggest that this is what he has in mind. Though the idea of equilibrium certainly has its place, he eschews the idea that there is only one kind of equilibrium, for there is the type known as the moving equilibrium, commonly found with respect to living organisms. An organism can be in equilibrium in that its organs or parts are all healthy and functioning well, but it does not mean that the organism does not change, for, of course, the organism, whilst remaining healthy and surviving, grows and ages. It is this kind of equilibrium which Parsons had in mind for society and change is integral to this idea. Amongst his very last works were two short books (1966, 1971) prepared for an introductory series in which Parsons sought to give a general account of the long-term evolution of Western society, from its origins in (particularly) ancient Greek and Judaic culture (a conception much influenced by Weber).

Parsons on change

The process of long-term change was to be understood in terms of the *cybernetic hierarchy*. Parsons drew this analogy from the design of systems to provide automatic control for machines such as heating systems, dishwashers and automatic weapons. The idea is that the control and direction of such machine systems involve an inverse relationship between information and energy, i.e. the higher levels of the system use little energy but are rich in information, whilst the lower levels use less information and more energy. The heating thermostat uses little electrical energy to operate, but it is sensitive to information (in the technical, engineering sense of that word); it responds to fine variations in temperature, and sends out signals as the temperature rises and falls. The central heating unit, however, uses much more energy than the thermostat to run its output, the heating, and does not use much information in its operations.

Parsons proposes that the social system can be understood as structured in a similar way.

Cybernetic hierarchy in society

Culture is itself mostly information and little energy; e.g. symbolic codes, such as language, are a major component of culture, and they are very rich in information, but they are not much dependent on physical energy. The social system, however, is much more intensive in its use of energy.

Sending someone a page of instructions can initiate and direct them through a very large task, immensely energy consuming. Parsons argues that culture is quite like the specific kind of control device represented by the thermostat in the heating system or the programme in the washing machine; it has little energy in its own right and yet provides enough information to point the whole system in a given broad direction, thereby guiding it towards its goals.

In summary, Parsons's account of the evolution of the West is very much dominated by the formation of new ideas and outlooks, by *cultural attitudes*. Having adopted much of his characterisation of the principle cultural attitude of the modern Western society as a type from Weber – an attitude which he calls *instrumental activism*, i.e. the desire actively to dominate the world in pursuit of practical purposes – he naturally follows Weber in placing great emphasis on what Parsons calls the 'seed bed' societies of ancient Greece and Israel. With respect to the latter, he argues that the Jews' idea of a god who prescribes morality eventually became, through Christianity, the basis for the concepts of generally applicable (i.e. universal) laws and standards, which are such an important feature of our contemporary outlook.

In adopting an evolutionary approach to cultural change, Parsons is recognising that culture is a long-term phenomenon. Cultures are considerably more long-lasting that social systems, personalities or organisms. Personalities and organisms last only a human lifetime while social systems can survive over many generations. Nevertheless, the pattern of social structural arrangements tends to change many times during a period in which a culture may be judged to continue and to be relatively unchanging. For example, in two hundred years or so US society has undergone many changes, from a small, agricultural society to a huge industrial and then post-industrial one. In this period key cultural elements like the Constitution have remained the same and the Protestant ethic has continued to provide the dominant ethos of the society. Social systems may also change in evolutionary rather than revolutionary ways, with basically the same culture being adapted to quite different social structural arrangements, which is what Parsons alleges has happened in the West. Parsons does not, however, rule out either drastic shifts in culture or revolutionary changes in society as such. His close associate, Neil Smelser, studied the conflict-afflicted, near-revolutionary change in the cotton areas of eighteenth- and nineteenth-century Lancashire, and also wrote a general book on the theory of revolution (Smelser 1959, 1962).

Parsons on power

Parsons complained that his critics saw power as the base for social conflict because they conceived of it in what he termed a *zero-sum* situation, i.e. some-one's gain must mean another's loss (the classic Hobbesian view of things). If someone wants a bigger piece of the cake, then someone else must have a smaller one. The potential for conflict in dividing up a cake is apparent, as there may not be enough to satisfy everyone's desires. The picture is clear, but it depends on an assumption: that a fixed quantity is being shared out. If the quantity is not fixed, if it can increase, then it is possible for the amount available to everyone to increase. For example, the overall amount of wealth can expand through economic growth, enabling everyone to have more (though not necessarily in the same proportions). Just as we can look at wealth from the point of view of the whole system as an aggregate and can talk about the wealth of the society, so, too, Parsons argues, we should first of all look at power from the point of view of the system rather than from that of particular individuals or parties.

Taking the societal perspective, it is easy to see how the amount of power available overall can increase; it is clear that the total amount of power available to and required in a society will increase as the society grows, as it becomes both larger and more complex. For example, more power is involved in the modern US than in a small hunter-gatherer group. Therefore, the total amount of power in a society is not a fixed quantity. Further, looked at from the point of view of the system, the necessity to regard power as a means of domination, as a matter of one person having power over another (which is an assumption that usually goes with the zero-sum conception), also dissolves. The distribution of power is to be understood not in terms of individual possession, but as a distribution relative to the functional needs and internal exchanges of the system. Power *is* a way of controlling people, but not of controlling them just for the sake of domination because it is a means of directing and co-ordinating them in the pursuit of collective objectives. Basically, power is a means for getting things done.

The idea of 'exchange' amongst the four AGIL phases suggests an analogy with economics, for economic exchange is the very paradigm of exchanges (Parsons had started his career as an economist). Economic exchange through barter is a difficult, problematic and inefficient system; money greatly facilitates exchanges. We exchange things for money with a view to using the money in exchange for other things in its turn. Money is a medium of exchange and is not itself the object of exchange. Further, money is standardised and therefore can be exchanged for anything. In barter, one thing is exchanged for another, and we have to find the right person who wants what we have and is willing to give it up for what we can offer to effect an exchange (i.e. a mutual coincidence of wants), but money eliminates this problem: money will exchange for anything, it is a generalised medium. However, not all the exchanges in society are economic or take place through money. If these other kinds of exchanges are not to be undertaken on a barter basis, presumably immensely inefficient and perhaps entirely impractical for any moderately complex society, then there must be other *generalised media* to facilitate the four phases to exchange.

Power, Parsons suggests, is one such generalised medium. He names *influence* and *commitments* as another two of the four generalised media he thinks necessary and, though he published essays on power and influence (1969), he did not elaborate his thoughts on commitments before his death.

Power as a generalised medium

Power is to be understood as playing a role in facilitating the pursuit of *collective* objectives, rather than as being essentially used divisively and in pursuit of sectional interests (though it can be, of course). Like money in economic affairs, it oils the wheels of society's organisation. Hence power is heavily concentrated in the polity sector of the social system and is related to the G phase, or goal attainment.

The criticisms we have discussed so far were not the only objections to Parsons's systems theorising. In fact, the reaction of so-called conflict sociologists to his work came relatively late in the day in comparison with objections from other directions. Thus though predominant in American sociology for a time, Parsons's approach also met widespread and fierce opposition from the early 1950s. Symbolic interactionists and ethnomethodologists (see Chapters 6 and 7) objected to the level of abstraction from observable, everyday activities, and even Parsons's functionalist colleague, Robert Merton, was critical of the very high level of generality of the theory. However, in terms of its impact in shaping the general direction of sociological thinking, it was the attack on Parsons by his conflict critics which was the most influential. At the centre of it was the charge of conservatism: by neglecting possibilities of change and conflict, Parsons's theory was guilty of purveying an ideology which justified the status quo.

The reaction to Parsons: conflict theory

We have noted that many of sociology's current concerns – as well as its current troubles – have their beginning in the 1960s, with the resurgence in the popularity of Marxism and also the 'interpretative turn' in sociological thought, discussed in Chapters 6 and 7. Parsons's work forms a crucial background to these developments, for it served as the principal butt of criticism for the conflict school and incited much alienation from the whole idea of sociology as it was developing in the USA at that time. As much as anything, the criticisms were directed at the perceived political implications of mainstream American sociology in general and of Parsons's thought in particular, which were seen essentially as the acceptance of a – very broadly defined – conservative attitude to contemporary society. Yet, as we have pointed out, Parsons did deal with power and change. Not only did he address what he called 'strains' in systems, he also wrote on the conflicts of his time. For example, he wrote on Nazism, on the tension which the contemporary family structure (of the 1940s and 1950s, that is) was creating for women, on the problems in integrating Blacks into American society and culture, on the rise of the radical right, on the nature of social stratification, and on the causes of social deviance. In political terms, Parsons was a liberal, not uncritical of many aspects of American society, albeit a loyal and conventional enough citizen. He looked to the solution to such problems as the position of blacks or of women in terms of adjustments of the system, rather than in its total, revolutionary overthrow. For many of his critics, however, a liberal was not significantly to be distinguished from a conservative; anyone who did not totally oppose the status quo was perceived to defend it.

Such was Parsons's stature that conflict theory virtually defined itself by its wholesale opposition to his ideas. The complaints about change, power and conflict were themselves expressions of deeper objections, of which we can identify two main ones:

* Parsons was an idealist and neglected the importance of material interests.
* Parsons failed to give any account of *systemic* sources of change.

Idealists are, of course, the *bête noire* of Marxists. Hegel had been one. His inspiration for Marx had been on the basis only of the thorough rejection of any idealist elements (see Chapter 1). Hegel believed that the nature and change of reality results from the emanation of ideas and is a product of thought. In *The Structure of Social Action* (1937), Parsons explicitly dissociated himself from such idealism at the very start. His position was very much influenced by Weber, to whom Marx has also often been preferred on the grounds that Weber is too much of an idealist as well. The basis for the accusation against Parsons is his strong emphasis on culture in the solution of social order, especially the stress on concepts of values and norms. However, this is certainly not idealism in the Hegelian sense and it is, of course, Parsons's point, just as it was Weber's, that it is not ideas alone, it is not culture by itself, which provides or regulates social order. Weber emphasised the importance of ideas in relation to what he called 'material' interests. Parsons throughout emphasised that it was culture as *instititutionalised* and *internalised* which mattered, and that the processes of institutionalisation and internalisation required articulation with many other phenomena. Even though the cybernetic hierarchy awards a broadly directive role to culture in regard to long-term change, it is not Parsons's view that culture, as some ghostly emanation from the skies, produces such change. Rather, the explanation is to be found in the way the institutionalised cultural patterns are interwoven into the organised affairs of the whole society, thereby providing the second nature of socialised individuals.

It might be suggested, however, that to take the picture of society as Parsons paints it, in terms of shared values and expectations, is to give a very partial and distorted portrait; it presents society in a misleadingly abstract way, and fails to highlight the fact that these values and norms are shared (if they are) in the context of considerable *material* inequalities. In other words, Parsons played down the role of inequality, especially in the form of social stratification, in his portrait of society. As already noted, of course, Parsons was well aware of the existence of social stratification (and of ethnic and gender inequalities as well), but he regarded stratification as just one institution amongst others and not as the central or essential institution in society. While important, it is not given pride of place in the analysis of a social system, but is analysed in terms of the four-phase model, just as any other feature might be. Parsons himself, his one-time associate Edward Shils (1978), and Robert Merton (in his notorious account of deviance as anomie, 1957) all wrote papers in which stratification figured significantly. Parsons himself wrote two directly about it (1940, 1953).

Accounting for stratification and change

Taking Shils and Merton as expressing at least parallel, if not strictly Parsonian, views, their position may be summarised as follows: the society is *unevenly* structured around its core values, and there are certain institutions within the society which are very closely articulated around these main values. Indeed, some institutions are taken as representatives and expressions of these values, e.g. the established church and monarchy in the UK. The monarchy was taken – until recent events – as not merely being a family, but representing the ideal of family life for many people. Hence the enormous impact made by the revelation of royal marital trouble and strife, inducing an unprecedented erosion of support for the monarchy.

Stratification

Institutions in this position in society are what Shils termed 'the centre', whilst other sectors stand in a more attenuated relationship to them, providing a 'periphery' within the society's overall value system. The ranking of people in terms of closeness to the centre of the society is certainly a matter of the prestige in which they are regarded.

In Durkheimian terms, the values of society are the sacred element; the more people are associated with the sacred core, the more highly they are regarded. Though the Parsonian scheme presupposes shared values and norms, they are not supposed to be simply and evenly distributed; it recognises that the intensity of attachment and position relative to values are a variable matter.

Further, Merton attributed deviance to the fact that stratification involves not only variable esteem, but also the sharing out of resources. Of course there can be a discrepancy between what the values and norms of society (the culture) prescribe and the actual, real social circumstances of people in society. It is all very well to hold up certain cultural ideals to all people, but it is more than likely in a complex society that stratification will make a difference in the extent to which people can realistically hope to live the kind of life prescribed in those ideals. For example, the ideal of economic success through hard work is, Merton argued, widely disseminated in US society, an ideal which (in the guise of the American dream) has reached all corners of the society. For most people, it is unrealistic to expect such success, given where they start in the stratification system and what opportunities are open to them. For most, rising out of poverty by legitimate means, through employment opportunities, is well-nigh impossible. Consequently, under certain circumstances there are pressures on individuals to deviate from the ideal of success through honest hard work, and to resort to illegitimate means, such as gangsterism and racketeering.

However, Parsons does not see society – and certainly not American society – as centred upon class conflict: the relationship between stratification and social values means that the inequalities in the society are accepted as legitimate, as expressions of the respective social worth of people ranked in their terms. Hence, class conflict as such is not a significant, let alone a systematic source of social change. The idea, bequeathed from Marxism, is that an account of social change has to be given, and that it must involve systematic change from within the society. Marx's idea (taken from Hegel) is that each society contains the seeds of its own destruction, the source of its transformation into another, different form. *If* we take this idea as the essential form of a theory of social change then, certainly in its terms, Parsons has no account of social change. But Parsons has a very different idea of what gives rise to social change.

Social change

Parsons's root notion is that there are many different sources of social change. Social revolutions and civil wars are not inconceivable in society – there is no guarantee that any society will meet its functional requirements – but whether or not such situations develop depends upon the particular character of a society, its mechanisms of integration and so forth. In reality, most social changes do not result from revolution or overt class warfare.

Of course, there are, sources of conflict built into society itself, in the very way culture, social system and personality fit together: in the internal contradictions of culture, in the discrepancies in the organisation of social systems, and in the inadequacies of human personalities. What they are, and how serious, depends on the case. However, there will be problems of malintegration in any society, and some of these problems might be so stubborn and persistent as to give rise to frustration, alienation and even organised dissent, whilst others may work themselves out so that dissatisfactions do not continue to build up. In either case, changes will occur, but characteristically they will be changes *in* the system that are compatible with its general character, rather than changes *of* the system into another, i.e. very differently organised, system.

Not all sources of change, however, originate within the social system. They originate in the system's environment. One major source of change for a given social system is other social systems. A social system can be invaded in a military or a cultural sense; it can be colonised by an army or by a religious or political ideology, producing social conflict and change, but there is no *internal* or systemic source for such a change. Similarly, a system can be affected by changes in its technical or natural environment. Since Parsons conceives of a social system as the pattern of relationships between people, then such things as technology and the environment are *external* to that system. Patently, changes in technology (as with the origin of capitalism itself) can have a major role in producing social changes, but they do not originate systematically in the structure of social relations themselves. Here capitalism is something of a special case, in so far as much of its activity is organised to generate techno-logical change, but the point remains that there is no generalisable basis for technological change from society's structure. The natural environment can also bring about social change. In the Middle Ages, the Black Death at least arguably reduced population, producing consequences for the agricultural labour force and resulting in changes in feudal relations. In short, there are many different sources of change. Some are internal to the society's organisa-tion, but many are not. That Parsons's theory does not offer a systemic account of change in the way Marx's does is merely to say that Parsons has a very different idea of what a theory can do.

These observations did not satisfy some critics. They reacted against Parsons's alleged consensus view of society by forming a loose front of arguments on behalf of a 'conflict' approach.

Consensus view of society

This sees society as centred upon agreement and dominated by co-operation rather than conflict.

Frequently the case for such an approach was made by default, i.e. pointing to alleged deficiencies in Parsons's approach. For example, he underestimated the importance of material interests and neglected the ways cultural elements such as values were the expression of sectional interests, imposed upon or instilled into others, as a rationalisation of their domination. Conflict theorists produced no body of work comparable to Parsons's in its systematic quality, perhaps because the central ideas of conflict theory were essentially a restatement of Marxian and Weberian conceptions.

Weber's concept of society as an arena of conflicts in which groups compete for domination through economic, cultural and political means (cf. Bendix 1960: 265–9) provides the essence of conflict theory. Whereas Parsons was concerned to provide an analytical framework applicable at all levels of social order, conflict theorists focused almost entirely on the level of the whole society. Like Weber, and to an even greater extent Marx, they emphasise the contest for domination within the system of social stratification as society's paramount phenomenon. Stratification is taken as the central organising feature of society, and the main objective is the demonstration of the degree to which other institutions and features of the culture are shaped in the image of the stratification system and structured to serve the interest of one stratified group rather than another. The Weberian view of stratification is more apt to be drawn upon than Marx's. Marx's theory of society, construed as holding that all social conflicts are, at bottom, class conflict, is regarded by many conflict theorists as reductive. Weber's view that classes, status groups and parties are all forms of stratification and can each be involved in contests for domination is to be preferred. Society comprises a plurality of conflicts, cross-cutting and exacerbating one another. Some centre on class inequality, but others are between what Weber calls status groups, involving ethnic, nationalist and gender conflicts. Domination and exploitation can take many forms, and Marx's account of nineteenth-century capitalism, with its emphasis on power as founded in economic position, is simply regarded as a special case by the conflict theorists. For them, economic position is only one form of the distribution of power. Weber argued that there can be a struggle for power itself. The reasons differ, e.g. possession for its own sake, or in order to improve one's position in society, or for the sake of some religious, political or economic purpose. In any actual case, of course, an individual's motives for seeking to dominate others are likely to be a mixture of these elements, though with one being somewhat more prominent than the others.

Parsons's contemporary influence

In the face of these assertions, disillusionment with Parsons's version of sociology became rife, and the emphasis upon conflict rose to pre-eminence. Although conflict theory itself did not develop into anything theoretically substantial, into anything beyond elaboration of Weberian points, it was influential in getting other schools of thought to try to draw in conflict more explicitly. For example, Randall Collins (1975), an American Weberian who talked about 'conflict sociology', certainly had an influence on the direction taken by latter-day symbolic interactionism (see Chapter 6), persuading many of its more recent affiliates to give more explicit attention to theory.

Parsons's sociological reputation reached its lowest point in the 1970s. After his death in 1979 and during the 1980s his theories made something of a comeback. Some sociologists – among them Parsons's former associates and students – talked of 'neo-functionalism'. Under this heading attempts were made to modify his thought in order to accommodate some of the objections from conflict theory. In addition, some serious revaluations of Parsons's work, e.g. by Jeffrey Alexander (1984), and by Robert Holton and Bryan Turner (1986), reject – as we have done – many of the standard criticisms as simply ill-informed and unjust. Furthermore, in recent years Parsons's work has had some impact upon important figures in German sociology, among them Jürgen Habermas (see chapter 13) and, more substantially, Niklas Luhman, who has sought to develop the idea of systems theory.

Luhman on the social system

Luhman seeks to combine Parsons's systems theory with his own *general systems* theory. It was derived (originally) from engineering, and the concept of *autopoiesis* as taken from biology (or, rather, from philosophy of biology), together with a *phenomenological* element. The Parsonian notion of system invites connection with general systems theory.

General systems theory

This proposes that many types of phenomena take the form of systems, for which there ought to be general laws referring to the properties of systems as such. If this were so, then many of the properties of social systems would result from the fact that they are merely systems, not *social* systems.

(For a counter-view that general systems theory is a spuriously mathematical pseudo-science, see David Berlinsky's *On Systems Theory* [1968].) The root idea of systems theory is that a system is less complex than its environment since, after all, the environment is everything which is not in the system, i.e. everything else, and in reality everything else must be more complex than just one item, however complex that item is as a system. Consequently, the properties of the system must be such as to enable it to relate to a more complex environment. The system cannot deal with everything at once; it can only survive by reducing the complexity of the environment with which it must deal.

To Luhman, a system is by definition a composite of interconnected parts. All systems have an internal organisation, but social and psychological systems, while fitting that part of general systems theory, also differ from mechanical or organic systems, for their parts are connected through meanings, not through causal interactions; i.e. the connections between different parts of the social system must be made through, must exist as, processes of communication. The parts of a social system do not exist only in contemporary connection, but derive part of their present connection from their relationships to the past and the future. Since human beings have both memory and foresight, to comprehend the nature of the connections between different parts of the system one must pursue a *phenomenological* approach, i.e. look at them through the eyes of society's members. Thus the interconnection between system parts is 'in the mind' of members, in the meaningful connections people see between them. The production and perpetuation of the system's *systemic* being demands that the connections in the minds of different individuals be the same; the individuals must understand things in the same way. The existence of social structures pre-structures meaning for individuals, i.e. these structures reduce the complexity of action situations by forming pre-given interpretations of and responses to them.

Luhman has been influenced by two philosophers of biology, Humberto Maturana and Francisco Varela. They formulated a notion – autopoiesis – designed to identify an essential property of *living systems*.

Autopoiesis

This is really the notion of systems as self-organising, and views a system's operations as being engaged only in reproduction of the system's own features, an important reversal of Parsons's approach.

Parsons's model conceives the system as being organised to sustain itself in the face of an external environment, while the idea of autopoiesis dispenses with the notion of any such independent, external environment. In its terms, the system defines its own environment relative to the needs of its own self-perpetuating arrangements.

For Luhman, the social system is something which exists as, which exists in, processes of communication. From this point of view, everything which is not communication is external to the social system.

For him as for Parsons, modern society is a differentiated entity with specialised functional sub-systems, specialising in such functions as producing economic resources, knowledge and trained individuals, which are discharged by the sub-systems of the economy, science and education respectively. These sub-systems simplify the complexity of dealing with the environment by specialising in one aspect of it, and also provide intellectual simplifications in their internal operations by each operating according to a simple binary opposition, e.g. 'true/false' in science, or 'guilty/innocent' in criminal law. Their operation provides simplification of the environment in that they point up the things to be taken notice of, the ones that matter, given the vastly multiple differences between any two things.

Further, modern society, contrasted with traditional society, is headless. In the traditional society, there is no functional differentiation; stratification is the only form of differentiation. Consequently, the dominant group in the stratification system could count as the 'centre' of the society; as such it could be regarded as capable of conceiving things for the society as a whole. Hence the system could be represented within the system. Modern, complex society, however, with its numerous differentiated sub-systems, has no comparable functional group; it therefore has no function of comprehending itself as a whole. Here again, albeit in a very different way from Althusser's (see Chapter 9), the system is 'decentred'. Consequently, there can be problems both in the interaction between the system and its environment, and between the various constituent sub-systems of the system, which do not automatically operate in effectively adaptive or reciprocally stable ways.

The issue of ecology and of ecological movements has provided one occasion for Luhman to apply his scheme since, of course, there are problems along both the external and internal boundaries of the system. Luhman is critical of environmentalism as such on the grounds that these movements involve sloganising and moralising; they suppose that a simple change in outlook is what is called for. Consequently they underestimate the complexity – the structured complexity – of the problem as it really exists in terms of the interface between the society and its environment, and at the interfaces of the numerous sub-systems involved in the collective movement of the system. For example, the very complexity of reductions of social systems can result in insensitivity to environmental consequences; the fact is that the autopoetic processes of the system are dedicated to their own perpetuation, regardless of their environmental consequences. Thus the system is to an important extent insulated against its environment.

With respect to internal sub-systems, however, it is a different matter, for these must be sensitive to one another, must be affected by and react to one another, but the ways in which they respond need not invariably be propor-tionate. There are disproportionately large reactions in one part of the system to small disturbances in other parts, e.g. when a potentially minor event such as a comparatively few deaths from Creutzfeld–Jacob's disease can precipitate a massive, indeed international, ethico-political explosion, as happened with the reaction to BSE (bovine spongiform encephalitis) in the mid-1990s.

Luhman contrasts his own sociology, in which the notion of 'relation to the environment' is a primary element, to that of other sociologists (such as his contemporary, Habermas) in which the main *social* (not sociological) problem was conceived to be the discrepancy between society's ideals (of freedom, justice, etc.) and its actualities, rather than the reciprocally destructive potentials of environment and social system.

Conclusion

Parsons was a crucial figure in the development of modern sociology, as much through the reaction against him as through his positive influence, though he continues to have contemporary adherents (cf. neo-functionalism, Chapter 13). However, the conviction that Parsons ignored conflict, power and domination in society moved these issues to central position, where, for most sociologists, they remain to this day. Indeed, the views which subsequent to the 1960s have had most appeal for the sociological community have been those which have given central significance to power relations.

Questions

1   Outline Hobbes's model of human action. What are Parsons's criticisms of it?
2   Illustrate Parsons's argument that society has to integrate culture, personalities and social systems with (a) the example about motorists, and (b) your own example.
3   'For Parsons, it is systems all the way down.' Discuss.
4   Does Parsons have a theory of social change?
5   Outline Parsons's concept of power. How does it differ from those of (a) Marx and (b) Weber?
6   Does Parsons produce a consensus view of society?
7   How does Parsons reconcile the stratification and the integration of society?
8. Outline Luhman's attempt to improve Parsons's systems theory. Does he succeed?

Further reading

Hamilton, P., 1983, *Talcott Parsons*. Tavistock. A good introduction. See also P. Hamilton (ed.), 1985, *Readings from Talcott Parsons*, Tavistock, for a useful selection of texts.

Parsons, T., 1966, *Societies: Evolutionary and Comparative Perspectives*. Prentice Hall. Parsons's analysis of historical change and the rise of Western societies.

—— 1971, *The System of Modern Societies*. Prentice Hall. Parsons's brief account of his social system theory.

—— 1978, *Action Theory and the Human Condition*. Free Press. His last collection of essays, notable for several taking a sociological perspective on fundamental ethical problems and tracing the historical and social origins of contemporary morality.

Savage, S., 1982, *The Theories of Talcott Parsons: The Social Relations of Action*. Macmillan. A more advanced study, influential in rehabilitating Parsons's reputation.

Smelser, N.J., 1959, *Social Change in the Industrial Revolution*. Routledge. Smelser's 'Parsonian' study of the nineteenth-century Lancashire cotton industry.

Worsley, P., 1970, *Modern Sociology: Introductory Readings*. Penguin. For Edward Shils's essay 'Centre and periphery' and Robert Merton's 'Anomie and social structure' (originally in *American Sociological Review* [1938], 3. Also contains Giddens's essay ' "Power" in the recent writings of Talcott Parsons' (originally in *Sociology* [1968], 2.

■   ■   ■

Chapter 6

Symbolic
interaction

Introduction: the reaction against scientism

During the 1950s and 1960s, developments in the philosophy of science combined with other developments in sociology and in philosophy to erode confidence in the ambition to create an objective method notionally modelled on the quantitative natural sciences. Summarising this opposition, it has been common practice to identify it as moving emphasis from the *objective* to the *subjective*. This characterisation is accurate only to a limited degree, and in many respects is quite misleading. However, the idea that the core opposition is between those who hold a view that sociology must adopt an objective approach and those who demand a subjective one has captured many people's imagination. One consequence has been the move on the part of a number of currently active, more traditionally inclined sociologists – such as Bourdieu, Giddens, Alexander, Habermas and Luhman, just to mention those discussed below – to make a main part of their theoretical effort that of reconciling this opposition, taking a middle way, and arguing that society is both an objective and a subjective reality.

Our present task is to explicate the reaction against the idea of scientific method, and thereby to offer an answer to the question once posed (rhetorically) by Egon Bittner (1973) as to how is it that a discipline committed to the goal of objective method came to abandon this in favour of something looser and more subjective?

The idea of method which became dominant in Anglo-American sociology after 1945 was controversial from the outset. We have already referred (in Chapter 3) to the *Methodenstreit* (or dispute over methods, i.e. whether the human and cultural studies should have basically the same, or very different methods to those of the natural sciences) in German thought around the turn of the century as the context which formed the problems that Max Weber sought to resolve. As early as the 1920s and 1930s, it had widespread impact on sociology at large by raising objections to the idea of basing sociological method on the natural sciences. Despite these objections, the positivistic view that all disciplines seeking the status of rigorous science must conform to the same broad methodological principles and assumptions proved compelling. The logic was simple: making sociology into a science – into the desirably successful science – required making it fit the pattern of science in general and, following the standard scientific method, to proceed methodologically in the same way as the natural sciences.

The misconceived idea of a scientific sociology

The controversy over whether sociology should try to be a science was renewed when Peter Winch's small book, *The Idea of a Social Science* (1990), appeared in 1958, followed later by a companion paper, 'Understanding a primitive society' (1964). These publications provoked what is often called 'the rationality debate'. They are frequently taken as his translation of the ideas of the philosopher Ludwig Wittgenstein (1899–1951) into arguments applicable to the social sciences. Wittgenstein was by any standards one of the major philosophers of the twentieth century, who played a massive role in the so-called linguistic turn which came to dominate intellectual thought during the period after 1945.

The title of Winch's book's conveys an air of contempt for the idea it names. He argues that the idea that we will not truly understand ourselves and our social life until we have created a science deserves comprehensive rejection. The attempt to impose a sociological method – a scientific method – modelled on natural science procedures on the study of social phenomena is precisely that, an imposition; it is misguided and can only distort the nature of the phenomena of social life, since their character is different to that of natural, physical phenomena.

As science would seem principally to be concerned with patterns and generalities (often thought of as laws), Winch tries to make his point by reference to *regularities*. He argues that in many prominent cases the regularities of social life are not the same kind as those of physics. The contrast is between *law-like* regularities and *rule-following* ones.

Law-like and rule-following regularities

The difference is between the way in which a billiard ball colliding with another, as a matter of invariant regularity, causes the second ball to move, and the way in which, when counting, we proceed 'one, two, three, four, five, six', etc. In the case of the billiard balls, the prior movement of the propelled billiard ball causes the other ball to move. It is not, however, the prior pronouncement of 'one' that compels us then to say 'two', with that in its turn making us say 'three'. Indeed, when we count, it is not inconceivable that we could actually go: 'one, two, three, five, six', or in some other way deviate from this pattern. We do not count in the order that we do because some physical law compels us to make these sounds, to make us say these words; rather, we just carry out the activity of counting, we follow a set of rules which prescribe the correct way of doing so.

The regularity of counting, just like the regularity of stopping at red traffic lights, is a *conventional* not a *causal* one. It is not the wavelength of red light which causes us to brake, but the fact that the colour red acts as a *signal*, an instruction to stop. In stopping the car at the red light, then, we are obeying a rule (in this case, one enshrined in a legal, not a scientific, law). There is, Winch maintains, another important difference between a natural law and a rule, namely that with respect to a natural law the phenomenon governed by it cannot do otherwise than the law states. A law in physics does not admit of exceptions, but we can violate a rule, e.g. we can miscount, or jump the lights. In other words, a rule often – not always, because there are different kinds of rules – states the right way to go about something, and it is possible for people to deviate from what the rule requires. Winch overgeneralises his case, but makes an important point when he emphasises that one of the defining features of rule-governed action is the possibility of *making a mistake*. By contrast, the tide on the beach cannot come in by mistake.

Winch next argues that the methods for identifying laws and rule-governed regularities are not the same. Thus the method of the natural sciences cannot be appropriate to the social studies (as Winch terms them, to avoid any carry-over association with the idea of science and its supposedly general method). Understanding a rule does not just involve seeing a regular connection but – to simplify a great deal – involves seeing the *point* of the connection. Traffic lights will do again as our example. We could establish a regularity by observation, noting that cars stopped at the red light, and on green moved on. Establishing this regularity would not give us understanding of 'stopping at a traffic light', for the colour itself is not the key to the regularity, but what the colour means, what the signal says to drivers. The red colour is not essential to the effect it achieves; the colours could be the other way around, with the green in place of the red. Yet the pattern could remain constant: when the top light showed, then cars would come to a halt. (In Chapter 9 we will find that structuralism has much to say about the arbitrariness of signs.) Of course, the position of the light is no more an absolute factor than the colour in achieving the effect of stopping the cars. In some rail systems, the same set of colour lights is arranged horizontally rather than vertically.

If we look only for some causal connection between the light and driver reactions, we shall never, says Winch, understand why the cars stop for the lights. We stop because the lights act as a remote means of conveying a message between people, between the authorities who regulate road use and drivers. The lights are signals, and the red light, as it happens, signals an injunction: stop now. To understand the point of the red light's power to bring traffic to a halt, then, we cannot simply study the regular connection between the light becoming red, and a car's stopping; instead we need to understand how this pattern is part of a much more inclusive one: a pattern of meaning rather than causation. The red light and the car form just a small part of a complex pattern involving road use, regulation by authorities and so on. By grasping this complex pattern we are able to see what traffic lights do: they serve a purpose, which is, of course, to secure safe transition for cars at road junctions.

Clearly, Winch is not suggesting that such observations come as revelations to us; we are not astonished to hear that traffic lights let cars alternate through road junctions to minimise collisions. He holds that as members of society we are aware of these patterns, but we do not find them out by studying concurrent events and seeking to infer causal connections between them. We become aware of these patterns and of the point of a particular activity within that pattern *by being taught the rules* (in the main).

Identifying rule-governed regularities

'Learning to understand and follow a rule' is a different sort of thing to 'establishing through observation and inference a law-like regularity', Winch maintains. Someone who studies a society – be it her or his own or an alien one – proceeds much more in the former way than the latter.

The anthropologist, for example, does not painstakingly observe the regularities of life amongst those native to the society he or she studies and then go on to hypothesise law-like regularities to cover them. Rather, the anthropological fieldworker more commonly talks to the people under study, and gets them to explain what the point of a particular (strange-looking, hard-to-understand activity) might be. In large part, the anthropologist characteristically learns *about* an alien society by learning *from* those who inhabit it. This is perhaps the pithiest possible way in which Winch's whole argument can be put, and it brings out the similarity with part of Weber's position on meaning (see Chapter 3). However, Winch does not think that the sort of explanation in terms of rule following that might be given of the role of traffic lights requires the sort of back-up in terms of casual laws that Weber deems necessary.

There is a further element to Winch's position which decisively separates him from Weber. One of the cornerstones of positivism is the notion that description and explanation are distinct activities. Crudely, on the one hand science consists in describing the facts to be explained; on the other hand, it shows how these facts are to be explained with reference to a general theory. Thus there is a *descriptive phase* and an *explanatory phase* to scientific method, each governed by different criteria. Although no positivist, Weber's thinking has some resemblance to this distinction. Here again, Winch finds an essential difference between science and the social studies.

Description and explanation

Winch argues that we cannot *first* establish any regular kind of connection between two activities and *then* appeal to or invent a rule-like relationship to explain that regularity. The making of the regular connection, of correctly identifying that connection and the two activities joined by it, cannot be done independently of the rule.

For example, to say that the traffic lights change to red and the cars stop does not properly, correctly, say what is happening , i.e. in stopping for the light, the drivers are obeying the injunction that the red light signifies. That the braking of the car is a *response* to the light is an integral part of what is happening here, and the idea of stopping as a response, complying with an injunction, etc., only makes sense if one already understands the relationship of the red lights to the rules of the road, and their role as signals. Thus to Winch, Weber's idea that one would need to observe causal regularities to confirm the connection in terms of meaning seems gratuitous, for, as just argued, getting the nature of the connection established aright in any one case requires the determination of the connection in terms of meaning, i.e. the traffic light signals 'Stop!' in the imperative mode.

Witchcraft and rationality

In his small but densely packed book, Winch says various other things, in particular about the relationship between language and reality. This relationship arises from the above arguments and has caused much controversy. By trying to clarify his ideas through the example of primitive magic in the accompanying paper, 'Understanding a primitive society', Winch perhaps only made things worse. Certainly he regenerated in sociology a debate which had been going on for over a century amongst anthropologists, and Lévi-Strauss, in his very different way, was taking up through his structuralist approach (see Chapter 9).

The debate was over the comparative rationality of so-called primitive people, on the one hand, and ourselves, the inhabitants of 'advanced' and 'civilised' societies, on the other. Winch's discussion of primitive magic rejects such a patronising view, holding that 'primitives' are no less intelligent and sophisticated than ourselves. Some early anthropologists had maintained that there was a distinct primitive mentality, that tribespeople were incapable of logical thought. Their use of magic was seen as proving the point: the fact that in such magic people would try to injure others by (say) burning the toenail clippings or hair of the person they wished to harm showed the lack of logical thought, since, of course, logic tells us there is no real causal connection between burning toenail clippings and injuring the person to whom they belonged.

In the 1930s Edward Evans-Pritchard had made a careful, very detailed study of the belief in witchcraft, and of the associated magical practices, found in an African tribe, the Zande. Evans-Pritchard argued that the very idea of people being harmed by witchcraft and of measures being taken to identify witches and to mitigate the effects of bewitchment might sound utterly bizarre to us. Yet he himself ceased to find these ways so bizzarre or unreasonable as practices for managing one's day-to-day affairs after living among this people for a period of time. Further, close observation of these people showed that they were not – as we might suppose – making childish errors about causal connections between natural phenomena. In many respects, the Zande made just the same causal connections as we do: if a building standing on wooden supports fell down then they checked, as we would (if we lived in Zandeland), for termites in the supports and, finding them, concluded that the termites were the cause of the collapse. And so on for all kinds of natural occurrences.

However, understanding these natural connections did not stop them wondering whether witchcraft might have played a role. Identifying the physical cause of some event did not necessarily exhaust their curiosity about it; if the event involved a trouble or misfortune for someone, then they asked the question 'Why did this building collapse and cause injury or death to an individual resting from the sun beneath it?' What explanation for *this* misfortune befalling *this* person can there be? After all, given that there are termites in the supports, the building might have collapsed at any time – why just now? As part of their culture, the explanation they were entitled to consider was that the misfortune resulted from witchcraft. Central to that culture is belief in both the existence of witches and the power of witchcraft to do harm. Since this explanation is not, as such, in direct conflict with the kind of ordinary, empirical causal connections we make, i.e. between the termites and the collapse, it is enough to justify Evans-Pritchard's major point: the practice of magic and witchcraft in 'primitive societies' cannot be attributed to the feebler mentalities of these so-called primitives, for they show themselves every bit as capable as us of grasping causal, empirical regularities.

However, having made this step, of which Winch approves, Evans-Pritchard provokes Winch's ire by taking a further one: he suggests that whilst we cannot say that these people are mentally more primitive than us, none the less, we cannot deny that their system of thought is misguided, whilst ours, based upon science, is correct. If we studied their witchcraft practices scientifically and statistically we should soon prove that these practices do not really work. They cannot work because, of course, science (which is the cornerstone of our system of thought) tells us there are no supernatural forces. The fact that their witchcraft beliefs are baseless and do not work is kept from these people by certain self-preserving features of their beliefs: they can explain away evidence. For example, the failure of witch-doctoring to cure a patient, in terms of the magical system itself, is due to witches acting to counter the steps taken to reveal their identity or remove their spells. Evans-Pritchard is, then, saying that in the end we *are* superior to them because we know what reality is truly like, while they are locked into a self-deceiving and false system of misconceptions.

By taking exception to Evans-Pritchard on this point Winch in his turn outraged those who thought he was denying the claim of science to tell us about the nature of reality, or at least was denying that science is any better at telling us about the nature of reality than witchcraft.

Consequently, Winch's work became one of the key provocations for worry about *relativism*.

Relativism

This is the view that the notion of truth is not universal, but relative. Rather than saying that one person (or group of people) possess the truth, and that other individuals and groups are mistaken, one should hold that what is true for one person or group of persons may not be true for others, for whom something different is true. Relativism asserts that it is up to each individual or group to decide for themselves what is true, and that their decision settles the matter.

Such views are anathema to those (we might mention Stephen Lukes [1982] and Ernest Gellner [1985], and more recently the biologist Lewis Wolpert [1992]) who think that science is something entirely distinct in human history; it *does* attain to the truth – or comes as close as anything can – and one cannot say that witchcraft is as good, or anywhere near as good, as science at explaining things.

However, Winch himself does not actually aim to say what the critics accuse him of. As his book title is meant to indicate, he has deep doubts about *The Idea of a Social Science*, on the grounds that the kind of explanation supreme in the natural sciences is not appropriate to understanding the kinds of things about social life that require explanation. This view is very different, however, from arguing that witchcraft is as good as science. The temptation to assert or to deny this is due to the inclination to think that religion/magic and science are competitors in the same kind of business. Thus we must either say that one is better at this business than the other, or that each is as good as the other. Winch's point is that religion and magic, on the one hand, and science, on the other, are actually different kinds of businesses. It is absurd to ask whether one is better at its business than the other. In other words, the persistent tendency to make an invidious comparison of religion or magic with science (which is the basis for the argument about relativism) supposes that religion/magic competes to provide the same kind of understanding as science. This premise makes it seem (if we adopt the standpoint of science to view the situation) that no one could possibly believe magic could work, for in scientific terms there is no way it could work. Therefore, anyone who does believe in magic must be less than rational.

Winch complains that though Evans-Pritchard has eschewed many of the grounds for patronising 'primitive people' as irrational, his study none the less contains residual elements of such patronising. Evans-Pritchard supposes that the scientific version of how things work is obvious and the fact that witchcraft does not work is equally obvious. It is only because the witchcraft system provides various means of explaining away the failures of their witchcraft practices that the Zande are able to sustain their belief in it. Without recourse to such *secondary elaborations*, they would be forced to acknowledge what any rational person knows: witchcraft is simply false.

Winch is not concerned to counter Evans-Pritchard's argument for science and against witchcraft by arguing the opposite case on behalf of witchcraft against science. Winch's argument actually consists in two elements, one concerning similarities between the Zande and ourselves, the other concerning differences between witchcraft and science as social practices.

The first element queries whether in respect of his own beliefs in science Evans-Pritchard stands in any different relationship to these from the Zande people's to their beliefs in witches. Would Evans-Pritchard be likely to give up his confidence in Western medicine because it often fails, because people have incurable illnesses or die? No, he no doubt accepted in particular cases of illness and death the doctor's explanation as to why it was not possible to cure the illness or prevent the death. Let us remember, too, that the natural sciences themselves are constantly getting things wrong. After all, the refutation of scientific theories and the making of new findings often involves asserting that previous conceptions were mistaken: Newton has been displaced by Einstein. The explanation of what was wrong with the previous ideas is, of course, given in new scientific terms, yet by the logic Evans-Pritchard applies to witchcraft we should conclude, that in the cases of both medicine and science, it is only by the explaining away of the facts that these ventures claim to grasp reality, since plainly they are always making mistakes. Of course, Winch's point is not that we should dismiss science and medicine as well as witchcraft, but only that we should not dismiss witchcraft as obviously mistaken on these grounds.

It might seem that Winch is saying that witchcraft is not mistaken, or not obviously so, and thus committing himself to the view that there are (or might well be) witches. He has been criticised in this way, but to make that objection is to suppose that his argument is directed towards judging whether either witchcraft or science is right when, plainly, he is entirely concerned with whether there is any formal difference in the reasoning pattern of someone brought up within the system of science who takes it for granted, and of another raised within the system of witchcraft who takes this different system for granted.

Winch's second – and even more crucial – point is that the determination to compare witchcraft with science results not in demonstrating the superiority of science, but in distorting the understanding of witchcraft. Hence it is seen as a perverse kind of science when, Winch maintains, it is not any kind of science at all. Since it is not any kind of science, it cannot be better or worse, or even just as good as, our science. Religion and magic (including witchcraft) are not centred on the matters which preoccupy science, but have to do with other matters which pertain to the meaning of life and to the ethics of how people should relate to one another. We would understand this latter point better if, instead of approaching religion and magic on the basis of science-derived presuppositions about what they must be, we were simply to try to understand them. To do so does not involve us in actually accepting their terms. We do not have to believe in witches in order to grasp that believing in them is not a stupid mistake. Neither should we take our own disbelief in them as testimony to our superior rationality. On Winch's argument, the possibility of championing witchcraft against science, an approach which has caused so much agitation, is one which simply does not arise.

Alternatives to scientistic sociology

Winch's capacity to cause agitation within sociology was complemented by provocations from two American-spawned schools of sociology, both having intellectual roots extending back to the 1920s, but not much noticed until the 1960s. These two schools were symbolic interactionism and ethnomethodology.

Symbolic interactionism originated in the work of the social philosopher George Herbert Mead (1863–1931), whose ideas were translated into a sociological doctrine principally by one of his students, Herbert Blumer (1900–86). Mead published little during his lifetime; his ideas mainly spread through his teaching at the University of Chicago, where there was a sociological tradition of field studies of urban life. This kind of *Chicago sociology*, initiated by Robert Park and Ernest Burgess, continued there through the 1930s, 1940s and 1950s under the leadership of Everett C. Hughes. The symbolic interactionist school was the product of a loose amalgam of Mead's theories – mainly as interpreted by Blumer – and a commitment to field studies championed by Hughes.

Ethnomethodology is also commonly associated with a geographical base, being frequently derogated for its Californian origins with the intendedly disparaging implication that its mode of thought reflected the disreputable, irresponsible, drug-crazed culture of late 1960s Hippie movement. Its actual origins, however, were in 1920s Germany, where a young scholar, Alfred Schutz (1899–1959), undertook a systematic criticism of the philosophical presuppositions of Max Weber's account of the meaning of social action. Here Schutz based his criticism on *phenomenology*, which was founded by the German philosopher Edmund Husserl (1859–1938). Schutz became an exile from the Nazis, escaping to America, where during a career as a banker he continued part-time to publish in sociology, though his work was little known until after his death and the publication of his *Collected Papers* (1962, 1964, 1966) in the 1960s. During the 1940s, Schutz's work was very influential upon a student of Talcott Parsons at Harvard University, Harold Garfinkel, who was to develop Schutz's ideas into the position of ethnomethodology. Garfinkel published little, and in relatively obscure places, until a number of his papers were collected into *Studies in Ethnomethodology*, published in 1967. From the 1950s Garfinkel was based in Los Angeles, and in the early 1960s his influence was spread across many campuses of the University of California, attracting a large number of graduate students, amongst whom the most notable was to be Harvey Sacks. Largely through lectures delivered (between 1964 and 1972) at the Irvine campus, Sacks developed an original extension of Garfinkel's ideas, which became known as *conversation analysis*.

Like Winch, though in different ways, both these schools raised the questions of meaning and rationality, doing so in ways which challenged received conceptions of method as being akin to the procedures of natural science. They often contend against a notion of rationality very similar to the one opposed by Winch. It was, however, given specific form in, for example, Talcott Parsons's influential theories (see Chapter 5) against which in the 1960s both symbolic interactionism and ethnomethodology in their different ways were reacting. Essentially, Parsons defined rationality as conduct which accords with the best scientific information. Thus the findings of science are made the yardstick of rationality, whose application is to be undertaken by the sociologist. The sociologist will judge whether the conduct of members of the society is based upon conceptions which correspond with, could be endorsed by, the most up-to-date scientific knowledge. If it does not, then the action involved is irrational. Both schools dissented from this approach in favour of what we might call a *contextual* judgement of rationality.

Contextual judgements of rationality

Whether some action or pattern of activity is judged rational is decided by reference to the particular conditions within which it is undertaken rather than to some abstract, general (scientific) standard.

If we isolate an action from its context, simply describing what someone does without any reference to its circumstances and comparing the understandings which the action seems to express with those of up-to-date science, we may find – almost certainly *will* find – that there is a considerable discrepancy between them and consequently declare the action to be quite irrational. However, this approach simply shows that an action undertaken in a particular context may well look bizarre if taken out of context and described in a way insensitive to its circumstances. This was precisely the point of Winch's objection to Evans-Pritchard.

Action in context: an example from Goffman

We can take an example from symbolic interaction's most successful exponent (in achievement, influence and commercial terms, i.e. his books achieved an unprecedented best-seller status), Erving Goffman. Goffman, studying mental patients, noted that they often seemed obsessive about trivial things such as pieces of string or tin foil, often hoarding them. How are we to think of what they are doing? Seemingly, a good way is to think that this behaviour is a symptom of their mental illness, perhaps manifesting obsessions or anxieties.

However, Goffman's point is that though such a description mentions the fact that the patients are in hospital, it says nothing more about the circumstances which life in the mental hospital provides for them. If we fill out some of those details and also consider them from the point of view of those patients as the conditions under which they have to live, a very different picture emerges. At the time of Goffman's study, patients in large mental hospitals were typically deprived of all personal possessions upon committal, e.g. made to wear hospital garb in place of their own clothing, and were neither allowed easy access even to trivial things (such as string, toilet paper, tin foil, etc.), nor provided with secure places for storage. In these circumstances, small, otherwise valueless items become significant, either as commodities (as cigarettes do in prison) or simply because they are one's own; they come to stand for vestigial autonomy in face of powerful institutional authority. Therefore, anything can become desirable to possess; even if one does not use something oneself, one can exchange it. Being desirable, they are things which other people may try to steal. If one cannot lock one's personal cabinet, then it is not a safe place in which to leave anything – the sensible thing to do is to keep things close, to carry them about in one's pockets, for example. Far from being irrational then, the patients' behaviour begins to seem perfectly rational in the circumstances; it is conduct as much imposed upon them by the institution's administrative arrangements as by any expression of their mental state.

Goffman argues that we can understand a great deal of inmate conduct in mental hospitals on the assumption that the inmates are psychologically normal rather than that they are insane. Goffman's study makes more the general point that judgements on the rationality of conduct are best made by relating the conduct to its circumstances and considering how the circumstances confront those involved as the perceived circumstances of their conduct.

Rethinking sociological enquiry

Both symbolic interactionism and ethnomethodology, then, raise the possibility that a conception of sociological method centred upon a general, abstract and *a priori* conception of rationality will encourage the sociologist to misunderstand and misdescribe social life. What purports to be objective and scientific descriptions can turn out to be partial and distorted, lacking a grasp upon the contextual conditions of the activities concerned and the meaning of those circumstances and activities for those who are situated in them. Thus the main trouble with a theorist like Parsons, according to these arguments, is with the very way he went about putting together a theory. The objection, articulated explicitly by Harold Garfinkel, was that Parsons's theory (like so much sociological theory) was built up in advance of acquiring an understanding of how actions relate to their context or circumstances, and how circumstances and actions acquire or possess their meanings. Rather than argue with specific parts of Parsons's theory, this response requires us to step back from the very starting point of such theorising and to set about sociology in a different way. We must seek general theory in a very different way, or even go so far as to give up the search altogether for a so-called general theory.

One of the most influential statements on method, deriving from a broadly symbolic interactionist outlook, prescribed how to achieve *The Discovery of Grounded Theory*. The very title carries the implication that most sociological theory (such as Parsons's) is *ungrounded*, i.e. it is not rooted in an understanding of what actual situations are like.

Grounded theory

Barney Glaser and Anselm Strauss, the authors of *Grounded Theory* (1967), held that sociological theory was usually preconceived, then situations were selected and studied in order to provide data to test the theory. Consequently, the theory was based on only a limited grasp of actual social settings, since the research attended to the nature of situations only in very selective ways, normally those relevant to testing the theory. Sociologists complained widely about the weakness of theory, but why, then, did they not seek to ground their theory? Why not build theory starting from case studies? Why not first make close and intensive observation of some domain of life and then seek to work out a theory which would capture the nature of the area of social life that the case study has revealed?

Not everyone was persuaded by the idea of grounded theory, though it has had considerable popularity over the years and contributed to a broadening of the conception of sociological method. Ethnomethodology, however, sees no need for theorising in the traditional sense at all, and certainly does not accept the need for a method for grounding its theory. We will have more to say on this in the following chapter, where we set out its ideas in some detail. However, the current point is: one way or another symbolic interactionists and ethno-methodologists reacted against the tradition of building all-embracing theories for sociology in advance of getting to know the social phenomena to be covered by the theory. Instead, what was needed – and both ethnomethodology and symbolic interactionism agreed – was to break away from the traditional efforts to construct an apparatus of mock-scientific theory and method. Instead, we should seek to observe social life as it occurs, to observe people as they go about their affairs in order that we might, at least, have access to the circumstances in which their actions are done, to the meanings employed in perceiving their circumstances, and therefore to the basis on which actions are undertaken. In other words, abstract theoretical schemes (based largely upon how theorists imagine how people would act) were to be replaced by much fuller depictions of actual conduct in real circumstances.

The origins of symbolic interactionism: Mead's conception of behaviour

In the remainder of this chapter we consider the approach of symbolic inter-actionism in more detail. Symbolic interaction is a very loose categorisation not particularly welcome to many of the sociologists commonly counted as part of it. The name itself provides a succinct summation of the key claim of Mead's social psychology, which holds that interaction between people is a matter of communication, through *symbols*. Mead aimed to understand how the capacity for communication by symbols developed amongst humans, and how it develops in the maturation of each human individual. He aimed to establish through this argument two (anti-Cartesian) points: the mind is a *natural, biological* phenomenon and, also, an *essentially social* one. René Descartes (1596–1650), a French philosopher, had contributed immensely to the formation of Enlightenment ideas through his emphasis upon the acquisition of knowledge through reason, and upon the regulation of the search for knowledge through rigorous method. He had also contributed the view (known thereafter as *Cartesian dualism*) that the human being was composed of two distinct elements, the mind and the body, which had to be understood separately. Mead thus set himself against the traditional dualism and, equally, against the idea that the mind is a purely individual phenomenon.

Mead's view of the self

The human mind – which Mead termed *the self* – develops in and through the process of symbolic interaction, enabling an individual to acquire a sense of himself or herself *as* an individual.

The development of the human mind was to be understood in strictly Darwinian terms as a product of the evolutionary process; the evolution of the human organism and the social nature of human individuals were both part of their biological nature. Hence Mead was certainly confident that social life could be studied scientifically, since his social psychology was in essence an application of biology, but he was none the less critical of many attempts to understand human social life scientifically. This was not because they sought to be scientific, but because they had an impoverished conception of:

- what science involves; and/or
- what the science is to study in the case of human life.

For Mead, the mind can be studied scientifically, for its workings are displayed in people's conduct, not concealed behind it.

The capacity of humans to respond in a more complex and flexible way to their environment than other animals do is a product of human biology and its evolution into its specific form. For example, no small part of the crucial linguistic/symbolic capacity of humans is a result of the evolution of the vocal chords. Mead emphasises the contrast between the way animal response is tied to the immediate situation and the way humans can transcend it; they are able to reflect upon and respond to past situations well after they have occurred, and can anticipate and prepare for future situations before they happen. How we shall react in a situation can depend on our preparation and planning, not just on an automatic link between a certain occurrence and a fixed, instinctual reaction as in the case of a reflex action, e.g. the knee's reaction on being hit. We do have reflex reactions, but not only those. Thus Mead is putting the case that we ourselves can control our own behaviour; we do not simply react to a stimulus which provokes our reaction.

The capacity to transcend immediate circumstance in this way requires the development of symbolic capacity.

Symbolic capacity

This is the ability to be able to represent, i.e. recall or envisage, past and future situations to ourselves, to conjure them up when they are not actually present, are in the past, or have not yet happened.

Part of this capacity for representation involves our ability to represent *ourselves* to ourselves. If we are to prepare our conduct for future situations then we must be able to imagine not just those situations but, also, what we would do in them. Thus we must have the capacity to think of ourselves in the way that we think about (other) objects; in Meadian terms, we can be objects to ourselves. That is, we can think about ourselves in just the same way as we can think about the objects (including other people) in the world about us, we can step back from our immediate involvement in a situation and reflect on it, and we can also envisage how others in our situation will look upon us and see ourselves as others see us. This, then, is the capacity for self-consciousness.

The individual is not, of course, merely a body, but an identity, a person with a distinct core of psychological character, which Mead terms the self. This is the basis of, the driving force for, an individual's conduct. Mead refers to 'the social self' to emphasise that the self develops in interaction with and is modelled on other people and their ways of acting. The child, for example, learns first by imitation, by copying the behaviour of others in playful form, acting now like the postman, now the shopkeeper, then the mother, and so on. In this way, the individual learns what is involved in social roles, i.e. learns what people expect of one another. Through imitating these roles, the child is learning how other people look upon the world, how they see it relative to their role responsibilities. The child is learning to take account of things not only from its own situated, particular point of view, but also to assess its situation from the point of view of others. Such assessment is a basis for the co-ordination of activities with others, allowing one to adjust one's own actions to what one can expect/anticipate, because one can consider things from their point of view as well as one's own. The child does not develop a detailed conception of how every other kind of person in a society would view things, for that is far too complicated a task, but forms, rather, a general sense of how other people, broadly and typically, look upon things. Mead called this general orientation the generalised other.

> **The generalised other**
>
> This is an important element in the individual's psychology. The standard outlook of the community in which the child grows up and the attitudes that are shared within it form part of each individual's personality.

Blumer: a method for symbolic interactionism

Herbert Blumer formulated a version of sociology strongly affiliated to Mead's theories. Like Mead, he was critical of the misapplication of the idea of science, and he wrote several papers criticising the 'scientistic' method then widespread in American sociology, one which prided itself on its use of mathematical symbolism. Blumer did not object to every use of mathematical symbols in sociology, but argued that there was an indiscriminate and meaningless imitation of the natural sciences in its use of mathematics. Mathematics was fine in areas like demography (the study of populations), where it plainly had real application, but it was often out of place in other areas of sociology, where the mathematical representations had no genuine grip on the phenomena they purported to represent.

For example, it was common for sociologists to talk about variable analysis as though they were doing the same thing as natural scientists. Variable analysis entails breaking down a complex phenomenon into a number of specific dimensions, which could vary – hence 'variables' – along those dimensions. For example, an object can be located by variables such as speed and direction. Blumer observed, however, that the so-called variables of sociology failed to meet the minimal requirement for comprising a variable, since they did not have actually measurable dimensions with clearly defined properties. In fact, they were not variables at all; rather they were 'abbreviated terms of reference' for complex patterns of social organisation, which the researcher had not described and, usually, could not describe. Thus the use of these pseudo-variables to describe social life unduly simplified and arbitrarily represented it. The methods involved in attempting to develop variable-type schemes cannot capture the true character and complexity of social relations: the ways society through communication is built up of elaborate chains of co-ordinated activity amongst many individuals. Moreover, such schemes tend to reduce the very concept of individual action itself to the stimulus–response relationship that Mead had decried.

Sociology needed to get away from playing with mathematical models of phenomena with which it was not really familiar in order to get on with increasing its familiarity with the range of social phenomena by making first-hand acquaintance with them *in their course*. In particular, it should attend to the ways individuals manage to co-ordinate their activities within the complexes of activity which make up organised social settings. Instead of setting out with ideas of rigorous and precise measurement, sociology should acknowledge that its theoretical concepts are vague and loose; they give no precise expectations about what we can expect to find in any actual situation. We should think of sociology's concepts as sensitising ones, rather than as elements in definite social laws which specify invariant regularities. They point researchers towards a broad range of diffusely identified phenomena, perhaps enabling them to be more sensitive to connections between phenomena, and to notice relations that otherwise might have been missed. The notion of *career* employed by Blumer's contemporary, Everett Hughes, is just such a sensitising concept.

Career

This invites us to look at a range of social situations in terms of the notion of the professional or bureaucratic career, even though such a notion may seem initially to be inappropriate.

For example, we might notice that even in the most supposedly irregular life, such as that of the criminal or the insane, there is orderly arrangement and progression, as illustrated by Edwin Sutherland with *The Professional Thief* (1961) and Erving Goffman with 'The moral career of the mental patient' in his *Asylums* (1968).

Blumer held that recognising the vague state of sociological thought is not an acknowledgement of disgrace, but a realistic appraisal of where sociology stands in the process of building its body of knowledge. The fact is that precise knowledge is the *goal* of empirical enquiry, not its starting point.

Blumer maintained his dissenting position in American sociology from the 1930s to the end of his career, albeit reformulating his arguments to encompass newly appearing sociological theories, prominently those of Talcott Parsons. Symbolic interactionism's critique was that many techniques, especially of the quantitative kind, were inappropriate to the nature of the phenomena they were intended to capture; they involved basic misconceptions about the nature of social life. Blumer held that symbolic interactionism, drawing upon Mead, had a distinctive conception of social life. He maintained that it was more inclusive than either of those involved in the conflict-versus-consensus debate, which, as we saw in Chapter 5, is the way that the major lines of dispute between Parsons and his critics were framed. Blumer argued that symbolic interactionism recognised that people come together in very different ways, sometimes co-operatively, sometimes competitively and, sometimes, in conflict. It is absurd to attempt to reduce the variety of possible forms of human interaction to one essential or basic form, e.g. either consensus or conflict.

Society and individuals

As viewed by symbolic interactionism, society is nothing other than people living their lives; it is a large-scale construction produced out of and through the actions and interactions of many individuals. There is, then, no basis for conceiving of 'society' as a self-sufficient entity with needs of its own that could be satisfied by 'functional' arrangements.

Here again, Parsons's views are put aside. If society is viewed as a vast network of individuals, each of whom responds from his or her position in that network and in terms of his or her picture of that situation, the problem of social order is not to be solved by treating society as a centralised entity engaged in the production of its own existence; rather, it is to be understood by treating it as a distributed network, to use contemporary computing terminology. To use terms rather closer to Blumer's, the need is to see society as a product of joint action, to examine it and its other constituent patterns of complex organisation as being assembled out of the independent, but (frequently) concerted lines of action put together by the individual members of society.

Blumer accepted that if one were to give what he called a 'skeletalised' picture of the complex of institutions and organisations which comprise society at any one time, then the picture given by symbolic interactionism would not look very different from that provided by functionalists or their Marxist critics. The difference lies not in the mapping of society's gross, molar organisation, but in the understanding of how that large-scale pattern comes about. Even though it is a very large structure, it is nothing other than the pattern of individuals going about their lives and, particularly, the understanding of society consists in understanding the way action, and joint action, are organised.

The significance of process

Blumer's dissenting view has two aspects: one pertains to the relationship of structure to what we will call process; the other pertains to the emergent character of lines of action.

Talcott Parsons made a distinction between, and affirmed the (analytical) priority of, structure over process. Parsons analogised his procedure to anatomy, where we seek to understand the (static) layout of organs. First, we describe the locations and physical interconnections of the heart, kidney and spleen. Then we attempt to understand the processes, the changes which take place in the organism, and the ways those changes interconnect and contribute to the functioning of the organism, e.g. the flow of blood and the production of oxygen. Blumer reverses Parsons's priority. It is true that a society can develop a relatively enduring set of institutions and organisations, which then stand in relatively stable arrangements to one another, but to give these structural patterns priority is, once again, to seek to present social life as simpler than it actually is by making out one aspect of it to be the basic, even essential element. True, some social phenomena do stabilise out, but many do not. There are many phenomena within society which are transient, short-lived and ephemeral, or which do not settle down into stable patterns, and a properly comprehensive account of society would encompass both kinds of phenomena. Blumer himself took a keen interest in *collective behaviour*, the name given to a heterogeneous assortment of ephemeral phenomena, ranging from the spread of rumour, demonstrations, riots and insurgencies, to the movements of fashion; they do not crystallise into a stable structure during the course of their (typically brief) existence. These phenomena, however, should be directly comprehensible in terms of the same theory which explains the development of stable, structured arrangements. Thus society in general consists of the *process* of social action.

The process of social action

People undertake actions through which they build up patterns of joint action in many cases. Some of these activities may comprise and sustain long-lasting patterns of joint action, but others do not.

The point is to understand the dynamics of both and not to treat one or other situation as the leading instance.

It is Blumer's complaint, then, that the picture of stable, shared expectations as the basis of action is best fitted to – in Parsons's case, developed for – the analysis of stable, structured arrangements of joint action, where activities have become routinised into patterns that are highly familiar and predictable to participants. It is not suitable, however, for those fluid, developing and changing situations which involve the rise, transformation and disappearance of some instance of collective behaviour. In the latter cases, joint action does not settle down into stable patterns, yet people are none the less able to organise and carry out their affairs. Indeed, Blumer argued that though a concept of shared expectations like Parsons's might best fit the stable, structured complex of joint action, it did not fully fit even the case for which it was designed. It overestimated the degree to which action, even in the best-regulated circumstances, is (so to speak) worked out in advance, thereby underestimating the need to make problematic what we have above termed 'joint action in a distributed environment'. (This point is perhaps best illustrated by considering symbolic interactionist approaches to the study of formal organisations, such as Anselm Strauss's conception of organisations as negotiated orders, in which people work out the arrangement of their relationships and work practices through person-to-person bargaining. (See Strauss et al. 1964.)

We can now turn to the second aspect of this part of Blumer's position, i.e. the emergent character of lines of action. With respect to the organisation of action and joint action, he argues three points:

- Action involves interpretation (or definition).
- The course of action is emergent.
- There is a process of formation of joint action.

Symbolic interactionism is often associated with a slogan formulated by an earlier Chicago sociologist, W.I. Thomas (1863–1947): 'If men define situations as real, they are real in their consequences.' Making much the same point, Blumer himself talked about the issue of 'interpretation'; hence this kind of sociology is often called 'interpretative' sociology. The key point is that people do not respond to situations as they are identified in terms of the latest scientific categories; rather, they respond to situations as they perceive (or define) them, even if they may not be real in scientific terms.

Reality

What people take to be real and what according to science may actually be real may differ, but people respond to what they perceive as real.

For example, it may be that witchcraft does not exist, but, as we have already seen in this chapter, it remains the case that people in some societies take witches to be real, and many of their actions are, therefore, undertaken as protection against or repair to the damage they believe witches can cause. In Thomas's terms, the fact that people define witches as real has real consequences, i.e. it has a tangible effect on their behaviour, leading them to engage in witchcraft-preventive action.

If, however, the way people perceive situations does not accord with the scientific determination of their character, then it cannot be that the ways people perceive those situations are, so to speak, inherent in them, since these situations are not in reality at all the way they are perceived according to the scientific scheme. How, then, do people come to define, to interpret, their situations in the ways that they do? The meaning of the situation for the actor is viewed, then, as *originating* with the actor, as being a meaning with which the actor endows the situation. Consequently, the investigation of defining the situation involves exploring the actor's interpretative procedures.

Obviously, the way people define or interpret their situation must draw upon their culture, but that culture cannot anticipate all the possible situations which can confront the individual, nor even the full detail of any one of the specific situations which will confront him or her. It follows, then, that the actor's interpretative efforts have to go beyond what is given by the culture.

Culture and action

Culture does not predetermine action; even in a situation which is so familiar and recurrent in an individual's life as to be readily defined, to be identified in a rapid and unreflective way, action will have an element of *improvisation*, since a current situation will never be precisely the same as ones previously encountered.

Of course, many situations which an individual will experience even in the course of a day will not be of this familiar, recurrent kind and defining them will be, for the actor, more or less problematic. Thus cases of collective behaviour can often consist in a co-operative effort of individuals defining together, inter- preting, and giving meaning and sense to some new phenomenon with which social change confronts them. For an example – ours, not Blumer's – the 'Cargo cults' involved Polynesian islanders in reacting to the imposition of colonial domination, generating beliefs that the Europeans had magical powers to produce material things – the Cargo – through access to the Bible. These cults were the indigenous people's way of defining, making sense of, their relations with the Europeans. The practices of the cults comprised an amalgam of tradi- tional native and Christian rituals, together with elements copied from the conduct and way of life which they had observed among Europeans.

Emergent action

The conception of action which was cultivated in Parsons's scheme, as throughout sociology more widely, seemed to Blumer to suppose that all that was needed to understand why people acted in the ways that they did was to identify whatever initiated action. For example, the idea of status/role seemed only to involve individuals in a situation identifying one another and thereby knowing which roles they were playing. Then everything else followed automatically, rather like the acting out of lines from a script. By contrast, Blumer held a conception of a course of action which we shall term *emergent* (to use a term coined by Blumer's intellectual mentor, Mead, to refer to the way a course of action is built up as it goes along).

Action characteristically involves a *course of doings*, some sequence of behaviour on the part of its performer. Blumer's point is that though we may have a rough idea of how and where some course of action is going when we set out on it, we do not start with the whole situation of action defined and the course of action fully set. A situation in which we act will itself change or evolve as we act. Therefore, defining the situation is not done prior to and preparatory of the course of action, but must be a continual part of the course of action itself, involving the further defining and redefining of the situation. Further, the way a course of social action develops has to respond to aspects of the situation over which we have no control, e.g. other people may not react to our actions in the way we anticipate. In doing something which requires their co-operation we may have to adapt our intended actions to their responses.

Emergence

How a course of action will turn out is very commonly something which develops over the course of action, i.e. it *emerges* over the spontaneous development of the course of action itself.

This property (we have called 'emergence') means that the building up of lines of joint action is also something to be rendered (analytically) problematic, not treated as simply following from a set of pre-given relationships, however long-standing and well entrenched these might be. Blumer suggests that even a longstanding, perhaps officially and organisationally prescribed, course of action must be renewed on each occasion; because we have done something the same way every day for a long time does not guarantee that this time everything will go as it has previously. At the outset of the occasion, whether it will or not remains to be seen. Even when things go exactly as anticipated, their transaction none the less requires interpretation; it may often prove an effortful matter to keep matters on their usual footing and course, since the capacity to reproduce them is

> subject to pressure as well as to reinforcement, to incipient dissatisfaction as well as to indifference; they may be challenged as well as affirmed, allowed to slip along without concern as well as subjected to infusions of new vigour . . . A gratuitous acceptance of the concepts of norms, values, social rules and the like should not blind the social scientist to the fact that any one of them is subtended by a process of social interaction – a process that is necessary not only for their change but equally well for their reten-tion in a fixed form. It is the social process in group life that creates and upholds the rules, not the rules that create and uphold group life.
>
> (Blumer, 1969: 18)

Interaction, then, is the basic notion for symbolic interactionism.

The basis of symbolic interactionism

This means that the regularity and repetitiveness in social patterns, in rules, norms and values, must be understood as produced by and imple-mented through action and interaction which must not be treated as the product of underlying rules, norms and values themselves. The production of large-scale, enduring complexes of repetitive actions is not to be viewed as automatically arising out of joint actions; instead they are endlessly built and rebuilt, worked and reworked.

After Blumer, the title 'symbolic interaction' acquired its significance much more from the emphasis upon processes of social interaction as the very stuff of society, and no longer quite so much from the emphasis upon the symbolic nature of interaction amongst humans.

Lastly, Blumer's conception involves viewing the complex patterns of joint actions as being produced from within themselves by individual people in their positions and situations. To quote Blumer again, it is a mistake to think of society as some kind of system, for one should

> recognise what is true, namely, that the diverse array of participants occupying different points in the network engage in their actions at those points on the basis of using given sets of meanings . . . the sets of meanings that lead participants to act as they do at their stationed points in the network have their own setting and localised process of social action – and that these meanings are formed, sustained, weakened, strengthened or transformed, as the case may be, through a socially defining process.
>
> (Blumer, 1969: 20)

Symbolic interaction as an urban anthropology

The other key symbolic interactionist played a different role to Blumer. Everett Hughes wrote little of a theoretical kind, but promoted a tradition followed by many distinguished colleagues and students – including Howard Becker, Erving Goffman and Anselm Strauss – of producing case studies, which were often written rather informally and in the form of essays. Hughes favoured the idea of sociology as a scholarly rather than a professionalised scientific pursuit, which should welcome contributions from wheresoever they might come. It should not attempt to construct exclusive barriers around itself and impose uniformity within. He disagreed deeply with Parsons and Merton on this point, a decisive one for the future of American sociology and resulting in Hughes's defeat. Attitude as much as ideas made for the difference between these Chicago sociologists and those who were becoming the establishment in American sociology. In particular, Blumer and his followers regarded theory as more of a limited, modest enterprise aiming partly to provide lightly developed, guiding concepts to bring some direction and order into studies, but primarily serving to open the sensibilities of researchers to aspects of social life that might otherwise seem beneath notice. For them, theory was not an end in itself. There was much reflective concern with the practice of fieldwork since research could itself be understood in terms of symbolic interactionism, for example, as an interactional and an emergent process. Fieldwork was not to be reduced to a strict method, to be followed recipe-like. Rather, the role of the field researcher was loosely defined and open-ended, its actual character being determined through interaction between those under study and the one(s) doing the research. The sense was, very strongly, of research as an *exploratory* activity, especially when the field studies were of areas of social life remote from the day-to-day experience of middle-class professional sociologists. Thus the studies sponsored by Hughes typically have an 'anthropological' character and have been characterised as *urban anthropologies*.

Urban anthropologies

Studies were often of people remote from conventional middle-class lives, either in class terms, e.g. people in 'low-class' occupations such as janitors and assembly-line workers, or in moral terms, e.g. drug addicts, thieves, prostitutes, the mentally ill.

Studies were also made of those middle-class professionals themselves, often focusing on their ways of dealing with the aforementioned socially remote groups, and there was a marked tendency for the tone of these studies about the professionals to be much more sceptical. This orientation gave rise to disputed accusations – as in a famously heated debate from a conflict-theory perspective between Alvin Gouldner (1968) and Howard Becker ([1967] for the inter-actionist side) – that they were based on an excessively sentimental identification with the underdog and the outsider.

The studies of occupations were no doubt motivated by the fact that in modern society the individual's sense of self, of identity, of who one is, has been tied up with one's occupation.

The sense of self

A main element in the sense of self is the degree of self-worth (1) one feels one has, and (2) one is regarded as having. It is, of course, closely interwoven with the occupational system, given that occupations are ranked in terms of prestige and people are judged to be high or low in the scheme of things according to (though not only) the kind of work they do.

For example, the professional is someone of high standing, while the janitor or the rubbish collector will be looked upon as a lowly type. Barney Glaser and Anselm Strauss, in one of their studies of medical work (1968), pointed out that one's life could well depend upon where one stands in the status scheme of things. Life-preserving resources are often scarce relative to the demands made on them. When overwhelmed with cases needing emergency medical treatment, staff have to make decisions about whom they are going to try, seriously, to save, and whom they will have to let die. Glaser and Strauss call the criterion they use 'social loss', seeking to capture by this term the practice among medical staff of making such judgements about social worth, i.e. who matters more in and to society, and whose death will represent the least significant loss. For example, a prominent citizen or business person, or a family member with dependents, will be chosen over a vagrant.

The occupational studies undertaken by Hughes, his colleagues and students covered both highly esteemed and humble jobs, but the attitudes which the researchers took towards each was rather different. The professions are jobs which have higher ratings and advertise themselves as occupations involving such levels of competence in their routine practice that they can only be carried out by highly skilled individuals who have been prepared through long and arduous training. Because the work requires such skill, the occupation seeks what Hughes called 'licence and mandate' from the society; i.e. it seeks to have itself recognised as dealing in matters requiring such expertise that it needs to be given independence from broader forms of social supervision, and allowed to regulate its own ethics, practice and training. Many sociologists used these features as elements in their models of professions, but the symbolic interactionists took a more sceptical view: the professed high-mindedness of the professions, setting themselves out as virtuous servants of their clients, was often a cover for justifying the elevation of their occupation in the competition for prestige and prosperity, and was to be contrasted with their exploitation of the client's ignorance about what was involved in order to deliver inferior service. For example, Abraham Blumberg (1969), writing about the criminal law as a 'confidence game', described how lawyers would organise their defence work in such ways as to send the client away (even to prison) happy with their lawyer, even though, in fact, the outcome was not the best, but simply the one the lawyer could get with least trouble. Similarly, the claim to expertise and the necessity of training was questioned: legal work is often done not by the lawyer who heads the practice but by clerical staff with no legal training or supervision. Howard Becker's 'The nature of a profession', in his *Sociological Work* (1970) is a sustained polemic against the usual, admiring concept of a profession.

On the other hand, the studies of the humble occupations and of socially degraded groups was sympathetic, being motivated to take the viewpoint of those in these lowly positions, to ask how they defined their situation, and to look at things from their point of view. The inclination was to emphasise the unappreciated aspects of these positions in society and, as with the studies of professions, to attempt a corrective to popular conceptions. People in lowly positions and social outcasts were subject to unfairly derogatory popular conceptions, which dismissed their lives as disorganised, irrational and disgraceful. In these cases, the point of the studies was to claim that the lives were very much *ordinary* for those who lived them, i.e. organised and routine. Those who live them face and practically contend with much the same array of problems of living as anyone else; crime, for those who do it, involves work no less than do other occupations. Just like the legal profession, crime too might have a kind of professional career structure. At the same time, though, these studies recognised that the people involved had low or negative esteem in the eyes of the world at large. An interest was therefore taken in how people in these positions contend with it: how could they maintain any sense of self-worth in a society which told them they were worthless individuals?

Goffman and the interaction order

Many of these studies were drawn together to provide the empirical stuffing for Erving Goffman's conceptual structures. As we mentioned above, Goffman was the most successful symbolic interactionist in terms of the distinctiveness of his conceptions, the influence they have had, and the financial rewards from his best-selling, well-received books. In a series of linked books, Goffman gave an account of the way the individual constructs and communicates a sense of self in the course of interaction, and how interaction is produced as an autonomous order of social organisation.

An example Goffman favoured was taken from restaurants. It concerned the abrupt change which would overcome the waiters as they moved through the door dividing the kitchen from the dining area. Before the public, the waiter's behaviour was courteous, constrained and respectful, but entry into the kitchen would transform it into a less restrained mode, often manifesting contempt for those who, only a moment before, were treated in a servile way. For Goffman, this example illustrates a widespread pattern, common to organisations of the form he termed 'establishments', which included hospitals, department stores, hotels and business offices. These establishments are open to the public and tend to be divided into two separated areas, one part on display to the public, the other closed to it.

The presentation of the self in establishments

In an analogy with the theatre, Goffman termed these areas the 'front' and 'back' regions, using their existence to argue that the presentation of the individual self is a collective affair, very often the work of a team. As with the theatre, what goes on before the public is organised to convey a particular conception. In the case of organisations, it is often the competent, professional delivery of the relevant service, accompanied by an appropriate attitude.

For example, clients and customers often want not only the specific service, but its delivery in a manner which treats them with respect, if not subservience. People visiting hotels do not want merely to be provided with a room; they also want to be treated as important and with courtesy. The staff, then, mount a collaborative performance to project themselves as the capable and committed deliverers of that service; they play back the clients' own self-conceptions as the well-regarded, gratefully and gracefully serviced clients. Putting on this performance is often stressful, for the attitude being projected is not actually held. Further, it involves withholding all negative reactions, like irritation, as well as having to fulfil physically demanding and mentally wearing responsibilities such as standing still impassively for long periods. The back region, private to the staff, is where they can physically and emotionally relax, let off steam, loosen tight clothing; they can express the reactions they have restrained during the performance, especially by reversing the relationship of servility they have been acting out. In the back region, they can reciprocally express and mutually sustain feelings of disdain for their clients, thereby reinforcing their sense of themselves as being more and other than they must appear to be in the front region.

Goffman on the mental hospital

The 'asylum', i.e. the large state mental hospital, was of interest to Goffman because it did not conform to the front/back region pattern, at least for those who were its inmates. From the point of view of those consigned to mental hospital, the place was not experienced as a therapeutic environment devoted to the repair of their damaged psyches, but, rather, as custodial, dedicated to attacking their self-image and eradicating any remaining residue of self-respect. For the inmates, notions of psychiatric treatment seemed like mere rationales for an oppressive, disciplinary regime. Medical and psychiatric procedures seemed to be used more as modes of control, even punishment, than of healing; their application seemed to be dictated more by the requirements for administering a large and unruly population than by patient symptoms. As previously mentioned, Goffman held that the inmates are better understood on the assumption that they are psychologically normal, rather than psychologically disorganised; much of their behaviour can best be understood as a perfectly reasonable reaction to a depriving environment. The earlier example of hoarding behaviour was construed by psychiatrists as mentally symptomatic, but it can as well – if not better – be construed as a reaction to a lack of privacy and a paucity of resources.

For Goffman, the lack of privacy for inmates was crucial. For them, there was no obvious division between front and back region; they were continually under surveillance and in the presence of many others. Affairs were so organised as persistently to thrust upon the inmate a conception of himself or herself as a flawed, failed individual, deservedly reduced in the social scheme of things to a most humble position, someone crazy or insane. Any protestations that inmates might make that there was nothing really wrong with them were criticised and undermined in the name of therapy until the patient came to realise that the only way out of the institution was to accept the judgement of the staff. Indeed, a first, necessary step in 'progress' towards release was to 'admit' that one was mentally ill; it was deemed 'insight'. Goffman records the detailed, marginal ways in which the inmates none the less struggled in the face of such an assault on their self-esteem to maintain some shreds of self-respect. Even in such a rigorously controlled environment they were adept at creating and exploiting opportunities for shielding themselves and their activities from surveillance:

> Free places are backstage to the usual performance of staff–inmate relationships. Free places in Central Hospital were often employed as the scene for specifically tabooed activities: the patch of woods behind the hospital was occasionally used as a cover for drinking; the area behind the recreation building and the shade of a large tree near the centre of the hospital grounds were used as locations for poker games.
>
> (Goffman 1968: 206)

The assumption behind symbolic interactionism's analytical strategy can be understood thus: the formal patterns of social organisation are general and remain the same across the whole range of behaviour; they do not alter as one crosses the line between respectable and disreputable social groups. Combined with the objective of seeing things sympathetically from the point of view of those under study, this approach encourages playing down the difference between those on different sides of morality or the law. Out of it (especially through the work of Edwin Lemert (1967) and Howard Becker (1964)) emerged a concept of *deviance* which was to be notorious, controversial and influential: as developed by Becker, it became known as the *labelling theory*. It was a theory of deviance rather than crime, even though crime is often the leading instanceof deviance, in order to include all kinds of socially disapproved behaviour and outcast groups, i.e. all those infringing social rules, not only those breaking the law.

Theories of deviance traditionally sought to establish just how deviants differed from 'normal' people, i.e. taking it for granted that they did. A common tactic was to look for characteristics – biological, psychological or social – which distinguish 'deviants' from 'normals.' The attentive reader will have noted that such an assumption would not appeal to symbolic interactionists. Goffman explicitly rejects this as a supposition for his study of the 'insane.' Further, symbolic interactionists noted that studies which sought to compare deviants with normals did nothing of the sort. Instead they compared *identified* (i.e. convicted or diagnosed) deviants with a general population which would also contain unidentified deviants. If a deviant is defined as someone who has broken a social rule or law, then there can be few of us who are not deviants, for we all break rules and laws at some time or other. For most of us there are no consequences – we do not even get fined for parking illegally.

Labelling theory

Labelling theory picks up on a Durkheimian conception, though developing it to very different effect: deviance is very much a public matter, and deviants, as they have traditionally been studied, are people who have been publicly identified as such, i.e. they have been taken through the courts, the psychiatric admission process and so on. The difference between deviants and normals is not, then, in their individual characteristics. The difference between them is how they have been treated by, broadly, the agencies of social control, i.e. the various administrative bodies engaged in enforcing social rules.

Some people who break rules or laws may be picked out by the police, social workers and so on, whilst others who break the same rules or laws may continue their lives unmolested. If we want to understand the difference between someone who is convicted or diagnosed, say, and someone who is not, we do not need to study their individual characteristics; instead, we need to look at the practices of the administrative organisations which publicly identify someone as a criminal or as mentally disturbed. The difference between a deviant and a supposed normal may result from how they are treated by the staffs of such administrative bodies. An outcome might be as incidental as, say, the fact that police patrolmen, bored and wanting a change from sitting in their car, might decide to arrest somebody for an offence that, under other circumstances, they would have done nothing about.

Becker's arguments responded to an issue raised by Durkheim about the fact that all societies create 'crime' (as Durkheim called it, or 'deviance' in Becker's terminology), as a class of prohibited actions. Becker took a different tack to Durkheim's in understanding this fact; we must study the ways people in society (not society itself) create and enforce rules. This approach involves recognising the frequently political nature of these actions, since rules are formed out of contests amongst social groups; the ways favoured by some social groups are enforced on other groups. The outcomes of such contests are not the expression of any will of society, but are very much prone to the contingencies of the (literally) political process. For example, unrepresentative groups, such as temperance movements, can gain a very strategic position, and get their policy imposed generally, e.g. prohibition of alcohol in this case. We can say, then, that the making of the laws *creates* deviance. It does so in two ways:

- by making a set of previously legal actions illegal;
- by giving rise to new kinds of actions which are also criminal, and respond to the new situation created by the prohibition of the first action (Lemert called them 'secondary deviance').

For example, prohibition brought into existence a gangsterism organised to bootleg liquor (as, some argue, the prohibition of drugs today creates and sustains the illegal drug trade).

The understanding of how the rules are brought into existence, however, is only part of the necessary programme of study, for the fact is that those who enforce the rules once they are made are not the same people who create those rules in the first place.

Moral entrepreneurs and bureaucratic professionals

Becker wrote of 'moral entrepreneurs', who campaign to obtain new law, and noted that the interest of these enthusiasts often extends as far as securing a prohibition. Those charged with enforcing the prohibition are often bureaucratic professionals, who are less likely to care as strongly about the merits of the rule than those who made it since enforcement is only their job, not their passion. They adapt the enforcement of the law to the practicalities of their work: their interests are in job-relevant considerations like career advancement, a quiet life, avoiding distasteful work, providing amusement during dull periods, keeping the boss happy, etc. In short, the way a rule gets enforced may be very different from how it was envisaged by those who framed it.

Jerome Skolnick's *Justice Without Trial* (1966) provides a compelling portrait of the way the police typically traded off law enforcement against peace keeping. Police officers treated as first priority the calming of difficult, disturbed situations, and mollifying the upset and angered parties to them; they preferred to disregard the fact that there had been an arrestable offence. That a law had been broken, allowing the possibility of an arrest, was often used as a threat to control the immediate situation. The police knew that if they made arrests every time they could, they would overwhelm their own and the court system's capacity to cope. Also, in many cases, they would refrain from arrest because it would cause them unnecessary work; they believed that having satisfied the demand of an injured party for an arrest, and having done all the paper work, the injured party would probably then drop the charges.

Thus an understanding of the difference between deviants and normals will not result from a focus upon the individuals who are publicly labelled as deviant. Instead, we must focus on the operations of the individuals, groups and organisations in society which promote and install rules, policies and standards, and on the organisations which implement and enforce these standards. Rather than ask what makes a deviant do deviant things, we might – Becker suggests – ask what stops people from engaging in such acts. We all are subject to impulses to do 'wrong' things at one time or another, but most of us do not follow through on these impulses, or not sufficiently frequently or carelessly to fall foul of the authorities and thereby have our lives transformed into those of outcasts. He suggested that many of us are careful to avoid this outcome because of the *commitments* which we have accumulated in our lives. Even though we have the impulse to do something, we are prevented by thinking of the risk involved to the things we value in the life we currently lead.

Defenders of more orthodox conceptions responded to labelling theory as a form of relativism, for which it was often fiercely condemned. The theory maintained (or seemed to maintain) that deviance existed purely in the eye of the beholder. Deviance was thus a purely subjective state; deviance was what people believed it to be, and nothing else. Since people had different beliefs, then they would believe different things to be deviant and, by this logic, these things *were* deviant. In a way, everything would at once be both deviant and not deviant. Becker explicitly argued that the characteristic 'deviance' is not intrinsic to a given action because a certain action, such as drinking alcohol, can be legal before midnight and illegal after it, can be legal in one state of the US and illegal in another, can be legal if done by an adult and illegal if done by an adolescent.

Defining deviance

If, then, deviance does exist in the eye of the beholder, any action can be deviant, for in the eyes of one group an action may be normal, but in the eyes of another abnormal. According to labelling theory, something is deviant only because there is a law (or rule) against it, and someone is a deviant only if the law (or rule) is enforced and she or he is publicly identified as infringing it.

Here critics complain that if there were no law or other prohibition against, say, beating up old people in the street, it would not be a deviant action. Despite criticism, however, labelling theory was influential, and its studies of the way the identity of deviant was conferred through the workings of the bureaucracies of social control contributed to the formation of the influential and even more controversial *social constructionist* doctrines, which emphasised the role of organisational arrangements in bestowing all kinds of identities, not just deviant ones. Consequently, the way people were identified as 'mothers' or as 'sick' or even 'dead' would be studied in this way.

The heyday of symbolic interactionism was in the 1950s and 1960s, when the pioneering thought and work of Blumer and Hughes was applied in highly creative and imaginative ways by many investigators, including Goffman, Becker and Strauss. The approach has continued to be productive, and there is a substantial and constant flow of writings, characteristically based on field studies, on a wide range of everyday activities. However, these are mostly conducted under the auspices of the general and reasonably well-defined approach, rather than involving real innovations in its nature. Recently, there has been an attempt to reassert the relevance of the approach with the claims that (1) it is reconstructing itself in such a way as to enable it to deal with topics which are now regarded as essential elements in sociological understanding – social structures, institutions, power and ideology – which hitherto, symbolic interaction, could have been accused of neglecting; and (2) it can accommodate to recent postmodern sensibilities, which have tended to minimise the significance of the subject or, in interactionist terminology, 'the self' in modern society, treating it as an illusory phenomenon. Against this poststructuralist and postmodern dispensation with the self it is argued that the self remains a proper topic for empirical investigation, that can be done in a way which is compatible with some main features of the postmodernist position.

Conclusion

Symbolic interaction continues to be practised and remains productive of research investigations, but it has become marginalised relative to the mainstream of sociological thought. Credited with making an important contribution to the relativising of social thought, especially through the ideas of labelling theory it is none the less regarded as having been left behind by the more drastic and all-encompassing relativism of poststructuralist and postmodernist doctrines.

Questions

1 What are the main points in Winch's argument that a science of society is misconceived? Do you agree with his argument?

2 'Modern popular beliefs in astrology are parallel to the Zande's belief in witches.' Discuss in relation to the Winch/Evans-Pritchard debate about science and rationality.

3 Does symbolic interactionism provide an alternative to positivism?

4 Outline Mead's concept of the self. Why is it considered to be important for sociological method?

5 How does Blumer's attempt to restore individual meanings into sociological analysis differ from Weber's?

6 Illustrate with contemporary examples W.I. Thomas's slogan, 'If men define situations as real, they are real in their consequences.' Do you agree?

7 Is the symbolic interactionist approach a crucial insight into the workings of the social world or merely a restatement of the obvious?

---

8   Some symbolic interactionists view, for example, lawyers and prostitutes as both having careers. Is this approach more the politics of egalitarianism than an attempt to do scientific sociology?

9   How does Goffman describe the fate of the self in mental institutions?

10 What is labelling theory? Does it extend Durkheim's notion of deviance? Is it an invitation to relativism?

Further reading

Baldwin, J., 1986, *G.H. Mead: A Unifying Theory for Sociology*. Sage. A good, short introduction.

Becker, H.S., 1964, *Outsiders: Studies in the Sociology of Deviance*. Free Press. The classic statement of 'labelling theory'.

Blumer, H., 1969, *Symbolic Interactionism*. Prentice Hall. Contains his essays 'Society as symbolic interaction', 'Sociological analysis and the "variable" ' and 'The sociological implications of the thought of G.H. Mead'.

Goffman, E., 1968, *Asylums: Essays on the Social Situation of Mental Patients and Other Inmates*. Penguin. Goffman's classic account of the mental hospital as a 'total institution'.

—— 1983, 'The interaction order', *American Sociological Review*, 48: 1-17.

Hammersley, M., 1989, *The Dilemma of Qualitative Sociology: Herbert Blumer and the Chicago Tradition*. Routledge. A useful critical study of Blumer's thought.

Rock, P., 1979, *The Making of Symbolic Interactionism*. Macmillan. A useful historical account.

Winch, P., 1990, *The Idea of a Social Science*. 2nd edn. Routledge. Still essential, controversial reading, with a new author's preface.

■   ■   ■

Chapter 7

Ethnomethodology

Introduction: Ethnomethodology – a relativist, subjectivist sociology?

In the debates surrounding symbolic interactionism, a recurrent charge was that it endorsed a relativist stance which denied any objective reality whatsoever to social life by reducing it entirely to the perceptions or definitions of individuals. In so far as the notion of *defining the situation* was taken seriously and to its limits, it was seen to combine with other arguments, e.g. Winch's, in inducing a relativist current into sociological thought. The accusation was most prominently made in relation to the notion of labelling, which, as we have shown in Chapter 6, can be seen as adopting a strange attitude to social reality, i.e. deviance exists only in the eye of the beholder. If symbolic interactionism appeared to encourage such relativist developments, then ethnomethodology was regarded as carrying them even further, to the extreme.

As we noted in the previous chapter, in some ways ethnomethodology is close to symbolic interactionism. Yet in other, and generally more important respects, it is very far removed. It certainly derives from different sources, i.e. directly from European philosophy, and most particularly from Alfred Schutz's application of the phenomenology fathered by Edmund Husserl to the problems of the social sciences. For Schutz, the *locus classicus* of these problems was the methodological writings of Weber. Therefore he began by subjecting to critical inspection Weber's most basic assumptions about social action. Weber put the actor's point of view, i.e., the subjective point of view, at the centre of his project, but he made no sustained effort to reflect on the way that point of view must be structured, and did not try to give any systematic account of how society appeared to someone situated within it. Nor did he resolve adequately the implications of the assumption of the actor's point of view for sociology's stance towards its subject matter. Schutz proposed to fill this gap. He began his critique of Weber in the 1920s, publishing it in the early 1930s before going into exile in the USA.

Basics of ethnomethodology

The starting point for the study of ethnomethodology is the writings of Schutz since, in key respects, ethnomethodology is nothing more than the working out of the implications of Schutz's arguments about the nature and foundations of sociological knowledge. In particular, ethnomethodology focuses on how we study the world: the issue of *method* best elaborates its ideas. For ethnomethodology, the notion of method goes far beyond sociological methods conventionally conceived, such as fieldwork and the social survey. The key to an adequate understanding of ethnomethodology lies in comprehending just why it is called what it is, particularly the significance of 'methodology' in its title.

Schutz and phenomenology

Schutz owed inspiration to the *phenomenology* of Husserl, which, in its way, had been critical of the 'positivist' spirit in Western thought, especially in science and philosophy. As we have seen in Chapter 3, at the heart of this positivist tradition lies the view that the new, immensely successful natural sciences are the source of a definitive conception of reality, one which is secured by scientific methods. The epitome of these methods are to be found in physics, the most successful of the sciences. At its limit, then, this view holds that if we want to know what reality is really like we had best look into the textbooks of physics. But there we shall find a world very different from the one that we ordinarily know. The natural world familiar to us in our daily life does not appear in such books; many thinkers of a positivist persuasion have read these books as telling us that this world of daily life does not really exist: it is a form of illusion.

The prevailing stance in sociology throughout much of its history has been shaped by such positivist assumptions, i.e. if sociology follows the path of the natural sciences, then it too will come to define reality in terms of scientific methods. Genuine social reality will be defined *through* these methods so that only when we have finished our sociological studies shall we know what social reality really is. On such assumptions we can expect it to look like nothing we now take it to be. Our current perceptions of social reality will come to be seen as the result of false beliefs.

This contrast was strongly opposed by Husserl. He did not accept this picture of the relationship between the world-according-to-science, on the one hand, and our lived-in-world (*Lebenswelt*), on the other. Husserl certainly did not reject (did not even question) the achievements of the natural sciences as sciences, for his doubts were about the way its findings were being construed. In particular he argued that serious misconceptions about the way science relates to our pre-scientific understandings had crept in, giving rise to a false picture of the two in conflict. Crudely, science does not provide a picture which displaces the lived-in-world as we experience it: it cannot do so, for the scientific picture both originates in and depends upon the lived-in-world itself. An X-ray photograph does not compete with or displace our passport photograph.

To start by comparing an X-ray with a snapshot and asking which is the correct picture of someone is to go about things the wrong way. Rather than starting with the (supposed) scientific picture already in place and then asking how that compares with our experience of the lived-in-world and how there can possibly be room for both, Husserl thought we should not take the presence of the scientific picture for granted. Instead we should ask about its *origins*, i.e. how the possibility of looking at the world in a scientific way as opposed to a common-sense way developed.

Husserl linked the rise of science as a way of thinking to Galileo, who most influentially promoted the idea that inquiry into the nature of things could begin from assumptions quite distant from those we common-sensically accept. Furthermore, Galileo argued that the development of scientific understanding involved the questioning and, if necessary, abandoning of reliance upon perceptions provided by our unaided senses. Here then were the origins of a distancing of science from everyday ways of knowing the world; they were built into thinking about the natural sciences and what was necessary to their success virtually from the start. Husserl's inquiries comprised the backdrop to Schutz's thinking about the relationship between science and common sense as ways of knowing. Schutz, however, shifted the focus from completely contrasting the world-as-portrayed-in-science, on the one hand, and the world-as-seen-by-common sense, on the other.

The natural attitude

Instead, Schutz emphasised differences within the *natural attitude*, i.e. an attitude which begins by taking the existence of an external world for granted. It has two forms, the *common-sense* attitude and the *theoretical* (or *scientific*) attitude. They are very different and in important respects incongruous, but even so they are far from being altogether distinct.

The reason – and the deep implication of Schutz's argument – is that we cannot give up the common-sense in favour of taking up the theoretical (or scientific) attitude. Consequently, we cannot replace the common-sense with the scientific. Here he connects with the approach of Descartes (see Chapter 6). Descartes recommended the *method of doubt* as a means of reaching the ultimate, unquestionable certainties for which he thought philosophy should search. This method involves doubting everything that can possibly be doubted in order to determine whether anything remains which cannot possibly be doubted, i.e. leaving us with certain knowledge. Descartes thought that one can doubt almost everything, even the existence of the external world. The one exception – the only thing seemingly capable of this kind of resistance – is one's own mental existence. In doubting, one is thinking, and being able to think presupposes one's own existence, or, more strictly, it presupposes the existence of one's own mind.

However, the Cartesian method of doubt has its function within the strictly defined domain of pure philosophical inquiry in order to establish the grounds for certain knowledge through the operation of pure reason. Someone who wants to do other than merely think, who wants to *do* something, cannot operate with Descartes's the method of doubt – a point that Descartes appreciated, as he was concerned purely with philosophical questions concerning how to establish certain knowledge. Acting requires dependence upon one's body and the external world: these are presupposed in action. The *method of doubt* can be taken in philosophical reflection, for this is something which can go on entirely in the mind and without the use of the body or its movement in the external world. Hence, it cannot be that the lives in society are lived on the basis of the method of doubt. They must be conducted on some other basis.

The natural attitude

The natural attitude is counterposed to the method of doubt. As they go about their lives, people do not doubt the reality of everything that could possibly be called into question. They take most things for granted. However, to notice this attitude is not to point to a failing on the part of people going about their daily lives. Of course, people in the natural attitude do doubt, but do not, in practical terms could not, make doubting anything like their first priority. They only doubt when they have need to, when something goes wrong in their practical affairs. We might suppose that people could doubt whether when they do something this time things will happen the same way as last time. For example, if they turn on the tap which last time produced water, will it this time produce water, or nothing, or poison gas? If we have a serious doubt about it, truly think that a fatally poisonous gas is as likely as water, we would not turn on the tap without first trying to ensure that water will come out. At the very least, an ordinary, routine activity would be made deeply problematic and extraordinarily time consuming. But note what follows if we assume such scepticism, not about a specific activity in particular, but in general. It is not simply that the problem would be an endless one if we adopted a comparably sceptical view towards everything else that we might use; the problem would be where and how even to begin the task. How are we to be sure that what we take as a tap actually is one? But if we do not assume it is a tap, then what possible sense can be given to the idea that we cannot trust what might come out of it?

Of course, the key point is that we do not carry on like good Cartesians because in our normal lives we just assume, just take it for granted, that this time will be like last time and the tap will deliver water we can drink and wash with. Doubt occurs if we turn on the tap and nothing comes out, or foul sludge drips forth. Then we have doubts, and start to check things out, but, even so, we do not start to doubt everything, only those things relevant to the tap's working properly, e.g. we look out of the window to see if the water-service repair crew might have dug up the road. Doubt in the natural attitude is an occasioned, stimulated occurrence and not the general condition of our lives. The implication for sociology, of course, is the need to study how people *operate under the natural attitude* if we want to understand how their social lives are organised. Schutz's career was entirely devoted to this enterprise.

Importantly, Schutz is analysing an *attitude*, i.e. an approach to their affairs which the members of society not only overwhelmingly exhibit, but are required to exhibit. When we refer to 'common sense', we are neither recommending nor supporting particular actions or beliefs. Otherwise, we would be open to the objection (often made by those who misunderstand even the elementary features of this line of argument) that common sense is a localised matter and that what is considered common sense in one place or at one time is not considered so in another locale or epoch. This putative objection is more of a confirmation, however, of the point being made here about understanding how actions are organised.

The common-sense attitude

The argument is that:

- it is an inescapable feature of the organisation of actions that their course depends upon what people take for granted;
- among any given set of people there is a vast multitude of things that they will take for granted, that between themselves they treat as obvious, apparent, as going without need of comment or explanation, as transparently and without question plainly the case, and readily known to anyone and everyone, i.e. as common sense.

Neither of these contentions says anything about what is treated as common sense in any given case. They are entirely comfortable with the idea that what is common sense in twentieth-century America would not be the same – certainly not entirely the same – as what was common sense in fourteenth-century China. The reference to 'anyone and everyone' has its own localised applicability: what Californian teenagers of the 1990s treat as matters that 'anyone and everyone' knows will refer to people like themselves, and these terms are often likely to exclude parents, teachers and other adults.

The dominant element of the natural attitude is its concern with getting things done, its practical character. People in society are not concerned with finding things out for their own sake, with accumulating knowledge of how things work in order to have the most organised and comprehensive stock of knowledge possible. Observably they are more concerned with getting certain sorts of things successfully completed by their actions, such as making the lunch, getting to work, buying a new coat, filling in forms, checking the stock, and, protecting garden plants against frost. Their occasions of doubt arise within the context of such practical enterprises. We do not sit in the living room all day wondering whether water will come out of the tap when we eventually turn it on. The issue only arises when we want some water, and only then if the usual expected flow does not materialise. What people know and take for granted is organised, for them, around the things that they are doing. The question they put to conditions is: are they good enough, can they be relied upon, *for all practical purposes*? The extent to which they doubt, and the degree to which they take measures to resolve doubt, are both characteristically set within practical limits. If water does not come out of the tap, then the kinds of questions which arise pertain to what kinds of causes could interrupt the water supply, and any inquiries into these matters will characteristically terminate the moment that the water supply is restored.

These aspects are not shared with the scientific or theoretical attitude, but, as noted above, we should not conclude that the scientific and the natural (or common-sense) attitudes are entirely distinct. The scientific attitude lies part way between the philosophical method of doubt and the common-sense natural attitude.

The scientific attitude

Simplistically put, we can say that the scientific attitude is concerned with knowledge rather more than with practicality, with finding out as opposed to getting done, and with knowledge for its own sake, rather than with knowledge that enables the fulfilment of a here-and-now practical task.

Further, the scientific attitude is more motivated by the possibility of doubt than is the common-sense attitude, making it closer to the philosophical posture of systematic doubt. Unlike the common-sense attitude, science does tend to doubt things which can be doubted, just to see what doubting them might reveal. However, it cannot doubt upon the global scale of the Cartesian 'method of doubt' since the objective of science is to inquire into the 'world-out-there', and that, of course, means that the existence of that world-out-there cannot be doubted as it can in philosophical reflection. For this reason, science is included within the natural attitude.

Moreover, the working scientist's doubt is much more specific and focused than the philosopher's, for the working scientist doubts that some specific thing is the way it seems or has been taken to be in order to investigate and settle this particular doubt. In so doing, scientific inquirers must exclude many things from the (immediate) possibility of doubt and must take for granted very many things as matters of so much common sense, just like ordinary members of society. Similarly philosophers can (and do) doubt whether words can have meaning, whether it is possible that if one person says something another can understand the words at all, but the scientist makes a study with every intention of reporting it to fellow professionals, and therefore cannot enjoy such doubts!.

Hence the picture of the scientist as the thoroughgoing and comprehensive sceptic about common-sense understandings makes science out to be unduly like philosophical scepticism, and does not note how selective actual scientific inquiry is and must be about its doubting of common sense. The extent to which it both (and simultaneously) doubts and depends upon common-sense understandings is especially consequential for sociology. The attitude of a real scientific investigator may indeed allow doubting of certain accepted features of the common-sense understandings of the world in which the scientific investigator dwells, e.g. in Copernicus's day the notion was that the earth was at the centre of the universe. Nevertheless, the conduct of the scientific examination itself has to be subordinate, in many respects, to the natural attitude. In fact, the scientific attitude has to take many things for granted and to count upon them as conditions for doing scientific work. It has to treat things as so much common sense for those within the world of science and, in many respects, for those outside the scientific community also.

Intersubjectivity

The frequent criticism that Schutz makes the social world into something which exists entirely inside the head of the members of society has often led towards the criticism of ethnomethodology as itself an extreme form of subjectivism. Again, this reading of Schutz is far from accurate, since he argues that social reality is an *intersubjective* matter, i.e. the individuals making up a society do not each occupy her or his own, personal, distinct, mental world; instead, they all exist within (allowing for adjustments of perspective) one and the same reality. In short, that the social world is a world known in common to its inhabitants.

Schutz thus emphasises the following:

- The extent of each individual's understanding of the world is dependent upon the *social distribution of knowledge*: individuals make sense of the world around them in terms of what they know. Of course, most of what people know is acquired not by learning through or from their own first-hand experience but by learning from others, who, in turn, did not learn most of what they know through or from their own first-hand experience, and so on. For example, we all know, i.e. take it for granted, that the world is round, but we have found it out in school, not by trekking round the globe.
- The individual acts upon the basis of a *stock of knowledge to hand*, which (1) has been built up by being handed down from other members of the society, (2) has been derived from the social stock of knowledge, and (3) has been transferred to the individual through social arrangements such as child rearing in the family, teaching in school, on-the-job training and, conversation amongst peers.
- The individual's rock-bottom assumption is not of living in a unique, private world, perceived entirely differently from the way others perceive it; on the contrary, the world is also known by others, and is known to them – other things being equal – in the same way as it is known to the individual. Of course, things do not appear identical from all points of

view, but fundamental to each individual's point of view are assumptions which co-ordinate the differences associated with each individual's specific experience.

Concerning this third point, Schutz identifies two crucial suppositions:

1   the reciprocity of perspectives;
2   the interchangeability of standpoints.

In (1) people simply assume that the way they see things will be matched, reciprocated, by other persons, allowing for their different locations in space and their different places in the course of action. In our familiar example from Chapter 6, motorists driving at high speeds entrust their lives to this assumption: they expect and assume that drivers they can see behind them through their rear-view mirror will have a view of their own car in front, and that their perception of the front of the car behind will be matched by the perceptions of those behind of the rear of their own car.

Assumption (2), the interchangeability of standpoints, entails that two or more parties, although in different places, see different but matching things, and, vitally, that if they were to change places then they would also exchange perceptions. In effect, if the drivers were to be magically switched between cars, then the driver previously in front would now see exactly what the driver in the rear car had previously been seeing, and vice versa. For example, the driver at high speed intending to change lanes switches on the indicator, and though that driver cannot personally see the rear indicator light flashing, he or she nevertheless assumes that the driver in the car behind can see it and can see what the first one would see if positions were to be swapped, thereby receiving adequate warning of the manoeuvre.

For Schutz, it is an analytical problem to understand how people maintain their sense of inhabiting an intersubjective world, how it is the same for you as for me, allowing for various differences of position and background between us. Of course, maintaining this sense of the world known in common can sometimes be a problem for people in society; taking for granted the reciprocity of perspectives and the interchangeability of standpoints and routinely counting on these assumptions does not always work out. On occasion people can find themselves confronted with persons who do not behave in ways which accord with these assumptions. Schutz's own example, 'the stranger', is one type of person with whom such expectations are likely to fail.

Multiple realities

Although Schutz emphasises the extent to which the meaning of events in the social world is routinely shared, with subjective variability being the exception rather than the rule, it might appear from the title of one of his essays in the *Collected Papers* (1962), 'On multiple realities', that he does encourage the opposite view. Such a view would stress that the things people understand to be real can and do vary widely amongst individuals, that each different individual does inhabit a very different reality; but that would once again be an entirely misleading way to read the essay. For Schutz is concerned, in the first instance, with the episodic nature of each individual's experience; over the course of a routine day the quality of our experience is not uniform, but variable, and we are likely to pass through a set of quite different states, all of which are experienced as real at the time they are undergone. For example, there is the contrast between being awake and dreaming while asleep. While we are awake, the events of daily life around us are understood as real, but when we are asleep and dreaming the events in our dream are also experienced as real: we are frightened by frightening things in our dream, we fear for our life and so on.

These differences are two extremes. Our participation in various spheres of waking life, however, also involves variations in the kinds of things we treat as real and the ways we treat them.

Finite provinces of meaning

Schutz refers to these different spheres of life as *finite provinces of meaning* in order to indicate the extent to which different (and, in a way, independent) standards of what is real routinely apply in daily life, e.g. in theatricals, science and religion.

Here Schutz is not being a relativist; he is not arguing that reality in any one of these provinces of meaning is just as authentic as reality in any other. Rather, he is attempting to describe the way people understand their own experiences, how they switch (so to speak) from one frame of reference to another within the round of their activities. Nevertheless, within people's experience, they treat one of these provinces of meaning as the paramount reality, namely, the world of daily life. He gives two reasons for this claim:

1   The switch into and out of the other provinces of meaning involves movement into and out of the world of daily life.
2   When events in the different spheres are compared, the standard of reality in daily life characteristically overrides the others.

We illustrate (1) with the example of going to the theatre, parking the car there, getting the ticket, finding the seat and waiting for the lights to go down: all are events in our daily life. After the curtain rises, we may become engrossed in the world – in the reality – projected by the play and treat as real *whilst watching the play* the fact, say, that a Martian visits a human household and exerts various kinds of strange effects on people and events. When the curtain falls we return to the world of daily life, to the mundane activities of leaving the theatre, finding the car, and so on. We go home, put the cat out, lock the doors, and do other everyday things before going to bed, where we fall asleep and then enter the reality of dreams, where, again, all kinds of strange things (from an everyday point of view) occur and are experienced as real occurrences *while we are dreaming*. In brief, we move from one finite province of meaning to another by way of the world of daily life.

With reference to (2), when we are in the theatre we are witnessing the presence in an ordinary household of an alien being treated as a real event, but on leaving the theatre we do not rush to a phone to tell friends that there is now proof that Martians are living amongst us. One knows very well that, in the world of daily life, the events on stage as part of a theatrical performance do not count as real occurrences. Similarly, we know that dreaming that we have divorced our spouse is not going to be recognised in the waking life as having actually gone through a divorce.

Finally, the relationship between science and common sense can also effectively be dealt with in terms of these arguments. Science is another of the finite provinces of meaning accessed from the world of daily life; it too accepts the paramountcy of the world of daily life. Note carefully, however, how we intend this point. It is illustrated by the physicist who starts the day by getting breakfast, reading the mail or the newspaper, driving to work and chatting around the coffee machine, before entering the world of science, i.e. getting down to serious scientific work. Of course, for the working scientist the world of science is embedded within the world of daily life. This relationship between the world of daily life and the world of science as the working scientist's daily routine is nicely captured in a remark by a professor of physics, quoted by the anthropologist, Clifford Geertz:

> Physics is like life; there's no perfection. It's never all sewed up. It's all a question of better, better yet, and how much time and interest do you really have in it? Is the universe really curved? It's not that cut and dried. Theories come and go. A theory isn't right and wrong. A theory has a sort of sociological position that changes as new information comes in. 'Is Einstein's theory correct?' You can take a poll and have a look. Einstein is rather 'in' right now. But who knows if it is 'true'? I think there is a view that physics has a sort of pristineness, rightness, trueness that I don't see in physics at all. To me, physics is the activity you do between breakfast and supper. Nobody said anything about Truth. Perhaps Truth is 'out'. One thinks, 'Well, this idea looks bad or looks good for general relativity.'
>
> (Geertz 1983: 162–3)

When engaged in the serious, scientific work, the scientist may deem irrelevant and may set aside from consideration certain routine matters of daily life: worrying if the pay cheque has come through is not an integral element in physics. While at serious work, the standards of the science decide what is real and what is not, whether the physicist has found some hitherto unknown particle of matter or whether the marks on the plotter are merely results of ink leakages in the machine. But notice, even here, Geertz's physicist describes how disagreement on these matters is resolved by reference to recognisably ordinary ways of deciding who is right or wrong: such things as taking a poll. At the end of the working day the physicist returns fully to the world of daily life and abides by its standard of reality: e.g. not arguing about needing to have a salary or to pay taxes because the notions of 'salary' and 'taxes' are not recognised as real in physics, and do not even appear in the vocabulary of physics which is used to define reality when at work.

Garfinkel: rethinking social order

Though Talcott Parsons (see Chapter 5) and Schutz had corresponded (Grathoff 1978), but mainly to their mutual frustration, it remained to Harold Garfinkel to work out the extent to which Schutz opened up a very different set of problems from those posed by Parsons, albeit the road he took was perhaps not one that Schutz himself did comprehend. In fact working through the project initiated by Schutz carried Garfinkel far away from the kind of concept advocated by Parsons or any other sociologist and made the doing of sociology itself the main focus of attention. Initially Garfinkel applied to sociology itself the point about the relationship between science and common sense as finite provinces of meaning. Garfinkel wanted to draw out the implications of the sociologist engaging in this back-and-forth movement between the world of science and the world of daily life. Interestingly, the world of daily life for sociology, unlike other disciplines, is also the topic of inquiry for the sociologist and the subject for her or his use of the scientific attitude. Sociology is a research pursuit into the world of daily life, yet its systematic investigations are not only into daily life, but carried out within the world of daily life itself. A dangerously oversimplistic statement of Garfinkel's position is that this back-and-forth movement between the world of science and the world of daily life, i.e. between the scientific and common-sense orientations, leaves sociological thought, particularly its reasoning, in a profoundly ambiguous condition. Clearing up this ambiguity involves giving much more direct and explicit attention to the common-sense elements in sociological reasoning.

A main difference between Schutz and Parsons, who was taken as an exemplar of sociological thought and practice more generally, is in what they regard as analytically problematic. Remembering that talk about common sense and communication as problematic entails the *sociologist* wondering about such matters rather than simply taking them for granted; it does not at all suggest that people in society do or should find them difficult or impossible to do. For Garfinkel, Parsons just takes it for granted that sociological research can be undertaken within society and that society is available as a world known in common between the members of society, a world which the sociological investigator can readily share with them. The fact that the investigator can assume that the world of daily life is (largely) known in common with those being researched is an essential assumption for communication between the investigator and those being researched, for it is only on the basis of their shared understandings, their mutually knowing what they are talking about, that people can communicate. Communication with those under investigation is not a trivial matter; but it is an essential requirement for sociological research, the great bulk of which involves talking to, listening to or reading things by the members of society. Sociological research itself takes place within the world of daily life and its conduct involves the researcher in finding his or her way around relationships based on everyday understandings. Whereas Parsons took for granted this set of conditions for doing sociological work without the need for further reflection upon them, Schutz engendered the idea of making these conditions of sociological work themselves part of the field of study. After all, the sociological investigator making sense of the everyday environment and undertaking mutually intelligible communication with (other) members of society is only a special case of the fact that social life in general is conducted under the natural attitude.

Garfinkel used Schutz to transform the nature of the problem of social order, which was at the heart of sociology for Parsons and others.

The problem of social order

As he posed it, Parsons intended the problem of order to be set at the deepest, most fundamental level of inquiry. For Garfinkel, however, Parsons solution to the problem of order – shared values – itself presupposed the prior existence of a social order and so did not go deep enough. Values can only be shared if they can be spread from person to person, if people can make sense to one another, if they share enough understanding to be able to communicate with one another. The attempt to understand the conditions under which people can make sense of one another's activities thus becomes the content of Garfinkel's rethink, in terms of Schutz's notions, of Parsons's problem of order.

Garfinkel was convinced that this repositioning of the problem separated the fledgeling venture of ethnomethodology from all other kinds of sociology. These other kinds overwhelmingly took the existence of a world with a common sense for granted. It was a given in their theories and a simple, unexamined presupposition of their research work. His approach, however, would be different in both respects and would not be directed at the same kinds of problems that other sociological theories sought to pose and solve. Whatever ethnomethodology was trying to do, it was not directly continuing the line of argument that stretched from Hobbes to Parsons.

What is ethnomethodology?

We begin by reverting to the topic of reality. People acting under the auspices of the natural attitude and within the finite provinces of meaning treat many features of their environment as 'real' in the required ways, distinguishing them from other candidate features which are 'not real'. One of the key questions Garfinkel poses for ethnomethodology is that of the basis on which people decide whether something is real or not. For him, it is a topic of study. He is not asking whether people are right to proceed in the ways they do, or whether one way of deciding these things is better than another. He does not evaluate at all the ways people decide what is really going on before their very eyes. His exclusive intent is to describe and analyse the ways people decide 'what is really going on' and 'what has really happened', whatever these may be.

Ethnomethodology and symbolic interactionism

On the face of it, ethnomethodology seems to be similar to symbolic interactionism. After all, symbolic interactionism shows much concern with the definition of the situation, and the idea of examining how people define the situation might seem almost identical to the conception we are now putting forward. Symbolic interactionism treats the definition of the situation as an interactional matter, emphasising the way defini-tions – shared meanings – are worked out between people interacting together in a certain setting. Garfinkel's ethnomethodology certainly accepts the focus on interactional matters, but its own programme is to treat them as methodical. The very label 'ethno-method-ology' can be simply translated as 'the study of the methods in use amongst members of the society', or more fully as 'the study of the methods for sense making and fact finding in use amongst the members of the society'.

Members' methods

Ethnomethodology's attention, then, is focused upon identifying the methods that members of society employ in deciding whether something is real or not, and upon understanding how the methods are employed in doing so.

Members' methods

In daily life, deciding what is real and what is not amounts to making one or more of an extensive range of distinctions: between the real and

---

the imagined, between fact and fiction, between truth and lies, between correct and incorrect results or conclusions, between true and false accusations, between the possible and the impossible, between what really happened and what was merely a dream.

Ethnomethodology, at its core, involves nothing other than the study of these things. It can obtain access to them by looking at those aspects of an activity which involve the making of such distinctions, i.e. the ways people, in going about their affairs in their daily lives, in their work, leisure, family or other activities, settle whatever questions arise as to what is 'actually the case', 'really so', 'surely a fact', 'unquestionably correct' and so on. The conduct of affairs in daily life is pervaded by the constant need to respond to such questions, to settle them, very much and quite routinely as a basis for *organising action* – for deciding what to do next. Therefore it provides us with a way into studying how action is organised in daily life. Clearly, then, the approach does not mean isolating one particular and limited aspect of people's sense-making and fact-finding methods, since these members' methods extensively pervade everyday activities.

These methods are quite ordinary, familiar and unsurprising ways that people enquire into and determine the reality of various things. For example, a very common method is the simple and familiar checking of one source of information against another. If, say, someone tells you about some event which sounds implausible, you might look in the newspaper or watch the TV news to see if this supposed event was reported there. If so, that would confirm what you were told. The reverse might work: seeing something reported on TV or in the paper, you might check with someone you knew who would have been involved in the reported matter in order to find out whether what you read in the newspaper was true, exaggeration or mostly made up. Obviously, there is a multitude of such methods, some of which involve considerably more elaborate activity than those we have just outlined, e.g. current work in physics checks out whether postulations about sub-atomic particles are correct and involves the use of machines (accelerators) which are many miles long and staffed by dozens if not hundreds of researchers. More mundanely, deciding the correctness of accusations of legal offences involves a dozen jurors listening to the adversarial presentation of evidence and argument in the courtroom prior to sequestration in a private room where, through perhaps protracted joint discussion, they have to arrive at a conclusion about the accusation.

For ethnomethodology, the definition of the situation and the determination of social reality are just abstract terms which refer to the quite ordinary and, to the members of society, entirely familiar ways of deciding whether something is true or false, correct or inaccurate, objective or prejudiced, factual or just made up. Such questions arise in many different areas of social life and are resolved by methods which have many features specific to the kind of activities about which the decisions are to be made, e.g. the jury operation in courtrooms, the experiment in scientific laboratories, and checking and double checking the figures can be found in all kinds of financial transactions. Ethnomethodology's central proposal is for the close, detailed examination of the ways the members of society go about defining social reality in their everyday affairs. It aims to identify these ways very specifically. A main rationale for this approach is that much of the stuff of social life is missing from sociological analysis; sociological descriptions of this or that activity characteristically display what Garfinkel has termed a 'missing whatness'. In other words, what makes the affairs carried out within the world of daily life the affairs they are is simply taken for granted. The fact that the people under study are engaged in specific work, e.g. medical treatment, repairing some technological equipment, teaching elementary mathematics, or arguing guilt or innocence, is often taken as the pretext rather than the focus for sociological analysis. For this reason, symbolic interactionism is more interested in similarities between different kinds of work and aims to emphasise the extent to which common social processes are to be found in all or many kinds of seemingly different work, while ethnomethodology is more interested in identifying details of the specific kind of work.

For example, the sociology of science traditionally concerned itself with the structure of the scientific community, the shape of scientists' careers, the prestige hierarchies used to rank disciplines and scientists, and the reward and award systems which motivate and acknowledge scientific achievement. There was very little about scientific *work* in this literature. The fact that working scientists spend immense amounts of their time carrying out observations and experiments in laboratories, observatories and similar places of work, was barely noticed until ethnomethodological studies helped to stimulate a now thriving field of sociological studies of laboratory science.

Further, while there may be respects in which the work involved in, say, diagnosing disease or identifying a scientific finding may have similarities in terms of the way the actions involved are organised, the fact remains that gynaecology is sufficiently different from astronomy for workers in each not to be interchangeable. From the point of view of understanding how actions are organised, it is entirely reasonable to suppose that such organisation may be *endogenous*, i.e. specific to the activity under consideration. Consequently we have to understand how the actions are organised to do that work and not some other kind, in turn requiring us to identify the methods participants use to carry out the work; e.g. how doctors make a provisional diagnosis, confirm it as correct and prescribe further action; or how in an observatory the astronomers suspect, then confirm, that they are on the verge of a major astronomical discovery, i.e. how their work in the observatory establishes the reality of a galactically remote celestial object.

The situatedness of action

Another key reason for this focus of attention is the concern for the analysis of action as practical action. It is an ineluctable feature of people's actual actions that these are *situated*, i.e. they must be carried out amongst and through particular circumstances; those performing them cannot adopt a take-it-or-leave-it attitude to these circumstances. For example, potential bank robbers wishing to make use of an escape vehicle face a parking problem. The streets in city centres are crowded and densely parked and it is difficult to find a legal parking space. Given one is about to rob a bank, one might not want to draw the attention of the law to a vehicle which is double parked, or in a prohibited area (see Letkeman 1973). Bank robbers cannot, then, shrug off or set aside as 'trivial' or 'uninteresting' or 'inessential to bank robbery' the need to park their car, and to park it in a way which will not attract undue attention. To be successful, they need to deal with this problem which, of course, may vary between one city centre and another.

Situatedness

Any real course of action involves responding to the specificities of its circumstances; it must be shaped to the particular conditions which are its environment and use them as 'the materials' for its accomplishment. In so doing, it must contend with *exigencies* or *contingencies*, i.e. unruly conditions which arise unexpectedly and even unforeseeably amongst a given set of circumstances, in order to achieve success.

Thus understanding the organisation of action involves understanding the ways its course is structured by those carrying the action out and under the practical circumstances, the situated conditions, within which the action is to be done.

Recognising the practical situatedness of action brings out the *improvisational* element in even the most routinised, standardised and rigidly prescribed of action sequences. Practical contingencies can afflict even the best-planned arrangement of affairs and, of course, the overwhelmingly large proportion of things people do is far from being rigidly prescribed or highly standardised. On this view, understanding the organisation of action is a matter of understanding how its perpetrators work out the course of the action sequence even as they engage in it, how they work out what to do next over the course of any sequence of activities. Such understanding necessarily involves the sociologist in paying just as close analytical attention as the participants pay practical attention to the specific circumstances of any chosen course of action, for, as noted, those perpetrating the actions have to handle or manage innumerable and assorted features of their acting circumstances in order to produce and succeed in their elected course of action. The attention to particulars may need, then, to be intense and close indeed.

Attending to the immediate situation is also crucial for resolving issues of meaning and sense. One of Garfinkel's most notorious usages is the concept of *indexicality*. This term had been coined by philosophers of language – *not* by Garfinkel – to note the fact that ordinary language contains many terms whose meaning is tied to the particular occasions of their use. An obvious example is the use of pronouns, e.g. 'it', 'that' or 'theirs'. Garfinkel noted that the point can be generalised beyond specific classes of words. Any remark can be taken in different ways according to how it is heard contextually. The question thus becomes precisely how someone hears a remark as having an unambiguous, obvious meaning; precisely how is it understood in relation to the relevant circumstances of the context in which it is produced?

What is conversation analysis?

A well-known exemplification of these concerns is *conversation analysis*. Originating as an offshoot of ethnomethodology's inquiries, it is now a quite independent venture and occupies a significant position amongst disciplines concerned with the study of language, albeit – like ethnomethodology itself – currently marginal within sociology.

The motivations for developing conversation analysis were those ethnomethodology proposed for the study of action: to examine action for its practical, endogenous organisation. Conversation is an interactional activity in which participants fit their conduct – in this case their talk – to one another as the activity proceeds. Harvey Sacks, the founder of conversation analysis, saw that conversation must be practically organised, i.e. organised in and over its course by those conducting it.

How conversation analysis works

The use of audio tape recordings of people's conversational activities makes it possible to study in close detail the step-by-step organisation of courses of action, since the audio tapes can be played over and over again and the most careful transcriptions of their content made. These transcriptions capture a vast amount of detail about the precise form of the utterances constituting the conversation and the way they fit together, yielding the kind of detail which would simply evade, say, the taker of field notes.

The study of conversation allows, too, for the examination of sense-making operations, for, of course, carrying on a conversation involves making reciprocal sense of each other's contributions, of understanding what each is saying. The possession of a retrievable record of the talk allows inspection of utterances to see how, from the form the utterance takes, it can be understood as it was understood by the parties to the talk. Such sense-making is, of course, an *embedded* affair, done (so to speak) under conversational conditions and in conversational time, i.e. the parties to the exchange have to understand each other and decide what to say on their own behalf while keeping the conversation going, so that virtually an immediate response is required the great bulk of the time. Further, the organisation of conversation has a thoroughly improvised character; it is worked out over its course. Although conversations do have an ordered course, moving from openings through a middle phase to closings, and often involving an orderly progression from topic to topic, it is not decided before the conversation commences what is going to be talked about or how the matters talked about will be spoken of. Although the parties co-ordinate their moves from phase to phase and from topic to topic of the conversation, they do not do so according to any explicitly worked-out procedures decided in advance. At each point in the conversation, they work out what to do next and how to do whatever must be done next in ways which contribute to and achieve an order for the organisation of the talk – not merely its order at this point now reached, but its overall order.

Last, but not least, the formation of a contribution to a conversation is very specifically circumstanced, and the production of a conversation's orderly progression involves managing, during the conversation, the contingencies, the exigencies, which afflict it. The specificities of what has been said and done up to this point in a given conversation are essential to deciding what a current contributor should say and how he or she should say it in order to ensure that it is appropriately understood in the light of all that has been said before. For example, he or she may have to respond to the exigency of being joined by a newcomer when the discussion is in mid-topic. From the point of view of how conversationalists understand the current talk, the analysis proceeds on the assumption that they operate with two central questions:

1   Why that now?
2   What next?

Conversational turn-taking

From studying conversation in terms of the practical asking and answering of these two questions, conversation analysis came to give pride of place to the *turn-taking* organisation of conversational talk, eventually developing an elaborately systematic account of the way turns at talk are shared out amongst participants in talk.

> ## Turn-taking
>
> Whatever conversationalists talk about, they do so by each taking turns at talking: one says something, another replies to that, a third comments on the second response, the first speaks again, and so on and on. Whatever the parties to a conversation are talking about, the way they talk must be done within the framework of such an 'ongoing' distribution of turns.

Consequently, one task for the investigation of talk must be into the allocation of turns with respect to two principal problems in such a distribution:

1   that the person now speaking can complete a turn at speaking; and
2   in such a way that as soon as the first has completed a turn the next can immediately commence a turn.

Thus extensive attention is paid to the ways the form of an *utterance* (the talk occupying a turn-at-talk) conveys information about when it will be complete. As a simple example, the question (and utterance)

A: Can I ask you a question?

provides an opportunity for A to speak again. The question format calls upon another speaker, B, to answer and, perhaps, to give permission to ask the question:

B: Sure.

A:can then ask:

A: Are you married?

'Can I ask you a question?' is characteristically understood as a request preliminary to the asking of a somewhat unusual, delicate or personal question; it would be surprising if the question projected by 'Can I ask you a question?' was 'Do you know today's date?'

In such a simple sequence the production of information about when an utterance will be complete is interwoven with the *turn-distributing operation*, i.e. the initial question occasions that another person should speak next, e.g. A asks the question, but it also provides him or her with a chance to speak again. After B's response to the initial question, there is the opportunity to ask the question prefigured by it. The recognition of completed turns-at-talk and of opportunity for turns-at-talk involves also the examination of *speaker selection* arrangements, i.e. the ways either the current speaker selects a next speaker, or a next speaker self-selects. 'Can I ask you a question?' selects a specific person as next speaker, while 'Does anybody know where Tom is?' indicates what a next speaker should do – say where Tom is, if she or he knows – but does not indicate which of the persons addressed should answer.

In this way, the forms for circulating turns amongst conversationalists can be treated as highly general; they operate regardless of the specific character of the utterances comprising them and of the activities they might be carrying out. Notwithstanding this, through a succession of alternating turns-at-talk conversationalists do produce an orderly organisation of talk about whatever they might be talking about. They differentiate the conversation into *episodes*, which they open and close quite naturally. Conversation analysis focuses also upon this episodic organisation of conversations and the ways such episodes are built and bounded. For example, the opening episodes of conversation often involve exchanges of greetings. Again, progressive moves can be made from beginning the conversation to arriving at its first *topic*, involving the way participants to a conversation organise their talk so as to be talking about the same thing, i.e. addressing a common topic. There are also ways for moving towards closing the conversation. For example, careful and extended attention may be paid to an exchange, early in a phone call:

A: Are you doin' anythin'?
B: I'm just watchin' *The X Files.*

Where the availability of the parties for conversation is dealt with by A's question, indicating that A has called up for a prolonged conversation and is giving B the opportunity to say she is not available for conversation just now. The answer provides that B is indeed doing something – watching a TV show – but that this is nothing much to be doing, and not something that takes priority over conversing with A. Perhaps A has not called up to talk about anything specific, but just to talk; then A and B face the issue of finding something, a topic, to talk about. Here the fact that B has *The X Files* on the TV provides a possible something to be talked about.

Of course, it is simply not possible, within the few pages we can devote to it, to convey anything of the detail and intricacy with which conversation analysis has examined the finely detailed course of conversation's structure. All of its questions are asked and answered in terms of the portrayal of the ways the conversationalists themselves confront and manage conversation as a practical matter. For example, just how do you say things so as to ask for something without seeming to have rung someone up only to ask them a favour? As stressed earlier, conversation has an organisation which is in use amongst conversationalists themselves to produce the very conversations that are so ordered. The orderliness correspondingly exhibited is recognisable and intelligible to the conversationalists. Arrangements for turn-taking do not result in a succession of turns-at-talk which are meticulously alternated, with one beginning immediately upon another's precise completion. There are frequent gaps and overlaps between turns-at-talk. Very commonly, there are either brief pauses between utterances or brief periods when people talk simultaneously. The conditions under which it will be a gap or an overlap are themselves topics for conversation analysis, but for the conversationalists the occurrence of such pauses and over-laps is a feature of conversation that is natural, unremarkable and orderly.

In conclusion, the analysis of conversation is that of a *self-organising* system. This brings us to a point at which it is useful to return to the question 'what is ethnomethodology?' and consider it as the study of the self-organisation of activities.

Studying activities as self-organising: neglecting the big picture?

The examination of the intricacies of stretches of quite ordinary – even very dull – conversation does not draw the attention or approval of many sociologists.

Criticism of conversation analysis

The determination of conversation analysis to engage with the minutiae of conversation seems to many to be a matter of taking to a logical extreme the more general position of ethnomethodology, i.e. focusing on the concrete and specific details of localised instances of interaction with-out attention to the big picture of social life within which they are located.

To many sociologists, it is self-evident that though two people might be having a conversation about what they did on their day off, they will be having it in the context of (say) their daily work for the corporate giant IBM, which is a major international company, part of American society in the latter part of the twentieth century, and involved in the progressive globalisation of capital. How can one understand what people are doing in particular cases without reference to all this complex environment?

We did say that ethnomethodology does not agree to play the game of sociological theory. One of the rules of procedure for ethnomethodology precisely prevents it from adopting such a course of argument; for to adopt it would be to abandon the concept of social scenes as self-organising. From ethnomethodology's point of view, sociological theory has a deeply ambiguous character: the sociological researcher is conceived to be someone who can not only inhabit the world of daily life like anyone else, but also step out of this world and observe it from outside, from above. In order to eliminate such ambi-guity, ethnomethodology treats sociology as done entirely *within the world of daily life*; sociology acquires its materials and its reported observations from within this same world.

Further, it is commonplace for sociological theory to assume that the solution to the problem of social order is to be found outside the immediate social scene or situation. For example, the orderly behaviour of persons is assumed to be due to some prior event, such as socialisation into role expectations, or to some structural condition, such as a hierarchical system of mechanisms controlling the present situation. These ways of conceiving social order, however, tend to result in taking for granted the presently observable orderliness of a social scene, e.g. people waiting to board their holiday flight, seeing people off, waiting for people to arrive at an airport. There is no concern with the way the people involved act in order to make their activities visible to an observer, *any* observer (including one another), as elements in such an orderly arrangement. Given the points we have made above about the exigencies and contingencies of activity, how exactly do those present within a social scene know just what to do in order to fit into its routine, standard organisation?

Mutual intelligibility

It is not an incidental feature of the organisation of actions that they are produced in ways which exhibit their sense or *intelligibility* to others. It is not an accidental fact about our actions that they are recognisable for what they are to others; much of our activity is directed towards or conducted for witnessing by others. Intimately interwoven into our actions is a concern that we perform so that others should be able to identify our actions, to see what we are doing, to understand what we are saying. Since actions are very widely oriented to others and produced in co-ordination and collaboration with them, this concern for the identifiable, intelligible, recognisable character of conduct is a feature not just of utterances, but of conduct more generally.

The attempt to express this concern has given ethnomethodology one of its 'terms of art', namely, the *accountable organisation of actions*, i.e. the way one aspect of the organisation of courses of actions is a concern to make them observable, intelligible, recognisable, identifiable, and amenable to being talked about and otherwise reportable. To say action-arrangements are accountable is not to say that they are so in the sense in which the term is often used, i.e. subject to and responsive to overseeing, as when governments propose to make 'what teachers do in classrooms' accountable to the electorate. Rather, the notion of 'accountable' used here means only 'so organised as to make it possible for those involved in the activities to describe and otherwise report the organisation of these activities'. Describing and otherwise reporting encompasses all imaginable forms: charts, diagrams, tables, brochures, sets of job specifications, remarks in casual conversations, and so interminably on. Accountability *makes visible* the organisation that activities have. Necessarily it involves recognising the circumstantial constraints which impinge upon someone's possible courses of action. How is it, for example, that in producing an activity the person displays awareness that there is a task to be done here and now which cannot be put off until later, that he or she is answerable to others for this task, that doing it adequately means coping with various constraints which are beyond his or her own control, and so forth? Someone's reasoning about these matters is displayed in his or her actions, and it frequently provides for their – the actions' – intelligibility.

This concern with the mutual intelligibility of activities means that attention is paid to what can be called the *visibility arrangements* of social settings, the ways people arrange the environments of their activities, and the activities themselves, to make readily available to others a sense of what is going on, thereby enabling others to understand how the setting works. For example, courtroom hearings of traffic offences in the US are so organised that those waiting for their case to come up can observe and overhear previous cases and, from the way those are dealt with, learn how to behave when their turn to enter a plea comes around. In these ways, ordinary members of the public show themselves to be 'practical sociologists', i.e. they can and do engage in practical sociological reasoning.

Doing sociology from within

Ethnomethodology's own proposal, then, is to make practical sociological reasoning its main, even exclusive, topic of study.

Practical sociological reasoning

This is found to inform and organise activity of all kinds and in all areas of life. Regardless of the position of activities within the status and moral ranking of societies, any and all activities in society can be examined as applications of practical sociological reasoning. Of course, the fact that they are looked up to or looked down on itself enters into the practical sociological reasoning involved in them.

Not unexpectedly, practical sociological reasoning also pervades professional sociological work, so that the work of those who make their living under the occupational title 'sociologist' can also be examined in the same way as, say, divining water, shoplifting and the work of ethnomethodologists themselves. The pursuit of this interest defines ethnomethodology's programme and has led to studies of such occupations as those of astronomers, musicians, dentists, the police, salesmen, truckdrivers and air-traffic controllers at work; and of such activities as mathematical calculation, plumbing repairs, coping with the effects of blindness, using a metronome to keep time in piano playing, training in kung fu, telling a story to a class of 6-year-olds, and eliciting a confession from a murder suspect. In addition, studies have been made of professional sociological activities such as interviewing an educational psychologist about his work, and doing an ethnography of a half-way house for drug offenders.

Relativism again, and reflexivity

We now return to the issue of relativism posed at the outset of this chapter. The charge of relativism might seem to be justified by the remarks which we have just been making. After all, water-divining and advanced physics have been mentioned in the same breath and it has been proposed that magical and scientific activities should be studied in the same way. In so doing, we have also transgressed the status rankings by employing putatively crazy or deluded ideas, e.g. equating divination with paradigms of respectability like medical work. In addition, there is the 'disprivileging' of the professional sociologist *vis-à-vis* the other members of society: in comparison with other members of the society, the only distinctive feature of the kind of sociological reasoning done by the professional sociologist is that it is done for a living, whereas everyone else does sociological reasoning as an unreflective part of whatever affairs they carry out in society. According to those who hold a relativist (mis)conception of ethnomethodology, the lessons ostensibly to be drawn are that:

- scientific sociology is no better than common-sense sociology;
- physics is no better than water divining and
- therefore, any way of thinking is as good as any other.

Worries about relativism connect with a further problem: *reflexivity*.

Reflexivity

This point derives from one further element of the above remarks. According to ethnomethodology's logic, the work of professional sociologists (including ethnomethodologists themselves) is amenable to study in ethnomethodological terms. This point is understood in terms of a notion of reflexivity, which means 'applying to itself'.

It is fashionable these days to note that the doing of sociology is itself a social activity and therefore sociology's concepts and theories should be applicable to itself. For example, it is a criticism of, say, functionalist arguments that they do not apply to themselves, that functionalist analysis is not readily provided of functionalist arguments. Ethnomethodology is seen as pioneering this kind of view, i.e. maintaining that its arguments should apply to itself. As understood, however, this notion carries heavier freight, for it is also argued that self-application of arguments all too often results in self-subversion.

Self-subversion

If functionalist arguments were to be applied to functionalist arguments themselves they would be discredited. For example, Durkheim's model functionalist account of religion reveals that religion is not really about religion and is not really about God and worship; it is about something else, namely, sustaining social order. Presumably, the application of functionalist arguments to functionalism would show that functionalism is not really about science and knowledge, but really about something else, namely, sustaining social solidarity among sociologists. Hence, in their very application, the arguments would effectively deny their own validity.

In the view of those currently excited by reflexivity, the fact is that sociological approaches generally simply cannot afford to apply this principle, since it would undermine their very character. The only valid possibility would be to recognise openly that sociological knowledge is impossible because, on the principle of reflexivity, all sociological positions are self-subverting, and a properly reflexive attitude would embrace this unavoidable fact. Reflexivity would bring out the self-subverting tendencies in all other sociological views, while ensuring that it kept to the fore the fact that ethnomethodology itself is no exception to the principle of reflexivity and must therefore undermine itself.

Ethnomethodology is, alas, a disappointment to those who see the potential merits of reflexivity for challenging professional sociology, for it does not seem too keen to develop its full force. As already suggested, however, there are reasons to hesitate in attributing any such notions to ethnomethodology. Garfinkel did give the word 'reflexivity' a prominent place in his initial exposition, 'What is ethnomethodology?', (in his *Studies* [1967]) but he quickly came to rue the fact even though he did not himself use the term in the manner others currently use it.

Garfinkel and reflexivity

Garfinkel used 'reflexivity' to draw attention to the way practical socio-logical reasoning is embedded in the very activities it concerns, e.g. the way practical sociological reasoning of jurors is done in the jury room, as part of the jury's work and in and through the jury's organisation. Practical sociological reasoning is not done in abstraction from activities, but from their very midst and as an integral part of them. Hence the examination of such reasoning cuts both ways: it considers how the practical sociological reasoning goes into organising, into carrying out, an activity; reciprocally, it considers the way in which the reasoning is itself shaped by the organisation of the activities it is involved in.

Consequently, the *substance* of such practical sociological reasoning will vary from activity to activity. A group of software engineers meeting to review progress on a software engineering project reason about the software, whilst what is reasoned about among jurors is the guilt or innocence of a defendant. What is reasoned about in sociology and also in ethnomethodology is 'social order', but, as we have seen, the terms in which the problem in common is conceived are very different. There is no discomfort or self-subversion for ethnomethodology in accepting the fact that it too employs practical sociological reasoning to get its work done, thereby providing just another exemplification of the kinds of phenomena it likes to inspect. Of course, ethnomethodology's practical sociological reasoning is itself reflexive to ethnomethodology's own work activities, something embedded, organised in and organising of these activities.

Congruently, the mention of physics and water-divining in the same breath carries no relativistic implications, for the point being made is not epistemological, i.e. about the merits of these activities as bearers of truth; it is simply methodological, i.e. about the way the organisation of these respective activities may be viewed. Each has its ways of practical sociological reasoning and each, along with any other social activity including sociology (and ethnomethodology) itself, is a candidate for examination in terms of its use of such reasoning to organise its daily affairs. At the same time, it must be noted that while physics and water divining both involve practical sociological reasoning, the substance over which such reasoning is done, the problems that such reasoning confronts, and the ways such reasoning is organised are distinctive in many important respects from the activities of which the reasoning is a constituent part. There is no inclination here either to obliterate the difference between physics and water divining or to deliver any judgement on their worth. Such judgements figure for ethnomethodology only in so far as they enter into the practical sociological reasoning of the respective activities; perhaps water diviners feel hard done by because their work is regarded as dubious and misguided relative to that of physicists, who are held in such high esteem, even though water diviners cannot see why they themselves are denied such status. Ethnomethodology simply does not say that water divining is as good as physics, or that physics is only as good as water divining. Since ethnomethodology's concern is with the organisation of activities, such judgements are irrelevant; the only comment it can make is, simply, 'No comment!'

Small and big pictures (again)

For those who would radicalise sociology towards relativism and self-deconstruction (see Chapter 10), ethnomethodology proves a disappointment. If appropriately deemed a pioneer of relativism and reflexivity, then it has failed to develop further its pioneering moves. Worse, it seems that they might be misattributions, i.e. ethnomethodology has been neither relativist nor reflexive (in the required sense). However, if it is a disappointment on that side, then it has also been a disappointment to those who would continue the 'classical tradition' of sociological theory. Their disappointment is often expressed as a criticism.

Critics' views of ethnomethodology

Ethnomethodology involves only the study of face-to-face relationships, and has nothing to say about the complex social systems which have been the main topic of the classical tradition of Marx, Durkheim and Weber. It is not just that ethnomethodology is silent on these matters, but rather that its silence involves (allegedly) a denial of the existence of such structures. Ethnomethodology sets out to be a comprehensive sociology, not just a specialist branch, but assumes (wrongly, say the critics) that the only social reality is face-to-face interaction amongst individuals. This view denies the existence of real phenomena which provide the causal conditions for the very face-to-face interactions studied by the ethnomethodologist.

For example, ethnomethodology cannot explain why the software engineering business has grown up in the Western world and why computerisation has been so rapidly and widely accepted in business and many other fields. Hence it cannot explain why or how in the first place the software engineers mentioned above are gathering in an engineers' meeting to talk about it. Rather than being a full-scale, fully comprehensive sociology, the best ethnomethodology can hope to be (the argument goes) is a specialism within sociology, which focuses upon small-scale social phenomena and face-to-face situations. For many such critics the logic is this: there is a need for a *synthesis* of sociological thought, which will find a place for ethnomethodology that actually complements the theoretical approaches of its ostensible rivals. (See the discussion of synthesising thinkers in Chapter 13.)

However, it is something of a misnomer to talk about the situations ethnomethodologists study as face-to-face situations, with the attendant suggestion that they are hermetically sealed against the larger social environment. For it is plain that the nature of that larger social environment frequently, and in a multiplicity of ways, enters into the practical sociological reasoning of those engaged in a situated activity.

Ethnomethodologists' views

It is in and through face-to-face situations that this social environment is made visible to those involved (and to sociological researchers sitting in). Indeed the expression 'visibility arrangements' has been coined to identify those aspects of face-to-face situations which serve to display to the participants the relevance and organisation of the larger social complexes within which they are situated, acting and themselves organising.

Finally, what appears to critics as the wilful neglect of the wider social structure is to ethnomethodologists themselves the product of a principled theoretical decision: to treat as the context of social activities the one that is oriented to as such by those they study. Ethnomethodologists have repeatedly explained the connection between the point made above about how they treat social order as something done within the local scene and their self-imposed denial, i.e. their self-discipline as they see it, in declining to solve the problem of social order by appealing to facts external to the local scene, e.g. personality, norms and social structures. Nevertheless, the charge of neglecting the wider context refuses to go away. For ethnomethodologists, however, the charge carries no weight, since it amounts to nothing more than a refusal to recognise the difference at the *theoretical* level between ethnomethodology's assumptions and those of other approaches. It amounts to criticising ethnomethodology for not being a more traditional sociology. For ethnomethodology there simply is no big picture to be had, since there is no standpoint outside the common-sense world of daily life upon which the would-be painter of this picture can rest the canvas. The sociologist's big picture purports to be constructed from outside, but our discussion of Schutz should have made clear that ethnomethodology has no truck with this assumption.

Conclusion

Ethnomethodology is both credited and blamed with making one of the most critical contributions to the destabilising of the sociological orthodoxies that had established themselves in Anglo-American sociology, being understood as presenting a direct challenge to the possibility of any kind of 'objective' understanding of social reality, and, consequently, to the realisation of any sociological dreams of grand theory. Ethnomethodology, like symbolic interaction, has been marginalised within sociology, and it continues to flourish most extensively in terms of conversation analysis, which is a busy area of work, but one as often as not having ties with linguistics rather than sociology. Whilst marginalised, ethnomethodology none the less remains controversial, something that very commonly has at least to be noticed, to be either commended as a precursor of poststructuralist and postmodern attitudes within sociology or condemned for playing such a disruptive role within sociological theory. In this latter respect it has intensified many of those oppositions which the 'synthesists' of sociological theory (see Chapter 13) must now attempt to reconcile, with some of ethnomethodology's insights having to be incorporated into the theoretical mix.

Questions

1 What are the main differences between ethnomethodology and symbolic interactionism?

2 Outline Schutz's concept of the natural attitude. How does it shape his view of the relationship between science and commonsense?

3 How does Garfinkel relate the natural attitude and members' methods?

4 What is the problem of social order? How does Garfinkel redefine it?

5 Does conversation analysis exemplify ethnomethodology as a way of studying the everyday world, or does it rather provide a way of studying conversational structures?

6 What is meant by 'the mutual intelligibility of activities' and 'practical sociological reasoning'? How does ethnomethodology seek to relate them?

7 What do you understand by 'reflexivity' as used by (a) Garfinkel and (b) his critics?

8 'Ethnomethodology is forever condemned to trivia.' Explain and discuss.

Further reading

Boden, D. and **Zimmerman, D.H.** (eds), 1991, *Talk and Social Structure: Studies in Ethnomethodology and Conversation Analysis*. Polity Press. A collection of conversation-analytic studies around the relationship of talk to its social context.

Button, G. (ed.), 1991, *Ethnomethodology and the Human Sciences*. Cambridge University Press. An advanced text which considers how ethnomethodology 'respecifies' fundamental issues in the human sciences.

Eglin, P. and **Hester, S.**, 1992, *A Sociology of Crime*. Routledge. A useful comparison of ethnomethodological work on crime and policing with symbolic interactionist and Marxist approaches.

Grathoff, R. (ed.), 1978, *The Theory of Social Action: The Correspondence of Alfred Schutz* *and Talcott Parsons*. Indiana University Press. For Schutz's review of Parsons's *The Structure of Social Action* and the correspondence between them on the nature of social action and sociological theory.

Heritage, J., 1984, *Garfinkel and Ethnomethodology*. Polity Press. A major study of Garfinkel.

Livingston, E., 1987, *Making Sense of Ethnomethodology*. Routledge. A useful introduction, especially the early chapters.

Schutz, A. 1970, *On Phenomenology and Social Relations: Selected Writings* (ed. H. Wagner). University of Chicago Press. A useful selection from Schutz's writings.

Sharrock, W. and **Anderson, R.**, 1986, *The Ethnomethodologists*. Tavistock. A brief and informative introduction.

Turner, R., (ed.), 1974, *Ethnomethodology* Penguin. A classic collection of studies.

■　　■　　■

Part three

.

Chapter 8

Western Marxism

Introduction

By 'Western Marxism' we mean the tradition of Marxist scholarship originating around the early 1920s, whose central contentions emphasise voluntarism and reading Marx as a humanist thinker. Western Marxism gained impetus from opposition to 'vulgar' interpretations of Marx, and the issue was, from the start, that of the relationship between the economic base and the superstructure of society. What critics found unattractive about vulgar Marxism was its reductive character, i.e. reducing social life to nothing more than economic interests, so that the way to understand any social phenomenon is to identify the class interests lying behind and animating it. Similarly, the vulgar view of Marx's base-superstructure notion was of a strict formula, stipulating that the culture and intellectual life of a society are wholly and directly shaped by the causal power and functional needs of the economic substructure. These cultural and intellectual phenomena are, at best, simply means of dressing up the most unattractive features of human lives which are exclusively concerned with economic matters. This crude, unsophisticated reading of Marx provoked a reaction among those who argued that, if read correctly, his work allows a more elaborate and flexible interpretation of the base-superstructure relationship.

Western Marxism began with the work of George Lukács (1885–1971), a Hungarian philosopher and literary critic, in the early 1920s. It involved a marked shift in interest towards the analysis of cultural phenomena such as literature, art and music, and contrasts with the heavily technical economic analysis which fills Marx's later work, *Capital* (1976). It also involved the attempt to develop a more sophisticated view of politics than was available in vulgar Marxism. By the time the first major works of Western Marxism appeared, Marxists confronted a new problem: how to explain the failure of Marx's key prediction that a proletarian revolution would occur in the advanced industrial societies. The one country in which the anticipated Marxist-led revolution had occurred was not in highly industrialised Western Europe but in predominantly peasant, hardly industrialised Russia.

This failure was treated as itself needing to be interpreted in Marxist terms rather than as disproving Marx, whose work was rethought in the light of this development. Here, a key element was the reflection that the working class had been unable to perceive the true nature of capitalist society and hence its own real interests, which, on Marx's premises, required the overthrow of capitalist society. Marx's basic model held that the development of capitalist society would make its own ruthlessly exploitative and dehumanising character ever more starkly apparent. The improvement of communications as part of its infrastructure would make the formation of a working-class revolutionary consciousness that much easier. The problem was, then, to understand how working-class consciousness had actually been shaped, what had prevented the rise of revolutionary consciousness, and how, if at all, such consciousness could be prompted among the working class.

Lukács: a Hegelian reinterpretation of Marx

Marx's publishing career suffered many vicissitudes and a great deal of his work was not published in his lifetime. The manuscripts with the most overtly Hegelian character were written while he was young and not published until after his death, some as late as the 1930s and 1940s. It was, therefore, one of Lukács's achievements to have figured out from the published writings just how much Marx's thought owed to Hegel, and he gave a new interpretation in this light. The context in which Lukács mainly applied this interpretation was literary criticism, for a large proportion of his books were about the history of the novel. However, *History and Class Consciousness* (1971), by far the most influential of Lukács's writings and the one we focus on here, was effectively a contribution to epistemology, i.e. to the theory of knowledge.

The idea of totality

For Lukács, the key idea in Marxism for the understanding of human life, the object of knowledge, the thing to be known, is the *social totality*.

Social totality

Lukács saw Marx as essentially teaching that the true identity of things is provided by their relationship to a whole. For example, the individual characteristics of a person do not make that person a slave, and nothing in the constitution of a particular machine makes it an item of capital. These items acquire those identities only as part of a system, as part of an arrangement of slave-holding or of capitalist production; i.e. they have their identity only in relation to the social whole.

In Lukács's view, Marx's most fundamental lesson is that the whole most decisively comes before the parts; the parts cannot be the things they are except in relationship to the whole. In order to spell out the connections making up the complex whole, Lukács introduced the influential notion of *mediations*, which refers to the steps of social relations linking a particular item (in a kind of nested series of larger, more complex units) eventually to the whole; e.g. the child can be linked by the family to the wider world, and the individual can be linked via the political party to the life of the state.

Since the whole is prior to the parts, vulgar Marxism or any simple idea of the causation of consciousness by economic conditions cannot be valid, for it is the system as a whole, the totality, which is the primary cause, and which produces the interrelationship of its constituent parts. The idea of one part of society determining the form of all the others is, on Lukács's interpretation, distinctly un-Marxist. The parts of society (through mediations) determine one another's nature in relation to the totality.

What has this argument to do with knowledge? Marx had shown that we do not understand a particular thing, a given fact, unless we grasp its relationship to the totality. Of course, Marx himself had achieved precisely this, not merely by showing the necessity to understand phenomena in relation to the totality, but also in actually revealing the nature of the totality itself. In order to understand anything, then, we need to understand it in relationship to (in the modern world) the capitalist system as a whole, grasped in Marx's terms. Lukács criticised the prevailing idea of knowledge in society, particularly as embodied in science. He termed it *empiricism*, which is very close to what is elsewhere in this book called positivism (see Chapter 3). The prevailing idea in empiricism lays emphasis upon the importance of facts, i.e. we come to understand reality through the acquisition and accumulation of facts. For Lukács facts were merely individual items; they record specific features of reality in ways which isolate them from their true identity, thereby preventing the proper recognition of their nature. Unless these facts are comprehended in relation to the totality, they are misunderstood. Further, the totality is not something fixed and unchangeable; it has potential for development. Therefore to understand the totality's true nature is to understand not simply how it currently is, but also how its current state contains its future possibility.

In Lukács' view, the fact that only a comparative few subscribed to Marx's ideas shows only that the rest did not truly understand things. The vast mass of the population is subject to what he called *reification*. This concept reinvokes Hegelian terminology and is a term found in Marx.

Reification

This suggests that people misrepresent the world to themselves, that they come to understand the world that they themselves have made through their own actions as though it exists and operates quite independently of them and beyond their influence, according to its own laws.

For example, Ludwig Feuerbach, whose critique of religion heavily influenced Marx, argued that religious consciousness involves the creation of ideas of God and other supernatural forces which provide a seriously distorted expression of human powers. In effect, religion displaces these human powers and projects them on to imaginary supernatural beings instead of attributing them to their true source. Having created these ideas, people then use them to understand their own situations and fates, which are then not seen for what they truly are, namely matters of their own responsibility. Instead, people imagine themselves to be ruled by the wishes, even whims, of deities and other supernatural forces. Comparably, the idea of the market provides another example of reification. In so far as people understand the market as something with its own laws and demands, something which decides people's fates, e.g. by throwing them out of work, then they misunderstand its real character as a human product. The market is, after all, no reality in itself, but only the relations of individuals to one another in the producing, selling and buying of goods.

Lukács argues that capitalist society is pervaded by such reifications; they are fundamental to the system, since the mystification of reality disguises the real social (i.e. class) relations of capitalist society. The mark of this process of mystification is that persons are unable to perceive the totality; they experience reality in a piecemeal fashion. A visual metaphor seems to be implicit in Lukács's argument: the particular location of persons within the system serves to restrict their 'view' of the whole; their position prohibits them from adopting or achieving a holistic perspective, a bird's-eye view of the whole scene. Consequently, even if they have some grasp of the objective character of particular elements, their understanding is seriously distorted by an inability to connect and link them into the whole.

The working class as the universal subject

Lukács asserts, however, that one group within capitalist society is privileged with respect to understanding the totality, namely the working class. This assertion is not as arbitrary as it might seem when placed in the context of the Hegelian legacy in terms of which Lukács comprehends Marx.

The universal subject

Hegel's theory required the *universal subject*, i.e. the one who (in a way) stands for all humanity. In so doing, a comprehensive understanding of the whole of human history, from beginning to end, can be achieved.

By this device, Hegel seeks to get around what he sees to be a misleading opposition in the theory of knowledge, namely treating knowledge as a relationship between a subject and an object. In this relationship, subject and object are treated as quite distinct and separate, so that they must be brought into *correspondence*. If knowledge is a relationship between two distinct things, knowing subject and known-about object, then knowledge is only possible if there are indeed two distinct things in this relationship. The effect, though, of this *subject–object dualism* (which, as we noted in discussing Mead in Chapter 6, was enshrined in the Western philosophical tradition by Descartes) is to cut off human beings from 'external reality'. Humans, as subjects of knowledge, stand over against the 'external world' of objects; the idea of the human subject seeking to know the objects which make up external nature is the leading idea of knowledge in this approach.

Against it, Lukács argues that subject and object are not really separate in the case of humanity (or, for Hegel, in the case of nature either); humanity is both subject and object, it is that which seeks to know and that which is to be known. The philosophical tradition following Descartes is therefore another example of reification. Yet the dualism of subject and object is not false, for it reflects in intellectual terms the *historical* separation of people from the social systems which they themselves have created and perpetuated by their actions. The separation of subject and object, therefore, is at root the social separation of human beings from their world. As a Hegelian Marxist, Lukács argues that history reaches its end point when the opposition of subject and object is overcome, when someone produces the knowledge which is the proper, full self-knowledge of humanity. In Hegel's account, this 'someone' is the philosopher (i.e. Hegel himself). Following the early Marx (see Timothy McCarthy 1978), Lukács identifies this universal subject not with particular individual philosophers but with the working class; it is their historic mission to overcome the opposition between subject and object (along with all the other false but persistent oppositions of thought).

The working class as the universal subject

Within capitalist society, the working class is that group which represents humanity as a whole. After the revolution, it will abolish the capitalist class and will then literally constitute all of humanity. Thus the position of the working class in capitalist society is special in virtue of its historical mission to emancipate humankind, thereby enabling it, or at least its intellectual representatives, to comprehend the totality truly.

It is important to note that 'working-class consciousness', as Lukács employs this notion, is not a descriptive concept: it does not describe the outlook of actual workers, but rather involves an understanding which is constructed on their behalf and in a way correctly formulates their position and interests in society even if they are not aware of them. Lukács was not the first to propose this idea; it is a cornerstone of Lenin's revolutionary theories. In arguing that Marxism correctly and objectively defines the nature of working-class consciousness – that Marxism, properly understood, *is* this consciousness – Lukács endorses Lenin's doctrine (1963) that the Communist Party is the vanguard of working-class thought and action.

Gramsci and hegemony

As well as the Hungarian Lukács, Antonio Gramsci (1891–1937), an Italian, was a main figure in the Western Marxist reorientation. In terms of subsequent impact, Gramsci was most influential in maintaining that the struggle of ideas is as important in social life as economic interests. Indeed, the struggle over economic interests is itself conducted through the battle of ideas. Lukács was concerned to combat the idea of Marxism as a science – at least in terms of the conventional view of a science as being quite distinct from values. According to this conventional view, e.g. one held by Max Weber, science is capable only of describing, incapable of prescribing; it tells us how things are, but not what we should do in the face of the circumstances. Lukács held this to be another of the false oppositions which Marxism destroys, for the understanding of the nature of the totality involves an understanding of what it has the capacity to become, of how to bring it about and, thus, of what to do, namely take the action to realise the potential of the totality. Gramsci argued rather differently: the interest of science in relation to social life is characteristically from the point of view of whether the social life *must* be understood in science's terms. But this approach is the wrong way round: science as an ensemble of ideas is created in the course of and through human history. Therefore the question concerns the role science can have in the perpetual struggles of social life, rather than in seeing it as providing the one true way of understanding reality.

In Gramsci's conception, ideas are virtually weapons whose important role is the part they play in the struggle to change society. Relative to this role, worries about their objectivity and truth are incidental. The important thing is the struggle for *hegemony*, i.e. the intellectual domination of the society. This domination is just as important as economic power to the persistence or over-throw of a regime, e.g. capitalism. Hence Marxism is of importance not simply as an economic analysis of capitalism, but also in its role of providing ideas to fight against the current hegemony of capitalism, providing the basis for overthrowing capitalism and installing a new society.

Hegemony

Gramsci's idea is that cultural and intellectual activities do not merely operate as functions of economic changes, but comprise an arena of social struggle, of domination and resistance. Therefore the struggle of ideas is a crucial part of the general pattern of struggle.

This conception has been very influential upon recent sociology (and especially on the formation of media studies, now a virtually independent area of academic work).

The Frankfurt School

The next element in the delineation of the Western Marxist legacy is the development of the Frankfurt School. This is the name given to a loosely knit collection of scholars associated with the Institute for Social Research, which originated at the University of Frankfurt in the 1920s, moved to the US in the 1930s and returned to Germany in the 1950s. The main figures associated with the school during its heyday, from the point of view of subsequent effect upon sociology, were Max Horkheimer, Theodor Adorno, Walter Benjamin and Herbert Marcuse; more recently its leading associate is Jürgen Habermas. The school identified its work as *critical theory*, a name we will explain later.

It should be stated at the outset that although it is widely perceived as part of the Western Marxist tradition and will be so treated here, some qualification is needed on this point. The attachment of the school to Marxism was variable from individual to individual, and over the career of different individuals, and the attachment was often to Hegelian (or even religious) forms of thinking as much as to specifically Marxist ones. All the figures associated with the School were united by a concern to critique capitalist society, and their shared dissatisfaction with capitalism was in terms not so much of the economic injustice and exploitative nature of its relationships as of its psychological and cultural effects. Common threads running through the writings of members of the Frankfurt School concern such issues as the cost to people's psychic lives as a result of reification, the threatening nature of an increasing kind of political gangsterism that they saw in the thirties, and – in some ways the most important thing – the decadence of modern culture. At the heart of the Frankfurt School's critique is the idea that capitalism involves the destruction of the critical thought that is capable of challenging its whole system, resulting in the perversion of human reason.

We noted above that by the 1920s and 1930s Marx's account of capitalism arguably had been outdated by changing events. Capitalism had not immiserated and pauperised its working class, but had given them levels of economic prosperity which, while not always consistently expanding, were generally far in excess of those imaginable in the mid-nineteenth century. Yet if economic developments had the effect of blunting orthodox, 'scientific' Marxist analysis of capitalism, they did so only in so far as capitalism's evils were viewed predominantly in economic terms. In common with Lukács, members of the Frankfurt School placed greater emphasis on ideas than on economics. If orthodox, scientific Marxism concerned itself with the economic foundations of society, the Frankfurt School is more concerned with its intellectual foundations.

The School's basic view

Its attitude was, to put it rather crudely, that there is more to life than bread alone; a considerable price had been paid for economic prosperity, for though economically well catered for, working-class lives were spiritually and psychologically stunted. The spread of economic well-being may have served to render the working class unavailable for the communist revolution, but it had left them living lives of a much more impoverished and inferior quality than they need be.

The task, then, was to engage in *Ideologiekritik*, i.e. to understand how the superstructure of society worked to restrict people's lives and reconcile them to their *spiritual* pauperisation. This pauperisation was manifest in many spheres of life, but nowhere more clearly than in politics. Throughout Western Europe, the rise of democratic parliamentary structures during the late nineteenth and early twentieth centuries had transformed the political landscape, rendering obsolete the orthodox Marxist view that the industrial working class could not possibly achieve power through parliamentary processes. Far from being excluded from the political process, the working classes, by virtue of the introduction of the universal franchise and the growth of mass, popular parties, seemed to have a genuine possibility of political power. Yet, across Europe, the working classes seemed unwilling or unable to avail themselves of this possibility. Not only were they uninterested in revolutionary political action, in being the basis for the advancement of humanity through participation in a revolutionary Marxist movement, but they seemed equally unwilling to sign up in support of parliamentary Marxist parties. In so far as they were available for political activity, they were just as likely to be recruited by demagogues such as Hitler. Such developments as the rise of Nazism only served to confirm the urgency of the task of understanding how and why the working class had become reconciled to and included in capitalist society, since it seemed to many as though European societies were entering a new age of darkness, in which irrational and immoral forces had been unleashed. Far from opposing such forces, the working class had been mobilised in their support.

Capitalism and Enlightenment reason

The key to the Frankfurt School's understanding of the origins of this situation was their analysis of the link between capitalism and a particular historical version (or perversion) of human reason. In essence, their view was that 'Reason' had been captured by capitalism; both reason and human lives were significantly reduced as a result. Thus their conception of modern capitalism owes almost as much to Weber as to Marx. Like Weber, they looked upon it as, in many ways, a puritanically repressive regime within which human relations and affairs were conceived in terms of – were reified into – the kind of calculated, impersonal, instrumental connections characteristic of bureaucracies. It is conceivable that human lives could be richly fulfilling and have a free and sensual relationship to the world around them in which people would recognise themselves as natural beings, as belonging to nature. However, the capacity for such a life is denied under capitalism. It is within the capacity of reason (a Hegelian element) to provide this kind of existence, to reveal to humanity its unity with nature, and to enable people to develop their full, rich, sensual existence. However, capitalism has defeated reason's ability to do so. In part, under the name of *Enlightenment*, reason has taken a wrong turn. Indeed, it is the role of the critical theorist to act as a bastion of reason, using it to criticise existing society, revealing the possibility for truly free existence, and revealing how this possibility is denied and defeated by capitalism and its culture.

Reason and the Enlightenment project

The position of the Frankfurt School can be summed up in two principal points:

- The *Enlightenment project*, whilst ostensibly aimed towards delivering human freedom, had in fact served as a vehicle for repression of human potential, even (metaphorically) enslavement.
- Reason, rather than playing a sovereign part in the evaluation and reorganisation of society for human betterment, had been co-opted into serving the purposes and defending the interests of one particular form of society, namely industrial capitalism.

The illusion of freedom

In order to make their case, the Frankfurt School were necessarily involved in showing that many of the features of modern society which seem to embody, express or enable freedom do not, in fact, really do so. The highlight of this kind of demonstration is a relatively late (1964) product of the school's work, *One Dimensional Man*. It was written by one of its affiliates, Herbert Marcuse (1898–1979), and had a strong effect on the intellectual climate of the late 1960s. In it Marcuse coined the expression 'repressive tolerance' to exploit precisely the apparently contradictory nature of the conjunction of its two terms.

Repressive tolerance

Modern industrial societies are claimed to have a much-vaunted tolerance and freedom of expression, allowing the formation and communication of all kinds of ideas and the acceptance of a widening diversity of life styles. All these apparently amount to a massive liberation, a truly extensive realisation of freedom and the very opposite of repression. On the contrary, Marcuse argued, this tolerance is one of the forms of repression, rather than being the opposite of repression; it is one of the ways in which the *system* inhibits the possibility of change in itself by effectively drawing the teeth of any challenges to it.

Thus to tolerate diversity is not to tolerate real revolutionary determination; instead, it is defused, and dissent is regularised into merely another and inconsequential activity within the system. Dissenting ideas are turned into commodities, into commercialised products of the system: they can be harmlessly (and profitably) disseminated as books, television programmes and films. Critical, even revolutionary, thought is reduced to a kind of leisure activity.

Marcuse's book was an expression of the Frankfurt School's attachment to a Hegelian interpretation of Marx's ideas, which emphasised the dialectical element in this thought, especially its negative character. Here 'negative' is not used as any derogatory characterisation. To talk about 'negative thinking' can be to emphasise something virtuous, since the point about dialectics is their initial assumption that things are to be identified not only as what they are, but also as what they are not. To say what something *is* also says what it is *not*, e.g. to say that a number is the number 'nine' is equivalent to saying it is not 'eight' or 'ten,' and so on. In this way, dialectics attempt a massive break with classical logic as the basis for thought, providing a profoundly different mode of thought. For our purposes, classical logic can be thought of as resting upon the *law of identity*: a thing is itself and nothing else or, in formulaic terms, $A = A$. In this logic, it would be a contradiction to say that $A = $ not A, but this is just what Hegel's dialectic does say: that a thing is what it is not or, more precisely, a thing contains its own opposite. It is not a contradiction or a paradox, but Hegel's way of attempting to come to terms with the idea that change is inherent in the nature of things, i.e. something is both itself and its own opposite, in the sense that it is in the process of becoming that 'other' thing. For example, a seed is and is not a plant: it is not now a plant, but a seed, but it will become a plant, will cease to be a seed and change into a plant, i.e. something becomes what it is not. Hence Hegel is offering a drastically different conception of logic and of thought.

From the vantage point of the Frankfurt School, then, it is a defining feature of thought that it can think not only about what is, but also about what is not but *might be*. In this alternative logic, Marcuse (1955) and other Frankfurt

School theorists see the opportunity for thought to burst out of the narrow range of considerations, set by the unquestioning acceptance of the status quo, to question the givenness and inevitability of 'what is', and to contemplate the possibility of radical changes in the nature of 'what is' as it becomes 'what is not'. In short, they value dialectics as a source of *oppositional thinking*. In Adorno's late *Negative Dialectics* (1973), the 'negative' role of critical theory was more or less reduced to revealing the necessary incapacity of other schemes of thought to attain the comprehensive grasp of reality to which they aspired.

At the heart of the school's critique of Enlightenment reason is the claim that it has virtually nullified the power of oppositional thinking, that it has remained (so to speak) within the limits set by classical logic and thus within the limits set by bourgeois capitalist society. Even Marx had remained partially captive, as evidenced by his concern to provide an analysis of the 'scientific' economic laws governing the workings of the capitalist system. Only by freeing oneself from the assumptions inherent in the orthodox conception of reason and logic can one hope to regain the power of critical thought, with its possibility of genuine freedom.

Science as control

For many, and certainly for the Enlightenment, the development of science is taken to be the equivalent of the development of reason, and the progress of science is seen to provide a truly rational basis for the conduct of social life, with humanity achieving control of its affairs and enjoying authentic freedom. So much for the ideal; but the School alleges that the reality is somewhat different. The Enlightenment took up rather than originated the idea that nature and humanity are in opposition, i.e. existence is a struggle between the two, and that the condition of humanity's well-being is the domination (for purposes of exploitation) of nature. Very deeply rooted in the Enlightenment idea of reason is the aim of domination. The natural sciences are presented as valuable as a means to enable humanity to shape nature in the service of its own ends.

In practice, the most important of these ends has proved to be economic productivity. In consequence, the achievements of the natural sciences have resulted not only in the domination of nature, but in the domination of some human beings over others. The practical realisation of natural scientific knowledge in the form of technology has given humankind control over nature and, at the same time, exploited it by creating organised forms of labour in which the many are dominated by the few. Furthermore, the tools of logical thought and mathematical calculation, so effective in developing laws of nature, have been transformed into the basis for a whole 'world view'. This view is a general way of thinking which includes an emphasis upon uniformity, leading in turn to further domination and the impoverishment of many people's existence. The tools of logical thought and calculation have been adapted from their successful development in scientific inquiry into the means for the administration of society, throughout the whole of life and not just in work. Far from delivering freedom, the development of reason provided people only with the illusion of greater freedom, whilst subjecting them to ever more rigorous and thoroughly disciplined administrative regulation.

Thus the actual role of science has been a rather one-sided application of reason for practical purposes such as economic production; it has not served as the basis for true human self-understanding and the development of full human potential. Science exemplifies what the school characterises as 'instrumental reason', to which reason has been entirely reduced as a consequence of the Enlightenment.

Instrumental reason

Reason is used simply as an instrument and considered to be a mere means to practical purposes.

Such instrumental reason is incapable of questioning the way things are, of seriously challenging the social order; it essentially takes the way things are as simple givens within which it must formulate its inquiries and set its tasks. Perhaps we can see why the Frankfurt School had a considerable resurgence of popularity in the 1960s amongst student radicals who challenged the role of scientists working for the military. Such scientists were seen to be in the grip of instrumental reason; they could not – on the basis of their science – raise vital questions, e.g. should humanity be producing weapons capable of its self-destruction? Should it be providing the tools for the competitive self-aggrandisement of nation states? As a part of the 'military-industrial complex', the scientists were incapable of doing other than taking the military objectives of producing bigger, more destructive weapons for granted.

A *critical theory* was necessary to grasp the big picture and challenge the idea that science should be in servitude to politicians. Science was condemned not only as the plaything of politicians, but also as a means of manipulating and controlling people rather than contributing to human welfare. Similarly the social sciences were critiqued, since they too were seen to be involved in seeking to control people, to make them into happy, passive and manipulable beings. The social sciences showed their perversion by capitalism and their lack of independent critical inquiry by the way they applied knowledge in the form of their input into managerial control, advertising and other propagandistic media.

The struggle to master nature had been largely successful, but not as a struggle on behalf of human freedom. On the contrary, it had required the continued and improved domination of some people by others, as well as the imposition of a rigorous ordinance of self-denial on individuals. Science had contributed to the status quo, and its mind-set had been immensely helpful to the advancement of what Weber had termed the 'rationalisation of social relations', i.e. their reconstruction shaped by the kind of law-like, predictable, controllable regularities of the natural sciences. According to science of this kind the image of the world of strict, remorseless regularity had also been impressed upon and demanded of individuals as a condition of their participation in the so-called progress of society and of reason. People had been induced into thinking of themselves in terms of, and to imitate the ways of, law-like regularities and to exist as, so to speak, mere mechanical cogs in a great social machine.

To satisfy the demands of such a restrictive existence, it is necessary for people to renounce essential elements of their nature, to forego their individuality, spontaneity and sensuality, and to act as interchangeable, utterly predictable, entirely impersonal entities. However, whilst people can to some extent deny aspects of their own nature, their real human needs are not diminished; the frustration of these needs generates unsatisfied yearnings and a fund of undirected but aggressive resentment. The widespread distribution of such unhappy individual minds ensures fertile fields of recruitment for *gangster-politicians*, who can vent these resentments by providing a sense to individual lives which have otherwise been reduced to the meaninglessness of small cogs in vast machines. These gangster-politicians can offer something of greater significance through (at least the illusion of) involvement in something greater, in a movement with large political significance.

Instrumental reason

The Frankfurt School's account of industrial society links two classical sociological analyses: Weber's account of rationalisation and a Hegelian–Marxist reading of capitalist development. Marx's own thought is criticised, for he too places prime emphasis upon the use of knowledge for domination; his economic theories unquestionably favour the unlimited expansion of productive powers in the exploitation – the domination – of labour. Weber's emphasis on the spiritually debilitating effects of rationalisation was picked up and his critique taken further by Frankfurt School writers. Philosophies inspired by and derived from natural science attempts to reduce all phenomena to the physical and is therefore seen to express the extent to which reason has become debased. Its application has subjected people to oppressive administration and, in so far as its influence permeates every aspect of social life, people's very existence is devalued, their position in the world diminished and their experience impoverished.

The Frankfurt School accepted Weber's idea of the 'disenchantment of the world' and also agreed with him that, *pace* claims about the beneficial effects of the Enlightenment, reason does not in fact result in progress towards a true understanding of things. Instead the process divests human life of meaning and all relationships are reduced to the merely instrumental. Human relations with nature and with one another come to be nothing more than means to some (materialistic) end. Enlightenment reason has become instrumental reason. It is not defined by a radical, questioning confrontation with the world 'as it is', setting out to show that the world could and must be otherwise. Instead, it accepts the way things are as if this is how they must inevitably be. It is compliant in the service of the needs of that world 'as it is'.

Ironically, then, Enlightenment reason was self-deluding, was much less of an embodiment of reason than it thought itself to be. Setting itself up as the unrelenting debunker of myths, it was itself the avid perpetuator of one such myth, i.e. the myth of the God-like being, which was at the root of the will to domination. With the secularisation of industrial society, the myth of God who was master over everything had superficially been abolished, but only in so far as the notion of God had been displaced by that of 'Man', the essence of whose being was to seek total domination of the world (through reason and its application in technology). The dialectical result of Enlightenment's self-realisation was its finding its greatest fulfilment in the regimes whose drive towards total domination over their populations endowed them with the title *totalitarian*, rather than in societies of emancipated human beings. The Frankfurt School saw a clear link between the development of Enlightenment reason and the twentieth-century emergence of totalitarian regimes in Europe, as exemplified by Nazi Germany and Soviet communism, both of which had risen to prominence in the 1920s and 1930s, in the formative years of the Institute for Social Research.

The culture of capitalism

Reason had been captured by capitalism. This was one cause for despair. Another was that reason had served to capture and tame the working class. A main task which the Frankfurt School set itself was to understand the way in which the working class, especially the industrial part, had been rendered content with capitalism. The analysis of this phenomenon had several facets. One concerned psychological conformity: how people could develop personalities of the sort that would put them loyally at the disposal of totalitarian regimes. *The Authoritarian Personality*, published in 1950 and based on collaboration between Theodor Adorno (1903–69) and a group of social psychologists at the University of California, was a major study of this topic. This theme is less relevant, however, to the flow of our discussion than a second one, the role of the culture industry in promoting mass culture.

Modern society has become *mass society*.

Mass society

This concept was widely employed in American social science during the 1940s and 1950s in order to emphasise once again how individualised industrial society has become. In many ways, this idea accords with the condition of egoism described by Durkheim, i.e. individuals have become isolated from one another, separated from social ties and the support of relatively intimate groups; instead of making up an organised society, they are simply an undifferentiated mass, which stands in direct relationship to the large political, administrative and economic structures of the society. In the view of the Frankfurt School, this relationship is increasingly one of regulation; more and more aspects of individual lives are subject to direct or indirect control by centralised administrative bureaucracies, with the result that the difference between 'private' and 'public' life is largely obliterated.

(As we shall see in Chapter 11, this theme is taken up by Michel Foucault.) In addition to regulatory bureaucracy, the other key institutional feature of mass society is the *culture industry*.

The culture industry

Whereas administrative bureaucracies enforce control over people's lives, the culture industry provides those lives with (superficial) meaning. Since there are no intermediary groupings to command individuals' allegiance and provide their lives with meaning, the institutions of the culture industry, or, more appropriately, the mass media, fill this gap; individuals, being without strong ties and social supports, readily turn to the mass media for their ideas.

Not all aspects of culture were condemned as conformist by the Frankfurt School, e.g. they regarded 'high culture' favourably. Their view of mass culture was that it is 'low' culture, a 'mockery of what had been striven after in the great bourgeois works of art' (Adorno and Horkheimer 1979: 126). Mass culture effectively masquerades as Enlightenment but actually operates as mass deception. In sum, their critique is that art has been replaced by entertainment, imagination by technology and technique.

Components of mass culture

First of all, mass culture is produced as a commodity. As such, its character is derived from the calculations of its producers as to what its consumers can be induced to want: production is governed by the kind of calculation associated with marketing and comprises a kind of manipulation of those consumers. Mass culture is antithetical to high art. It is produced by organisations which are weak and dependent relative to the major economic and political organisations. Consequently, the culture industry must appease the more powerful industries and services which provide them with their technology and finance. Its products are homogenised, sharing predictable, undemanding formats, which themselves are effectively calculated, showing that the culture industry is thoroughly commercialised and pervaded (and perverted) by the spirit of business. The audience's imagination is suppressed, and no independent thought is demanded. The mass media seek to purvey an image which accords with their audience's notion of ordinariness, i.e. the audience's understanding is not stretched or challenged. Instead, it is reinforced in the passive, compliant attitude which the pressures of life in the society have already created.

Of course, the reproduction of the obvious, familiar world within the products of the culture industry confirms the ordinary world of the audience's experience as the *real* world. It is the only world there possibly can be, with no tension – let alone confrontation – between the outlook expressed in the product and that which is general in the society. At the same time, the culture industry flatters its victims with illusions, not least that they are capable of free and independent choice, even though the consumables they are presented with are ready-made, mass-produced and allow only the bare semblance of choice. For example, the production of cars, with its proliferation of makes and models, gives the impression of a huge range of choice, though in important respects cars are basically the same. An exaggeration of difference in service gives the illusion of choice. Spurious individuality is also conveyed, with the superficial differentiation of physical appearance or stylistic quirk, but within the context of a (contra-dictory) message which is (again crudely) that happiness is to be found through conformity. Indeed, mass culture is not even escapist, though its initial attraction may be that it appears to be so. For though it may even promise to be escapist, in fact 'in front of the appetite stimulated by all those brilliant names [of stars, etc.] and images there is finally set no more than a commendation of the depressing everyday world it sought to escape' (*The Dialectic of Enlightenment*: 139).

In support of this analysis, Walter Benjamin (1892–1940), another German scholar of the 1930s and loosely allied with the Frankfurt School, pointed out that the capacity of modern technologies to reproduce visible and audible 'realities' appears to authenticate the representations projected in media images, i.e. the technology effectively disguises from the viewer the fact that these images are selections or artificial creations. It enables images to be pre-sented in such a way as to convey the impression that reality is being neutrally reproduced rather than artificially simulated. In this way a particular cast is given to the portrayal of reality; it is effected through clichés and stereotypes, which – inevitably – conform to the prevailing ideology.

In reality, then, the Frankfurt School's critique is not actually of the *individualism* of modern society, but of its *false* individualism, i.e. the creation of fantasies of independence, choice and autonomy in a society which actually is uniform, thoroughly regulated, conformist and often strongly authoritarian.

Conclusion: defrauded by history?

Although the main writings of the Frankfurt School were produced in the period between the late 1920s and early 1960s, their *direct* influence was at its peak from the early 1960s to the early 1980s. As we indicated in Chapter 1, with the recent waning of interest in Marxist ideas in sociology, the critique of industrial society and its intellectual foundations in Enlightenment reason has moved on. The mantle of critique has now passed to the poststructuralists, whom we discuss later and whose thought often strongly matches Frankfurt School themes (see Chapter 10).

We have mentioned the Frankfurt School's doubts about the realisation of Enlightenment ideals, but in key respects the position the school took was ambivalent. The idea of reason enshrined in the institutions of industrial society is critiqued because these realisations amount to *perversions and debasements* of reason, rather than because any appeal to reason is suspect. The school was pessimistic about the prospect of a revolutionary overthrow of capitalism in accordance with orthodox Marxist doctrine, but nevertheless, its approach is essentially optimistic: if only some effective means could be found with which to oppose the prevailing institutions of industrial society and expose the falsity of their intellectual foundations, then there would be at least the prospect of reconstructing society along different lines, i.e. on the basis of genuine rationality and freedom.

We stated at the outset of this chapter that Western Marxism set itself the task of identifying the reasons for the incorporation of the working class into capitalist society. It wanted, however, to do more; it wanted to resuscitate the prospect of fundamental societal change and locate the source from which a transformation of the system might come. As Marcuse recognised, the crucial problem is in finding the vehicle for such a reconstruction once the revolutionary impotence of the working class is acknowledged. It might be argued that the 'failure' of the Frankfurt School was their inability to identify this alternative vehicle convincingly and, more profoundly, even to conceptualise the basis upon which its claim to rationality would stand.

Questions

1 Explain Lukács's concepts of 'totality' and the 'working class as the universal subject'. Do they improve our understanding of modern society?

2 Is Gramsci's concept of hegemony a refinement of or an addition to Marx's analysis of the role of ideas in society?

3 How do the Frankfurt School make use of Weber's idea of rationalisation?

4 What is the Enlightenment project? What are the Frankfurt School's main objections to it?

5 How can it make sense to argue that tolerance and freedom help to maintain repression?

6   Outline how mass society is viewed by critical theory. How does this view differ from Weber's account of the disenchantment of modern society?

7   What do you understand by the term 'the culture industry'? What are the Frankfurt School's main objections to this 'industry' and how valid do you find them?

8   'If Marx thought that the point was to achieve humanity's reconciliation with itself, the Frankfurt School came to believe that it was reconciliation with nature that was essential to human freedom.' Discuss.

Further reading

Benjamin, W., 1970, *Illuminations*. Cape. Includes his essay 'The work of art in the age of mechanical reproduction'.

Bottomore, T., 1984, *The Frankfurt School*. Tavistock. A good, short introduction.

Bronner, S. and Kellner, D. (eds), 1989, *Critical Theory and Society: A Reader*. Routledge. A useful reader.

Connerton, P. (ed.), 1976, *Critical Sociology: Selected Readings*. Penguin. A useful selection of texts.

Gramsci, A., 1971, *Selections from the Prison Notebooks of Antonio Gramsci*. International Publishers. Contains his discussion of hegemony.

Held, D., 1990, *Introduction to Critical Theory: Horkheimer to Habermas*. Hutchinson. A more advanced study of the Frankfurt School.

Jay, M., 1973, *The Dialectical Imagination: A History of the Frankfurt School and the Institute for Social Research. 1923–1950*. Heinemann. A full historical account.

—— 1984, *Adorno*. Fontana. A good, short survey of his work.

Kolakowski, L., 1981. *Main Currents of Marxism. Vol. 3: The Breakdown*. Oxford University Press. Ch. VII gives a more sharply critical assessment of Lukács. Chs X and XI give an assessment of the Frankfurt School.

Lichtheim, G., 1970, *Lukács*. Fontana. A good, brief introduction.

McIntyre, A., 1970, *Marcuse*. Fontana. A good, short survey of his work.

Marcuse, H., 1964, *One Dimensional Man*. Routledge. The key source for the theory of repressive tolerance.

Parkinson, G.H.R.(ed.), 1970, *Georg Lukács: The Man, his Work and his Ideas*. Random House/Vintage Books. A useful source, especially for Parkinson's introduction and Istvan Meszaros's essay 'Lukács's concept of dialectic'.

Critical overviews of the Western Marxist tradition are:

Anderson, P., 1976, *Considerations on Western Marxism*. New Left Books.

Jay, M., 1984, *Marxism and Totality*. Polity Press.

Merquior, J.Q., 1986, *Western Marxism*. Paladin.

■ ■ ■

Chapter 9

Structuralism

Introduction: the linguistic model

It is common in the social sciences for an approach in one discipline or field to adapt its inspiration and most basic assumptions from another discipline. 'Structuralism' has its origins in linguistics as a model for social and cultural analysis, drawing upon what was, until the 1950s, one of the most successful strands in linguistics (which was itself deemed in certain respects the most successful of the human and social sciences), namely structural linguistics.

Saussure's structural linguistics

The structuralist approach in linguistics originated in the work of Ferdinand de Saussure (1857–1913), somewhat under the influence of Durkheim's ideas. Writing at a time when the study of language was in its infancy, Saussure sought to define a subject matter for linguistics (just as Durkheim had done for sociology) and comparably sought it in a supra-individual phenomenon, the language system (which he termed *langue*), rather than in the individual one of speech (in his terminology, *parole*). His approach treated the act of speaking very much as a secondary phenomenon; order in language was to be explained in the systemic relations between words (or 'signs') which pre-exist any particular act of speaking, and not in terms of the ways individuals put words together to say things. Furthermore, the language system was to be understood quite differently to previous accounts, as a *system of differences*, of contrasts.

In the first instance, a language is a system of words, i.e. in this approach a system of *signs*. In the traditional, i.e. prestructuralist, view, the meaning of words is thought to result from the fact that they stand for other things, e.g. the names of things stand for the concrete objects themselves, or for the ideas in a speaker's head. Stable relations between words and their *referents* (i.e., the things or ideas that the words refer to) enable people to identify certain objects as the things the words stand for. Understanding a language is, then, understanding the ways the signs in the language can be combined to state new ideas and/or refer to complex things. However, Saussure's bold proposal was to dispense with this view in favour of considering signs entirely in terms of the (internal) relations between them.

Saussure's strategy can be seen as akin to Durkheim's treatment of totemism. Prior to Durkheim, writers on totemism characteristically had sought to understand the meaning of the totemic object in terms of its own properties, to figure out how people could see something especially valuable or awesome in the natural phenomenon (animal, plant, place, etc.) that was their totem. Against such accounts of totemism in terms of the practical or psychological importance of the totems, Durkheim argued that their meaning could not be accounted for in terms of their objective properties. All instrumentalist explanations fail, since there is nothing particularly practically useful or awesome about totemic objects. Instead the totemic object is a sign and stands for something. Its specific nature is itself arbitrary; it does not really matter what the particular totem is, any more than the sacredness of the national flag depends upon its design.

The role of the totem was to bind people together; it stood for the social group from which it derived its potency. For Durkheim, unifying the social group involves differentiating between sets of people. The role of the totem is to bind some people together in separation from others, therefore the totem must differ between groups; i.e. someone claiming to be a member of the emu clan is at the same time saying he or she is not a member of the parakeet (and vice versa). What is important about the totemic objects, then, is that they should be different from one another. The system of totemic symbols is crucial.

Similarly for Saussure, the meaning of a sign is only arbitrarily linked to the sign itself; e.g. there is no reason why we should use a particular configuration of sound, such as 'totem', to mean what it does. The same goes for any other word in the language: some other sound could have been used to carry the meaning. Language is about communication, about the conveyance of information from one person to another. The capacity of a system to convey information derives from contrastive relations built into the system itself. Thus the *whole system* is important, not any single unit within it. The meaning of a word does not derive from the word itself, nor from the thing it stands for. The important feature of a word is that it should differ from other words, that it should contrast with them, e.g. saying something is 'red' is to say it is 'not green', 'not yellow' and so on. Saussure viewed language as just one *semiotic system* (i.e., system of signs) among many. His larger project, never realised, was to locate language within the broader set of communication systems. Although Saussure never completed his project, it was taken up again after World War II as the goal of the structuralist movement.

Freud: The workings of the unconscious

A second source of inspiration for structuralism can be found in the writings of Sigmund Freud (1856–1939), the founder of psychoanalysis. The ideas of Freud are honoured – in conjunction with those of Marx (see Chapter 2) and

Friedrich Nietzsche (see Chapter 10) – both by structuralists and by their post-structuralist successors for contributing to the idea of the *unconscious* as a source of the determination of human conduct.

The unconscious and structuralism

The idea of the unconscious is important to structuralism since it proposes to discover the very structures which govern the nature of human thought generally and, at the same time, to be making an original discovery. In short, it proposes to find out things of which all people have been previously unaware. Structuralism is interested in the deeper, unconscious structures which operate within the mind. Individual thinkers are quite unaware of them, yet they shape the organisation of whatever individuals do consciously think.

Freud's ideas about the unconscious, especially when mediated by the influence of a Parisian psychoanalyst, Jacques Lacan (1901–81), was immensely influential on French theoretical ideas in the post-1945 period. By arguing that the unconscious was constructed like a language, Lacan offered the irresistible prospect of combining Freudian notions with the linguistic and semiotic ideas that also captivated theorists at that time.

Freud himself claimed to give a general account of the human mind. He maintained that it included two main parts, the conscious and the unconscious. The *conscious* is those workings of the mind of which we are aware and which we can control. It is accompanied by thoughts of which we are not aware, of which we are not conscious; they take place in the unconscious. The *unconscious* is – and here the connection with Nietzsche is apparent – the direct expression of our organic, biological, animal natures, of what Freud regarded as the basic, instinctual drives that demand satisfaction – drives for food, for sex and so forth. The animal nature of human beings is of an indiscriminate, insatiable desire for immediate pleasure, an unreasoning, uncontrolled demand for the easing of the unpleasant tensions which build up in us when our desire for food or sex is frustrated. Such a nature would be self-destructive if left to itself. Sheer, blind striving for immediate satisfaction would result in damaging, eventually fatal contact with the environment, because though human beings have instinctual needs, they have no instinctual ways of satisfying them. Therefore, it is necessary that the drives at the basis of human personality be controlled and directed, but this requires that the organism must learn (1) to postpone the demand for instant satisfaction in favour of less immediately but more safely gratifying responses, and (2) about its environment in order to grasp practically effective ways of achieving gratifications. Thus the human being learns to regulate its drives, and to adapt its reactions to its circumstances, something which it does through the development of its basic personality. This development takes place first within the family relationship and later within the larger society. The individual must learn not only how to relate to its natural environment – what it can safely eat, etc. – but also to its social one.

As part of developing its social nature, the individual will learn that certain of its reactions are not allowed, that they are not acceptable to others. The urge to be aggressive to other people, even the wish to see them dead, is a natural, atavistic reaction, but it is not one which is acceptable within society. The developing individual will come to share this general social attitude, though, at the same time, these natural, unacceptable responses will continue to occur. However, the individual will be unable to admit to itself that it has such wishes, and will deny them to itself by suppressing and forgetting them – in Freud's terms, will repress them. The individual will drive those thoughts out of the (conscious) mind, but not from the mind altogether. Instead, they are exiled to the unconscious, where they persist, and where they will continue to seek expression. If these unacceptable thoughts are to be expressed this cannot be done directly, in plain and open form, but must happen in some other way, in a form which does not look at all like the original thoughts and which mis-represents, and therefore conceals, their socially unacceptable nature. Thus Freud accounts for dreams as the way in which unconscious thoughts gained expression in the mind; the dream was a way of trying to express and fulfil a wish which could not be expressed and fulfilled in an explicit way. However, seeing what wish it is that a dream expresses and fulfils is rather akin to break-ing a complex code; it can only be done by the trained psychoanalyst, who can see that the events in dreams are symbolic, and who understands what the symbols stand for.

Self-deception and the normality of neurosis

Freud's view was that many of the milder mental illnesses were the results of unresolved tensions retained in individual unconscious minds, tensions involving thoughts which could not be consciously admitted by their individual owners, and which individuals therefore consciously deny. These thoughts continue to be expressed in the form of *seeming*, e.g. a seeming physical paralysis for which there is no physical basis. The explanation given by Freud would point to this paralysis as really psychological, not physical; as the result of inner tensions, in which, say, very straitlaced individuals experience incestuous sexual desires, but are unable to tolerate the idea that they could possibly have such feelings. Such a psychological conflict could take the form of physical expression, with the distress caused by the paralysis being a kind of self-imposed punishment for having those forbidden feelings. The purpose of Freud's psychoanalytic clinical operation is to enable the patient to become aware of, to become conscious of these inner, unconscious, suppressed conflicts. Awareness provides the capacity to sort out the feelings and to overcome the conflict, which means that the physical symptom will evaporate.

Thus Freud argues that people are often unaware of the true psychological causes of their behaviour, of the unconscious impulses which can compel it.

When they seek to explain things which have such unconscious causes, they give explanations which they think are true, but are, in fact, false. Because the unconscious impulses are ones which they – after the fashion of their culture and of the standards they have come to share – cannot regard as acceptable or admissible, the explanations that they give seek to present these 'low', unacceptable motivations in improved, 'higher', generally acceptable terms; they therefore seek to explain behaviour as the product of the rational deliberations of the conscious mind rather than in terms of the irrational, impulsive, unconscious drives in which it actually originates.

In Freud's account, the discipline of the instinctive impulses and their subordination to conscious control, is an essential for the healthy development of the individual into someone capable of achieving satisfactions in a civilised way. Being reared within the family, and then the wider society, individuals learn to restrain their unconscious impulses. The self-denial of immediate satisfactions and the acceptance of a socially imposed discipline is the price of civilisation. Some individuals, however, can have their lives severely disrupted by psychological afflictions arising from the unresolved conflicts in their unconscious. The operation of science – the application of the scientifically derived doctrines of psychoanalysis – will enable reason to emancipate individuals from such afflictions, offering relief by providing people with rational, conscious understanding of the conflicts underlying their symptoms. Freud does, however, argue that the existence of civilisation involves a cost to the expression and satisfaction of human instinctual drives, though, as indicated, he himself thought the price well worth paying. As we will show, poststructuralist thinkers have particularly seized on Freud's point about the extent to which civilisation is antithetical to free self-expression, but they do not accept his view on the acceptability of this cost.

Lévi-Strauss on 'the savage mind'

Movements of thought are often associated with specific locations. Just as symbolic interactionism (see Chapter 6) was associated with Chicago, so the structuralist movement in social science was centred in Paris after 1945. The first major thinker in this movement was the anthropologist Claude Lévi-Strauss (b. 1908). His writings brought together the structuralist model of language with notions about the mind inspired by the Freudian idea of the unconscious.

The idea of contrast as the basis for systems of meaning was developed by subsequent thinkers after Saussure into a powerful and sophisticated linguistic scheme. On the basis of these successes Saussure's ideas were reimported into the social sciences, initially through the anthropology of Lévi-Strauss, who aimed to give an account of the system of unconsciously operating rules of thought built into the human mind. One of his first (short) works was on the subject of totemism. It reviewed the development of thought about totemism since Durkheim's time, to some extent turning the structuralist argument against Durkheim himself. This book, *Totemism* (1969), and another early work, *The Savage Mind* (1972), form a pair and we will consider them together.

Lévi-Strauss's concern with totemism has to be understood against the background of the longstanding anthropological argument over whether 'primitive' people think differently from people in 'advanced' societies. For some contributors to this debate, the presence of totemism and similar thought systems in tribal societies reveal that 'primitives' are incapable of truly logical thought. Lévi-Strauss refuses to regard totemism as something special and unique to tribal societies; it is only a small part of a more general phenomenon which has to do with the organisation of human thought and, particularly, with the way human and other natural phenomena are interrelated in thought.

Totemism

Against Durkheim, Lévi-Strauss argues that the key to totemism has to do with the organisation of thinking, with the operation of the intellect, not social organisation. He goes on to claim that studies of totemism show so-called 'primitive societies' use natural phenomena to think with.

According to Lévi-Strauss, the possession of totemism by tribal, 'primitive' peoples and its absence from our 'advanced' societies does not indicate a true division in the nature of the minds; it is only a superficial difference. The human mind works always in basically the same way, and the difference between the 'primitive' and 'advanced' societies is due only to the conditions under which the mind has to operate. The 'advanced' societies are marked by the development of a complex apparatuses for the abstract expression of thought, e.g. writing and mathematics. Such systems enable the expression, preservation and communication of thought, facilitating complex and abstract intellectual operations. The inhabitants of 'primitive' societies do not possess such systems, but are no less capable of sophisticated intellectual operations. Like us, they engage in abstract, rigorously logical and sophisticated thinking, but they have the problem of how to express and communicate it in the absence of the means available to us.

In *The Savage Mind* Lévi-Strauss employs what has now become a widely used expression, *bricoleur*, as an analogy to characterise the form of thought characteristic of tribal peoples. *Bricoleur* is French for a kind of handyperson, who will do a job with whatever materials there are to hand. A *bricoleur* has an accumulation of things, tools and materials collected up over time, and access to those things present on the scene where the job must be done. The *bricoleur*'s task is to find a way of doing the repair job with just those materials. In Lévi-Strauss's account, the situation of the 'savage mind' is comparable. It does not have access to specialised tools for the work of thought – such as writing and mathematics – and if it is to do the work of thinking then it must use whatever resources are to hand. The materials are those of nature – plants, animals and natural phenomena. The attempt to understand the totemic system must recognise, first of all, that the use of natural phenomena to represent social relations is only a small part of the general pattern of using natural phenomena as the medium for intellectual operations. To understand the totemic system and the other cultural forms of such societies is to see how complex and universal intellectual problems are posed and tackled in ways expressed through a particular content derived from the natural world.

Although Lévi-Strauss's approach owes much to Durkheim's emphasis upon the nature of the totemic object as a sign, he none the less turns his argument against Durkheim's fundamental ambition. Lévi-Strauss says that Durkheim 'affirms the primacy of the social over the intellect' (Lévi-Strauss 1962: 97), but though he, Durkheim, aimed at and stood by this overriding ambition, he was a scholar of integrity and he was on occasion forced to admit things which were not consistent with it, e.g. when he admits that 'all social life, even elementary, presupposes an intellectual activity in man of which the formal properties, consequently, cannot be a reflection of the concrete organisation of the society' (*ibid.* 96–7). Lévi-Strauss agrees with this observation of Durkheim's that the basic forms of thought are not derived from the social order. Instead, he insists that they reflect very general forms of operation which are characteristic of the human mind.

In Lévi-Strauss's view, it is hardly surprising that there are universal processes of the mind, since the operation of the mind is dependent upon the operation of the brain, which itself operates in terms of *binary oppositions*, i.e. electrical pulses which go on and off.

Binary oppositions

These are simply paired terms which directly exclude each other, which starkly and sharply contrast, e.g. 'on' and 'off', 'up' and 'down', 'left' and 'right', 'man' and 'woman'. Lévi-Strauss is a firm advocate of what philosophers call the *mind–brain identity thesis*, i.e. the nature of the mind is revealed by knowing the workings of the brain. Accordingly, he can assert that the human mind operates fundamentally in terms of such binary oppositions.

Therefore the way to understand totemism and other products of 'primitive cultures' is to analyse them in terms of this universal principle of operation.

The structural study of myth

Lévi-Strauss dedicated his subsequent career to this task. His work was dominated by the structural study of myth. The structuralist approach is worked out in and through detailed examination of a very large corpus of myths taken from 'primitive' – mainly South American – societies, climaxing in the production of four large volumes comprising *Mythologiques*, translated as *An Introduction to a Science of Mythology* (1970, 1973, 1978a, 1981).

These myths tell stories in which people, for example, pay visits to heaven, go on quests, are assisted by animals (which may talk to them), and sometimes even turn into animals. From our point of view, these stories seem quite hard to understand, involving a rather arbitrary series of events.

Myths as a system

Lévi-Strauss argues that if we were enabled to detect the underlying structure of the narrative, to discern its constituent elements and the way these are arranged, then we would see that these stories are not arbitrary, meaningless sequences of events. Through his structural analysis we would see that they are (1) concerned with deep, profound, intellectual problems, and (2) rigorously logical in their underlying structures.

Concerning what myths are actually about as opposed to their surface content, Lévi-Strauss argues that there are things in human life which deeply and persistently trouble us, for which it is difficult to obtain satisfactory, stable solutions. For example, and something which matters a great deal in his work, the problem of the relationship between nature and culture is a matter of considerable ambiguity in human thought, since we sometimes starkly contrast 'nature' and 'culture'. We think of ourselves as creatures of culture *rather than* nature, contrasting ourselves with other creatures which are part of nature only, i.e. merely animals. Yet we too are part of nature, we too are animals, and our capacity to develop culture could be said to be natural to us. Thus as human beings we both are and are not part of nature, and culture is both natural and unnatural: an unsatisfactory position from the point of view of logical consistency and symmetry. Lévi-Strauss holds that myths are often quite sophisticated attempts to resolve this unstable logical position and, indeed, other similar kinds of logical problems.

As for the organisation of myths, Lévi-Strauss insists that they only seem to consist of randomly sequenced occurrences; properly analysed, they can be seen to be highly and complexly structured. At one point (1963: 213) Lévi-Strauss compares our reading of the myth with attempting to read an orchestral score in which all the notes have been placed on the same line. We would not see much musical structure in such a document until the notes were redistributed on to different lines in order to separate the various instruments. Similarly, to read myths as just a linear succession of incidents will not reveal the logical structure which they embody. Structure is detected by redistributing the events in the story amongst the various patterns of *contrast* (or binary opposition) which fundamentally make them up. In doing so, we find the myths embody structures of intellectual thought which are so rigorous that they are like mathematics in character.

As an illustration of his method, Lévi-Strauss takes the Greek myth of Oedipus. He first decomposes the events into several collections of elements. Some events instantiate the 'overrating' of blood relations, e.g. Oedipus's marriage to his mother. Several events instantiate the opposite, namely, the 'underrating' of blood relations, e.g. Oedipus slaying his father. A third set of elements is of incidents in which monsters are slain by humans: a dragon has to be slain in order that humankind can be born from the earth. A fourth set pertains to the names of major characters in the myth; they are all names with meanings associated with difficulties in walking straight and standing upright, e.g. Oedipus's own name means 'swollen foot'.

Lévi-Strauss then attends to the way these collections of elements relate to one another. For him the key is the autochthonous origin in the third set of elements above ('autochthonous' means 'born from the earth'). The myth is an attempt to think through the contradiction found in a culture with (1) a belief in the autochthonous origin of man and also (2) the knowledge that we are born from man and woman. In Lévi-Strauss's own summary:

> The myth has to do with the inability, for a culture which holds the belief that mankind is autochthonous, to find a satisfactory transition between this theory and the knowledge that human beings are actually born from the union of man and woman. Although the problem obviously cannot be solved, the Oedipus myth provides a kind of logical tool which relates the original problem – born from one or born from two? – to the derivative problem: born from different or born from same? By a correlation of this type, the overrating of blood relations is to the underrating of blood relations as the attempt to escape autochthony is to the impossibility to succeed in it. Although experience contradicts theory, social life validates cosmology by its similarity of structure. Hence cosmology is true.
>
> (1963: 216)

In this way Lévi-Strauss has rearranged the elements in the myth, breaking up the narrative structure. He extracts from the story various elements of different kinds which stand in logically contrastive relations to one another, namely, overrating is the logical opposite of underrating. He can then seek to show further logical relations between these initial logical relations after the fashion of the algebraic formulation:

a : b :: c : d, (i.e. a is to b as c is to d).

With the Oedipus myth, this formulation shows that underrelating of blood relations is to overrating them as attempting to escape from autochthony is to the likelihood (nil) of succeeding. Through this mythic representation, thought is able to achieve the reconciliation of an impossibility: to provide an intellectual bypassing of a tension within the culture from which the myth is taken, i.e. the tension between the belief that humankind springs from the earth and the fact that we come from the womb, thereby allowing the preservation of the belief in the face of that knowledge.

In Lévi-Strauss's work the basic pattern of intellectual operations takes the form of binary oppositions, although they are often involved in a triadic nexus, i.e. two opposing terms have another mediating between them, bridging the gap between them, thereby providing a transition point from one to the other, e.g. rain can connect the earth and the sky, above and below.

An illustration: The Jealous Potter

Obviously, some 2000 cumulating pages of analysis of myths taken mainly from the cultures of Latin American tribes provide a much more intricate and complex structure than our brief illustrative reconstruction of the Oedipus myth can even suggest, but we will attempt to give some flavour of the major work by considering Lévi-Strauss's comparatively short study, *The Jealous Potter* (1988).

The Jealous Potter is a follow-on to his major, four-volume work *An Introduction to a Science of Mythology*. In it he dealt with one of his major themes: the demarcation of nature from culture as reflecting a preoccupation of human thought, apparent in some of the myths concerning the acquisition of cooking fire. The possession of fire was something which in the myths had to be striven for by human beings. Fire is the focus of a cosmic struggle between the people of the above – celestial beings – and those of the below – creatures living on the earth, including humans. Human beings were successful in their efforts and attained secure possession of cooking fire. The origins of pottery are also a topic of myth, for pottery is one of two great arts which the most basic human societies have, the other being weaving. The origin of pottery, however, must be a secondary or dependent matter, to the extent that it presupposes the possession of cooking fire (for pots must, themselves, be 'cooked' by fire) and the pattern in such myths is rather different from those analysed in his prior work. Humans do not acquire pottery by effort, but incidentally, as a beneficial by-product of another, unending, cosmic struggle between celestial beings (represented by birds) and aquatic creatures (represented by snakes). Unlike the possession of fire, the art of pottery is not permanently assured, but is constantly endangered; great care needs to be taken, otherwise it can very easily be lost.

Lévi-Strauss begins, then, from the way in which associations are often assumed made between a craft and the character of its practitioners, and he notes that one such connection commonly made is a tendency for potters to be viewed as jealous. What, he wonders, could be the basis for this association? By an elaborate, often roundabout, series of steps, he seeks to understand the connection between pottery and jealousy: how is it made by, and how does it fit into, the pattern of interrelationship amongst the elements of mythic tales? Much of the fascination of one of Lévi-Strauss's accounts of myth lies in following the seemingly tortuous argument by which he draws out complex connections between things which seem, initially, unrelated. (Note here the similarity with psychoanalytic method.) In this case, he is going to connect – at least – pottery, jealousy, the goatsucker (a species of bird), the sloth, the howler monkey, opossums, subterranean dwarfs, heavenly bodies (including meteors, the sun and the moon), and the relationship between life on earth and the after-life. Further, he is going to connect these different elements across considerable geographical distances, for one of his key arguments is that the mythical thought of the Americas was essentially unified. Even this short work encompasses myths drawn from tribes from Latin America, the North American plains and Californian region, and the west coast of Canada.

Consequently, he must face, for example, this question: since the sloth is a creature confined to Latin America, what creatures could fulfil its signifying function in the myths of North America? Although the fascination of the work may lie in following its convoluted unfolding, our brief exposition is best effected by first revealing the ending. The analysis in *The Jealous Potter* reveals that the structure of the constellation of myths involved is basically built around the treatment of the living body as a kind of pipe; things pass through a pipe, and the extent to which they can do so defines the elements which provide the key contrasts in the myths. The openings in a pipe provide means of entry and of exit, therefore it is through openings in the body/pipe that things enter and are ejected from the body. He notes that 'these openings can be at the front or back, above or below: mouth, nose, ears, vagina and anus. Each can perform three different functions: closed, open to receive, open to eject. The myths under study here illustrate only a few of these combinations' (1988: 163). For example, laughing, vomiting, eating, farting and excreting are amongst the bodily functions which figure prominently in the tapestry of the myths.

Lévi-Strauss summarises the main lineaments of the stories the myths tell:

> Plots primarily motivated by marital jealousy chose a Goatsucker for a hero or a heroine and connected this Goatsucker physically or logically with the Sloth, who 'originated in jealousy' and was also jealous of his excrement. Through the Sloth we were introduced to the image of the comet or meteor. In South America it issued from excrement over which the Sloth had lost his jealous control. For the Iroquois, the comet or the meteor was the immediate cause of the jealousy that prompted a husband to eject his wife through a hole as if she were his excrement. Jealousy can be defined as a feeling emanating from the desire to hold on to something that is being taken away from you, or as the desire for something or some-one you do not possess. We can say then, then, that jealousy tends to sup-port a state of conjunction whenever there is a state of threat or disjunction. All subsequent developments, however varied their themes, pertain to different modalities of disjunction, whose immutable nature is to break up formerly united terms by putting distance between them – a distance sometimes large, sometimes relatively small.
>
> (1988: 173)

Furthermore:

> The lesson taught in these myths is that earth must no longer be what men eat but must instead be cooked, like food, in order to enable men to cook what they eat. In the state of nature, earth was food; in its cooked form it becomes a vessel – that is to say, a cultural product

and

> [As] the function of fire becomes double (it cooks food or cooks pots in which food will be cooked) there emerges a dialectic of internal and external, of inside and outside: clay, congruent to excrement *contained* in the body, is used to make pots *containing* food, which will be *contained* in the body, until the body, relieving itself, ceases to be the *container* of excrement.
>
> (*ibid.*: 176, 177)

The way Lévi-Strauss works towards these conclusions is not as arbitrary as this bald presentation might suggest. After all, his mode of analysis is meant to treat connections made in the myths as themselves intelligible rather than arbitrary. At its heart, *The Jealous Potter* seeks to disclose the logic which links jealousy, excrement and meteors, e.g. in some myths the excrement of particular animals turns into meteors. He asks how such connections can be made.

Another key to Lévi-Strauss's analysis is provided by recognising the symbolic significance of pottery. At the root of all thought is the contrast between shape and shapelessness; pottery involves imposing shape on the shapeless, giving form to clay. The activity of pottery itself is risky, its operations can be very delicate and its objectives are easily frustrated if things are not done just so. Of course, the transforming of the shapeless into the ordered is involved in the very creation of the world (we might note here the role of humankind as 'clay' in biblical symbolism); that pottery reproduces this imposition of order marks it out as a special kind of activity.

In the myths, pottery is connected with jealousy in three ways: (1) the art of pottery is jealously guarded by those who possess it; (2) the art itself is a jealous one, i.e. it imposes strict requirements upon its practitioners if it is not to desert them; (3) it is specifically connected to marital jealousy: in one myth, clay, the material of pottery, originates from a woman who is the object of struggle between rival husbands. In South American myths, marital jealousy is often connected with the goatsucker, a bird with a wide mouth and voracious habits that stands for greed. For example, in myths of marital discord (which arises in some cases from the jealousy between wife and mother-in-law over sons who do not really want to leave their mothers) one of the parties involved in the relationship turns into a goatsucker. The goatsucker is associated with another characteristic, that of splitting, with both physical and social separations. On the physical side, in some myths the goatsucker dismembers other birds and smashes rocks; on the social side, it is linked with domestic separation brought about by 'jealousy among men over the same woman, the jealousy of the rejected lover (man or woman), the inability of two lovers to be together or marital discord' (Lévi-Strauss 1988: 52).

The mythical system is a relational one, and the association of the goat-sucker with other things is to be understood in terms of the way in which that creature stands to other creatures used in the myths: a prominent opposition of the goatsucker is with the sloth. Why opposition? Lévi-Strauss points out that the two creatures exhibit paired opposed characteristics: oral versus anal, conti-nent versus incontinent. Remember, the goatsucker's trait is greediness in its eating habits, so it stands, in the myth for incontinence connected with the mouth, or orality. On the other hand, the sloth is noted for the fact that it infre-quently excretes and is possessive about its faeces, exemplifying, therefore, anal continence. Just as the goatsucker is associated with pottery, the sloth is associ-ated with weaving, another of the great arts. As a small eater and infrequent defecator the sloth is seen as naturally well bred and therefore a suitable natural model for a culturally well-bred, technically refined activity such as weaving.

Lévi-Strauss insists that the myths of far-flung peoples are connected, yet the sloth does not exist outside a delimited area of Latin America. Since it is associated in myth with subterranean dwarf people who have no anus, then the way to find a connection is to search myths where the sloth is not available as a character, because of the absence of the real creature from the environment, for dwarfish subterranean people. Finding some such people, the next step is to ask what kind of animals they are associated with, e.g. the squirrel and the opossum in North American tribes.

Lévi-Strauss then notes that the creatures associated with the sub-terranean dwarfs are tree dwelling, thereby evoking for him a three-tiered world: those who dwell above (in the trees), those who dwell on the earth and those who dwell beneath it. This model for the relationship between super-humans and humans is conceived in terms of the problems that arise in respect of creatures living one on top of another, e.g. gods over people. Those who live up above are apt to make a dump and sewer of the space of those living below; of course, humans treat the world beneath them in the same callous way. In this way, defecation provides a connection between different levels of reality, as excreta passes down to a lower level.

This connection now evokes another animal contrast, this time between the sloth and the howler monkey. Again, the contrast is in terms of the orifices of the body, the mouth and the anus: the howler monkey is both anally and orally incontinent; it is a noisy animal, and also defecates frequently from high up in trees, unlike the sloth, which does its infrequent excreting close to the ground. In the myth, the sloth's care about excretion is connected with a con-cern for the preservation of the earth and life on it; if it were to defecate freely and incautiously from high up, its excreta would be transformed into a meteor, wreaking destruction.

To sum up, Lévi-Strauss uses the examples of cooking and pottery to show how lessons about the relationship between nature and culture are conveyed in myth. He makes connections between the structure of the cosmos and the excreting behaviour of animals through drawing on the pattern of orifices and their open/closed states. Excreta is treated as a (no pun intended) fundamental metaphor for separation, domestic separation being one form, and as a mechanism for interconnection between the different strata of reality.

Lévi-Strauss's anti-humanism

Clearly, Lévi-Strauss's approach is uncompromisingly intellectual, yet there is more to it than intellectual puzzle solving. The operations of the intellect are concerned with social matters, for the logical problems which the mind addresses arise from the contradictions within the life of the society, with the fact that social relations cannot themselves be organised with thoroughgoing logical consistency. Myth confronts these contradictions and draws out patterns of relationship in the form of the mythic analogies, which make it appear that these logical difficulties can be overcome, that their reconciliation is possible. Since, however, these contradictions in social life *are* contradictions, it remains the fact that they cannot be reconciled in real life. Myth creates the illusion that they can, making them easier to live with. Thus Lévi-Strauss's analysis of myth is not very far from Marx's concept of ideology and its functions; in the end it presents myth as a form of collective self-delusion.

However, we must be careful here not to take too humanistic a view of Lévi-Strauss's work. His structuralist approach is informed by a strong *anti-humanist* perspective; it was massively influential in promoting the *subject-decentring* movement which has been such an importantly unifying element in recent theoretical developments (see below). Lévi-Strauss's analyses of myth are not designed to provide us with an appreciation of the ingenuity of a teller of the myth able to conjure up such elaborate constructions, for the meaning structures of the myth are not the conscious contrivance of the teller at all. Rather, they are the product of unconscious operations of the mind, ones of which the teller is not aware. Lévi-Strauss sometimes sees himself as akin to a scientific observer of some natural phenomenon; its actual and lawlike order is just not discoverable to naive participants in its observable, surface detail. Only through complex analytic reconstruction of the phenomena can this order be found – compare the way laboratory scientists tear things apart in order to discover their true (inner) nature.

In fact, the individual tellings of the myths are only instances of the operation of the general, unconsciously operating pattern of the human mind. The tellers of the myths are therefore providing only partial realisations of a complex system of pattern possibilities. The individual teller does not create the basic pattern for producing the telling of the particular myth . Consequently we can only understand this basic pattern properly by seeing the way it is worked out across the whole range of myths.

Below we shall talk about 'the death of the author' and 'the abolition of the subject', explaining more fully what such expressions mean, but in these arguments of Lévi-Strauss's we can find some important contributions to the formation of these ideas. Note, for example, that Lévi-Strauss does not collect myths on the basis that we collect stories in our society, i.e. that they are the product of the same teller, the creations of the same author. Nor does he seek to understand them by making any reference to the lives or circumstances of those who tell the myths. Lévi-Strauss does not look for a pattern in some myths which results from their being the productions of one and the same creative individual, nor does he have the slightest interest in attempting to trace the cultural history of particular myths. Instead, he looks for a pattern which is present in *all* myths, regardless of who created them or from what geographical region they originate. The crucial question is whether logical connections such as opposition, inversion and mediation can be found between the structural components of the myths.

From Lévi-Strauss's standpoint, then, the 'authors' of the myths, i.e. their tellers, are unwitting operators of the structure of thought underlying the individual myths; they tell the myths as they do because of the nature of that structure. In this respect, the underlying structure can be seen to be in control of the telling of the myth and, thus, of the teller of the myth, rather than the teller being in control of his or her own conduct. The true meaning of the myth is, then, something created not, by the individual teller, but, instead, by the system which shapes the teller's behaviour. Further, the 'author' of the myth is not someone who provides the principle of unity amongst them. The 'author' is not a centre from which each myth singularly originates and derives its meanings, or around which the myths are assembled into unified collections, i.e. as the *oeuvre* of an author assembled into a 'collected works' in our society. Neither the pattern in the myths nor the principle which connects them together originates in any single focus or centre, for the pattern is distributed across the whole of humanity. Myths are connected with one another across considerable distance of time and space in that they represent the elaboration, the working out, of different, perhaps complementary possibilities within the general pattern.

Thus meaning originates from the *system*, not from the individual. The 'author' is anonymous and even unknown, an irrelevance from the point of view of understanding the meaning of the myth; we need to know more details about other myths in order to understand this one, not further details about the lives and intentions of the 'author'. Among structuralist and poststructuralist thinkers this notion in part is what is meant by talk of the *death of the author* and the *decentring of the subject*. In summary:

1   Reference to the figure of 'the author' is not essential to the understanding of writings and may, indeed, be obstructive to true understanding of the meaning of writings.
2   The individual (in the form of 'the author' in connection with writing) is not the centre from which the meaning of meaningful phenomena originates. The meaning of the phenomenon does not perhaps derive from any centre.

Thus the anti-humanist element is large in Lévi-Strauss's treatment of myth.

Reconfiguring the human sciences

Lévi-Strauss's appeal went far beyond the boundaries of social anthropology, his nominal discipline. Methodologically, his work seemed to many to prefigure a new approach to the social sciences, one which promised to realise the goal of a rigorously formal, generalised methodology and even point the way towards the often longed-for mathematisation of social analysis. The equations and diagrams which littered his texts projected an image of a discipline in which formal, algebraic-type mathematics could be widely used, rather than the measurement-oriented quantitative maths which was more usually entertained as the key to making sociology a genuine science – though Lévi-Strauss is at pains to point out that his formulae and diagrams are not true mathematical ones. On a more substantive plane, Lévi-Strauss seemed to offer an approach to the analysis of cultural phenomena which could be applied to all the cultural products of humankind, including those of our own society and, for example, all artistic creations. For example, disciplines such as (indeed, particularly) literary criticism could apply his methods to the examination of poems and novels. Lévi-Strauss might not himself entirely approve of this suggestion, but it was none the less quite natural to think that if the underlying structures of culture were universal, the outgrowth of one and the same human mind/brain, then the methods of structuralist analysis should be generally applicable. At the same time, Lévi-Strauss retained Marxist elements in his thought, and was willing to think of his analyses of myth and other aspects of culture as contributions to the theory of the superstructure. An important element of his thought about myth was a direct borrowing from Marx, namely the idea that ideology attempts to overcome in thought, in theory, contradictions in the organisation of social life which cannot be overcome in reality, in practice.

Though Lévi-Strauss's own studies were directed towards analysis of rather esoteric phenomena, there was no reason in principle why the self-same methods could not be applied to looking at everyday cultural phenomena of our own societies. For example, things as diverse as food, fashion, wrestling or a newspaper photograph could be analysed *semiologically*, i.e. purely as a form of communication and as a system of signs. Thus Lévi-Strauss's structuralism initiated tendencies which were to lead eventually to the formation of what nowadays are known as cultural studies. Semiological ideas have had a major impact in this field, albeit in ways now quite far removed from Lévi-Strauss's original scheme. The leading figure in this development was another French intellectual, Roland Barthes.

Barthes: semiology and contemporary culture

The work of Roland Barthes (1915–86) is broadly divisible into two phases, an early structuralist one and a later poststructuralist one. In this chapter we focus upon the first, leaving his later works for the next chapter, where we discuss post-structuralism. Even in his early writings, however, there are indications that

Barthes himself was never wholly comfortable with the commitment to structuralist ideas; he displays a somewhat ambivalent attitude, being at once drawn to the idea of a remorselessly all-encompassing science and also somewhat repelled by it. In this respect, even Barthes's early writings have a somewhat schizophrenic character; there is a strong contrast between those with a theoretical, systematic, scientific cast to them, such as *Elements of Semiology* (1967), and those more fragmentary and essayist, such as *Mythologies* (1973). Barthes's later writings (see the next chapter) become progressively more literary and self-consciously experimental, e.g. *A Lover's Discourse* (1978) or *Roland Barthes by Roland Barthes* (1977b).

In his early, anthropological phase, Barthes brings structuralism home to the analysis of contemporary Western, particularly French, culture. As for Lévi-Strauss, for Barthes too Marxist assumptions are important to the whole picture of what he is doing, though whether he was, strictly speaking, a Marxist is one of the many questions about his work that remain unsettled. The Marxist influence is, if anything, more pronounced than in Lévi-Strauss, in that Barthes's early studies are devoted to the analysis of French bourgeois culture in a manner very much akin to that of *Ideologiekritik* as developed by, for example, the Frankfurt School, as we discussed in Chapter 8.

Also like Lévi-Strauss, Barthes draws his major inspiration from Saussure, who, as we noted earlier, had envisaged linguistics as a part of semiology, the general science of signs. In *Elements of Semiology*, Barthes presents his programme for such a science, based on the idea – which originates in Saussure – that the words of language are not the only things which comprise systems of signs. For example, the various activities of eating, wearing clothes, owning and driving a car, etc., can all be conceived as such systems. Barthes argues, however, that it is impossible to think of cultural systems such as those of dress, dining, motoring and so forth independently of language (certainly in Western society). For example, part of the point of fashion (a topic to which Barthes eventually devoted a whole book [1985]) is to be talked and written about; therefore the account of language must be most general and inclusive. On that basis, Barthes proposed to develop the science of semiology to give central emphasis to language in accordance with the general *linguistic turn*, i.e. the emphasis on the importance, indeed centrality, of language which is such a strong feature of post-war Western thought, and certainly crucial for subsequent poststructuralist developments.

Mythologies of culture

The investigation of semiology was, however, interwoven with the considerations of ideology. A significant difference between Barthes and Lévi-Strauss is marked by their very different uses of the notion of myth. As we have seen, Lévi-Strauss was concerned with myth as a distinctive feature of so-called primitive societies; for him, myths are means by which pre-literate peoples utilise the world around them to build complex structures of thought concerned with universal human problems. While retaining the idea of myths as constructs, Barthes employs myth in more Marxian-oriented terms:

Barthes and myth

Myths are patterns of cultural activities and ideas which have a fundamentally ideological character, in that their function (in part, at least) is to obscure reality, by conveying a sense of naturalness about things which are integral to one particular cultural configuration, that of modern, bourgeois society.

Barthes's starting point, he declaimed, was a

> feeling of impatience at the sight of the 'naturalness' with which newspapers, art and common sense constantly dress up a reality which, even though it is the one we live in, is undoubtedly determined by history . . . I resented seeing Nature and History confused at every turn, and I wanted to track down, in the decorative display of *what-goes-without-saying*, the ideological abuse which, in my view, is hidden there.
>
> (1973: 11)

His purpose, then, was to reveal the extent things presented by the culture as purely natural were instead – or at least, were also – cultural phenomena: their representation as natural was, in important part, *mis*representation. Thus something as seemingly natural as eating and drinking was not to be seen as that alone, for eating and drinking are also meaningful, with the eating and drinking of certain kinds of things functioning as a sign. Thus one can examine eating and drinking (or the wearing of clothes) not only from its practical point of view, but also as a process of communication, and therefore as the functioning of a system of signs along the lines of the dichotomously contrastive mode stemming from Saussure. For example, Barthes emphasised the extent to which the drinking of wine is, in the first instance, associated with French identity. He described wine as 'the totem drink' (1973: 58) which provides the basis for French morality, in the sense that knowing how to drink wine is the mark of an admirable, controlled and sociable individual; it is integral to all the ceremonial activities of French life, large and small. At the same time, however, he points out that the admirable and agreeable features attributed to wine are also the product of French capitalism and its exploitative nature, involving, for example, the appropriation of Muslim lands in North Africa for a product for which the Muslims themselves have no use. As for steak and chips, the steak is a prestige food, associated with strength, whose eating can, for example, 'redeem' the effete character of intellectuals, make them seem more earthy and worthy people; the eating of steak and chips is (or was) associated with French 'national glamour'.

According to Barthes, the role of myth is to naturalise, to make things which are contingent and historical seem necessary and eternal, to make things, which could have been different and which may have their roots in dubious circumstances, seem as though they could not be otherwise, as though they are entirely innocent, i.e. entirely beneficent and harmless in their nature. Remember, the emphasis upon the character of wine, its fine and improving nature, makes people forget – in the sense of disregard – the fact that the wine itself is created through unequal and exploitative relations. In more of Barthes's own words, myth

> abolishes the complexity of human acts, it gives them the simplicity of essences, it does away with all dialectics, with any going back beyond what was immediately visible, it organises a world without depth, a world wide open and wallowing in the evident, it establishes a blissful clarity: things appear to mean something by themselves.
>
> (1973: 143)

In modern societies, then, the role of myth is to depoliticise, to present things in a way which can be taken-for-granted, simply and naively accepted as the way they must be, obscuring the fact that these things might, if seen in their full, complex and historical character, be recognised to be more equivocal and contested than they are seen to be. In this way, Barthes connects structuralism with themes which had been developed as part of *Ideologiekritik* (see Chapter 8); they have now become staple elements in cultural analysis across a whole range of social scientific disciplines.

Prisoners of language

In subsequent works, one of Barthes's principal targets was the literary style of realism, which seeks to present itself as though it is not a style at all but simply a natural way of writing.

Realism as ideological

Realism is essentially ideological in that it seems to portray how things really are in the world, merely providing a window on the world; i.e. the written text is like the pane of glass in the window, something which is looked through and disregarded for the purpose of seeing something beyond it. Realist writings thus are apt to deny their own status as involving a style. Style is thought of as something ornamental, to be attended to in reading for its own sake, for its own decorative qualities; and thus realist writings insist that the writing is of no interest in itself, that it is merely a functional vehicle for the relating of the facts. On the contrary,

---

Barthes counters that realism is no less a style of writing than any other, there is no such thing as prose which purely states the fact, and supposedly realist texts are, in fact, complex composites of literary style.

The grand master of realism in nineteenth-century French literature was Honoré de Balzac, and it is, therefore, certainly no coincidence that, in his book *S/Z* (1975a), Barthes subjects one of Balzac's short stories (which concerns two main characters, Sarrasine and Zambinella – hence Barthes's title) to a most detailed and extensive literary analysis, the intention being to reveal that this ostensibly realist tale is, in fact, constituted out of no fewer than five stylistic codes which serve to structure the story, creating suspense in the reader. They enable the invocation of references to, for example, locations in ways which make those references not merely the names of places but also symbolic of certain sorts of things, e.g. as, today, a reference to 'Hollywood' is much more than the mere mention of a place's name. The codes enable the building up of a thematic pattern in the story and the episodic structuring of the story into different sequences. Finally, the code which draws upon what is known in common, the common sense of the culture, serves to anchor – to secure – the story's conviction, attaining the reader's consent to aspects of the telling which hinge upon being known to be so because everyone knows that they are. Hence far from being a neutral medium through which reality is portrayed, the story is a complex contrivance, something which achieves its character as a transparent, style-free portrayal of 'reality as it is' through being a dense and elaborate construction out of stylistic elements.

In a less literary context, namely, the case of media coverage of the Tour de France, which is ostensibly the simple reporting of an actual event, Barthes argues that the coverage is in fact shaped by the way it draws upon a quite traditional literary form – the epic. For Barthes, then, the difference is not between those writings which are without style and merely report the facts, and those which involve an eye-catching, attention-attracting style. The contrast is, rather, between two different styles, which he terms 'the readerly' and 'the writerly'. The prime difference is in the relation the text has to its readership, whether – in the former case – it is written to be easy to read, making the reader into someone passive, a mere recipient of the message that the text delivers to him or her (many popular novels are obvious examples of this style), or whether the text is written in a way which demands a contribution of the reader, making the reader into an active participant in the reading and virtually transforming the reader into a writer, i.e. the reader has to put a lot of effort into reading, into figuring out what the text is saying, what the story is and so on. In short, the reader in the latter case has to make a contribution in determining how the text is to be read. Equally plainly this characteristic pertains to many so-called literary novels. For a simple example, the British writer B.S. Johnson published one of his novels (1969) in a box as a collection of separately printed chapters, with no indication of an order in which to read them; it was necessary for the reader to make a decision about the order, to work out for himself or herself whether there was any correct order for reading. Barthes, of course, approves of the writerly kind of writing, for it means that the text draws attention to itself, provides a perpetual reminder of the fact that it is a contrivance, thereby inhibiting any falling back into the illusion that one is looking through a window on to an external reality.

Barthes is arguing, in respect of literature (and, by implication, of all other kinds of texts, however non-literary they may be regarded as being), that there is no such thing as an authentically realist writing which provides unvarnished reports of 'the facts'. For all writing carries with it, and is made out of, the cultural codes under which it is produced. It therefore inevitably absorbs the real world into these codes in ways which cannot be extricated from one another. More generally, then, Barthes is sounding the theme of *prisoners of language*.

Prisoners of language

This is the suggestion that we can never know reality in itself, for our only access to it is through the cultural schemes (particularly the codes) which we have. It is impossible to represent (describe or otherwise portray) reality independently of those codes, for any representation must be done in terms of them.

Hence Barthes needs to subvert these modes of representation – not merely written, but also in the form of activities or artefacts, such as wrestling or the Eiffel tower – which seek to present themselves as natural, as simply given in reality. After all, he argues, we could not make contact with them at all except through our cultural code.

This theme of 'prisoners of language' is an important element in the epistemological/methodological travails of recent sociology. In shifting towards the critique of language and the idea of representation associated with language, Barthes was moving in the direction of poststructuralism; therefore we will take up his work again in that context in the next chapter.

Althusser: Marxism as science

The third major figure in the structuralist period was Louis Althusser (1918–90). However, Althusser was not really connected with structuralism in the sense in which Lévi-Strauss and Barthes were, i.e. engaged in applying the underlying idea of structural linguistics to the analysis of social forms. In his writings, which we briefly discussed in Chapter 1, Althusser was much more concerned with redefining the contemporary understanding of Marx. He did, as we mentioned, share the anti-humanist perspective displayed by Lévi-Strauss and Barthes, perhaps possessing it more strongly, but his primary concern was to establish and explicate the correctness of the theories to be found in Marx's late writings.

Althusser's work is essentially centred upon the problem of the relation between base and superstructure in Marx, involving him in two main, though interrelated, operations. One is establishing *the* correct reading of Marx, making an identification of what, in Marx's own writings, are ideas essential to Marxism, as well as what is properly Marxist in the writings of his successors. The other is to amplify the properly Marxist things that Marx had said, particularly in respect of the understanding of how economic and ideological elements figure in the understanding of society.

Unlike the case with Barthes, there are no equivocations in Althusser's commitment to the idea of science. His work depends on his assumption that Marxism (whatever it is) is a correct – indeed, is the first and paramount – science of *social formations*, i.e. of societies. However, though Marx may have created this science, he had not perhaps always been fully aware of what he was doing, and his writings, both early and late, are admixtures of scientific and ideological elements. For Althusser, there is a complete break between science and ideology; they are two distinct things. We can only establish a science (something which is true) by entirely breaking with ideology. It cannot be the case, therefore, that we can create a science by continuing and developing something with an ideological nature.

Consequently, Marx could not have developed his science on the basis of Hegel's philosophy, as many have argued, increasingly so at the time Althusser began to publish. Hegel's philosophy is ideology and Marx had made the transition to science, therefore Marx must have made a complete break with Hegel. But Marx's early writings were very much a continuation of Hegelian themes, and therefore Marx must have broken also and equally completely with his own early writings.

The break between early and late Marx

The break does not involve rejecting the kinds of answers which a Hegelian would give to Hegel's problems and substituting a different kind of answer. The break must be complete and it must, therefore, involve rejecting even the questions that Hegel asked: in Althusser's word, installing a completely new *problematic*.

On this basis, Althusser devotes much effort to locating the point in Marx's career at which the break was made, but the intricacies of this operation need not concern us here; it is sufficient to say that the scientific content of Marx's thought is to be found in the late writings, particularly in the volumes of *Capital* (e.g. 1976). Indeed, Althusser eventually came to the point at which the only writings of Marx he could find to be *totally and definitively exempt* from any trace of Hegelian influence were two very short and, otherwise, comparatively minor pieces: the *Critique of the Gotha Programme* and *Marginal Notes on Wagner* (Althusser 1971: 90).

Two things in particular about the Hegelian tradition were anathema to Althusser: (1) its humanism and (2) its notion of the social whole as an expressive totality. Althusser's objection to both can be seen to originate in his opposition to *essentialism*, i.e. the idea that there is a specific nature to an object (or phenomenon), an essence. The essence of a thing is the basis on which the object is to be explained and is an assumption crucial in Hegel. For example, the Hegelian account of historical development treated the mind as the essence of human beings, and therefore treated the history of human thought as the development, the realisation, of that human essence. Relatedly, Hegel treated any given period of history, and the organisation of a society, as a complex but internally unified thing made up of distinct parts, each of which was, however, an expression of some central theme or element. In Hegel's case, of course, a given historical period was an expression of the stage of development which the human mind (or spirit, as he would term it) had achieved, so that all aspects of life and thought were pervaded by the same kind of self-awareness. The level of self-awareness reached by the human mind, together with the intellectual dilemmas in which it was necessarily entrapped, provided the basic principle (or centre) on which the whole historical epoch and its societies were organised.

Althusser's position was a reaction to the extensive attachment of much of twentieth-century European Marxism to a Hegelian interpretation of Marx, which insisted on interpreting all his thought in terms of the (Hegelian inspired) humanism so fully expressed in his early writings. This interpretation of Marx emphasised and celebrated certain of his remarks, such as that human beings were the creators of their own history albeit not in circumstances of their own choosing. On this assertion, the history that people made was to be understood as the development or realisation of human potential through the material transformation – by means of productive activity – of their world.

Also in accord with Hegelian conceptions, Marx's conception of society and its development would be conceived as an expressive totality, unified by the principle of economic determinism, by the idea that the rest of society was shaped by the influence/need of its economic structure. Apparently, this assumption was the basis for Marx's base–superstructure theory and relatedly of the notion of ideology. Althusser's counter to this Hegelian interpretation involved reconsidering the nature of the relationship between base and superstructure and formulating a conception of ideology certainly very different to that usually attributed to Marx.

The notion of base and superstructure as it is often interpreted in Marx is an instance of the conception of expressive totality. Society is a complex, differentiated structure, but it is organised around a unifying principle, i.e. the determination of other forms of social organisation by the economy. Although a society involves not just economic institutions, but also political, religious, educational and other ones, they are all to be understood as expressions of the needs of the economy. They arise in response to the requirements of the economic structure to perpetuate itself, and thus create and recreate the legal, political and other conditions essential to its continued operation. For example, religious doctrines, political beliefs and legal conceptions come to be understood as ideological in the sense of being false conceptions which play the role of justifying or otherwise facilitating the operations of the economy, of reconciling those within the society to its ways, which they would have occasion to question and perhaps overthrow if they were not misled about their true character.

For Althusser, this conception of the social whole (or, in his terms, 'formation') is much too simplifying. It goes against obvious facts about society such as the features of the superstructure being not only, and certainly not simply, functions of the organisation of the economy. The notion that the economic base determines the superstructure involves an overly coherent conception of the society. Society is indeed a unity of some kind, but it is not unified with all of the parts being an expression of a single basic principle or influence. It cannot be so, because historical events such as the transformation of a social formation, e.g. from feudalism to capitalism, do not derive from one single cause but require many different causes – what Althusser terms an '*over-determination*'. That the Russian Revolution took place was in important part due to the weakened and dissaffected state of the army after prolonged warfare – among other causes – and not due to the development of the economy alone.

Althusser's key concepts

In developing this argument, Althusser attempts a delicate balancing act between relaxing the principle that the economy determines the rest of the social whole, on the one hand, and yet retaining the idea that the economy does exercise more than just a contingently causal role, on the other, since to abandon the economy's critical role would destroy virtually everything distinctive to Marx's thought. He attempts this balancing act through three notions:

1   the economy as *determinant in the last instance*;
2   the social formation as a *structure in dominance*;
3   the relation between parts of the society as being one of *relative autonomy*.

Together, these ideas constitute the core of Althusser's theoretical stance.

Althusser maintains that a general truth about the shape of societies is indeed their dependence upon the development of the economic base (point 1 above): if production in a given society were not organised in that way, then it would not be the same society, and the whole would not be structured like that. Consequently, the role of the economy is to be considered more fundamental than the other parts, not just as one part of society amongst others. However, there is no simple formula for deriving the organisation of the rest of society from the nature of the economy, or for deriving or explaining most, let alone all, features of the other parts of society by the influence of the economy.

Neither should it be supposed that within any given society the economy will necessarily be the dominating segment of its organisation. The idea of structure in dominance (point 2 above) refers to the tendency in any given society for one element to dominate, one set of institutions to prevail over and control other sectors of the society. Thus the social formation is a complex interplay of structures, but it has a dominant element, which is not necessarily – is not, in fact, even commonly – the economy. For example, in many societies in Western Europe, and for a long time, religion was the dominant force in society, and the Church was the institution which prevailed over all others, even over monarchs.

The social whole is a complex structure, as it is composed of different elements – economic structure, political structure and so on – each having its own different requirements and its own history and rate of development. These different sectors change, but they do not automatically change together in close conjunction and at the same pace. The recognition of this fact is termed the 'relative autonomy' of structures within the social formation (point 3 above).

Relative autonomy

This allows that, say, parliamentary arrangements can arise in different ways; their development has its own kinds of preconditions, which have nothing specifically to do with the state of the economic structure of the society. However, the autonomy is *relative*. It should be compared to the simplistic idea (in Althusser's judgement) that the structure of the society as a whole is a straightforward function of the economy's own development. But it can only be relative, given the notion of the economy playing the role of determinant in the last instance.

This point is anything but minor; without this idea Althusser's Marxism would hardly qualify as Marxist at all. If he were saying only that the different structures of society interact with one another, each possibly and certainly occasionally, exercising causal influence on the others, with causal effects between them being frequently reciprocal, then his position would amount to a version of Marxism which would differ not at all from the platitudes of sociology generally. Hence his insistence that the economy is not just one structure among others, composing society and causally interacting with other structures. Instead, it is *primus inter pares* (first among equals). Thus Althusser differs from those he criticises by arguing that the economy does not directly determine the form of other structures within society; their form depends in part upon the nature of their own internal development and upon the ways they interact with one another, i.e. they have autonomy from economic determination. He does, however, set limits to its extent and to the conditions which determine how independent of the economy some other structures can be. In this way, the nature of the economy can determine the dominant element in a social formation; it may be the economy which is to be dominant or it may be some other component.

The development and workings of the social formation are to be understood in terms of *structural causality*.

Structural causality

This was meant to emphasise that the determination of the form and development of a social formation and its constituent parts was a phenomenon in its own right, not something that could be understood in (so to speak) a bottom-up way, i.e. arising from the intentions and actions of individuals.

Althusser's anti-humanism was resolute; the minimal constituents of social structures were the positions and relationships, e.g. the positions of worker and manager and the relation of employer–employee, prescribed by the structure, in this case the economy. Actual individuals are of no significance in Althusser's theory; they are merely the occupants of these positions, the bearers of their responsibilities. Althusser would argue that he is not displaying his own theoretical predilection in respect of capitalism; it is capitalism itself which has reduced people to the merely incidental occupants of the positions and relations it prescribes, ensuring that it does not matter whether one person rather than another occupies and fulfils the requirements of a given position; all that matters is that someone does.

Rather than the structures of the social formation being created by individuals, it is the other way around; the individuals are mere products of the society.

Individualism as ideology

Once again, in the argument we have met often before in the French tradition, the idea of 'the individual', so often the foundation for attempts at social theory, can be seen as an ideological construction, the product of a specific period and its culture. As signalled at the outset of this section, Althusser declares this idea to be a part of bourgeois ideology. The reciprocal of this argument is, of course, that ideology (bourgeois or otherwise) cannot be a product of individuals.

Ideology as structure

Althusser generates a revisionist – what he would call 'authentically Marxist' – account of ideology. Ideology is often thought of as created by particular individuals or groups and serves as a means of communication and persuasion, whereby those individuals or groups induce others to believe certain things, thereby duping them into accepting otherwise unacceptable conditions. On Althusser's terms, this account cannot be correct, for it underestimates the extent to which ideology is structured; it is not what individuals think so much as something that individuals think in terms of. Language provides a model here. Individuals communicate with one another in a language and may persuade one another through such communication, yet we do not suppose that they contrive the language that they speak. In the same way, though individuals may think in an ideology, they do not contrive it. Furthermore, actual individuals are not aware of the extent to which their own existence as 'individuals' is drawn from ideology.

Althusser shares the standard Marxist view that ideology and science are counterposed and Marxist science is a critique of ideology, but he does not draw the usual conclusion, namely that science can result in the abolition of ideology. It cannot do so because science is not an adequate basis on which practical life can be conducted. Science is a purely specialised pursuit with an entirely impersonal point of view; it cannot, therefore, be used as the basis for someone's personal view of her or his situation and of its practical requirements. There is no room in science for a personal point of view. Further, science is purely concerned with the pursuit of knowledge, but a person's conduct in society also has many practical concerns; what is required for her or him cannot be derived from the theory of science. Since the only alternative to science is ideology, then life in society necessarily requires it. As Althusser suggests, in every society people must be shaped, reshaped and equipped to respond to the demands of their conditions of existence. Since this demand cannot be met by scientific theory it must be fulfilled by ideology. However, under conditions of relative autonomy the particular forms which individuality will take vary across the different spheres of the social formation.

On the other hand, while there may be varying ways for individuality to develop (because of relative autonomy), none the less, in a capitalist society ideology must serve to ensure the reproduction of the conditions of capitalist economic production (because of determination in the last instance). Thus ideology is structured, albeit in different ways and to different degrees, around the general requirements of the economy. Althusser argues that, in a modern society, it is achieved through *ideological state apparatuses* (ISAs).

The traditional Marxist theory of the state has treated it as a means of achieving domination for a given, ruling class within the society as an instrument of class power and, therefore, as primarily a repressive agency, capable of resort to violence in order to keep things under control. However, the needs of the reproduction of capitalist conditions of production require that the subordinate classes be equipped with the skills requisite to their work, and also with the attitudes and outlook which will make them well-behaved and compliant participants in the productive process. Consequently, control of the society cannot be simply on the basis of the threat – and sometimes the actual use – of physical coercion alone. It must involve control of the mind, i.e. hegemony, as Gramsci termed it. Althusser's distinctive move is to propose that the *state* achieves hegemony, by two means: through coercion but also through ideological control. The state consists in two distinct (though, of course, related) apparatuses: the *repressive apparatus* (the police and armed forces particularly, under the single, central direction of the political authorities) and the *ideological apparatus* (a heterogeneous assortment of social forms not united under any central direction).

Ideological state apparatuses

The list of ISAs which Althusser provides is:

- the educational system;
- the family;
- the legal system;
- the political system;
- the trade unions;
- the mass media;
- the cultural domain and leisure spheres.

They are clearly a mixed bag, involving very varied activities, and there is certainly autonomy amongst them, i.e. they have their own independent, internal developmental tendencies. However, Althusser makes two general points about them:

1   The autonomy is, again, only relative, and the heterogeneity of the assorted ISAs is quite superficial, for they all operate under and emanate a single ideology, that of the ruling class.
2   These seemingly independent spheres of social life have in common the crucial fact that they are all part of the state apparatus.

We might think that claim (2) is odd: while we count the government, its police and army, and its civil service bureaucracy as part of the state, we would not normally count the family or the trade unions as such. For Althusser, it manifests perfectly how we are captured by the ruling ideology – the bourgeois ideology. After all, this separation of the state and these other spheres is founded on the distinction between public and private sectors, which is internal to bourgeois ideology and therefore dispensable from any Marxist theory.

Not only does relative autonomy figure in Althusser's formulation of the ISAs but so, too, does the notion of dominance. Not all ISAs are equal. In a given social formation, there will be some – in the cases he discusses, a pair – of ISAs which are dominant. In the Middle Ages, it was the church and family which were the dominant ISAs, and in capitalist society it is the education and family pairing which has replaced them. If we take the governmental arrangements of democratic parliamentarism to be the dominant ISA, we might not think that this latter point is so, but we would be wrong. Modern history has shown that democratic parliamentarism is by no means essential to capitalism, which has proved itself to be compatible with quite other types of governmental arrangement. Althusser briefly states the essence of his argument on behalf of the dominant position of 'the school' over the other ISAs, which also instil the appropriate capitalistic attitudes: 'no other ideological State apparatus has the obligatory (and not least free) audience of the totality of the children in the capitalist social formation, eight hours a day for five or six days out of seven' (Lenin and Philosophy, 148).

For Althusser, then, ideology shapes who and what we are as members of society. Our whole existence in society, lived as it is in and through participation in the various ideological apparatuses, is permeated with ideology. In Althusser's conception, ideology is equivalent to what in other, non-Marxist traditions would be called *socialisation*. Little wonder, then, that capitalism has proved so resilient as a system. It is built into each of us at an early age and reinforced in all aspects of our daily existence. Such an all-encompassing view of ideology inevitably led to complaints that Althusser's conception left no space to develop opposition to the status quo. If ideology is built so deeply into the structures of social existence, if, indeed, it is the thing underpinning them, if it is itself the foundational structure, then what has become of the idea of resistance? These concerns, perhaps more than other more philosophical objections to Althusser's structuralism, had the effect of creating disenchantment and paving the way to poststructuralism (see next chapter). If this was what Marxism had come to, arguably its usefulness as a critique of society was outlived.

Conclusion

Structuralism played a powerful part in reorienting Anglo-American sociology towards European social thought, and also in breaking down disciplinary barriers, in so far as the structuralist method, originating in anthropology and linguistics, appeared to be a means of analysing cultural phenomena generally (with a specially strong influence on literary work, where 'theory' was to become a key term as a result). Combined with the influence of Western Marxism's concern with cultural hegemony, structuralism's nature as a form of cultural analysis heavily shifted interests towards the analysis of what were, in Marxist terms, superstructural phenomena. A little like Talcott Parsons, however, structuralism will, perhaps, be more influential in terms of the effects of the reaction against it, rather than through its positive achievements. Poststructuralism (whose name reflects the fact that it does follow from, and owe some of its ideas to, structuralism) now exercises a much greater and more far-reaching influence on contemporary thought than structuralism ever attained, and whilst there are continuities between them, these are minor relative to the differences.

Questions

1. What is structuralism? What contribution to it was made by (a) Saussure and (b) Freud?

2. How did Lévi-Strauss develop Durkheim's concept of totemism? Why does he lay such stress on it?

3. 'The stress on the unconscious calls for a new approach to the study of society.' Discuss with particular reference to Lévi-Strauss's treatment of myths as a system of signs.

4. Compare and contrast Lévi-Strauss's binary oppositions with Marx's and Hegel's dialectic as critiques of traditional logic.

5. How does Barthes's use of the concept of myth differ from that of Lévi-Strauss?

6. Discuss Barthes's view that realism is always ideological.

7. Argue for and against, the case that we are all prisoners of language.

8. Why is Althusser so anxious to separate the early and the late Marx? Analyse the problematic that he claims to find in the late Marx.

9. Evaluate the claim that the economic base has relative autonomy.

10. Outline Althusser's argument that the individual is an ideological construct. How does it compare with similar views by other thinkers you have encountered in this book?

Further reading

Althusser, L. 1969, *For Marx*. Allen Lane. Gives his arguments about the proper understanding of Marx's theory.

—— 1971, *Lenin and Philosophy*. New Left Books. Includes the key essay 'Ideology and ideological state apparatuses'.

Badcock, C., 1975, *Lévi-Strauss, Structuralism and Social Theory*. Hutchinson. Gives a general account and connects structuralism to issues in social theory.

Barthes, R., 1973, *Mythologies*. Granada. A very readable collection of short writings.

—— 1977, *Image, Music, Text*. Fontana. A selection of early essays.

Benton, T., 1984, *The Rise and Fall of Structural Marxism*. Macmillan. Explains and appraises Althusser's thought.

Callinicos, A., 1976, *Althusser's Marxism*. Pluto Press. A good introduction.

Clarke, S., 1981, *The Foundations of Structuralism*. Harvester. A general and critical account.

Culler, J., 1976, *Saussure*. A brief introduction.

—— 1990, *Barthes*. Fontana. A good introduction.

Elliott, G., 1987, *Althusser: The Detour of Theory*. Verso. A more advanced discussion.

Freud, S., 1971, *Introductory Lectures on Psycho-Analysis*. Penguin. A key source.

—— 1986, *The Essentials of Psycho-Analysis*. Penguin. Another good introduction.

Glucksmann, M., 1974, *Structural Analysts in Contemporary Thought*. Routledge. A general and critical account of structuralism.

Harris, R., 1987, *Reading Saussure: A Commentary on the Cours de Linguistique Génerale*. Duckworth. A more substantial introduction.

Jenkins, A., 1979, *The Social Theory of Claude Lévi-Strauss*. Macmillan. A fuller account.

Leach, E., 1974, *Lévi-Strauss*. Fontana. A concise and sympathetic introduction.

Lévi-Strauss, C., 1962, *Totemism*. Pelican. A very short book, arguing against Durkheim on totemism.

—— 1978, *Myth and Meaning*. Schocken Books. A very brief and popularised statement of his ideas on myth.

—— 1987, *Anthropology and Myth: Lectures, 1951–82*. Blackwell. Summarises some of the content of the massive, four-volume *Mythologiques* (1970, 1973, 1978a, 1981).

—— 1988, *The Jealous Potter*. University of Chicago Press. A small companion study to the main work on myth.

—— 1995, *The Story of Lynx*. University of Chicago Press. Another companion study.

Pace, D., 1983, *Claude Lévi-Strauss: Bearer of Ashes*. Routledge. Paints a general picture.

Smith, S., 1984, *Reading Althusser*. Cornell University Press. A readable account.

Wollheim, R., 1991, *Freud*. 2nd edn. Fontana. An excellent introduction to his thought.

■   ■   ■

Part four

Chapter 10

Poststructuralism: abandoning reason

Introduction: background and some provisos

In Chapter 1 we mentioned the way the critique of capitalism gave way to a critique of the culture of modern society and, eventually, to a condemnation of one particular but very prominent and influential aspect of it, the so-called Enlightenment project, i.e. the aspiration of bringing people to freedom through the use of reason. Poststructuralism has put the challenge to the Enlightenment at the centre of contemporary debate, and stated a most thoroughgoing scepticism about reason.

Previously we mentioned the Frankfurt School's doubts about the legacy of the Enlightenment, pointing out its position is ambivalent. It critiques the idea of reason enshrined in the institutions of industrial society because these realisations amount to perversions and corruptions of reason, rather than because any appeal to reason is intrinsically suspect. Thus its position has an optimistic aspect, in the sense that if only some effective means can be found to expose the falsity of the intellectual foundations of the prevailing institutions, then there is at least the prospect of reconstructing society along different lines, i.e. on the basis of genuine rationality and freedom. With the poststructuralists, however, the critique of the Enlightenment is radicalised; they replace the ambivalence towards reason displayed by the Frankfurt School with outright rejection. Poststructuralism expunges all traces of such optimism.

In order to understand the character of this scepticism we need to examine the intellectual foundations of poststructuralism, in particular its relationship with structuralism, out of which it developed and in relation to which its view of language was forged. Before doing so, however, a word of caution is necessary. Giving any general characterisation of poststructuralism is problematic for two reasons. First, the poststructuralist movement is anything but unified. Indeed, several of those most prominently associated with it, whose ideas we discuss below, have expressed their reluctance to accept the label. They have complained of being lumped together with other thinkers with whose thought they see no strong affinity. For example, Michel Foucault was uneasy about the classification of his early work as 'structuralist' and his later work as 'poststructuralist', and he and Jacques Derrida, another poststructuralist, by no means always see eye to eye. These complaints alert us to the fact that there are significant differences among the positions of those conventionally assigned the label 'poststructuralist', and that in giving a general characterisation of poststructuralism we can do little more than identify a set of themes, some broadly shared, but others understood quite differently by different thinkers.

Second, more difficulties stem from the complex, unconventional and often elusive nature of poststructuralist arguments themselves. Poststructuralists often defy the usual conventions of academic/scientific discourse, intending their work directly to challenge these, but there can be much – even calculated – ambiguity about the extent to which they have withdrawn from these conventions. Just how radical poststructuralist positions actually are is also ambiguous since they are sometimes presented as though they are quite extreme, and at other times are set out in a much more moderate way. For poststructuralists themselves, ambiguities and inconsistencies in their own ideas do not necessarily count against them. They are disdainful of scientific aspiration and academic convention. After all, they are engaged in a profound critique of reason with its demands for logic and system; rather than comply with those demands, they resist them, embracing, even cultivating ambiguity, contradiction and paradox. In this way, poststructuralism disarms its critics by celebrating inconsistency.

With these provisos to the fore, we sketch the origins of the poststructuralist movement. It was another predominantly Parisian development, which both reacted against structuralism and also, in important respects, grew out of it. In the earlier part of their careers, two prominent poststructuralist thinkers, Roland Barthes and Michel Foucault, had structuralist allegiances, seeking in some ways to take the structuralist arguments to their extreme. That is not to say that they were taken to their logical conclusions, since taking them to that extreme involves going beyond their logical limits, even into paradox.

The debt to Nietzsche

As mentioned in Chapter 1, following the failure of Marxists such as Althusser to give a positive lead in the disturbances of 1968, thinkers like Foucault and Derrida repudiated Marx's work as a basis for their own efforts. (Derrida has recently been pointing out, in response to criticisms of his work as apolitical in nature, that he has always had an affinity with Marx's views.) Despite the emphasis upon the determination of people's conduct by social forces of which they were not aware (through the workings of ideology), Marx had remained an Enlightenment-minded figure in that he had retained his faith in the value of conscious, rational thought to overcome the domination of these unconscious determinants. Reason alone could not emancipate humankind – Marx's rejection of Hegel was in no small part due to Hegel's assumption that it could – but reason could guide effective class action to deliver this result. Though acclaimed for his contribution to the discovery of unconscious forces in human life, Marx was now being criticised for underestimating the extent to which such unconscious forces pervaded it, and could not be overcome.

The rejection of Marx, however, did not represent a step towards the reduction in the dependence of contemporary social thought upon nineteenth-century theory. Another nineteenth-century thinker, Friedrich Nietzsche (1844–1900), was assigned the tutelary role which Marx had previously occupied.

239

Nietzsche had much more profound doubts about the nature and capacities of reason, and the significance of modern civilisation, than did Marx.

Nietzsche's primary importance in relation to poststructuralism is in terms of his attack upon the spirit of modern civilisation, i.e. that of the nineteenth century in Western Europe. Nietzsche referred to his work as 'philosophy with a hammer' to indicate that the task he had set himself was substantially destructive: to tear down the two 'false gods' of religion and reason. In Nietzsche's opinion, the culture of Western civilisation had become sterile and oppressive, making individuals living under it timid, unadventurous and repressed creatures. Nietzsche blamed Christianity for teaching people to be meek, compliant and dependent. Human nature had two conflicting sides. One, the wilder, uncivilised side, is instinctive, impulsive and undisciplined, but also vigorous and strong. Nietzsche termed it the *Dionysian* element, naming it after the Greek god of drunkenness. The other, contrasting side of human nature, however, is the *Apollonian* (after Apollo, a Greek sun god of great beauty); it is concerned with discipline, control, order and form, but is also insipid and constricting. One of these sides – the Apollonian – had markedly gained the upper hand in the nineteenth-century West, an unhealthy situation for civilisation and culture.

For Nietzsche, the great prestige accorded to reason at that time and in that place was a perfect symptom of the dominance of the Apollonian outlook; reason was conceived as the apogee of discipline, control, restraint and neat and tidy order, yet it was neither so valuable nor so beneficial as it was made out to be. Rather than being the fullest and most extensive fulfilment of the capacities of the human mind, reason obstructed its most adventurous, creative, imaginative and powerful uses, which could only be released if the Dionysian side were to be given much greater rein. Within modern society, the representative figures were business people and scientists, who were dull, uninspiring and unimpressive people in comparison with the great and heroic achievers of earlier civilisations.

In short, the vaunting of reason was a matter of self-deception. The point about the predominance of the Apollonian mode was not merely that it sought to contain the impulsive, Dionysian side, whose anarchic spirit would threaten to destroy the structures of order and discipline that had been developed, but it also sought to deny the very existence of this element of human nature. It would not admit that human beings have these two sides, and that the expression of the Dionysian qualities is essential to a healthy situation. The mind was elevated over the body, and the culture of nineteenth-century Western Europe would not allow that people have more physical, earthy, animal urges and needs which also call for satisfaction, as well as the need to satisfy their 'higher' intellectual powers. The picture of human beings painted in that culture was one-sided in ruling out the existence of the Dionysian aspect. However, the fact that the culture would not admit to its existence did not mean it had ceased to exist, for human beings continued to have the same two-sided nature. It did mean, though, that the outlet for the impulsive, wayward side of individuals could not be open and direct.

> # The will to power
>
> For Nietzsche, the roots of individual motivation were in what he termed 'the *will to power*', i.e. in the instinctive human drives to grow, to develop in strength and potency, and to be increasingly powerful and dominant. This will to power was the natural, biologically rooted source of all human activity and achievements – including those of reason itself – but its nature made it the sort of thing that contemporary culture could not acknowledge or approve.

The modern Western mind, i.e. that of Nietzsche's time, could not think of itself as driven by instinctual urges and was, therefore, unable to admit to itself the true nature of the underlying forces which propelled it. Therefore, the culture had to misrepresent itself as the product solely of the 'higher' mental powers, entirely dissociated from those 'lower' drives rooted in the animal nature of human beings (including, of course, the will to power). As a result, the culture it had created could, in more modern terms, be said to act as a rationalisation, i.e. explaining the nature of human beings, the ways their minds work and the reasons for their activities in a way which makes them seem better, more high minded, objective and public spirited than in truth they actually are. A rationalisation is sincerely given, but is false because the mind is divided against itself. In a situation in which the Apollonian inclination is so dominant, the suggestion that Dionysian tendencies have any contribution cannot be accepted, cannot be allowed to enter into conscious deliberation, cannot even be thought.

Thus reason commonly sets itself up as the pure product of its own operations, something created entirely out of the impartial, reflective and dispassionate desire to know, thereby setting itself out as entirely in opposition to passion and impulse. It was Nietzsche's intention to dispute this opposition.

Nietzsche's scepticism about the source and nature of reason as an expression of the will to power and as something which has been applied to achieve the subjugation of the more Dionysian side of human existence greatly influenced the poststructuralists. Far from regarding science as enabling the triumph of reason over unreason, of rational thought over unconscious processes, Nietzsche's approach encouraged the view that science is itself only one more manifestation of the unconscious, just another product of the will to power. Rather than being a vehicle for the emancipation of humanity, science, along with the heritage of Christianity, played the part of forming the docile, sheep-like character of people in modern society. This Nietzschean idea can be clearly seen in the work of Michel Foucault (see next chapter). Foucault adopts this view in stressing the extent to which social life involves the disciplining and suppression of the wilder, more disorderly aspects of human existence. In particular, his later work immensely emphasises how the growth of social scientific fields (such as psychiatry and criminology) has been interwoven with the development of complex administrative structures which make people docile and easily controlled by producing an elaborate and detailed set of techniques of social organisation.

From structuralism to poststructuralism

The difference between structuralism and poststructuralism can be (crudely) reduced to the following points.

Differences between structuralism and poststructuralism

- Poststructuralism abandons the scientific aspirations of its structuralist forebears,
- because it sees an insuperable paradox in providing a critique of the inescapable ideological contamination of language by means of that same ideologically contaminated language; with Althusser it sees (virtually) no means of escaping ideology.
- Poststructuralism adopts a conception of language as a species of power; its use inherently involves domination, which we may term 'the prison house of language' (cf. Jameson 1972). This expression is often used to convey the idea that people are unable to get outside of language in order to encounter and truly comprehend reality in itself and independently of all human preconceptions, but can only perceive it through the medium of language with its inbuilt preconceptions. This is certainly the case made by poststructuralists, but to this conception they add the idea that language is a vehicle of social control, i.e. the way it regulates people's thought serves the social purposes of regulation and domination.
- Consequently, poststructuralism develops an anarchist, rather than a Marxist, politics.

Everything is political

Politics is at the top of the poststructuralist agenda. As mentioned in Chapter 1, it involves the attempt to find an alternative way of criticising bourgeois culture from that provided from a Marxist basis. The difficulty the poststructuralists see (in parallel with the Frankfurt School: see Chapter 8) is that the relentless following out of structuralist arguments disables the prospects of oppositional thinking. At its core, the poststructuralist rejection of structuralism asserts the political character of everything, language most of all. By contrast, structuralism is perceived as having a comparatively apolitical stance. This arises directly out of structuralism's view of language. Poststructuralists like Barthes sought to solve the problem of how to retain structuralism's *anti-representational* view of language without succumbing to political quietude.

Representationalism

This is the label given to a traditional theory of language which, as we noted in the previous chapter, understands that the function of words is to name, or stand for, things. In this traditional view, language is understood quite literally to re-present, to enable us to make absent objects present to us, to enable us to speak of and relate to things even though they are not actually, physically there. On this theory, at the basis of language exists a connection between the linguistic (words) and the external to language (things).

The poststructuralists understand Saussure to have severed the tie between language and any world outside of language. His account features the signifier and the signified as only elements of the sign. The *signified* is the idea in the mind of the speaker, i.e. the concept associated with the *signifier*, which is the physical (aural or graphical) vehicle, e.g. a sound or letter. Some words *do* stand for things, but the relationship between the word and the thing it stands for is an arbitrary and conventional one. Hence, the relationship between words cannot reflect anything essential about the nature of external reality, and about the relations of the things that comprise it. It is, of course, the inherently essential nature of things that philosophers have (fruitlessly) sought to capture through language. The meaning of words is given through the organisation of the language itself, through the pattern of contrasts which makes up the system, and not by words' relationship to physical things, by their standing as names for things. Thus the nature of signs – which we will largely treat as words – is determined internally within the system of language; it has nothing to do with any external world outside language. From this view, the poststructuralists draw the epistemological conclusion: since language is not a vehicle of representation (there is no room for a representational function in Saussure's account) then it cannot be used to represent the external world. Hence it cannot be a basis for knowing the external world, for saying things about how the world truly is.

The problem with which poststructuralists grappled can be briefly stated as follows. If social reality is entirely constituted out of sign systems, then the idea that there can be any 'outside' to those sign systems ceases to have any meaning. Consequently, the idea that there can be any tension between the sign systems and reality itself disappears. By definition, sign systems cannot misrepresent reality, if reality consists in these sign systems. Nor can these sign systems operate repressively if there is nothing outside them to be repressed. Yet much criticism of capitalist society is based on the discrepancies between reality and its representation, between people's true needs and the ideologically instilled ones. The structuralists Lévi-Strauss and the early Barthes had many Marxist elements in their general social thought and were certainly inclined to criticise capitalist society, yet in terms of thoroughgoing structuralism, it seems that they were not entitled to do so. Persistence with the logic of structuralism seems to take away what was regarded as its point, namely, to critique bourgeois culture. After all, from this critical standpoint, there is no place outside society from which to criticise it.

Abandoning aspirations to science

Poststructuralists part company with the legacy of structuralism on another key point: the aspiration to scientific status. Like their structuralist forebears, post-structuralists reject humanism, insisting that the system of language operates independently of speakers' intent. Speakers may appear to be in control of the meaning of language, but in fact they are quite unconscious of the system of language within which their speaking takes place. Therefore they are essentially unaware of much that is going on when they speak. Hence language operates according to its own ways, beyond the conscious control of speakers.

The structuralists were certainly keen to deny significance to the *subject*, and talked about the structure of language operating according to its own laws, thereby emphasising their own allegiance to the project of achieving a scientific understanding of language and culture. Here the poststructuralists discerned a dilemma.

> ## The dilemma over science
>
> By continuing to aim to be scientists, the structuralists operate in defiance of Saussure's idea that language is not a vehicle of representation, yet the very idea of science is representationalist, i.e. it manifests the conviction that language can be used to re-present things outside itself. In short, the structuralists aim to talk about the external world which is inaccessible through language.

The poststructuralists resolve this paradox at the heart of structuralism by giving up on the idea of trying to be scientists. They regard the scientific pretensions of structuralism as yet another manifestation of the Enlightenment project; making a clean break with it involves abandoning such pretensions entirely.

The critique of representationalism and the rejection of scientism are linked moves. Structuralism failed to think through rigorously the ideological connections between language, representationalism and science. From its standpoint representationalism was treated simply as an incorrect theory, which would be replaced by a more adequately scientific understanding of language. Poststructuralism asserts a much stronger connection between language, representationalism and ideology. Representationalism is not just an incorrect theory but a master ideology which pervades language and shapes its use. The idea of representation, i.e. that language speaks about the external world, is so deeply rooted in language – and so interwoven with relationships of domination in society – that it is virtually inconceivable that its control can be entirely or even substantially evaded. Thus the ideology of representation is built into the whole way Western society is organised, so that people pick it up without its ever being explicitly or deliberately taught; it is not formulated or advanced by any group within society, and it is not a position espoused by any party as a political cause. Language is entirely saturated with this ideology, not merely contaminated by it; that it could be purged of ideological elements is not conceivable. Consequently, while it is essential to expose the falsity of representationalism wherever possible, it is hard to conceive how this ideology could be thoroughly eliminated. Ideology is the framework within which the individual thinks; it is imposed upon the individual through language. This view is much akin to Althusser's conception (see Chapter 9), though not necessarily in explicit alliance with it. Although his concept of ideology moves away from the traditional one in this respect, it was none the less used as part of the quite traditional contrast between ideology and science, which has now collapsed.

Far from being in stark contrast to it, science must be seen as a prime instance of ideology – indeed the leading exponent of the ideology of representation. The whole notion of science as capable of giving genuine knowledge of the nature of the external world, e.g. telling us how things are at the further end of the universe or down at the most inconceivably minute levels of matter, is entirely at odds with the idea that the external world is inaccessible to us, i.e. that words cannot really categorically capture reality. Thus science itself is one of the central candidates to be exposed as falsely presenting itself as representational. By the same token, those who make it their business to expose this falsity must themselves eschew any conception that what they do is any kind of scientific enterprise; despite continuities with structuralism, they must distance themselves from it. As Barthes put it:

> precisely because all thought about the historically intelligible is also a participation in that intelligibility, structural man is scarcely concerned to last; he knows that structuralism, too, is a certain form of the world, which will change with the world.
>
> (1972: 219–20)

The point, then, is to turn the arguments of structuralism against structuralism itself and to subject to analysis not only what are patently mythologies, but also what is ostensibly knowledge, including science.

The rejection of science is related to two other points on which poststructuralism differs from its structuralist parent. First, structuralism inclines too much towards one side of the traditional body–mind dichotomy, being *mentalistic*; it is an approach concerned with tracking the abstract, immaterial operations of the mind, and thereby excluding from its attention the physical, bodily existence of human beings and the material conditions of living. Second, structuralism has a problematical relationship to history, arising from its natural focus on identifying the general and unvarying principles of the structure. For example, in Lévi-Strauss's approach these principles result from the universal physical structure of the human brain. Consequently, structuralism did not develop a way of dealing with the historical character of social existence. On both points, the poststructuralists adopt a more radical stance. For them, the separation of language and thought from the body and its life in a practical world was as the product of structuralism's failure to free itself entirely from the legacy of Cartesian dualism (see Chapter 6). Here the poststructuralist concept of *discourse* crucially refers to ways of speaking and thinking that are patterned and socially accepted.

Discourse

For the poststructuralists, discourses are conceived historically; they are not fixed and universal, but rather emerge at certain points in history; the relationship between discourses is not predetermined but historically contingent.

The concept of discourse is not reconcilable with that of science, since the very notion of science as conventionally understood is itself a cornerstone of one particular discourse, namely the one established in the seventeenth- and eighteenth-century Enlightenment. Therefore there cannot be a science of discourse.

The unruliness of language

Another general element crucial to understanding the broad poststructuralist position is its emphasis on the *unruly* nature of language.

Unruly language

Although language is put to the service of social ends, it never can be identified with such ends and should never be regarded as straightforwardly ideological. Similarly, while language is socially controlled, it is used as an instrument for the conduct and organisation of day-to-day affairs within society, and is almost by definition, in the poststructuralist scheme of things, an instrument of domination, none the less it has the potential for disruption, tending to escape from and/or subvert the arrangements which seek to contain it.

This view gives us a picture of a struggle between language and social arrangements. Existing social arrangements strive, so to speak, to straitjacket the language, to regulate, control and discipline its operations and, to a very significant measure, succeed. Eventually, however, they exhaust their capacity for control and reach a point when their schemes for the control of language break down. Better put, the schemes of control reach their limits, since the breakdown is not of the whole system of control, but, rather, at its borders and peripheries, the limits beyond which enforcement cannot extend. Now the energies and potentialities of language itself exceed what is allowed for within the socially imposed scheme. The conception of the sign perhaps brings out most starkly this contrast between structuralism and poststructuralism. For structuralism, the sign is well behaved in terms of the requirements of the orderly, structured schemes of scientific categorisation; it can be described in terms of elegant, formal, almost mathematical systems of generalities. For poststructuralism, it is a most unruly element, whose nature is only superficially captured by such neat and tidy – Apollonian – structuralist schemes. Moreover, its potential cannot be contained within these or any other such schemes. In the poststructuralist view, the notable consequence for method involves recognising the ultimately uncontrollable nature of the sign and, therefore, doing everything that will allow it full rein and let it run free.

For poststructuralists, then, the structuralist account of the system of signs is partial rather than wrong. It emphasises the extent to which meaning is socially imposed and controlled and how it is produced through *conformity*. This structuralist approach is certainly acceptable, but at the same time it is necessary to recognise that the system of signs is not entirely controlled and that there is the potential to evade and resist social regulation. The system of signs is two-sided, i.e. it has a socially regulated aspect and also an undisciplined, uncontrollable side. The undisciplined aspect of the sign system is not to be thought of as involving individuals resisting social regulations which are imposed upon them, for this notion brings back the very idea of the subject as a centre, and the poststructuralist tendency is towards the thoroughgoing decentring of social phenomena. Consequently, the poststructuralist account is still as anti-humanist as the structuralist – if anything even more so. The ambivalent nature of meaning has nothing to do with individuals and individual intention. The undisciplined behaviour of meaning is an expression of its nature, i.e. its true nature. While meaning is systemic, it is also inherently unstable, motile and multifarious; it is too fluid to be captured in any fixed, stabilised and rigid arrangement. This undisciplined character is, so to speak, the true nature of the sign system. The socially organised, conformist government of it goes against the nature of the system and, therefore, is only problematically (and often unsuccessfully) dominant over this unruly potential. The crucial element for the poststructuralist position is, then, to demonstrate the disruptive potential within the sign systems, with the purpose of highlighting the dogmatic, repressive, even dictatorial character of the conventional side.

Here the notion of language as unruly owes much to Nietzsche's ideas, especially his discussion of the conflict between the Dionysian and Apollonian elements in human life to which we referred earlier. While the terminology used by Nietzsche is abandoned, poststructuralists retain the contrast it expressed, together with his tone of strong disapproval for the way the vigour of exuberant, inchoate, erratic energy is stifled by the imposition of lifeless, impersonal, restrictive order. Order is conceived as involving the suppression – but not the elimination – of this energy, which retains the potential of transgressing the boundaries set out to contain (and constrain) it.

Poststructuralists aim to bring out how much the ways we talk and think consist in (effective) attempts to coerce language, to exercise violence on and against it, to force it into patterns that will not fit. The approach involves identifying those points where this control breaks down and drawing out the ways the actuality of language cannot fit within the restrictions being imposed upon it. Further, these points threaten the structure of the whole, i.e. they do not just occur at the limits of the system, but reflect back (and reflect negatively) on the principles underpinning the whole system. The boundaries or margins of both language and society – in poststructuralism these are often the same – are sites of crucial significance, places where the tension between the straitjacketed forms of language come under strain and where the straitjacketing of meaning becomes manifest. *Transgression* is another key word in poststructuralist discourse; it refers to the refusal to fit within conventional classifications and divisions or to respect prohibitions on the crossing of boundaries.

Barthes as a poststructuralist

Thus Barthes in his later phase viewed language and reading as repressive, as means for imposing upon readers the conventions of the society (and of language, and the institution of literature itself). In fact, readers were often only too willing to subordinate themselves: language, he remarked at one point, is Fascist. Barthes's efforts at exposing the ideological and repressive character of the meanings of French bourgeois society had, however, themselves been conducted within that same language and in compliance with the conventions of science. The thorough logic of Barthes's later position meant, of course, that his own analytical efforts could not be exempted from his critique. Therefore the structuralist attempt to develop a science of culture and a scientifically based literary criticism was futile.

Looked at in this way, structuralism looked more like an operation inimical to the nature of literature than a method for grasping its true nature. Barthes now came to feel that structuralism was seeking to assert uniformity over diversity and plurality, and attempting to make the vast multiplicity of all the stories there have ever been into mere variants of one and the same basic story, i.e. to reduce them all to one single, underlying, basic and general form. There was need, then, for a reversal of strategy: rather than seeking to reduce diversity and ambiguity, the purpose became, instead, that of defying this structuralist proclivity by not merely emphasising diversity and ambiguity, but increasing and intensifying them – indeed proliferating them. The role of the reader must be transformed from that of the passive recipient of a preformed and delivered message into that of an active, creative participant in literature.

Barthes's later poststructuralist stance was criticised by those who wished to defend the view that creativity is in the hands of the author of the text, and that the literary critic, for example, is merely someone whose role is to understand and appreciate the creativity of the author. His critics could not accept Barthes's implication that literary criticism is just as creative as the production of literary works; the reader is on a par with the writer – in a way, the reader *is* a writer. Accepting this view undercuts the possibility of objective standards of literary criticism and therefore any basis of agreement on a canon of works of recognised literary worth. Rejection of such a canon was indeed Barthes's point. Given his attitude that conventions and passively received forms repress and inhibit the spontaneity and creativity of individuals, it is not surprising that he argues in this way.

As we outlined in Chapter 9, a key work in Barthes's transition from structuralism to poststructuralism is his book *S/Z* [1975a], in which he analyses a Balzac tale of tragedy resulting from gender stereotypes. Barthes's treatment retains some structuralist features. He claims to identify five *codes* at work in the text. These are:

1   the *hermeneutic*, which deals in the puzzles posed by the narrative;
2   the *seme*, which regulates the metaphors and allusion;
3   the *symbolic*, which deals with symbolic oppositions such as 'indoors/outdoors' and 'dreaming/waking';
4   the *action*, which deals with the actions of characters in the story and provides them with a logic of events;
5   the *reference*, which involves all the references to the culture and draws upon the common knowledge of the reader.

However, if Barthes is using structuralist ideas such as 'codes', i.e. underlying, generative rules, he is using them in a less-than-systematic way: the book itself is made up of ninety-three short commentaries – albeit variable in length and rather arbitrarily assorted – on parts of the text, some including criticisms of structuralist ideas. The problem of reading is spelled out as more of a moral than a scientific one. It confronts the reader with the choice of either being a merely passive dupe of the text, ingesting from it a (for Barthes, nauseating) diet of received conceptions and spurious, illusory solutions to the problems of life, or adopting an active, creative approach which effectively recreates the text being read. See how Barthes's commentary on 'Sarrasine' recreates the story so that the reader is becoming a writer. To live by convention is to lead an inauthentic life. The challenge is: do you want to live authentically? The aspiration to the creation of coherent, integrated, logically structured works is common to classic literature and to structural analysis. When found, it is to be attacked and disrupted. Barthes hereafter (in, for example, *The Pleasures of the Text* [1975b]) champions what he calls 'the Text'.

Barthes's conviction that the institutions and conventions of society are antithetical to the true, free, spontaneous nature of the individual means that to be confronted by the Text the reader must be non-social, i.e. he or she has to operate outside the social realm with all its laws, rules, structures and other orderly, regular, coherent divisions that make up its hierarchical, authoritarian and regulatory structures. The satisfactions for such a reader will derive more from physical and sensual responses than through any meanings of the text, since meaning is too intensely interwoven with convention. Thus the words themselves will be the object of attention, rather than their meanings and any purportedly guiding authorial intentions and schemes; the reader can revel in a babel of language. What the reader seeks is a state surpassing pleasure, which Barthes terms '*jouissance*'. It is translated as 'bliss' or 'ecstasy' and is a sensual, not an intellectual experience. The Text that offers the opportunity of such ecstasy, such a sensual, heady and vertiginous experience, cannot be found in the easy pleasures of reading provided by the transparent, smooth and comfortably engrossing best-seller type of story, which draws upon and reconfirms our stereotypes and prejudices.

Literature, however, does provide one of the places where it is possible to evade the burden and pressure of social conventions. Text will offer us the language itself as an object of our attention, rather than as a medium for the thoughtless presentation of our culturally given comforts and in such a way that it will not be our familiar, taken-for-granted tongue. It will be so presented as to be disturbing, challenging and unsettling, provoking us to linger on the Text, to brood intensely over it and to relish our responses to it. The bliss engendered by such poring over the Text will, of course, be a personal and incommunicable response, for such bliss itself takes place through transgression, i.e. moving outside, the settled conventions of language. It cannot, therefore, be reabsorbed into language for expression to others. To be in the state of bliss entails the patterns and segregations shaped by the culture losing their hold over the individual, who is thereby deprived of the conventional supports of self and security. The self, in any conventional sense, is disintegrated (which is to border upon madness, in conventional terms) and the blissfulness derives from the extremity of this condition. In summary, Barthes has displaced literature from being an object of analytical, scientific work to being a source of self-absorbed hedonism.

In his last works, Barthes practised what he had previously preached, producing, for example, an 'autobiography', *Roland Barthes by Roland Barthes* (1977b). The autobiographical form is a personal one, but in this case the form of the genre is tampered with, the demarcation between the true and the fictional is muddied and confused, and the requirements of an orderly structure are displaced by a string of separate thoughts arbitrarily arranged, i.e. set out in an approximately alphabetical manner. It is playful and humorous in style; it declines to be assertive or argumentative, rejecting these moods as forms of violence, of imposition on the other; and it refuses also to locate itself within the dualistic oppositions which are the points of reference of conventional thought, e.g. 'self' and 'other', 'subject' and 'object'. The real Roland Barthes is not the character who is the (often obliquely approached) topic of the book, but the one encountered in and through the writing, which ensures that any suggestion that the identity of Roland Barthes is fixed, stable and continuous is constantly unsettled, e.g. by switching between the first and third person terms, i.e. 'I' and 'he' are both used to refer to 'Roland Barthes'.

This account of Barthes should readily convey how he conceives language as the leading instance of social convention, and how he regards convention as inimical to individual well-being. In these respects Barthes is representative, and reflective, of the general poststructuralist position, for he was influenced in the formation of his later views by the work of Foucault and Derrida, whose ideas will be discussed in Chapters 11 and 12.

Poststructuralist ambiguity

Representational writing

The notion of language as inherently unruly connects with the intellectual unruliness of poststructuralism itself. As noted above, poststructuralist ideas do not comprise a straightforward and consistent body of propositions; ambiguity and even contradiction are its characteristic features. Indeed, they can be seen as essential, given its antagonism to the classical, linear, logical modes of thinking identified as part of the Enlightenment legacy. We should not be surprised, then, to find ourselves faced repeatedly with ideas that seem to run counter to one another; for the poststructuralist such outcomes are not only inevitable – they are to be celebrated.

A first ambiguity relates to representationalist forms of writing. Poststructuralists explicitly forswear such writing and seek to foster a new attitude towards a language which is concentrated on the sensual pleasures inherent in its uses, regardless of meaning or communicative function. Even so, and even though they might not claim any scientific status for what they do, none the less poststructuralists frequently write in ways which are apparently representational. For example, Michel Foucault, as we shall see in the next chapter, writes about previous historical periods and subsequent changes with respect to the formation of modern penology or the development of the contemporary Western treatment of sexuality. His critics and defenders debate whether or not his historical studies are sound and they do so in quite conventional ways, arguing over the extent to which the facts correspond to Foucault's assertions. However, Foucault himself is (at least sometimes) prepared to disown any representationalism, to deny that he has written anything other than fictions, works which have no representational ambitions. Yet his own occasional disclaimers do not resolve the question of how far his actual practice is consistent with these declarations; certainly, the merits of his work are widely understood in traditional academic terms as being in substantial part representational. Moreover, they are even advocated and opposed in much the same ways as some purportedly scientific theory.

Other poststructuralists, such as Barthes and Derrida, make a much more obvious attempt to break with the conventions of representationalism. A thorough and consistent rejection of representationalism must involve undermining these tendencies in one's own writing, not only in the work of others. Similarly, in contemporary fiction it is commonplace to find that many aspects of a novel are designed to remind the reader that the work is fiction, i.e. an artificial contrivance which must not be mistaken for some kind of factual report. The idea of admiring a novel for its realism, i.e. its attempt at a faithful portrayal of the nature of life as actually lived, has been completely rejected by many contemporary novelists. Instead of realism, their novels are presented as objects to be admired as works in and of language, to be relished for the pleasures that can be derived from the ways the words are assembled. This kind of writing tends to be approved – and emulated – by poststructuralists.

Barthes's disruptive play with the conventions of the autobiographical genre has been mentioned above. Jacques Derrida (b. 1930) continues to write scholarly pieces, albeit often in forms which disrupt conventional expectations. For example, a book called *Jacques Derrida*, jointly authored with Geoffrey Bennington (Bennington and Derrida 1993), has a quite unusual format. Bennington attempts, in his commentary on the top half of the page, to give a systematic account of Derrida's thought, while Derrida's comments, at the bottom of the page, are specifically constructed to frustrate Bennington's effort to encapsulate Derrida's thought in a system. Another work, *Glas* (Derrida 1986), has its pages divided into two columns: in one Derrida discusses Hegel's writing, in the other that of Jean Genet (see Chapter 12 for more on this).

We hasten to note that the rejection of representationalism is not meant to suggest that scholars should write fiction rather than fact or novels rather than reports, since the rejection abolishes the difference between fact and fictions. Alternatively put, it asserts that there are (and can be) only fictions. Foucault's contention that he had written only fictions does not reflect some decision on his part but, rather, only his acceptance of a necessary situation, i.e. he wrote only fiction because that is all that anyone can write. All writings are fictions, there is no other kind. Works which look as though they are factual reports, the results of researches, findings about the real world, i.e. works which take themselves seriously in this respect, are only prisoners of the ideology of representation.

Critical consciousness

A second area of ambiguity or contradiction, bringing us back on to the territory of the Frankfurt School (see Chapter 8), concerns the issue of critical consciousness. The contemporary vogue for poststructuralism in sociology undoubtedly has much to do with the fact that it is perceived by many as offering a critical stance towards society distinct from a Marxist tradition which was once strongly associated with the critical theory of the Frankfurt School and is now widely discredited.

Poststructuralists themselves seem to be ambivalent on such questions as the following: can they provide the basis for an oppositional politics? Is their approach any longer consistent with a critical stance towards the status quo? What are the grounds for such a critique? Here poststructuralist thought owes much to Durkheimian conceptions, albeit reproducing them in a rather inverted fashion. Durkheim has a strong claim to being the pioneer anti-humanist in sociology. His writings show individualism as a social product; a sense of one-self as belonging to a society is created by processes of inclusion and exclusion. It involves recognition of common membership among some, while at the same time other people are treated as excluded from the society or group. For example, as we saw in Chapter 4, the basis of his account of crime is that the moral community of society can only exist because there is a difference between those who do and those who do not belong within it; the existence of society demands the existence of criminals, those who fall outside society's moral limits.

The poststructuralists concur that identities are defined contrastively. They use the expression 'the Other'.

The Other

This term is used to convey the message that any given form of existence requires its Other. For example, we can only be a superior people if there is an inferior one and can only be sane if there are mad people.

But whereas Durkheim looks at the necessity of this Other from the point of view of society, as a kind of sacrifice of some people on behalf of the existence and solidarity of society and, thus, of the well-being of those within the society's boundaries, the poststructuralists are apt to look at things from the other point of view. They concur with the idea of the exclusion of individuals as a kind of sacrifice on behalf of social solidarity, but in taking things from the Other's point of view, they are not inclined to see the making of such sacrifices as a satisfactory solution. Instead, these are viewed as an infliction, an imposition upon the Others; their position on or outside the boundaries of conventional society is coercively endowed and punitively enforced. The poststructuralists do not see why some individuals should pay the price of other people's comfortable and comforting sense of themselves; they do not see any justice in the sacrificing of one set of individuals on behalf of the psychic well-being of others.

Yet in some ways, rather than continuing Durkheim's arguments, the poststructuralists fulfil his prophecies about the development of an extreme cult of the individual in modern society, whereby each individual becomes a sacred object. Despite its denunciation of the subject, poststructuralism has such a strongly individualistic cast to it that it can reasonably be interpreted as expressing, or at least implying, not only an anarchistic moral and political theory which is rigorously and thoroughly anti-hierarchical, but even an extreme form of it. Anarchists characteristically oppose the existence of government, supposing that if individuals were left freely to conduct their affairs, a more beneficent situation would develop. However, poststructuralism sees life in society as oppressive not merely because of the existence of a governmental apparatus, but because of the pervasively coercive nature of social relations in general. They often write as though the attempt of one person to influence or affect another involves violence and terror. Here, then, coercion means simply imposition, the making of demands by some persons on others rather than any overt force or compulsion. For example, they sometimes dub as 'theoretical terrorism' the demand for logical consistency, a demand which can result in criticism of people for their inconsistencies in intellectual argument. In post-structuralist arguments, then, coercion is given such a wide definition that virtually all social relationships, even the most localised and transient such as conversational exchanges, are seen as involving the use of power, i.e. the attempted, coercive imposition of one person's will – and, through it, of social conventions – upon another. From this point of view, asking someone a question involves attempting to compel her or him to honour and abide by the (socially established and enforced) conventions of the language. Having so widened the coverage of terms like 'power' and 'terror' they have, of course, at the same time intensified the problem of how can it ever be possible to achieve truly non-hierarchical, uncoercive relations, since domination and coercion are now seen as pervasive of social relations.

For example, Foucault has been characterised as holding a Hobbesian conception of social life (for Hobbes, see Chapter 5), involving an eternal and universal struggle of all against all, the very conception which Durkheim sought to eliminate conclusively. Whether this characterisation is true or not, Foucault certainly did see even the finest details of social existence as permeated by the workings of domination, and expressed this idea in talk of the *capillary actions of power* (capillaries are the innumerable small tubes of which plants are made and through which move the substances which they metabolise). Similarly, Barthes held to the ideal of a language which could operate independently of the exercise of power, but came to the despairing conclusion that it could only be utopian, i.e. unobtainable; what little non-coercive contact could be sought between human beings was only attainable outside language altogether, e.g. in the literary text, only through the sensual contact with the voices of another as embodied in the Text. The poststructuralists, then, seem to accept an anarchistic individualism in so far as they treat all conventional social relations as coercive, restrictive and essentially an unnecessary imposition upon the individual. But they are not hopeful anarchists, for they see little prospect of lifting the overall burden of oppression, save at marginal points and to marginal degrees. The Marxist idea of a full-scale confrontation with and shattering of the status quo has been left behind.

Conclusion

Critics of poststructuralism often warn that its acceptance is associated with the rejection of belief in science and in the superiority of our scientifically based, technologically supported civilisation. They argue that such notions threaten to unleash irrationalist forces which will hasten the end of civilisation as we know it. Rather than seeking to counter such objections, at least some poststructuralists seem to delight in them, revelling in the idea that by their writings they could bring the massive edifice of Western civilisation crashing down. As for its replacement, they might perhaps welcome the collapse into anarchy as for the better rather than the worse, but they do not count on it. After all, ranged against them is the vast, deeply entrenched and all-pervading network of oppressive forces which, for the great bulk of the time, succeed in portraying themselves as improving, progressive, liberating influences; they cannot be confronted or overturned on a general scale, for they are thoroughly interwoven with even the details of life in the society (remember the capillary metaphor), but can only be challenged at particular points and in fairly specific ways. Poststructuralists have to seek victories at the margins, sometimes through direct political action by particular groups, e.g. Foucault himself was associated with a prisoners' organisation agitating for reform. Usually, however, they work through intellectual activity to expose the pretensions of the dominant forces and to violate and subvert their conventions and divisions .

The result is ambiguity: however opposed poststructuralists might be to the idea of a political programme, all talk of oppression and control seems only to make sense in relation to some vision of freedom, some idea of what human life could be like in the absence of the repressive forces of language, reason and power. A worked-out version of this alternative, or even a clear statement of its possibility, is no more forthcoming in poststructuralist writings than in the work of the Frankfurt School. The difference is that whereas the Frankfurt School believed in this possibility – it was their *raison d'être* – the poststructuralists are more cynical. Indeed, a generalised and deep attitude of cynicism might plausibly be said to be their defining outlook, the crux of their anti-Enlightenment stance. But without some commitment to at least the possibility of an alternative, positive vision of social life, what sense can there be to the notion of critical consciousness? What point can there be to political action if its likely outcome is a Hobbesian (non-)society? However, we are jumping the gun somewhat; before developing this conclusion we need to consider in more detail the work of the leading poststructuralists, beginning with the writer who has been most influential in sociology, Michel Foucault.

Questions

1. What is the significance for a science of society of Nietzsche's stress on feelings? How does his argument about them differ from Freud's?

2. How does poststructuralism differ from structuralism?

3. What is representationalism in language? How can its rejection lead also to a rejection of science?

255

4   What are the implications of the unruly sign for (a) individuals and (b) social systems?

5   In Barthes's view, is the author dead?

6   To what extent does the poststructuralist emphasis on the Other resemble the symbolic interactionist concern with the underdog?

7   Can poststructuralism be critical?

Further reading

Barthes, R., 1975, *The Pleasures of the Text*. Hill and Wang.

—— 1991, *The Grain of the Voice: Interviews 1962–81*. University of California Press. An informal expression of his changing views.

Bauman, Z., 1992, *Intimations of Postmodernity*. Routledge. A clear review of general issues.

Culler, J., 1990, *Barthes*. Fontana. A clear, brief account.

Dews, P., 1987 *Logics of Disintegration: Post-Structuralist Thought and the Claims of Theory*. Verso. A more elaborate account.

Frank, M., 1989, *What is Neo-Structuralism*? University of Minnesota Press. A thoughtful, though long and demanding, account of what we have called 'poststructuralism'.

Harland, R., 1987, *Superstructuralism*. Methuen. A brief and lucid account of the transition from structuralism to poststructuralism.

Lombardo, P., 1989, *The Three Paradoxes of Roland Barthes*. University of Georgia Press. An account of Barthes's changing views.

Nietzsche, F., 1967, *The Birth of Tragedy*. Random House. Makes the contrast between Dionysian and Apollonian modes of being.

Norris, C., 1990, *What's wrong with Postmodernism*? Harvester Wheatsheaf. A critique of postmodernism.

—— 1996, *Reclaiming Truth: Contributions to a Critique of Cultural Relativism*. Lawrence and Wishart. A further criticism of postmodernism's relativist inclinations.

Schrift, A.D., 1990, *Nietzsche and the Question of Interpretation: Between Hermeneutics and Deconstruction*. Routledge. An excellent, though more advanced, source.

Stern, J.P., 1978, *Nietzsche*. Fontana. A good introduction.

■   ■   ■

Chapter 11

Michel Foucault

Introduction: Foucault's first phase

Foucault (1926–84), like Barthes, made a transition from initially structuralist to eventually poststructuralist ideas. Throughout he was exclusively concerned with historical investigations, centring on the changing nature of knowledge and the creation of categories of outsiders in society. His studies counter the regular accusation that structuralism cannot comprehend history and change. In this first section we consider his first four major books, which together make up what might – and against his objections – be called his structuralist phase: *Madness and Civilisation* (1967), *The Birth of the Clinic* (1973), *The Order of Things* (1970) and *The Archaeology of Knowledge* (1972). They form a kind of quartet centred mainly upon fundamental changes in the nature of thought in Western Europe in the period leading up to present times. They deal with the way the order of the world is conceived and how thought makes connections between the things in the world. However, a note of caution: it is possible to exaggerate the continuity between these studies. It is worth noting that Foucault's own attempts at linking them were made retrospectively and in a manner which suggests this unification was somewhat sardonic rather than fully serious. In the fourth, methodological volume, *The Archaeology of Knowledge*, the systematic formulation is something of a self-caricature; perhaps it is an at least partially parodic exercise in the vein of systematic, abstract theorising, an approach eschewed in the other three volumes. Ostensibly, the three preceding historical studies depend on certain key concepts, particularly 'archaeology', 'episteme' and 'discursive formation', but these ideas enter into the historical analysis progressively, and the notion of discursive formation in particular is only developed in any thorough way in the retrospective *Archaeology*. None the less, for ease of presentation, we will begin with the last book of the four and consider the set of abstract concepts presented there. The central question concerns their relationship to Foucault's largely debunking purposes, which mainly aim to provide a new, structuralist way of writing the history of ideas.

Unearthing epistemes

In Foucault's view, the development of structuralism marked a new point in the history of systems of thought. Its appearance around 1950 marked the beginning of the end for the period of modern thought and the start of a postmodern period (see the next chapter). For Foucault the key feature of structuralism was that it decisively decentred the subject, especially through the contention that unconscious structures rather than the conscious mind of the subject explain conduct (see Chapter 9). The intriguing question arose: how could one write a history of ideas if there were no subjects? Foucault rose to this challenge by applying the notion of the unconscious on a collective level, proposing that for any given historical period there is a kind of unconscious structure to the whole organisation of thought generally, i.e. thinkers are very much of – are captives of – their age. Attention is directed to the unconscious forces which guide and direct the explicit theories and other ideas thinkers come up with, and not to the thoughts which individual thinkers consciously form. There is an underlying matrix of presuppositions which confines the mind in a given period and makes only certain kinds of thoughts thinkable. This matrix is what Foucault terms the *episteme*.

The episteme

Foucault presents the episteme as a common structure within which the various, sometimes conflicting, ideas of individual thinkers, their schools and disciplines are formed. Furthermore, these epistemes are socio-historically situated: the development of any given set of ideas can take place only in certain highly specific conditions which involve a combination of features of the episteme with other socio-historical conditions.

If a particular conjuncture of conditions does not hold, then the ideas will not form, indeed *cannot* form because the conditions are not ones under which it is possible to think them.

Foucault aims to *historicise* the history of ideas thoroughly.

Historicism

The development of ideas is socially and historically situated. Alternative versions of historicism emphasise (a) contingency, i.e. there are no underlying laws, no general pattern to history; or (b) laws, which give history a determined path and pattern.

Two vital elements distinguish Foucault's argument from previous approaches: he divests the development of ideas of any notion of (1) necessary, predestined development and (2) progressive movement. The history of ideas seems naturally inclined to trace a continuing succession of ideas, one set leading to others, preferably as part of a logical, cumulative sequence. Foucault rejects this view: epistemes do succeed one another, but they are discontinuous, i.e. one episteme abruptly displaces another, with no continuities between them. He also rejects any notion of a progression that would enable us to look back upon the less enlightened conceptions of our predecessors. Consequently, his work is strongly relativist. He shared with the English historian E.P. Thompson, himself no relativist, the ambition to rescue people of the past from 'the enormous condescension of posterity' (Thompson 1968: 13). Ideas from the past often seem bizarre, misguided or unnatural to us, and we may flatter ourselves that this is because we now understand things better. On the contrary, we only think this way because we do *not* understand things better than our predecessors. Indeed, to assume the necessary superiority of our ideas shows that we understand these Others (and ourselves) hardly at all. We are not really aware of the successive epistemes within which our European forebears lived. The extent to which we can be aware of them is problematic but, if we were attuned to them, then we should see that things which seem strange to us were, for those inhabiting the episteme, every bit as natural, comfortable and right as our certainties are to us. Foucault inclines towards portraying people within an episteme as being its prisoners. Yet they are not conscious of their confinement; they think within the episteme, not about it. Therefore they cannot consciously comprehend the episteme. Persons in a later episteme are no better placed; those in a successor will not be aware of the previous episteme. After all, they are not conscious of their own, let alone of that of a previous age, given that the episteme does not figure explicitly in the thought it enables. Hence people from a later age are not really able to understand the previous one or even themselves.

One consequence of this approach is an element of paradox, since Foucault attempts to get us to understand ourselves through understanding previous ages and their epistemes. One of the ambiguities of Foucault's work is its purposes: are his studies intended as genuine histories or as fables, for want of a better term, albeit fables of a complex, sophisticated and documented kind?. In fact, the title 'archaeology' suggests that a purpose is to dig up the buried layers of preconceptions underlying previous periods of thought, i.e. the widespread, unconscious structures not explicitly held by individual subjects but framing the possibilities of what those individuals can think/say (thinking is something which is done in and through language). Foucault's continuity with structuralism is apparent here; it provides the basis for referring to his early works as his structuralist phase. In contrast with Lévi-Straussian structuralism, however, Foucault's studies do not seek to identify any universal unconscious structures; rather, they are concerned with very specific configurations, historically localised to an age and a region. This historical proclivity provides one reason why Foucault would not affiliate himself to structuralism, despite his affinities with it.

The structure of discourses

We have coined the expression think/say to bring out Foucault's notion of *discursive formation*, which emphasises that sets of ideas cannot be divorced from language. In line with structuralism, Foucault regards thought and language as two sides of a coin. He does not want to treat ideas and thought as mental phenomena, occurring in the privacy of the individual consciousness, for to do so would put the subject back in the position from which Foucault strives to displace it. Therefore he attends to what is explicit and public, that is, what is said (or, more accurately for historical studies, what has been written).

Discourses

Discourses are ways of speaking/writing and operate according to rules, and these rules articulate with socio-historical arrangements and circumstances.

The Archaeology of Knowledge attempts to spell out the general dimensions of the rules of discourse.

Foucault provides a battery of concepts for analysing the constitutive features of discourses. A discursive formation consists in the first instance of objects, the things that can be talked about. For example, 'mental patient' is an object of the discursive formation of modern psychiatry, something that can now be talked about and acted towards in various ways, e.g. identified, treated therapeutically and so forth. Prior to the development of the formation, this object could not be talked about; the persons nowadays identified as 'patients' could only be spoken of in the prior discourse of madness as 'madmen' or 'mad-women'. Additionally, the discourse has certain concepts for talking about the properties of the object, e.g. the mental patient may be spoken of in terms of various 'mental illnesses', such as paranoia or manic depression. Further, Foucault's *enunciative modalities* (explained in point 2 of the list below) are the ways of discursively marking the cognitive worth of what is said. Finally, *themes* can develop within these enunciative modalities; they are expressed in these concepts and talk about these objects; they are strands of thought relating to some given conception, e.g. the idea of evolution is a theme of biological discourse. Foucault insists that a discursive formation is not to be thought of as an internally coherent unity. He uses the notion of *field* to emphasise that a discourse is open to various possibilities and elements which are *dispersed*. His whole point is that the kinds of positions which seem to set individual thinkers at odds with one another are none the less contained within the same discursive formation and operate under the formative influence of a common episteme. Thus the discursive formation of psychiatry involves many different conceptions of the basis of mental illness and different notions of how mental illness should be treated; they are often at odds, if not in open warfare.

In more detail, then, Foucault identifies four processes which determine the distribution of the 'field' of a discursive formation:

1   *The formation of objects*, i.e. what things can be talked about within the formation, what kind of objects can be introduced into it, who controls such

admission. Here *grids of specification* provide the criteria for recognising, classifying and relating these objects, and also for differentiating them from other kinds of objects. For example, within the discourse of psychiatry they involve the symptoms which manifest particular types of illness such as schizophrenia, and the specific syndromes or illness sub-types which are medically recognised, such as catatonic schizophrenia and paranoid schizophrenia.

2   *The formation of enunciative modalities.* Just as not anything can be said, so not anyone can say particular things; they can be said only in certain sorts of settings, under certain conditions by certain kinds of people. For example, psychiatry involves the giving of diagnoses, which are only properly given within the context of a professional relationship by people who are qualified on the basis of their observation of the patients' behaviour. These rules also govern the formation of concepts regulating the relationship between statements, and whether or not the statements are accepted, excluded or awaiting definitive assessment. For instance, the statements of the psychiatric patient are often treated as symptoms, as expressions of the patient's illness, and not as potentially true statements about actualities.

3   *Procedures of intervention.* These regulate the way new statements can be produced or the ways they can be transformed, as when verbal statements are converted into mathematical symbolism, or spoken statements are transcribed into written form. For example, in psychiatric medicine there are professional rules about who is qualified to describe and record a patient's symptoms in reports which count as medically authoritative.

4   *Strategies.* These are the development of themes, the selection and development of certain lines of possibility, e.g. the formation and development of treating mental illness through talk or, alternatively, through drug regimes.

The dispersion of statements across the field of the discursive formation can obviously be a complex matter, further compounded by (1) the interaction of one discursive formation with another and (2) the interaction of the formation with non-discursive constraints. In forming the concepts of one discursive formation, people frequently draw upon another, e.g. the idea of psychotherapy through talk drew upon the religious model of the confession. Of course, discourses are socially regulated; they are subject to constraints of authority or normative restriction, in respect of what they can say.

These general ideas – archaeology, episteme and discursive formation – notionally underlie Foucault's three early studies of madness, medicine and classification. We say 'notionally' since these ideas are more prominent in *Archaeology* than in the previous three, and because the details of these studies are not necessarily explicitly arranged around them. Nevertheless, these studies certainly exemplify the broad directions indicated by these abstractions. They do have some theoretical linkage and, taken together, they present an analysis of some of the main elements of the Enlightenment transformation of Western thought. As one commentator remarks:

Foucault maintains that his histories of madness (disorder), disease (orderly disorder) and epistemic fields (order) in the classical period together expose the 'deepest strata of Western culture', the strata that mark the threshold of modern thought and the emergence of the concept of Man.

(Poetzl 1983: 153)

Further, though Foucault may be said to be delving into the archaeology of thought systems, his work from *Madness and Civilisation* onwards is underpinned by a conception of the pattern of social change from the sixteenth to the twentieth century. It shows a development which conforms broadly to Weber's story about the progressive disenchantment and rationalisation of the modern world (see Chapter 3), leading to the development of what the Frankfurt School calls the 'administered society' (see Chapter 8). As we shall see later, this theme provides the main connecting link between Foucault's early studies and his later ones.

The discourse of the asylum

Madness and Civilisation (1967) is an ironic comment upon the way the formation of the modern notion of reason, which counterposes itself to coercion and repression, has itself contributed to these. If this is the abstract story that Foucault seeks to tell, the concrete one concerns the transformation of what was defined as madness in the Renaissance into what has become mental illness in the modern world.

In the fifteenth century madness was conceived in two disparate ways (remember, epistemes are not internally uniform or coherent). The first was in cosmic terms: when human animality breaks out of social control, it places an individual in communication with awesome, tragic forces which drive towards destruction, yet also give the mad person special and secret knowledge. The second was satirical: madness was conceived as a kind of comment on reason, making mock of human fallibility and frailty. In this period the mad were outcast from regular society, but they were left free to wander, and they remained in connection with society in so far as they deserved to be listened to. The cosmically mad could give voice to wisdom, and the satirical form of madness could have its own wisdom: there was the idea of 'the wise fool'.

With the change from the Renaissance to what Foucault calls 'the classical age' (beginning in the later part of the eighteenth-century) there is a profound alteration in the conception of madness, which ceases to be something authentic in its own right. Now it is defined as entirely outside of reason and is rejected as antithetical and dangerous to it. No longer a fate befalling the individual, madness now is thought of as chosen by the individual; thus mad people reject the standard of reason. Consequently, they are not open to rational persuasion, so that the only mode of treatment to which they might respond and through which they can be controlled is physical confinement and coercion through brutal treatment. At the same time as the mad were being rejected from social life, the attempt was being made to conceive madness in terms of science, i.e. to bring it within the reach of reason. Hence madness could not be treated as entirely devoid of reason (otherwise it would defy comprehension in terms of reason); instead it was represented as a *perversion* of reason. In this way the concept of madness developed as a misapplication of reason; the mad have the power to reason, to develop logically ordered thought, but they apply it on the basis of falsehood, misconception and delusion. They are incapable of comprehending the world correctly not because they have turned their back upon reason but, rather, because they have faced it too fully and been dazzled by its light.

These changes were interrelated with other changes in the society of the time. First, there was the 'great confinement', a period early in the classical age when all kinds of socially troublesome individuals – the poor, the sick, the vagrant, the criminal and the mad – were indiscriminately locked up. This development in part was an opportunistic response to the fact that lazar houses (buildings designed to house lepers) had become superfluous with the disappearance of leprosy from Europe, thereby creating the opportunity to confine all those who might threaten social order. Subsequent changes in social values, however, produced pressures for the separation of the mad from other inmates, e.g. the growing belief in the need to make productive use of all possible labour and, associatedly, a conception that poverty and unemployment were not necessarily the choice or fault of the poor and unemployed. Hence there was more discrimination between those confined, separating those who could be returned to gainful work from those who, like the mad, could not. In a moment delicately poised between two possible directions for confinement of the mad – prisons or hospitals – it so happened, though by no means inevitably, that the hospital was deemed the appropriate option.

The differentiation of the mad from the general population of the undesirable and their relocation to the hospital context is widely advertised as a progressive development, involving both more humane and better-informed treatment. The madperson was becoming the patient, and the patient was no longer treated through brutal discipline but through medical regimes based upon scientific knowledge. Foucault maintains that this appealing image is not true.

The treatment of the mad

This image conceals the fact that the change was no improvement; if anything it was a continuation of the deterioration in the situation of the mad. Since the Renaissance they had lost their freedom and dignity and had been reduced to silence: nothing they had to say was worth listening to. Further, the treatment was not truly medical in nature and was not based upon genuine scientific knowledge. The doctor controlled inmates with power, not expert knowledge. The hospital was an intensely moralised environment for compelling the inmates back into conformity with social rules through the manipulation of their guilt.

The origins of the clinical gaze

With respect to physical disease, Foucault argues that again the conjunction between developments in fundamental concepts and social currents gave rise to the discourse of modern medicine and to its site of operation, the clinic. *The Birth of the Clinic* (1973) holds that the French Revolution with its associated wars was a major precipitant of medical reorganisation. The involvement of all experienced doctors in military medicine left a vacuum in civilian medical treatment which was rapidly filled by quacks, in turn giving rise to demands for administrative measures for ensuring good medical treatment. These measures set medical competence based on observation of actual disease as the standard. The provision of the clinic, i.e. a site where doctors could acquire experience of illness and study it systematically, was another contingent development, going rather against the grain of the prevalent idea that illness should desirably be treated at home. Nevertheless, the charity hospital did develop, gaining the necessary financial support from the wealthy because they considered it a worthwhile investment in their own self-protection. The poor gained medical treatment and, through studying them, doctors could develop a better knowledge of disease from which, eventually, their sponsors could themselves benefit.

On the epistemic level, the development of modern medicine involved the displacement of the classical conception of disease. Put simply, Foucault's case is that the classical conception is only incidentally connected to the human body, i.e. disease manifests itself in the body, but the fact that it occurs in one place or another in the body is not relevant. Indeed, the true nature of disease is only to be grasped by abstracting its essential nature from surrounding, accidental circumstances which may be concealing this essence rather than revealing it. Moreover, the idea of treating disease in hospital makes no sense either, for the hospital is an artificial context further complicating the business of abstracting the disease itself from the setting in which it is incidentally located. As a first step, then, this classical conception of disease as a hidden essence is displaced as a result of a wider shift in ideas about the nature of the sign at that time. Instead of differentiating between signs of the disease, which are not essentially connected with it, and symptoms which are part of its essence, the change involved the abolition of this distinction of symptom and sign; now all the observable occurrences associated with the disease were a part of it.

However, the observable occurrences of disease remained those which were on the surface of the skin, and the second step in shifting from the classical to the modern concept of disease was to adopt the dissection of corpses as a method of inquiry into disease. This method was far from being the most obvious way to learn: those who studied disease could not have seen any sense in dissecting corpses prior to a certain point in the development of ideas. Here Foucault argues against the more accepted view that the adoption of dissection was delayed beyond a point at which it might have been introduced due to popular (religiously inspired) prejudice against the use of corpses in this way.

> ## The clinical gaze
>
> In the eighteenth century there was no problem in obtaining corpses, but medical practitioners needed a change in their concepts to see any relevance in the practice. It required a change in ideas to bring dissection into conjunction with the investigation of disease, since prevailing conceptions saw diseases as occurring on the surface of the bodies of living creatures – quite a difference from the inspection of corpses! An extension of the idea of 'surface' made possible the introduction of dissection because it now came to be conceived as an examination of surfaces, i.e. the surfaces of the body's inner organs. This conception involved a new way of looking at the body, the *clinical gaze*.

In its turn, the clinical gaze made a profound shift in the conception of disease possible, for disease was no longer considered as only incidentally related to the body on which it was manifest; rather, it was now conceived as originating in the body's own nature, as part of life itself.

Words and things

The third and by far the most complex and demanding of this trio of studies is on general conceptions of knowledge, tracing again the development from a Renaissance conception, through a classical phase, to a modern one and beyond. The title was translated as *The Order of Things* (1970) to avoid conflict with an already published book entitled *Words and Things*, though this would have been more literal and more accurate. A main element in the study of changing concepts of knowledge is the role of language and the topic of representation, which will predominate in our summary of the story of Foucault.

The Renaissance was dominated by the idea of resemblance. The whole universe was seen as filled with and interrelated by resemblances; it was possible to pursue an endless chain between one thing and another, understanding one set of resemblances as a product of yet further resemblances. Thus the medieval 'doctrine of signatures' held that 'every herb was stamped with a more or less clear sign of its uses; so that, for example, a yellow blossom indicated a likely cure for jaundice, or a root shaped like a foot became a remedy for gout (Thomas 1973: 224). Language was unproblematically part of this world, for all things within it, including linguistic signs themselves, were part of the ubiquitous pattern of resemblances and were themselves to be understood in terms of relations of resemblance to the things that they spoke of. Therefore language did not present any special sort of problem; it was to be understood in the same terms as anything else. Further, the tracing out of the resemblances was a matter of finding the relationships which had been inserted and assured by God. The business of such tracing out was a putatively endless matter; it did not lend itself to systematic structuring, so knowledge did not show the kind of cumulatively structured character it has now acquired.

With respect to language, the change from the classical episteme involved the change from resemblance to representation. Rather than language being understood to be simply a God-given part of the pattern of creation and integrated into the all-pervading pattern of resemblance, it began to be conceived as something which existed within the human mind. Words stand in a relationship of representation to things. The conception of knowledge also shifted: now it was a pattern of strict similarities and differences rather than a notion of reality consisting in a set of (vague) resemblances. Language, too, was part of this reality, itself to be understood as such a pattern. The form which the depiction of such a reality could take was the tabular arrangement, the distribution of elements within a grid mapping the characteristics they did and did not share, thereby permitting the abstraction of the essence of a given phenomenon (see the classical concept of disease above). The grid brought in a crucial element of systematisation to the organisation of knowledge. At the same time, this approach engendered the possibility of – in the ideal case at least – an exhaustive description, i.e. one could notionally enumerate all the similarities and differences for a particular phenomenon.

The further change from the classical to the modern episteme, however, places language not in the mind but in history, along with life in general and human beings in particular. Phenomena are no longer to be understood as consisting in an abstract, timeless essence which can be arranged in a static tabular display, but as existing in time. This change is most vividly exhibited in the change from natural history to biology, from the portrayal in tabular classifications of natural history to the evolutionary conception championed by Darwin. Humankind and language, conceived as historical phenomena, can now become topics of scientific knowledge. They can be both the subject, i.e. creator, and the object, i.e. thing to be known, of knowledge and representations. However, the situation has become destabilised, because the effectiveness of representation is no longer assured and the link between capacity of words and the things they purportedly stand for is no longer guaranteed by the nature of reality itself, but has become problematic. In the Renaissance, the connection of words with things was forged by God, and in the classical age it was assured by the nature of things and by language itself. In the modern period there is nothing to provide such assurance.

Thus the modern period of thought prominently features two tensions:

1   People seek to reconcile the fact that they are both subject and object of knowledge.
2   They seek to secure the connection between words and things in the light of an awareness that this relationship can no longer be viewed as a necessary one.

How can people know themselves with any (scientific) certainty while at the same time recognising their own contingency? What language can secure such knowledge if language itself is a human product? For Foucault it is impossible to resolve or reconcile these tensions; the consequence is a fateful instability at the heart of modern thought.

These tensions are the background to Foucault's remarks about 'the end of Man'. These remarks may seem obscure and tendentious, but they merely refer – in the jargon of the *Archaeology of Knowledge* – to the formation of a particular *object*, Man. (Note that 'Man' here refers to humanity, not just to males.)

From subject to object

Within modern discourse, people are integrally identified as something that can be talked about as a potential object of knowledge; this way of talking was simply not possible within the Renaissance and classical discourses. These tensions within the modern discourse have been unresolved and the modern episteme is (perhaps) disintegrating. If so, then perhaps this notion of people will not even figure in the new discourse, i.e. since structures are becoming the objects of knowledge in human studies, the notion of 'Man' will not be employed in this emerging episteme.

Moreover, the notion of representation as well as that of 'Man' is losing its hold. In its place has arisen the realisation that language is an autonomous reality, which creates and runs the *subject*, rather than the other way about: language is an end in itself, rather than being looked upon as an instrument to be used to gain knowledge of an extralinguistic reality. These notions mark Foucault's shift towards his later, poststructuralist phase.

Later studies: genealogies of power/knowledge

No sooner had Foucault provided the account of his (supposed) methods of analysing discursive formations than he made a shift in his project, which led him to subordinate the idea of archaeology to that of *genealogy*. The discontinuity, however, did not require the prior studies to be jettisoned entirely; rather, something implicit and subordinate in them was brought to the fore.

Genealogy

Derived from Nietzsche, the concept of genealogy was concerned again with developing the buried history of thought, but this time with the specific objective of revealing a link between *knowledge* and *power*.

Foucault himself observed that he had paid attention to the connection between the different knowledges and the operations of power, e.g. in his work on psychiatry. Of course, he had been much concerned with the way people were marginalised within society, and with how discursive formations had been shaped by authority relations and changes in dominant ideologies. Nevertheless, the connection had not been fully explicit or central. Now his genealogical investigations were to be used to develop a new conception of power.

Foucault's historical perspective, his story of the development of the administered society or, as he preferred to call it, the *carceral society*, henceforth focused upon the way activities are brought under regulation. This process involves the development of bodies of professional and administrative functionaries equipped with a supposedly scientific body of knowledge on the basis of which activities are transformed into rational objects. The task of such functionaries is twofold:

1   to implement a process of redefinition whereby activities are turned into something that can be thought about rationally in the categories of a science;
2   to reorganise conduct along these purportedly more rational and efficient lines.

The task does not end there, since thereafter these redefined activities require continual management – in the sense of administration – in order to sustain and enhance their efficient organisation, thereby providing further rationalisation.

However, it is not the activities of professional and administrative functionaries themselves that are Foucault's main focus, but rather the nature of their *disciplinary power*. The creation of the various bodies of supposedly scientific knowledge that serve as the basis of professional and administrative practice has involved the formation and deployment of the idea of the normal phenomenon (here 'the normal' has more of a moral rather than a scientific force). The administrative arrangements are devoted to the maintenance and development of the normal phenomena. Of course, the notion of the normal involves its Other; the application of this idea across different activities serves to create more categories of deviants. For example, the formation of an idea of normal sex goes along with, is inseparable from, the idea of other, abnormal sexual practices. The attempt to manage activities (and even the whole population) so as to enforce and sustain that which is conceived as normal and to seek to regulate, if not eliminate, that which is conceived as abnormal in its turn requires monitoring of the activity – '*surveillance*' is Foucault's term (which can include all kinds of monitoring of people's activities, such as policing or administrative supervision). Consequently, activity is reorganised in ways which seek to make things more visible, more readily amenable to observation, investigation and supervision. Thus surveillance extends into more and more areas of society; it is itself increasingly rationalised.

As in the early studies, so in the later ones, Foucault's account of modern society is making a case about the formation of the modern subject. The term 'subject' now has very much the sense of one subjected, i.e. dominated and controlled. The theme is comparable with the argument about mental illness, i.e. the change towards modern society has replaced physical brutality as a means of discipline. Effectively it has produced individuals who are self-controlling and can think for themselves. They can live in the delusion that they are free, autonomous beings because they are not aware of the extent to which they have been shaped by the detailed, intricate and elaborate mechanisms of power.

The earlier studies sought to reveal the buried past underlying the formative stages in the development of the modern age, but the explicit use of the notion of power was not a central element in them, although it is not, after all, that difficult to see power at work in the incarceration of the mad and, later, their subordination to moralising control. In genealogical studies, however, Foucault directly speaks of power and seeks to trace the way bodies of knowledge – such as the human (social and psychological) sciences – have grown up in conjunction with, and as servants of, power.

Power/knowledge

In the modern world, the development of power and knowledge are so intimately interwoven that they cannot properly be spoken of separately, and the display of their interconnection requires the formation of a special mode of expression, namely *power/knowledge*.

The two develop together, and modern society involves new forms of power, whose recognition requires a new conception, i.e. power without a subject.

Previous conceptions have seen power as something in the hands of either individuals or groups, e.g. exercised by a ruler or by a ruling class – a conception of power *with* a subject. The point about power in modern society is that it is diffused throughout the affairs and activities of the society, not exercised on behalf of any individual or group in particular. Rather, the operation of power has become internal to the organisation of activities. This internality contrasts with sovereign power, the kind of power a ruler has over her or his subjects. This power is over their activities but is external to them, i.e. the sovereign is not concerned with or involved in the organisation of the day-to-day affairs of the society. In the spirit of efficiency, power is more effective if it does not regulate activities from a distance – as the sovereign does – but is interwoven into the very activities it is to regulate, for it can then operate closely and intensely upon these activities, e.g. a teacher can oversee, regulate and direct the detailed organisation of a small class of pupils. The spread of administrative arrangements throughout modern society has extended this kind of power in all directions, making it part of innumerable domains of life. All the different administrative domains of society do not connect up with one another and, even within each administrative domain, there is no extensively co-ordinated and unified direction. So though power pervades these environments, it does not serve any single purpose, nor is it in the hands of one or even a few individuals. It is everywhere, and/but it is undirected. It is disciplinary power not only in the sense that it involves punitive, disciplining measures, but more so in that it develops well-disciplined individuals who are prompt and obedient.

The carceral society

In his later studies, Foucault develops this analysis in relation to two fields of activity in modern society: the development of the prison, and the emergence of modern sexuality. The themes of surveillance and discipline are manifest in Foucault's next book, *Discipline and Punish* (1977). Foucault's account of the prison and of penology as a form of power/knowledge is best known for its reproduction of Jeremy Bentham's idea of the panopticon, a design for an ideal prison – at least in Bentham's eyes. It is a circular arrangement of individual cells dominated by a central observation tower.

Carceral society

Foucault treats the panopticon as a metaphor for modern society, the carceral or imprisoning society, an expression reminiscent of Weber's 'iron cage'. For this metaphor, Bentham's model has the relevant features of:

- being purportedly a completely rational plan for the treatment of prisoners, thus reflecting the extent to which thought is devoted to devising ways of controlling people;
- emphasising the extent to which the system is designed to encourage people to control themselves through reflection on their own conduct;
- conceiving the thoroughly constant and pervasive supervision of the inmate: the model represents the ideal of a totally administered society.

Foucault notes the value which the model places upon the purportedly rational, planned scheme as a basis for organisation, and the manifestation in the plan of the idea of all-encompassing surveillance; the central tower means that everything that the inmate does can be constantly and exhaustively overlooked. He also notes the idea of individual responsibility: the prisoner is an isolated individual left alone with his or her thoughts and given the opportunity to reflect upon his or her sins and to see the merits of better ways.

Foucault charts the development of penology in terms of a transformation in the notion of punishment. We have commented previously (see Chapter 4) on the strong Durkheimian threads in Foucault's work, and they are apparent here. In the pre-modern era, punishment was premised upon the idea that crime is an assault upon the collective body of society, as represented by the sovereign. Punishment, therefore, primarily consisted in some kind of retributive assault upon the (literal) body of the criminal, the nature and extent of which depended on the magnitude of the crime. Physical mutilation, torture and violent forms of execution, all normally conducted in public, were the legally required and socially accepted responses to various types of criminal actions, from theft to murder. Imprisonment was not viewed as a form of punishment, but simply as a means of ensuring that a criminal would be available for punishment, i.e. criminals were confined prior to their trial and while awaiting the carrying out of the sentence. Confinement did not have a unique connection with crime, many types of non-criminals being kept in prison in order to remove them from society, e.g. the poor and the mad.

With the development of penology in the eighteenth and nineteenth centuries, public ceremonies of trial and punishment gave way to administrative rituals conducted by specialised legal professionals, and incarceration came to replace physical mutilation as the normal form of punishment. This change involved a shift to a different conception of crime and of the relationship of the criminal to society. In brief, the logic of punishment became associated with the idea of control, i.e. control of the criminal by the authorities and of the individual by himself. The prisoner was required to conform to a disciplined regime of daily life in which everything he or she did was subject to monitoring and regulation.

As in the earlier studies, Foucault's account in *Discipline and Punish* is guided by the idea that, contrary to Enlightenment propaganda, the great shift in the nature of Western societies has *not* been towards the replacement of arbitrary power by rational organisation and the displacement of authority by knowledge. Instead, it has involved only a reorganisation of the way power is exercised. Very crudely, control by the royal ruler through the occasional administration of brutal punishment has been replaced by far-ranging, deeply penetrating and complex networks of regulation, including the self-regulation of individuals. Foucault refers to the change from sovereign power, where the locus of control is external to the activities and relations controlled, to *disciplinary power*, where activities and relations are, so to speak, controlled from within themselves. We have exchanged the loosely supervised existence of pre-modern society for a most closely, extensively and intensively supervised existence. As for its rationality, the purpose of many of the human sciences has been to contribute to the development of this network of supervision, to provide ways of more effectively controlling individuals. Foucault's linkage of power/knowledge refers to the way (often self-styled) scientific knowledge combines and collaborates with administration in the formation of new, refined and improved ways of keeping people under control.

As this last remark implies, it is important to note that *Discipline and Punish* is not simply a study of the origins of the modern prison. Foucault regards the penal regime as a model for the organisation of modern society generally; the prison is merely one institution of carceral society, in which individuals and their behaviour are subjected to – and subject themselves to – surveillance. Other, similar institutions include the school, the hospital and the business organisation. Nevertheless, even though disciplinary power has been dispersed throughout the society, power is still focused on, if not concentrated in the hands of, the state. This *biopower* has resulted from the changing nature of the state's power, which derives from its total population – large, healthy, educated and trained – and not from its military strength alone. The idea of the population as a whole as an asset of the state has given rise to efforts to manage and cultivate it, to enhance (so to speak) its asset value, to provide for the general welfare of the population.

Biopower

Biopower is the power involved in the management of the population.

In his series of books on sexuality, Foucault connects the development of modern sexuality to biopower, and also seeks to elaborate another aspect of power – what he calls its 'productive' side.

Sexuality as discourse

The volumes on the history of sexuality were Foucault's final and incomplete work. They usefully clarify the way discourse creates its object, since sexuality seems to be one of the most natural, innately human and, therefore, invariable facts. Foucault does not doubt that human biology is pretty uniform or that people everywhere engage in acts of sexual contact, but he does argue that sexuality is a socio-cultural creation. Sexuality as we know it is the production of a particular set of historical circumstances and obtains only within the terms of a discourse developed relatively recently i.e. since the seventeenth century.

The nub of Foucault's argument can be explicated with reference to a paradox. We are (or were until recently with the coming of 'sexual liberation'), we often tell ourselves, a sexually repressed civilisation. The highpoint of this repression was the Victorian era, and we are still living with the legacy of that time. Sex is, therefore, something that we are not allowed to speak of; its expression in discourse is inhibited and was then entirely forbidden. Note, then, that we are already talking (in Foucault's terms) about a discourse. The story of repression is not told (only) about the prevention of sexual activity itself, but also about what we are allowed to say about sex. The story is not just about behaviour, but also about silence, about limits on language. The paradox is that we continue to tell this story, to put into discourse the complaint about this suppression of discourse. In other words, we keep on speaking about that which we are (supposedly) forbidden to speak about. The paradox is somewhat fuller since we not only speak of the fact that we are (supposedly) forbidden to speak of sex, but we constantly speak of sex itself. Accordingly, the story of repression is simply not true; what is true is that there has been a change in the way we can speak of sex. There has not been an inhibition about speaking of sex at all.

Sex has become a particular type of discourse. The essence is (1) the way sex can be spoken of has changed; under the Victorians, there was certainly an inhibition upon the free expression of sexual feelings and reactions; but (2) there was an efflorescence of attempts to speak about sex in scientific and therapeutic ways, which (3) were intimately interwoven with, and constitutive of, efforts to make sex amenable and subject to regulation in order to create a healthy, flourishing and productive population. In the end, then, the very opposite of the traditional story of repression is true, for the whole development of the discourse of sexuality has been to get people to speak of sex, to incite – Foucault uses this word – them to talk about it.

The development of the discourse of sexuality builds upon the deeply entrenched Western practice of confession, an area in which talking about sex was already established. Confession has developed from a practice distinct to religion into one widespread in society and often employed by science, e.g. in psychotherapy. There is a change in its nature, though, in that originally confession was concerned merely with the fact of bodily transgressions, i.e. the sinful sexual acts performed; now the confessional relation has been psychologised, has come to attend to the thoughts, feelings, intentions and other mental concerns involved with sexual acts. Foucault's account here parallels his argument in *Madness and Civilisation* (1967) about the way control shifts from regulation of the body's activities towards manipulation of the mind. Another parallel is the medicalisation of sexual matters which, in his own words, meant:

> first of all that the sexual domain was no longer accounted for by the notions of error or sin, excess or transgression, but was placed under the rule of the normal and the pathological (which for that matter were the transposition of the former categories; a characteristic sexual morbidity was defined for the first time; sex appeared as an extremely unstable pathological field . . . This implied furthermore that sex would derive its meaning and its necessity from medical interventions; it [confession] would be required by the doctors, necessary for diagnoses, and effective by nature in the cure.
>
> (1967: 67)

Hence the new medical vocabulary is entirely continuous with the old moral vocabulary of sin, transgression and guilt, so patently associated with social control. The medicalisation of sexual discourse simply involves substituting newly coined, scientific-sounding words for previous, moralising terms; the concerns of social control are retained, but now less overtly as they are concealed in a vocabulary which is seemingly, but only seemingly, technical/scientific.

The development of the modern discourse of sex, formed in concepts of heredity and racial purity, originated out of a concern to ensure the thriving well-being of the bloodlines of bourgeois groups and not as a means of suppressing the sexuality and fertility of the 'lower orders'. It was only later (and in adjusted form) that the practices forming around such concerns were exported to the subordinate classes. Foucault characteristically notes that these developments placed a general moral obligation on people to subject their sexual conduct to surveillance so as to ensure that it would not detract from the purity or strength of the physical inheritance. These developments became fused with the formation of the idea of the state as a matter of population rather than of sovereignty, e.g. modern wars are fought on behalf of the population, not on behalf of the sovereign. In major part, the state's job has become the management of a population. Consequently, it requires administrative mechanisms to ensure the reproduction, health and longevity of the population, and to provide social welfare measures such as education and training to shape the population in response to the needs of the society's disciplined pursuits, such as participation in the military and in industry. Foucault draws an ironic contrast between those cultures in which knowledge of sex takes the form of a mastery of erotic arts and the modern Western one, where knowledge of sex is identified with medical and scientific information.

For Foucault, in this instance power was not repressive but *productive*; it did not inhibit either sexual activity or sexual expression, but created something entirely new, giving rise to a whole new discourse of sexuality and an associated set of new practices. While this discourse very much was rationalised around the requirements of biopower, it did not entirely ruin sex (as Drury [1994] puts it) by turning it into an instrumental activity to be overseen and regulated by medical and other bureaucracies. For the discourse also engendered new sexual pleasures and developed new sources of resistance to power. This resistance is important; the point conforms to Foucault's general claim that disciplinary power and resistance to it go together. The development of specific disciplines provides the opportunity for reactions against them, e.g. prison discipline creates inmate subcultures and prison riots.

To illustrate more fully, in the field of sexuality much effort has been devoted to the repression, even elimination of homosexuality. Medical discourse has contributed massively towards a conception of 'the homosexual' as a type of person suffering from an illness with certain characteristic symptoms and causes, and amenable to certain modes of curative treatment. This development is just what Foucault means when he talks of discourses as creating their object. Of course, prior to the formation of the contemporary medical discourse people engaged in same-sex relations, but 'the homosexual' as a conception of a person *did not exist*; it came into being with, was created by, the formation of that discourse. While the formation of the concept of 'the homosexual' was developed with the aim of repressing homosexual activity, it also produced counter-action, creating a basis on which homosexuals can think of themselves as people with something in common, as people who are badly treated, who should organise to achieve the acceptance and legitimacy of their sexual practices. An outcome of the medical discourse of homosexuality, therefore, is something unintended and unexpected: homosexuals have been able to think of themselves as a social category united by common interests. On this basis they have formed groups to oppose the stereotypical image of themselves and to fight for civil rights.

Summarising Foucault

Although Foucault may be seen as someone who moved away from an early structuralist towards a poststructuralist position, from the beginning his work was also importantly different from that of Lévi-Strauss and Barthes. Foucault did begin by seeking to isolate structures, but they are not the universal structures of the human mind; rather they are the general structures of thought – epistemes – which dominate and are tied to a particular epoch. These historically and socially situated structures are subject to displacement by quite different, successor structures. From the start, therefore, his thought was thoroughly relativistic; the transformation in Western society after the seventeenth century represents not any kind of progress or improvement but merely a change, a reorganisation. The Enlightenment's self-evaluation as a progressive force is directly challenged in an attempt to expose the human sciences, on which the Enlightenment set such store, as offering only a delusory prospect of progress. Indeed, the main platform of Foucault's arguments is consistently that knowledge does not entail liberation and does not contrast with power, or, more importantly, does not necessarily or automatically oppose it. Knowledge is complicit in power relations to the extent that in his later work Foucault routinely refers to 'power/knowledge' to indicate the fact that the two are – not in every case, but in the great preponderance – inseparably related to each other.

Foucault's work changed quite significantly over its course, but one element which plays a central part throughout is the notion of discourse. The increasing role which this concept played in his writings is perhaps the clearest index of his shift away from structuralism and towards a poststructuralist position. His studies are much concerned with language, albeit not as a general system of signs. Rather, language contains particular, self-subsistent sectors, each developing in connection with particular forms of social organisation, and each arising along with, and as part of, the reorganisation of activities and the elaboration of new social practices. In many ways, Foucault's investigations are into the ways the conditions necessary for the very idea of something may develop. These ways involve the development of a discourse, i.e. a way of speaking, constituent vocabularies, the rules regulating what it is possible to say, who can say things, under what conditions, and with what consequences. Only within such a discourse can the idea even be formed.

Foucault's main studies, then, are all focused upon the way some institution with which we are now familiar and take for granted could come into being. Further, it is important to notice that the development of a discourse is itself decentred: it does not arise from the efforts of one or two individuals, or even from any concerted effort to bring it into being. Rather, it emerges without anyone foreseeing it from a variety of dispersed and frequently independent developments, interacting with one another to engender as their entirely unintended end result the organisation of activity with which we are now familiar, e.g. the visit to the doctor's clinic for a medical examination. Foucault is apt to remark that discourses create (or produce) their objects, which may seem to imply that the development of language can of itself bring actual things into being. This perceived implication can enrage many sociologists for its apparent absurdity. However, his inclination to speak in this way does not create any real problems; there is nothing to strain at in the suggestion that only through the development of a discourse is it possible to have a particular phenomenon. For example, there have been sick people throughout history and people from remote times may well have suffered from many of the illnesses, diseases and afflictions which sick people now suffer from, but sick people were not always and everywhere patients. Only comparatively recently has the idea of 'the patient', as we now know it, come into being, i.e. as a person whose health is to be administered through participation in a clinic. This idea has arisen with the conjoint development of a physical site for the medical consultation, and of a professional grouping to regulate and manage such consultations. In this sense, 'the patient' can only exist through, is only thinkable in terms of, the discourse that has grown up, and out of, these organisational and occupational restructurings.

Foucault's diagnosis of modern society is akin to the mass society envisaged by the Frankfurt School (see Chapter 8), albeit emphasising much more strongly the extent to which individuals are subject to a regime of rationalised administration, making them into passive, acquiescent subjects who even co-operate in their own subordination. Modern society seeks to instil in each individual the disciplined self-control of his or her activities, combined with the elaboration of an ever-more-encompassing system of monitoring. In this way, things which might seem benign – such as the medical and caring professions – are to be revaluated as malign, part of the network of supervision and regulation. The medical and social services have ever-expanding mandates to investigate areas of social life, to find out more and more about people in society, to obtain inquiring entry into more and more formerly private areas of life, to accumulate records on them, to intervene in these areas of life, to acquire powers to reorganise people's private affairs and to subject them to disciplines, i.e. rules of and prescriptions for behaviour intended to bring their conduct into line with the general standard. In short, these services work to normalise people, i.e. to align them with the norm. Normalising in matters of physical health, mental outlook or practical conduct might superficially seem to be done to benefit the individual, but the ways these practices are built up derive very commonly out of a conception of the necessity for the authorities to manage the population; these normalising practices are ways of rendering the population tractable to the managerial activities of the (characteristically state) authorities. It is not what the individual wants, but what the system is deemed to need, that is the decisive consideration.

Despite the way these arguments may sound, there is another important difference between Foucault and the Frankfurt School. His notion of power is anything but a rerun of the (Marxist) idea of a ruling class or stratum using power – or power/knowledge – in order to maintain control over subordinate groups. To think in this way supposes a centre to the operation of power/ knowledge in society. This is anathema to Foucault's way of thinking, since he argues that power is not possessed by individuals and groups and exercised by one set over another. Rather, he holds that power is the milieu in which individuals and groups operate; the workings of power are not centred in any one group or source, they do not arise from any given location in the social structure, they do not all operate from any singular site. For him power is everywhere, it comes from everywhere – recall the all-pervading, capillary connections. The network of surveillance, the patterns of discipline and the knowledges that service them have all grown up outside anyone's control. The arrangements they have were formed quite independently of anyone's purposes; they just cannot be understood as being created in order to permit one group of people to control others.

The consequences for politics are significant. On this conception the idea of confronting power is absurd, for such an idea requires that there be a place within society where power resides. Since power is all pervading, there cannot be any focused, united assault upon it. In so far as modern society is portrayed as being almost exhaustively pervaded by supervision and regulation, there seems to be every reason to draw a conclusion, reached by some members of the Frankfurt School, that the possibility of extensive revolutionary activity within the society has been rendered nugatory. Certainly Foucault rejects the idea of any wholesale uprising of the sort that Marxists envisage. Is *all* point to political activity ruled out? Foucault produces somewhat like a rabbit from a hat, the contention that power generates resistance, that there are reactions against supervision and regulation almost as an inherent response to them, though these are only localised and peripheral within the society as a whole. For example, prisoners oppose in many ways the dominance of the prison system, through minor acts of disobedience, sometimes through prison riots, and through organising pressure groups to fight for their interests. In place of revolutionary activity the most that one can do politically is to align oneself with such struggles; Foucault himself devoted his political efforts almost entirely to agitating for prisoners' rights.

Conclusion

A final point: our discussion perhaps has shown that, notwithstanding its structuralist predispositions, Foucault's work involves a blend of Durkheimian and Weberian ideas (see Chapters 3 and 4). We have noted the similarities with Weber's preoccupation with the process of rationalisation and the development of what we might call the totally administered society. Durkheim's later writings on the social nature of knowledge and the origins of the categories of thought are other vital components in Foucault's work and clearly inform his investigation of the way the categories of (particularly) the sciences can originate. The significance of these classical sociological legacies shows Foucault in some respects making a sociologically comfortable adaptation of structuralism, consistent with dominant themes in the classical tradition. He goes some way towards a radicalisation of structuralism. Yet his depiction of modern society as a disciplinary society dominated by rationalist discourses of professionalised knowledge/power seems overwhelmingly to be characterised by coherence, system and order, despite his caveats about internal inconsistencies and sites of resistance. Consequently, for a fully radical, genuinely poststructuralist stance, we have to look elsewhere, principally to the writings of Jacques Derrida (see next chapter).

Questions

1   Explain and briefly illustrate (a) episteme (b) discourse and (c) archaeology.

2   Compare Foucault's treatment of the insane with Goffman on asylums.

3   Outline Foucault's argument that people shift from being subject to object in modern discourse. How close is this to Weber's rationalisation and disenchantment of modern society?

4   What is the clinical gaze? Is this concept simply another way of talking about modern medicine as an ideology?

5   What is carceral society? Illustrate with reference to (a) prisons or (b) sexuality.

6   Does Durkheim anticipate Foucault's decentring of individuals? Be specific in your answer.

7   Consider the relevance of Foucault's notion of power/knowledge for understanding the role of administration in contemporary society.

Further reading

Gutting, G., 1989, *Foucault's Archeology of Scientific Reason*. Cambridge University Press. Good but complex account of Foucault's views of science.

McHoul, A. and **Grace, W.**, 1973, *A Foucault Primer*. Melbourne University Press.

McNay, L., 1994, *Foucault: A Critical Introduction*. Polity Press.

Merquior, J.G., 1991, *Foucault*, 2nd edn. Fontana. Highly sceptical account.

Poetzl, P.M., 1983, *Michel Foucault's Archaeology of Western Reason*. Harvester. Complex account of Foucault's early work.

Rabinow, P. (ed.), 1986 *The Foucault Reader*. Penguin. Contains a selection of Foucault's own words.

Rabinow, P. and Dreyfus, H., 1983, *Michel Foucault: Beyond Structuralism and Hermeneutics*. Harvester.

Sheridan, A., 1990, *The Will to Truth*. Routledge. Introduction to Foucault.

■　　■　　■

Chapter 12

Poststructuralism and postmodernity

Introduction: Derrida – the project of deconstruction

Like Foucault's, Jacques Derrida's arguments are also primarily about language. Derrida not only rejects representationalism, but also comprehensively abandons any notion of meaning as systematic and of language providing a handle upon the world. Meaning is *imposed*, thereby committing an act of *closure*, which is a form of *violence* against language. Meaning always appears coherent and systematic, but this appearance is chimerical. Once set free from the violence of closure, language will show itself to be wild and unpredictable, magnificent in its disorderliness. Derrida's project, therefore, is to rescue language from the violence of ordering, to oppose closure by *deconstructing* meaning and thereby restoring openness to language.

These are exciting-sounding ambitions, but what precisely do they amount to? Derrida is a philosopher by training and occupation, and his writings are primarily intended as an attack upon philosophical positions. His arguments are essentially pitched against the dominant philosophical tradition, i.e. Western metaphysics, which aspires towards an ultimate or final knowledge of reality. Derrida holds that it is impossible to fulfil this ambition, which is counter-productive and oppressive. Derrida's arguments can be taken to be directed against Western thought more generally, against a world view shared by many more than a few philosophers, but having the same characteristics as his particular target in philosophy. Although distinctive, in its specific development Derrida's critique essentially involves many of the same points we have already considered in Barthes and Foucault (see Chapters 10 and 11), namely that the Western way of thought, expressed through language, is basically repressive; it seeks, particularly, to formulate a straitjacketing conception of language; it seeks to inhibit the unruly ways of language as part of a generally repressive orientation. It is to be countered (at least in part) by a practice which exposes this repressive dimension and cultivates the wayward nature of words. For Derrida, exposing some of the key assumptions underpinning metaphysics (even Western thought generally) contributes to undermining its credibility and contributing to its subversion. One such key assumption is the attainability of *presence*.

Opposing the metaphysics of presence

For Derrida, the search of Western metaphysics for ultimate, final knowledge comes down to the issue of the relationship between speech and writing. Such philosophers as René Descartes and Edmund Husserl (see Chapter 6) have sought ultimate, certain knowledge in the idea that it must be founded in the self-evident.

Presence

The self-evident is what is absolutely true beyond all possibility of doubt. Therefore it must be patently true immediately and merely on presentation. Certain knowledge must therefore be experienced directly without anything intervening between it and the perceiver.

For Derrida, the search for the presence of absolute certainty has proved elusive because it is not to be had. It is a chimera.

He alleges that the idea of presence has found one of its expressions in the way the spoken voice is regarded – at least as far back as Plato – as more authentic than the written word simply because the one producing the words is present when they are produced. Our spoken words are immediately tied to our presence, to our being there to utter them. Similarly, for our interlocutors they are tied to our presence; they must be with us for them to hear our words, and they can then and there debate our meanings with us, getting from our mouths our personal authority for what we mean by our words. With writing we may not be present to accompany our words, to clarify and elaborate upon them if that is required in order to understand them; indeed we may even be long dead when someone reads our words and wonders what we really meant by them. According to Derrida, on this basis many philosophers take speech to express the essential nature of language, i.e. speech is a matter of immediate contact between speaker and hearer and the speaker has the capacity to control the meaning of her or his own words.

Derrida seeks to reverse this relationship and thereby make his conclusive demonstration of the illusory nature of presence. A true understanding of the nature of language comes from writing, rather than speech. Here Derrida agrees with the post-Saussureans (such as the structuralists and his fellow post-structuralists) in rejecting the idea that the presence of the speaker guarantees security of meaning. This idea expresses the classic conception that it is the individual – the subject – who is the source or centre of meaning. Instead, the language system itself and not the individual speaker is the source of meaning. The notion that the speaker originates meaning and ensures it through being present at its production and in control of its interpretation must be rejected.

The subject decentred

The presence of the speaker (the author) is not necessary to the production of meaning.

Writing makes plain that we do not – cannot possibly in the case of dead authors – have access to the presence of the author, yet we are not prevented from reading or from satisfying ourselves that we have understood what was written. For us, 'Homer' and 'Shakespeare' are not actual persons who could enter into our presence; rather they are collections of writings. A better term is *texts*; 'writings' suggests the activity of someone who is doing the writing, whereas texts, suggesting the ensemble of words on the page, does not foreground this connection with an individual producer. After all, anything we say about Homer or Shakespeare as individuals arises primarily from the texts and not the other way around. When people try to decide whether Homer was a single, individual poet or whether *The Odyssey* and *The Iliad* are ensembles of different works, possibly by several authors, or when people argue about whether Shakespeare was the author of the plays under his name, the primary basis for their efforts is the reading of the epics, the plays and the poems, in ways which look for stylistic unities and breaks as part of a search for clues, allusions and hidden messages.

The text as source of meaning

Homer and Shakespeare as individuals emerge from the texts, though the way people commonly talk might make it seem that they hold the opposite view and that the text arises from the individual.

For Derrida, that the individual author is not essential to the meaning of his or her written words establishes a general point about language, i.e. that the subject does not guarantee the source of meaning. He then applies this idea to speech situations and concludes that the presence of the actual speaker is no more relevant than in the case of the written word. Consequently, the situation taken by metaphysical philosophers as the paradigm of presence is denied; for them, the phenomenon of presence ensures meaning, but presence is shown to be illusory.

Différance

Derrida has another main argument – again deriving from Saussurean origins – against Western metaphysics. It is often assumed that the true nature of things is to be found in their origins, that a grasp on their essence is to be gained by tracing them to their beginnings. The idea of the presence of the speaker as the guarantor of meaning is one example of this conception: to find out what the words really mean we must have access to the place whence they initially came, the mouth of the speaker.

However, such an idea is contrary in at least two ways to post-Saussurean views, views which identify two axes to language, the *paradigmatic* and the *syntagmatic*.

The paradigmatic

This refers to the fact that on any occasion of speech the meaning of spoken words is due to their relationship to words which are not themselves spoken, i.e. the contrastive element which we have noted before (in Chapter 9).

When we choose a particular word in a sentence, we do *not* use many other words which could have gone in that same position. For example, in developing the sentence 'the cat sat on the mat', in the position where we put 'cat' we have a choice of many other words that could have gone in the same place – 'dog', for example. The word 'cat' is chosen because of the way it *differs* from those other words.

The syntagmatic

This refers to the selection of words in sequence. A sentence is built up in a temporal sequence, and the meaning of a word in a sentence depends not only upon the words that come before it, but also on those which come after it. We have to wait to see what other words come after to see what a particular word does mean.

For example, if we have a sentence which begins 'The man ate' we shall have to listen (or read on) to see what follows; if the sentence goes 'The man ate his words' rather than 'The man ate the fish', we shall see that 'ate' is very different in the two cases. In other words, we ascertain the meaning of a word by moving further away from its point of origin. The point applies not just to words, but also to sentences. We find what a prior sentence means by hearing/reading what follows it.

In Derrida's hands, however, these arguments are taken further. We have spoken as if waiting for further words and sentences does enable us to decide what is meant, but Derrida wants to argue that we can never arrive at an absolutely definitive, final meaning, for the chain of words and sentences is never ending. We seek to establish what the earlier words mean by listening to or reading what comes later, but there will always be more signs, i.e. more words and more sentences. We can never be sure that the words will not take on a quite different sense by events occurring later.

For example, in Francis Ford Coppola's film, *The Conversation*, words to the effect 'He would kill us if he could' are replayed many times, and are understood to express the fear the couple have that the woman's husband would revenge himself upon them if possible. Then, in the closing sequences of the film, the way the situation is set up leads us to hear the words not as an expression of fear for the lovers' own lives, but as their justification for their decision to murder the husband. They now have the sense, 'We must kill him first, because he would kill us if he could.' Of course, we conclude that this meaning of the words is final, that we now know what they meant all along, but we do so only because Coppola's film draws to a close. There was nothing to stop Coppola prolonging the film and making other twists on this meaning. The chain of signs is endless, and since its elements can work retroactively, there is no point at which we can say utterly conclusively, absolutely finally, what a given string of words means. Thus the desire to establish the actual meaning of a word leads us not in the direction it is commonly supposed to, i.e. back to their initial minting, but in the opposite direction, further away from that point of origin, as we seek to ascertain what was meant by seeing what comes afterward, with the point of origin receding ever further in time.

Derrida coins the expression '*différance*' in a play on two relevant French terms.

Différance

Convenient for translation, this item pertains to the paradigmatic and syntagmatic axes of language: to the importance of *differing* (i.e. of contrasting) and of *deferring* (i.e. of postponing any final conclusions).

Neither at the beginning nor at the end is there a point at which the definitive, unequivocal meaning can be found, since, in a way, there is neither a beginning nor an end. In so far as the location of such a point is an essential to being able to ascertain meaning, and as there is no such point of origin or conclusion, then meaning cannot be ascertained.

Derrida's work has been immensely influential in literary criticism, which has very often given interpretative primacy to the author, seeking to understand literary materials better by assuming that she or he is the source of their meaning. For example, the meaning is to be found by investigating the biographical circumstances of the author, reading the author's letters, interviewing people who knew the author, sometimes interviewing the author in person if available. For Derrida, this approach does not ascertain the meaning of a text by means of other materials such as the life or opinions of the individual. Rather it attempts to ascertain the meaning of one text by reference to *other texts*. These texts can be written or spoken (remember, spoken words are also texts; they are a form of writing, not the other way around). The whole operation proceeds at the level of texts, of relating elements within a text to other elements in the same text, and of relating one text to other texts, and for this reason followers of Derrida speak of *intertextuality*. Thus traditional approaches to literary studies depend for their methods upon the assumption that writings are centred, i.e. their meaning originates with a subject, whereas acceptance of Derrida's line of reasoning involves a comprehensive decentring of texts.

'There is nothing outside the text'

Almost as important as his rejection of the subject is the fact that Derrida, like Barthes and Foucault, has emphasised the (so to speak) opacity of language, i.e. the extent to which it is important to respond to it for its own sake, rather than to treat it as a means to an end as in the representationalist tradition. The latter does so in effect by conceiving language as a window on the world, something we use to access a world beyond. Equally the literary critical tradition has been concerned with the meaning of the text as its message, i.e. what it intends to tell us about the world outside itself, the information or advice that it seeks to convey about how things are or what to do. Derrida, again, is attached to the common poststructuralist conviction that the understanding of language is not to be looked for through conceptions of it which are dominated by the idea that language is essentially a medium through which other things (such as the nature of reality or the intentions and purposes of individuals) are to be sought. The aim is, rather, to examine language as a phenomenon in its own right as found in texts, assemblies of written or spoken words, and indeed to examine any other phenomena which function as signs in human life.

'Nothing outside the text'

Derrida, no doubt provocatively, once made the notorious remark that 'There is nothing outside the text', which many have understood as some kind of denial that anything exists except words (signs), i.e. there is a language but no external world.

Perhaps Derrida might have meant that, from the point of view of understanding texts, the appropriate thing to do is to examine the texts themselves, to see what they are like and how they work, without supposing that the key to what a text is saying/doing is to be found somewhere else (such as in the mind of the author).

Another *possible* way of understanding the suggestion that 'There is nothing outside the text' might be to suppose that Derrida is trying to problematise the distinction between what we say or write on the one hand, and what we talk or write about on the other; to show that what are treated (in philosophy at least) as clear-cut, categorical distinctions, sharply separating different realms of phenomena are anything but. In short, 'words' and 'things' are not as sound, sharp and stable as they are there presented. On this reading, Derrida is not trying to demolish these distinctions, to do away with them altogether. He is no less impressed than Hegel by the fact that philosophy is preoccupied with seemingly irreconcilable oppositions. Hegel sought to show that they could be overcome through reconciliation over the full expanse of history (see Chapter 2), but, if we may put it this way, Derrida is determined to destabilise those oppositions (at least as they have been philosophically construed) and to show that what they attempt to demarcate cannot be contained within the boundaries laid out by the oppositional categories. As mentioned, with respect to the opposition of speech and writing, Derrida sought to show that the philosophers' criteria for contrasting the two did not really distinguish them. Indeed, in terms of these same criteria, writing, not speech, seemed best to embody the general character of language.

Hence he stands the previous contrast on its head: speech seems now to be a derivative and dependent on writing, rather than the other way around. Thus saying that 'There is nothing outside the text' might also be a way of problematising the language/reality distinction, which is a major staple of philosophical dichotomising. Here, the point would be to suggest that the distinction is more complex and much less clear cut than it sounds; separating out the world in itself from our ways of talking about it is easier said than done. If so, Derrida is not therefore doing away with the distinction altogether. After all, the attempt to make the separation (by way of distinctions and contrast) will itself have to be undertaken in language and subject to all the problems which afflict the attempt to set up stable, categorical distinctions. On Derrida's own account of the nature of language, the exercise will be ultimately frustrated. In the same way, Derrida does not set out to demolish the difference between literary and philosophical texts, thereby denying any difference between philosophy and literary theory. Alternatively, he does not set out to deny that there are any differences between literary and factual documents; rather, as part of his programme of destabilising dichotomies, he would want to challenge any claim that this distinction comprises a set of simple, pure, clear-cut and uncomplicated differences which can be given in any sweeping and general way.

To illustrate further we have mentioned Derrida's *Glas* (1986), in which the page is divided into double columns, each column being devoted to a different figure (see Chapter 10). The first is on Hegel, the great philosopher, the other on Jean Genet, a French literary figure of the 1950s and 1960s with an 'outlaw' past and identity as homosexual, thief and prisoner. Derrida's comments are intermixed with materials from the two figures he is commenting upon, and he draws their writings from diverse sources, including personal documents as well as their formally published work. The text is meant to induce uncertainties, both in the sense of doubts and questionings, and also in the sense of things which cannot be resolved or settled. The first is how to read it, for there is no right way of deciding how to alternate between the two columns. Further, the intermixing of the texts raises doubts about its authorship: who is to count as author of an assortment like this? There are doubts about its character as literature and/or philosophy. Hegel is a philosopher, but are his contributions to this book to be read as philosophy? Genet is a literary figure, but could his work be read philosophically in relation to Hegel's? And is *Glas* itself to be seen as philosophy, or as a work of literary art, or as a practical joke in the surrealist mode? And what about the relationship of literature to philosophy? Might Genet's writings have something to say to the philosophy of Hegel?

    Glas can thus bring out doubts about truth and its connection to authority. For example, perhaps Genet's 'outlaw' attitudes informing his own search for truth are a denial of the association that Hegel makes between truth and social authorities, such as the father as the figure of authority in the family or the state as the authority within society. Is, then, philosophy's traditional idea of its search for truth merely another expression of patriarchal domination? Thus *Glas* displays the sense in which deconstruction (see below) is not an attempt to depict or analyse any given text with a view to bringing out its coherent meaning. Rather it performs operations on texts which are disruptive of the quest for coherence and uses texts to create further and different texts which generate, perpetuate and proliferate ambiguities, keeping things unsettled and uncertain, and crossing and recrossing boundaries in ways which show that these cannot stably and unequivocally contain things within their limits.

    Philosophical work and factual reports may have many literary aspects to them and many fictional elements in them; that there is no principled difference between literary and other kinds of texts is not necessarily the same as saying that there are no differences between a piece of fiction and a factual report.

Redrawing the boundaries

The denial of a principled distinction between literary and other texts has an important methodological consequence: it offers the prospect of an extensive redrawing of boundaries within the social sciences and humanities and also makes a tremendous impact on the practice of literary studies themselves. It suggests a fundamental shift in the definition of subject matter, i.e. opening up the boundaries of textual analysis to incorporate many other ('non-literary') kinds of texts. Indeed, since every use of language is a text, there can be no principled grounds for drawing definitive boundaries between any of the disciplines concerned with language and its uses. Derrida's arguments have as a by-product the most profound disciplinary implications: it is no longer possible to treat literary criticism, history, sociology or any other of the human studies as discrete domains on the basis that they deal with different phenomena, have different intellectual concerns and characteristically work with different forms of data; e.g. literary studies address fictional and poetic writings; history studies historical documents; sociology works mainly with interview materials. From the standpoint provided by Derridian arguments about texts and intertextuality, such differences obscure a more profound truth.

Disciplines as convention

Since no text, and no (so-called) type of text, has inherent meaning, no distinctions between texts (or text types) can be treated as authoritative; they are nothing more than conveniences, impositions of arbitrary (and ultimately groundless) convention.

We will consider this point in more detail later.

As already mentioned, Derrida argues against the tradition in philosophy as well as literary criticism. This tradition (perhaps) dominates the broader culture, the general way of thought in the Western world. He is protesting against the effort to straitjacket thought within the confines of unity through logical consistency. His concern is not just to confront or to complain about the dominance of such traditions, but to undermine them and to contribute to the liberation (the free play) of the sign, i.e. to escape from these straitjacketing inclinations and to *empower* (so to speak) the discipline-resistant, uncontrollable nature of language.

Derrida's arguments also have significant methodological implications. As mentioned, the level of operation is, he insists, entirely at the level of the text. We are irreducibly dealing (in literary and philosophical work, and in other intellectual operations) with texts, either written or spoken. If anything is to be done about the straitjacketing of language it must be done in and through texts. Consequently, his arguments require the development of a way of working on texts which undermines the illusion of control over them and over meaning, releases the boundless, uncontrollable capacity of signs, disintegrates the apparent centres and structures in texts and, finally, proliferates the diversity of meanings. The methods developed by Derrida (and also independently by the critic Paul deMan) comprise strategies for dismantling accepted meanings and interpretations, aptly named *deconstruction*.

The policy of deconstruction can be intensely offensive – certainly to the project of the Enlightenment with its emphasis on reason – since it sets no store on logical consistency, usually considered the essence of reason. For Derrida, the unrelenting demand for logical consistency is merely so much dogma, an exercise of power through the attempt to create a structuring grid within which texts can be contained, into which they will be coerced. There seems to be a great deal at stake: the continuing pre-eminence of a whole way of thinking, and not merely disagreement about the policies of literary criticism. One way this thinking is exhibited in Western philosophy is in its dualisms, the oppositional pairing of terms, on which it focuses, e.g. 'truth/falsity', 'speech/writing', 'mind/body', 'philosophy/literature'. As we saw in Chapter 2, Hegel had also noted this usage, making it the basis for his own philosophical scheme, thinking that he could resolve these dualisms. For Derrida, however, they are not stable; the separations they make cannot be sustained. Furthermore, the dualisms are not just oppositions, they are characteristically inequalities; one element of the pair is considered the basic, more profound, or otherwise dominant element. Take Derrida's own argumentative starting point: not only are speech and writing counterposed, but writing is invariably the inferior element – a view which arouses his animosity.

Deconstruction

The operation of deconstruction works in the opposite way to conventional attempts to identify a coherently structured text, unified under its title and the name of the author. The conventional direction seeks out as much internal consistency as possible, trying to bring all aspects of the text within the scheme. Its obverse, deconstruction, cultivates incongruities and paradoxes, highlighting the ways texts are internally divided within themselves, showing how one part of the text counteracts the effect ostensibly sought in another, and revealing especially where aspects of the text resist, confound and unravel the order which seeks to impose itself upon the text.

Some of the operation of deconstruction can be very simply understood as showing that a crucial dualism, an opposition between two categories, cannot be sustained as an opposition. It also claims to demonstrate that the supposed priority of one element over the other cannot be defended and the usual hierarchy can be reversed. For example, the opposition of speech to writing is attacked as an opposition, since Derrida treats speech as a kind of writing (so speech and writing are no longer opposed but are the same thing); yet he also promotes writing above speech, since writing, not speech, most perspicuously exhibits the essential nature of language.

Towards postmodernity

In so far as poststructuralism involves the abandonment of the idea that there is an overall, rationalised order to social thought and progress in social development, it moves beyond modernity and becomes *postmodernity*. The terms 'poststructuralist' and 'postmodern' are often used interchangeably, but we have separated them here, at least (though not only) for presentational reasons. The poststructuralists have been concerned to provide arguments as to why the modernist conception, or the Enlightenment project, as they prefer to call it, cannot be sustained, to show how it is unsustainable relative to the historical developments of the modern period, and to formulate alternative conceptions. However, it would contradict their own arguments to suppose that the critique of the Enlightenment project was thinkable at any time, that the shift beyond modernity had taken place entirely as a result of the free development of the logic of thought and of discussion.

Postmodernity

If we are moving beyond modernity, we are not merely moving beyond a particular intellectual outlook. Rather we must be moving beyond the particular historical period (or epoch) in which the notions of modernity were thinkable into one in which those notions are no longer thinkable, i.e. a postmodern age.

We have chosen, then, to discuss under the heading of 'postmodernity' those thinkers who have rather more to say than Barthes, Foucault and Derrida about the specific character of contemporary society, about the extant or emerging postmodern world.

Lyotard on the postmodern era

However much those who argue for a postmodern approach may eschew Marxist influences in favour (usually) of Nietzschean ones, we cannot help but notice that their argument remains persistently Marxist in its mode. For both Lyotard and Baudrillard, the two key figures in the postmodern analysis, the legacy of Marxist thought – specifically, Marx's base – superstructure distinction – infuses their work, albeit in somewhat different ways.

Jean-François Lyotard (b. 1924) begins his analysis of contemporary post-World War II society from observations about the way the changing structure of economic production has transformed the position of knowledge, especially as a result of the rise of the computer. Here we have the idea of the information age, in which knowledge will itself become a productive force, perhaps the predominant productive force. There have been corresponding changes in the nature of science and technology, which have become particularly focused upon problems of language (as was illustrated in the trajectory from Lévi-Strauss to Derrida: see Chapters 9 and 10) and we note that the information industries involve technologies of communication.

Knowledge as a commodity

Not only does knowledge become a productive force, it also increasingly becomes a commodity, i.e. something produced for the purpose of sale. Knowledge as something to be instilled in the human mind is being displaced by the idea that it is something to be sold.

Consequently, the whole place of the production and dissemination of knowledge within contemporary society is being reorganised.

In the contemporary world, economies are increasingly globalised; economic activity is now beyond the directive control of individual nation states. At the same time, the production and control of knowledge have become an economic phenomenon and, as such, an increasingly political, i.e. governmental, question in so far as issues of control over the economy, including knowledge, increasingly arise. What possibility is there of rational control of these developments? Lyotard maintains that the thought that there might be any sense to these developments has become untenable; they are driven only by what Weber (see Chapter 3) called means–ends rationality, what Lyotard himself terms *performativity*.

Performativity

Essentially this is the standard of practical (particularly economic) efficiency.

The expansion of the economy has become an end in itself, quite independent of any of the standards by which we might otherwise seek to judge things. Usually we do not desire to judge things only by standards of efficiency; there are other standards such as moral goodness, beauty and fairness. Science, however, knows nothing of these things, and scientific knowledge is, of course, a driving force of the economy.

On this argument, it follows that if there is to be knowledge of what is good, beautiful and fair, it cannot be scientific knowledge. If such knowledge is to be found, it cannot be within the forms that scientific knowledge can take. It must take a different form, which Lyotard dubs *narrative*.

Lyotard thus provides yet another version of the transition from traditional to modern society, involving in this case the increasing displacement of narrative by science, making for fragmentation and the loss of wholeness. It is, again, a recounting of the triumph (the empty triumph) of rationalism.

Narrative

In traditional societies, narrative is the common, predominant form within which knowledge is conveyed. Lyotard asserts that knowledge of different kinds can be transmitted through stories. In these traditional societies the role of narrative is functional; it subserves and contributes to the needs of social solidarity.

By contrast, the modern or postmodern form of contemporary society is made up of isolated, atomistic, instrumentally connected individuals. It results from the dissolution of the social solidarity of traditional societies, a process which, in Lyotard's telling, is effected through the rise of the way of thought characteristically dubbed rationalist and pre-eminently embodied in science, i.e. it requires logical, formal, demonstrative reasoning sustained by empirical truth. In short, it requires theoretical structures, not stories. Narrative does not traffic in argument and proof and cannot therefore satisfy scientific standards. Rather than recognising narrative as signifying a different kind of knowledge, however, those enamoured of scientific standards disvalue it, denouncing it as a form of archaic or impoverished thought, e.g. as primitive thought or mere opinion.

Grand narrative

Paradoxically scientific standards are not, and cannot be, self-justifying with respect to such qualities as moral goodness, beauty and fairness, because scientific discourse explicitly excludes narrative discourse, the only form of language that can provide such justifications. Any legitimisation for scientific discourse must, however, be drawn from narrative forms; indeed they illicitly and surreptitiously (but inevitably) must intrude into it. Ironically, then, science cannot do without stories; the task of stories is to provide justification and legitimisation to science. For Lyotard, the modern age has been marked by a number of *grand narratives*.

Grand narratives

These have attempted to provide overarching, comprehensive stories of the development of science, thereby endowing the development of science with sense, with a guiding and worthy purpose.

For example, Marx provided a grand narrative of science, which placed it within the framework of the total history of the human species and attributed to it the purpose of contributing to the progressive freeing of individuals, on the way to the emancipation of humankind as a whole. Another grand narrative, usually referred to as positivism (see Chapter 4), tells of the advance of scientific knowledge, of a continuous movement towards the achievement of final, comprehensive and unified knowledge.

Such myths are often intertwined with the development and justification of the nation state. Lyotard argues that these grand narratives are themselves myths which have lost their hold. Now science has moved away from acquiring knowledge for such high-minded purposes and for its own sake, and into merely being bought and sold by business and the state. Knowledge is acquired for its practical (political or economic) use, and not for its own sake or its improving or emancipatory value. Further, the capacity to justify scientific activity by integrating it into judgements of goodness and beauty through narrative has diminished as the spheres of science, morality and art have been progressively differentiated out in 'modern-into-postmodern' societies. The possibility for artistic and ethical commentary upon science is drastically undermined as these spheres of social life become ever more separated from one another and from the direct, day-to-day experience of people in society; such matters are made over into the business of experts.

The redundancy of grand narrative

The modern outlook, with its hope in the all-commanding, all-comprehending power of reason, has been obviated. It is not now possible for people to place credence in grand narratives, for such attempts at overarching and unifying schemes simply cannot encompass the diversity, the fragmentation, of society today. Since this condition is not temporary, then the day of the grand narrative is over.

Signs in and out of control: Baudrillard

Having started as a sociologist operating within a Marxist perspective, Jean Baudrillard (b. 1924) later, by his own account, turned against Marx and sociology, asserting both to be outmoded and irrelevant. Nevertheless, despite these assertions we will suggest that his work remains in many ways quite continuous with both. Baudrillard's announcements of the end of things – 'reality' and 'the social' being only two (but main) examples – on inspection prove to be hyperbolic expressions of somewhat less exceptionable points. In a way, one could summarise – somewhat unfairly we admit – Baudrillard's main claim as being that contemporary society is dominated by television and advertising (and electronic media more generally), and this domination involves a dehumanisation reminiscent of the emphasis upon and condemnation of alienation found in Marx's early analysis of capitalism (see Chapter 2). Indeed, Baudrillard's claim appears to be that media dehumanisation *is* the contemporary form of alienation. Although Baudrillard does attempt an upturning of the fundamentals of Marx's thought by reversing the base–superstructure relationship, thereby making the production of culture the defining characteristic of contemporary society, Marx's concept of capitalism as a dehumanising force principally drives his arguments.

Similarly, the later Baudrillard professes intense hostility to sociology and categorically dismisses it, yet a central element of his picture of modern society amounts to a recovery of a central preoccupation of both the Frankfurt School and 1950s American sociology: the mass society (see Chapter 8). It was commonly held among both that mass society was marked by cultural superficiality and the political inactivity of the great majority of the population. Baudrillard's assertion of the *death of the social* refers precisely to the political and cultural indifference and unresponsiveness of people; correspondingly, the death of sociology follows only in so far as it involves a conception of sociology as consisting in theorisation of the dynamic and historical role of the masses (in the old Marxist sense). So understood, sociology is justified as a pursuit only so long as a case can plausibly be made for the imminent overthrow of the system by those it oppresses. Since Baudrillard (along with most contemporary sociologists) cannot find plausible grounds of this sort, sociology is dead. Baudrillard's notion of the mass into which society has collapsed (and therefore ceased to be) means that any source of organised opposition or challenge to the status quo has disappeared. In its place there can be, at best, nothing more than a quasi-dormant sullenness: an inert resistance to the persuasion of politics, the blandishments of advertising, the solicitations of the media. It is true that Baudrillard's later work is often more a series of cryptic aphorisms than an explicitly developed argument, but its preoccupations and insistences remain continuous with those of his more traditionally argumentative stances.

There are good reasons, therefore, for not taking too literally Baudrillard's pronouncements concerning the death of this or that. For example, Baudrillard proposes that a perfect crime has been committed, that reality has been disposed of without anyone (except, of course, our Baudrillardian detective) noticing.

The death of reality

How is the claim that reality has been done away with to be understood? Not, we think, as the denial that anything ever really happens, but, rather, much more as a denial that what does happen comprises real (in the sense of authentic) instances of things, as when people say that junk food is not 'real food' – they mean not that you do not get anything to eat, but that you do not get anything with the proper qualities and nutritional values that real food is supposed to have.

For instance, when Baudrillard argues that the Gulf War did not take place (Baudrillard 1995a), he is not denying that there was military activity in the deserts of Kuwait and Iraq, but is rather saying that this military activity did not represent a real war, i.e. amount to a war in the sense which has been traditionally understood. It was not, for example, a contest between two military forces, but between one side with awesome military power, and another side which was hardly well enough organised or equipped to amount to an army. It is a bit more complicated because Baudrillard uses 'real' to make a slightly different contrast, which is the kind that is used in computing with terms like 'real time' and 'virtual reality'. Much of the military activity which took place in the Gulf War was not real, in the sense that much of it did not involve first-hand military activity on the part of human beings, but, rather, was done through electronic, virtual media. So pilots never faced their enemies in reality but only through their virtual representations on electronic displays.

Reality has thus been disposed of in the sense that our actual experience of the world around us is now thoroughly interwoven with and overlaid by virtual representations. We 'watch Grand Prix motor racing' from our couches, on TV screens, and never go near the actual races, and we may well think that the television picture is better because we see more of the race, get replays of the actions and so on.

Lastly, as a fourth element, Baudrillard is arguing that there is (may we use the word) really a reversal of the relationship between the supposed media of representation and the reality those media purportedly represent. Far from what is shown on the television, cinema screen or video display being a representation of a pre-given reality, it is, rather, increasingly the case that what happens in reality forms itself in terms of, after the fashion of, its representation in the media. For example, actual, on-the-street police get their own idea of how the police, and therefore themselves, do/should behave from watching cop shows on TV; the virtual has become the model (or *code*) for the actual.

Similarly, while Baudrillard's beginnings with Marxist suppositions, which he subsequently denounces, show that his career has been one of movement, the idea that this shift involves a decisive renunciation would be misleading. There is much continuity in Baudrillard's career, and the changes frequently consist in taking further his previous positions, even of pushing them to extremes.

Baudrillard is centrally taken with the idea of modern society as *consumer society*, and the terms in which consumer society is depicted are what evolves through his work.

Consumer society

The cumulative picture he paints is of consumer society as one in which an extreme (possibly even the ultimate) form of dehumanisation has occurred and the objects have taken over. The response of people is to make themselves as much like these objects as possible.

The evolution of this view involves adopting the idea that objects themselves have become signs, and so it is no contradiction to say that Baudrillard both:

• sees society as being dominated by objects; and
• sees society as pervaded by signs.

In characteristic Marxist vein, Baudrillard sees the consumer society, with its apparently prosperous, comfortable and enriched lives for many, as a snare and a delusion, as a continuation of the traditionally exploitative nature of capitalism. People are not consuming because they want the things that they are consuming, because these things fulfil their needs. Rather, they are consuming because they are being made to. Were consumption an expression of human needs, then it would (at least on Baudrillard's estimate) result in the satiation of those needs; but it does not do so, and consumption continues to change and grow, following the familiar expansionist dynamic of capitalism. In the age of consumer society, human relationships are becoming more and more one with objects – one's house, car, television, wardrobe, etc. – rather than with people. The importance of objects in people's lives, however, has less to do with the use those objects have than with their meaning. Here is another aspect of the dehumanising effect of capitalism which Baudrillard's later work will emphasise: the essential meaninglessness of life in consumer society.

The turn against Marxism

Given these strong Marxist themes in his work, how is it that Baudrillard came so vehemently to reject the Marxist tradition? Two main elements are important in understanding Baudrillard's turn against Marxism:

1 Baudrillard attaches himself to a nostalgic picture of 'primitive' society involving symbolic exchange, a situation which denies the *use value* of objects.
2 He regards Marx as a perpetrator of bourgeois morality, particularly the work ethic, which is simply outmoded in a consumer age.

Marx's idea was, of course, that capitalism was a system which perverted the treatment of objects. In Marx's terms, objects have a use value.

Use value

This refers to the things one can actually use objects for, e.g. eating in the case of a banana, knocking in nails in the case of a hammer.

Under capitalism, objects are not produced for their use value, but for their *exchange value*.

Exchange value

This is their capacity for being bought and sold in capitalist markets.

Exchange value, rather than use value, decided whether objects were produced, how they were distributed and so on.

Furthermore, as we saw in Chapter 2, part of Marx's conception of human nature was that the essence of human existence is work. In this true human fulfilment may be found, albeit not under the degrading working conditions of capitalism.

Confronting these two points, Baudrillard turns Marx's own concepts against him

---

The rejection of Marxism

Baudrillard argues that the idea of work as a fulfilment of human essence is nothing more than acceptance of the bourgeoisie's own ideology; the idea that production and accumulation are natural features of human life is refuted by life in 'primitive society'.

Baudrillard takes his picture of this type of society partially from Durkheim's collaborator, the anthropologist Marcel Mauss (see Chapter 4). In such societies it is often the highspot of people's lives to engage in the wasteful destruction of property. For example, among the native peoples of British Columbia (as it now is) a ceremony called the potlatch involves the wealthier members of the tribe attempting to impress others in a competition by giving away and destroying their possessions. Mauss sought to explain such behaviour in terms of the symbolic meaning of possessions: what possessions signify about the possessor is important, not their material utility. Another element is also taken from Mauss: an emphasis upon the gift. The exchange of gifts in an elaborate and widely extending circle of relationships is a prominent feature of some so-called primitive societies. Such networks of reciprocal gift giving show, for Baudrillard, that the objects which are exchanged play a symbolic role: the giving of gifts requires exchange, with the object playing the role of making a connection – one of mutual recognition – between people. The objects themselves have this symbolic significance; they are not exchanged to be used, i.e. they are not valued for their capacity in use. Thus Marx's use value is not a necessary foundation for understanding objects, but is itself a creation of certain social conditions.

In these arguments against the foundational status of the material character of objects, we can see how Baudrillard is led to the claim that people carry a sense of a loss of the authentic human contact, that can be found in symbolic exchange. In Western societies, even if objects were not part of a process of symbolic exchange, they once were embedded in social relationships, but now they have been extricated from these, forming systems in their own right. For example, in more traditional Western societies, objects were closely linked with social stratification; whether or not people could possess certain sorts of things depended upon where the people stood in the social hierarchy; the significance of objects was entirely dependent upon the structure of social relationships. However, objects have now been abstracted from such contexts and have an autonomous standing. What matters now is how objects stand in relation to other objects, not how they fit into and facilitate human social relations.

> ## Objects and social relations
>
> The basic charge that Baudrillard makes against contemporary society is that objects and their meaning determine social relations, rather than the other way around.

The consumption of sign-objects

What does it mean to say that objects relate to one another rather than reflecting social relations? Baudrillard employs the example of interior decorating to indicate how a particular object is conceived as part of a system, how it is to fit in with other objects according to various principles, e.g. colour and textural matchings. He makes use of a notion of the *code*, which many commentators find obscure, but these kinds of principles, which articulate objects into patterns, can perhaps be seen as one kind of exemplification. Another is computers, which operate according to binary code. The idea of things as increasingly operating according to (one or another) code makes an analogy with the Saussurean view of language and fits with Baudrillard's contention that objects are operating as signs.

> ## Objects as signs
>
> The production of capitalism is now a production of signs, superficially seen in the way, quite literally, the productive resources of capitalism are increasingly devoted not to the production of physical objects, but to signs (words and images), e.g. with television, computer supplies and so forth. However, Baudrillard's point is that physical objects are also signs. This is the point at which his inversion of Marx takes place, when he insists that the nature of objects as signs is more basic, more fundamental, than their nature as objects with a use value.

Consequently, what is needed to displace Marxism is a political economy of signs.

People have themselves been, so to speak, absorbed into the system of objects. They have been removed from a society in which their sense of themselves was rooted in spatial and social location and are now governed by the codes which produce and circulate signs (including objects). Consuming them is governed by fashion. The possession of things is relative to the images they carry or convey, rather than to their use value. The fact that the images of things change means that new things are desired; the laws of fashion play a strong part in driving consumer behaviour. Consumer goods are being used as a way of forming social difference, not distributed as a consequence of it. In this sense, objects produce (kinds of) people, not the other way around. Thus social identities amount to nothing more substantial than a collection of signifying objects, e.g., wearing spiky hair, chains, safety pins and so forth marked someone out as a punk in the late 1970s.

If production is not the fulfilment of human essence (as it was for Marx), then consumption is certainly not its fulfilment either. Though Baudrillard might deny this is his intent, certainly the nature of his characterisation of consumer society conveys an impression of it as involving a loss of true meaning and an increasing shallowness of existence. We have already referred to the nostalgic contrast implicit in his writings; for him, pre-capitalist and earlier forms of capitalist society placed people in more stable and authentic structures of existence. We have not yet mentioned the way Baudrillard indicts consumer society for bringing about the loss of reality itself.

Baudrillard on Hyperreality

We have seen that one key element of the Marxist scheme which Baudrillard certainly retains is the role of ideology, though the term he uses is 'alibis', by which he refers to ideological justifications of the system.

Alibis

The idea that an object is wanted/possessed for its use value is an *alibi*, i.e. a misleading justification, for the object's real role is as a sign in circulation.

Comparably, the alibi for signs themselves – whose whole point is just to proliferate and circulate – is that they have a use, namely to refer to reality. Baudrillard goes along with numerous other poststructuralists in casting doubt on the idea that signs refer to anything outside themselves, that their role is to identify a pre-existing reality. Rather, it is the other way around, with the sign projecting the reality of which it speaks, a projection which already contains marked ideological elements. We cannot speak of nature, for example, in a way which is not deeply implicated with ideology. In many mouths the notion of nature is permeated with the conception of the unspoiled, though it might in other mouths carry the connotation of the raw and the ruthless (as in 'nature red in tooth and claw'). The central application of this element of *Ideologiekritik* (see Chapter 8) in Baudrillard involves the argument that the operation of culture (of signs) in consumer capitalism is such as to convey the impression (the alibi) that signs do refer to an external reality, when in fact that external reality has been lost by being displaced.

Baudrillard's main targets, and the institutions which principally exemplify these matters, are television and advertising. In both cases a similar alibi obtains: the impression is given that a broadcast or an advert is referring to something real, i.e. a newsworthy event or the use value of the advertised commodity. In fact, the broadcast and the advert have become ends in themselves, things which are consumed for their own sake, not for what they talk about. To fill out the example a little further, consider the way politics has shifted on to television, with television reporting of politics displacing the politics, reporting itself becoming the politics.

As we illustrated earlier, Baudrillard made himself notorious with his argument concerning the Gulf War. During the build-up to it, he asserted that it existed solely as a sign and not at all as a real world event, a real war. What was occurring was only a media phenomenon, not a war taking place in the desert. It was simply something shown on television, for everyone to see. Even when the Gulf War did 'take place', Baudrillard persisted. The war had not taken place, for the role of any actual fighting was merely to contribute to the virtual struggle taking place on television screens. The battle scenes were produced (in the desert) merely to be reproduced, i.e. to provide things to show on television in order to give the image of American supremacy and victory.

Signs as reality and hyperreality

In the modern world, the world as given in signs (especially as images on television and computer screens) is the reality. This reality has not only displaced the original reality but has transcended it, has become more real than real, has become, in Baudrillard's term, *hyperreal*.

Examples are the attempt to make video games more exciting than the racing or fighting activities that provide their materials, and the aspiration to develop virtual reality to a point at which it will give ever more intense and convincing experiences.

In a way, though, we are being a little bit false to Baudrillard's ideas by talking about the reality and the sign since, for him, they have imploded. They have become so involved with each other that it is no longer possible to separate what is real from that what is, say, fictional; though, of course, it is a feature of the ideological nature of the system of signs that it functions to project and protect the impression that there is a difference between the image and reality, that the reality exists beyond the image, thereby concealing the fact that the reality has disappeared. Witness the emphasis in television coverage of the Gulf War on eye-witness reports, pictures from near the front and so forth.

The simulacrum and the death of the social

According to Baudrillard, we live, in the time of the *simulacrum*.

The simulacrum

This is an image without an original.

The current era of hyperreality is the product of a historical progression in which the relationship between reality and sign has gone through various forms to arrive at this point. This four-stage sequence began with the traditional society, in which signs were installed within and governed by the social order, and where there is no problem about the relationship of signs to reality. The Renaissance was the time of the *first order* of simulacra, i.e. the sign independent of reality and produced a change with the loosening of social control over social position and concomitantly over signs. People could be socially mobile (unlike traditional society) and thus they could use signs in the competition for, and confirmation of, rises in status. The competition for signs inevitably gave rise to counterfeiting, ways of using signs to convey a reality to which they do not actually correspond. The *second order* of simulacra comes with the industrial age and the mechanical reproduction of images. Now images can be bought and sold freely, the difference between an original and a reproduction ceases to matter, and many industrial products are mechanical reproductions, but not of any original. For example, the mechanical line produces many motor cars, each reproducing the same design, but not reproducing some first, original, copied car. The *third* stage, in which we currently live, is increasingly dominated by digital technology, a prominent instantiation of the rule of code. In the age of the hyperreal, signs now generate reality rather than reflect or distort it.

Baudrillard is not wholly fatalistic; he does find some limited grounds for opposition to this state of affairs. However, it is not an active form of resistance; rather, it is an inert, sullen, resentfulness which is exhibited by 'the mass'. Mass communication contrasts with symbolic exchange. In the latter case both parties are active; a message is exchanged and the action of each is a response to the other. Mass communication, however, is a one-way process, with no real recognition of, or response to or from, the other; in Baudrillard's view 'the mass' in contemporary society has not absorbed the messages sent out through the mass media. It is resistant to them since, being only one-way, they are not truly communicating. Hence the mass neither absorbs nor responds to them. Somewhat as happens with the astronomical phenomenon of black holes (into which light is drawn but from which it cannot then escape), the output of the media is directed at and into the mass but no output is returned. The mass as such has no active part to play in the politics of the society, refusing to respond to the blandishments of the media, or to let itself be known through its own political actions. Hence it can be known only through research, e.g. opinion polls, which it may entertain itself by deceiving. The unresponsiveness of the mass does not show contentment, but rather discontent and resentment.

The death of the social

It is this change of the majority of the population into a television audience, and this audience into a privatised, non-communicative people, which comprises the formation of 'the mass' or, alternatively, the *death of the social*.

Incidentally, this death of the social signifies in its turn the end for sociology. Here Baudrillard echoes Durkheim since, without the social, sociology has no subject matter and no *raison d'être*.

As we said, Baudrillard's argument is about the meaninglessness of lives in contemporary societies, where all sorts of boundaries are collapsing, e.g. between fiction and reality, between science and art, between the sexes, between work and leisure, etc. A social order structured around differences has given way to a society in which characteristics are freely purchasable in the consumer culture. It is a society in which the point of differentiation is not to mark real differences, but to attempt to recreate differences which have disappeared or are disappearing, to produce boundaries which are no longer necessitated by the order of social affairs. There is a shallow nostalgia for that which is putatively lost, such as nature, but the nature which is yearned for is not one that ever really existed. Instead, it is an ideologically loaded conception of nature, a nature whose recapture is attempted through simulations, e.g. through wilderness parks, nature conservancies and the devotion of television time to images of animals in the wild.

Whatever might be said about Baudrillard being fascinated by and even relishing many of the characteristics of contemporary society, it is hard to read most of his writings as other than highly critical of such a society. He depicts its culture as an essentially aimless and enfeebled one, in which the point of many activities has been lost, displaced or confused; it is a stagnant, shallow and dispirited culture. Its tone is distinctly hysterical and many of its tendencies are out of control, as seen in *fatal strategies*.

Fatal strategies

These stem from their own logic of development, which will take them progressively to extremes and ultimately to self-devastation; e.g. the enthusiasm for the car has brought us to the point at which the roads are clogged by them.

The culture cannot resist the capacity of digitally encoded materials to proliferate across, and eventually to obliterate, all lines of separation, and to reduce things to the lowest common denominator. It is a culture devoid of real creativity; many of its strongest reactions are simply panic reactions. There is frantic pursuit of ephemeral fashion, the recreation of what has gone before; the mere and unimaginative recombination of available elements is the main base of further productivity. Such a 'culture' can hardly be credited with this title, since it is without real meaning, foundation or purpose. The great majority are alienated from a culture which, through its media of mass communications, seeks to maintain the great illusion, namely that the reality principle is still in operation, even though that reality has been displaced entirely by the burgeoning of simulations.

Conclusion

The work we have been reviewing in this chapter is often characterised as nihilistic, meaning that it rejects all established beliefs and values. The long-established and well-entrenched convictions bequeathed by the Enlightenment are certainly open to dismissal. In the context of theory, the very notion of discipline begins to sound inappropriate, with its suggestion of a well-demarcated, distinct and independent field of activity, and the further suggestion of regulation and self-regulation through subordination to controlling methods of inquiry. Thus the approaches reviewed in this part are often accused of bringing the academy into both intellectual and political disarray. At the least, the critique of the Enlightenment means, in respect of theory, the drastic redrawing of intellectual boundaries, and the abandonment of the traditional theoretical and methodological ambitions of the social sciences, especially the ambitions for rigorous and thoroughly standardised methods of inquiry, and for all-embracing, universal theoretical schemes. The desire to assemble growing bodies of positive knowledge is now confronted with approaches which are devoted, rather, to continual confrontation with, and subversion and dissolution of, all attempts to develop supposedly 'rational' schemes and promote 'rationally' based social arrangements.

Questions

1 'Barthes kills off the author, but Derrida makes him or her disappear!' Explain and discuss.

2 What are the implications for the study of society of Derrida's view that there is nothing outside the text?

3 What is deconstruction? Is it a method of research?

4 Why does Lyotard regard grand narrative as redundant? Is there a self-contradictory dimension to his argument?

5 Describe Lyotard's view of postmodern society. What are the main influences he sees as shaping it? Do you agree?

6 What is Baudrillard's view of postmodern society? Is it related to Lyotard's view? How much does it owe to Marx?

7 Discuss the view that the world given in signs is *the* reality and illustrate your answer with reference to a major contemporary event.

Further reading

Baudrillard, J., 1988, *Selected Writings*. Polity Press. A substantial selection of his writing.

—— 1990, *Revenge of the Crystal: A Baudrillard Reader*. Pluto Press. Another subbstantial selection of Baudrillard's writing.

—— 1995, *The Gulf War Did Not Take Place*. Power Press. Collects Baudrillard's commentaries on the Gulf War.

—— 1996, *The Perfect Crime*. Verso. One of Baudrillard's more accessible accounts of how reality has been 'disposed of'.

Bennington, G., 1988, *Lyotard: Writing the Event*. Manchester University Press. A good introduction.

Bennington, G. and **J. Derrida**, 1993, *Jacques Derrida*. University of Chicago Press. Bennington's part of this book is probably the best explanation of Derrida's views. Derrida's contribution, on the bottom half of the pages, is as good a source as any for a flavour of Derrida's style.

Boyne, R., 1994, *Foucault and Derrida: The Other Side of Reason*. Routledge. Recounts the disagreement between the two, and compares their thought.

Callinicos, A., 1989, *Against Postmodernism: a Marxist Critique*. Polity Press. An attack on poststructuralism and postmodernism from the advertised Marxist point of view.

Culler, J., 1982, *On Deconstruction*. Routledge. A short introduction to the idea of 'deconstruction'.

Derrida, J., 1991, *A Derrida Reader: Between the Blinds*. Wheatsheaf. Contains a substantial selection of writings.

Gane, M., 1991a, Baudrillard: Critical and Fatal Theory. Routledge. An introduction, but not at an introductory level.

——1991b, Baudrillard's Bestiary: Baudrillard and Culture. Routledge. A discussion of aspects of Baudrillard.

Gasché, R., 1986, *The Tain of the Mirror: Derrida and the Philosophy of Reflection*. Harvard University Press. A more difficult account.

Jameson, F., 1991, *Postmodernism, or the Cultural Logic of Late Capitalism*. Verso. Marxist account of the phenomena which are generally identified as postmodern. An article-length version of Jameson's argument appeared under the same title in *New Left Review* (1984), 184: 53–92.

Kellner, D., 1989, Jean Baudrillard: From Marxism to Postmodernism and Beyond. Stanford University Press. An introduction, but not a clear one.

Lyotard, J.-F., 1984, *The Postmodern Condition*. Manchester University Press. A short, though not easy, statement of his position.

May, T., 1994, *The Political Philosophy of Poststructuralist Anarchism*. Pennsylvania State University Press. An examination of poststructuralist anarchism in philosophical terms.

Megill, A., 1985, *Prophets of Extremity*. University of California. Contains discussion of Derrida.

Norris, C., 1987, *Derrida*. Fontana. A good short introduction.

—— 1992, *Uncritical Theory: Postmodernism, Intellectuals and the Gulf War*. Lawrence and Wishart. Critical onslaught on postmodernism, particularly provoked by Baudrillard's responses to the Gulf War.

Tallis, R., 1988, In Defence of Realism. Edward Arnold.

—— 1995, Not Saussure: A Critique of Post-Saussurean Literary Theory. Macmillan. Two attacks on postmodernism from a more traditional, realist point of view.

■   ■   ■

Chapter 13

Back to sociological theory?: theoreticism and synthesis

Introduction: Mouzelis – back to sociological theory

In 1990 Nicos P. Mouzelis published *Back to Sociological Theory*, which was followed in 1995 by another book, *Sociological Theory: What Went Wrong*. These were only one author's contribution to a number of books expressing concern about the state and identity of sociology – by which is meant, primarily, sociological theory – to appear in recent years. At the same time, books were also being published with highly indicative titles welcoming *The Return of Grand Theory in the Human Sciences* (Skinner 1985). Similar articles were also written. For example, Frederick Crews (1986) complained of the way theorising in the social sciences had virtually run away with itself and become *theoreticism*.

Theoreticism

Crew's complaint was that theorising had become an end in itself, dissociated from its original purpose and detached from empirical inquiry and evidence.

Such theorising very largely involved the theorists using recombinations of elements of one another's schemes. Crews's complaint was against the way theorising seemed to have dissociated itself from the business of informing and organising empirical inquiry (and its results). In losing sight of the connection to empirical work, it had also loosened itself from the constraint and discipline which this connection entails. In short, the need to relate the constructions of theory to (evidence of) the real world can provide a check upon the excesses of theory. Consequently, our original thought was to title this chapter 'The synthesists' in order to reflect the extent to which the theorists we shall look at – Mouzelis, Randall Collins, Jeffrey Alexander, Anthony Giddens, Pierre Bourdieu and, Jürgen Habermas – all contribute few new theoretical ideas to the schemes they propound. Their schemes are constituted by ideas taken from previous and diverse sociological theories and traditions. To this extent, our treatment confirms Crews's complaint about theoreticism.

The attempt by Mouzelis and others to reassert the importance of sociological theory against social theory is to seek to pursue – in principle perhaps rather more than in practice – the very project which has been dismissed as *demodé* by social theory, i.e. by proponents of poststructuralism and postmodernity. For Mouzelis one source of the difficulties which need to be corrected by the reassertion of sociological theory resides in the overreaction to Talcott Parsons, and we share, at least, his view that the critical response to Parsons was misinformed and misguided (see Chapter 5). In this respect, Jeffrey Alexander and the neo-functionalist tendency (see below) are mainly devoted to a rehabilitation of Parsons's thought and its adaptation to respond to certain criticisms. Mouzelis himself is critical of Parsons yet none the less wishes to see a resuscitation of the kind of theorising in which Parsons engaged. Mouzelis seeks to present it as a modest enough ambition, i.e. to provide a generalised conceptual apparatus for assisting empirical investigators, enabling them to give a systematic co-ordination of their work by means of a shared frame of reference within which to compare their results. At the same time, however, we also know that the idea of theory which derives from Parsons is of an all-embracing scheme, one which smacks of a would-be grand narrative of the sort that Lyotard tells us can no longer be credible (see Chapter 12). Moreover, it also retains the idea of sociology as a theoretically governed science. This idea is to defy (though not perhaps to defuse) social theory, which opposes the ambition to be a science. And, of course, social theory also rejects the concomitant notion that abstract generality can be a successful form of understanding.

Mouzelis and the synthesisers

Mouzelis and those he discusses have been struggling, then, against the tide of intellectual fashion, i.e. social theory, which sees itself as having largely left behind the concerns of sociological theory. The concerns of the synthesists remain much the same as those provoked by Parsons and the reaction against him – indeed, inevitably so, in so far as the synthesists attempt to construct theories which will overcome what they see as divisions within sociological thought. That is, they see that sociological thought has been riven with dispute, and that the various factions identify themselves in intellectually oppositional ways. Hence there are recriminations between determinists and voluntarists, between realists/objectivists and idealists/subjectivists, between macro or structural and micro or interactionist, between (methodological) individualist and holist, and between consensus and conflict sociologies, to name some of the main divisions. The theorists we discuss in this chapter have sought to construct unified theoretical schemes for sociology which transcend these divisions. We are apt to call them 'synthesists', however, because their efforts at theory construction have not involved any attempt at a fundamental reworking of sociology's problems and ideas; they do not seek to bypass the oppositions altogether.

Synthesis

A main objective of the synthesists' respective theories has been to achieve comprehensiveness by including the main disputing positions within their proposed new, single, unified theory in an attempt to incorporate and reconcile the ostensibly divided positions. Expressing this point in the simplest terms, the theory-building technique has been to replace 'either/or' with 'both/and'.

Efforts at these kinds of reconciliations began some time ago, in the late 1950s and early 1960s. For example, Ralf Dahrendorf (1958) tried to argue a way out of the consensus-versus-conflict opposition by proposing that society should be seen as 'Janus-faced', i.e. a 'two-faced' phenomenon. Peter Berger and Thomas Luckmann (1967) sought to dispense with the opposition between views of society as an objective phenomenon (e.g. the sorts of views that Marx or Durkheim exemplified: see Chapters 2 and 4) and society as a subjective phenomenon (e.g. as instantiated by such as Schutz, symbolic interactionists and ethnomethodologists: see Chapters 6 and 7) by maintaining that society was both an objective and a subjective reality. For them, indeed, social processes of reality construction could be analysed in a manner – highly reminiscent of Parsons's account of socialisation and institutionalisation – which would trace the way subjective experience became objectified, i.e. what Parsons would have called institutionalised. Thus it can be seen how the previous 'either/or' situation – *either* society as conflict *or* society as consensus, *either* society as objective *or* as subjective reality – is replaced by 'both/and', i.e. society as *both* conflict *and* consensus, society as *both* objective *and* subjective reality. Seemingly opposed views were to be reconciled within a single scheme, but both Dahrendorf and Berger and Luckmann merely offered indications of axes along which the combination of these views were to be attempted, without much effort at elaborating the scheme that could result. The attempt to spell out rather more elaborate schemes singles out most of the theorists we are dealing with here. Their schemes seek to reconcile and combine some (or even all) of the above-mentioned sociological oppositions. Nevertheless, we should perhaps note in all these theorists one characteristic which brings them into some correspondence with thinkers in social theory: their response to power.

Power

In the case of the sociological theorists, this characteristic lays an emphasis upon power and domination as key phenomena which any general theory must treat as of central concern, and represents a common reaction against Talcott Parsons. If anything, they are convinced that social cohesion and consensus originate in power rather than, as Parsons proposed, the other way around.

As already suggested, Mouzelis himself diagnoses a key source of post-Parsonian difficulties as resulting from the (over)reaction against Parsons, an overreaction which had, however, rightly involved negative responses to two failings of Parsons's theory: (1) underplaying the voluntaristic aspect of social life and, relatedly, (2) overconcentrating on the *macro* (large-scale), whole-system level of analysis at the expense of the *micro* level (face-to-face interaction between individuals). Mouzelis can therefore welcome, for example, the appearance of interactionist sociologies such as those detailed above in Chapters 6 and 7 (symbolic interaction and ethnomethodology). These sociologies, however, are accused of going to the other extreme: in Mouzelis's account they insist on treating face-to-face interaction as completely detached from the macro level, if they do not altogether deny reality to the latter. If we were to accept Mouzelis's own characterisations of Parsons, of interactionist sociologies, of his criticism of Parsons's failings, and of overreaction to them, then a middle road would be called for. Such a road would recognise that society has both macro and micro levels of structure; these levels are not independent, since micro levels of interaction are not between individuals considered as isolated entities, but between individuals considered as bearers (to use Weber's terms: see Chapter 3) of the affairs of larger social units, such as churches and schools. Mouzelis endorses Randall Collins's (1981) formulation of this position as *situationalism*, as opposed to individualism.

Situationalism

Collins argues that individuals act in terms of social situations, so that one acts within the context of a bank, a church, a scientific laboratory or some other socially organised environment, and that, therefore, micro and macro analysis can be connected by analysing the way activities, connected in chains of interactions, realise the organisation of larger social structures (as the relation of teller and customer enacts the affairs of a bank, the monetary system, and so on).

The approaches of macro analysis should be combined with the methods of micro analysis, for the study of the latter should proceed through the use of audio and video recording and examined through the kinds of techniques that have developed for analysing such materials in, for example, ethnomethodology, and not through, say, social survey methods.

Mouzelis's own agenda is to combine such observations about micro sociology and the formulation of this position as situationalism with a view of society as a complex, differentiated, articulated but, above all, hierarchical structure. He is convinced (falsely, we believe) that the above interactionist approaches have denied, neglected or understated the extent and importance of the fact that social life takes place within hierarchically structured arrangements. His objection to poststructuralist and postmodernist approaches is that they have overestimated the extent to which there is a demise of boundaries in their emphasis on the way contemporary society changes, i.e. in their focus on the disintegration of traditional social forms, the collapse of an overall organisation for society, and the concomitant evaporation of many of the established lines of social division. At the same time, by overestimating these changes, they have underestimated the extent to which reality can still be comprehended in terms of the traditional categories of sociological analysis. Indeed Mouzelis insists upon the relevance of these categories; the social theorists have not done away with distinctions between, say, macro and micro any more than they have really liquidated the boundaries between disciplines. Mouzelis cannot accept the poststructuralist idea that society as a differentiated structure of hierarchical relationships no longer exists. For him an alternative picture of society as a plurality of diversified, independent discourses or language games (to use Lyotard's adaptation of Wittgenstein's phraseology), which are not arranged in any stably hierarchical pattern, is quite unacceptable.

Mouzelis wants to maintain that society continues to exist in this traditional conception, and that it is within the hierarchical structure of social relations that discourses are formed and implemented. He suggests that the poststructuralists are less than consistent; while they disavow this traditional conception of society, at the same time it is at work in their actual analyses. The ultimate recommendation from Mouzelis is for a moderated functionalism.

Moderated functionalism

This respects the view of society as a structured whole, but employs this conception in a heuristic not a dogmatic manner, i.e. it is used as a tool for provoking questions about the sustaining conditions for particular institutions or practices in relation to the requirements of the society as a whole.

This conception of the social whole, the system, emphasises the systemic properties to a lesser degree than does (perhaps) Parsons, and recognises that the various levels of social organisation, macro, meso (i.e. middling) and micro are themselves interrelated within a hierarchically structured order. Mouzelis's efforts, then, are primarily akin to those of the neo-functionalists, who have sought, within their broadly Parsonian standpoint, to accommodate objections to Parsons's (supposed) underemphasis on disintegration and conflict within society. They also resemble Louis Althusser's attempts to relax the systemic conception of Marxism, through notions of relative autonomy (see Chapter 9). Mouzelis's moderated functionalism brings him close to the grouping of post-Parsonians known as neo-functionalists (perhaps most prominently represented by Jeffrey Alexander (1985).

Neo-functionalism

The neo-functionalists allow that Parsons's work is not entirely exempt from conservatism, from idealism (in the sense of giving too great an emphasis to the role of ideas/culture) and from excessive theoretical abstraction, though less so than many critics have alleged.

Neo-functionalism

Neo-functionalists follow a broadly Parsonian line, with the following guiding principles:

- Functionalism provides a descriptive portrayal of society as a relatively self-contained system, which is organised through the interaction of its parts, but without any suggestion that there is any overriding principle or force directing the system as a whole.
- Ideas of system equilibrium and system integration are analytical tools to help describe society, though without assuming that members of society are attempting to achieve these conditions. Alexander (1985) says that integration is a possibility and that deviance and social control are facts, thereby making it quite clear that there is no naive assumption that actual societies are fully integrated.
- It is assumed that there must be some degree of integration of culture, personality and social system. Naive assumptions about complete integration within culture, personality and social system respectively, as well as between them, must be avoided; within and between these elements there are tensions which create strain and provoke change.
- Change is not only a product of strain and tensions. Indeed, change can often produce strain and tension. There is a long-term evolution of Western societies through the progressive differentiation of previously undifferentiated features of the cultural, social and personality systems. These changes have moved the society as a whole from one relatively integrated level to another, and have become reintegrated at a higher level of adaptability.

But does this form of functionalism, however, represent its final denaturing? As we noted with Althusser (see Chapter 8), the idea that society is made up of a set of parts which interact with and affect one another is a general sociological idea, and certainly not distinctive to functionalism. Turner and Maryanski (1979) argue that what was both distinctive and also problematic about functionalism is the idea of explaining features of the society in terms of the needs of the whole system. This idea is absent from neo-functionalism.

There was also argument as to whether Marxism is a form of functionalism.

Marxism and functionalism

On the one hand, Jon Elster (1985) argued that the greater part of Marxist analysis was actually functionalist in nature. For example, Marx does analyse the organisation of capitalism in relation to meeting the needs for reproducing the capitalist system. For Elster, this part of Marx's work was invalid and needed to be reworked on the basis of an individualist approach. On the other hand, G.A. Cohen (1978) agreed that Marx's core theory did use functionalist analysis (of the kind which recognised that parts of the society could contribute to the maintenance of the whole) but, for him, it was a perfectly valid form of analysis.

Giddens: the theory of structuration

A critique of the shortcomings of functionalism was the starting point for one of the most notable attempts at theoretical synthesis in contemporary sociology, contained in the writings of Anthony Giddens. The work of Giddens is impossible to summarise in its totality, since it ranges across many different kinds of writings. There is Giddens the commentator, who has written essays on just about every major figure in the history of sociology (and many minor ones). There is also Giddens the substantive social theorist, who, over his career, has written on an immense variety of topics and problems, from suicide to social class in industrial capitalism and from violence and the nation state to modern identity. There is also Giddens the textbook writer, author of several of the most popular introductory works on general sociology and classical sociological theory. Since none of these is directly relevant here we shall pass over them and concentrate on the Giddens most relevant to our purposes, and also the most controversial in contemporary sociology, i.e. Giddens the general theorist. In a linked series of books from the mid-1970s onwards and culminating in *The Constitution of Society* in 1984, Giddens put forward a theory intended to provide a unifying framework for sociology.

Giddens's critique of functionalism centred on its failure to provide a convincing, overarching framework for sociological analysis. Thus, his principal target was Parsons. His criticisms of Parsons followed the lines with which we are now familiar: an overemphasis on the unifying structures of society and neglect of centrifugal forces; an unjustified assumption that normative consensus is the principal underpinning of social structure; and a failure to take adequate account of the interpretative dimension in human action. Notwithstanding these basic shortcomings, however, Giddens recognised the importance of Parsons's project in attempting to formulate an integrated set of concepts which would solve the basic problems of sociological theorising. The problem was not that Parsons had set himself this goal but that he had failed to accomplish it. Giddens took up this same challenge, i.e. to show how the divergencies and inconsistencies of sociological theorising could be overcome by building a systematic theoretical scheme which would bring together apparently different – even opposed – sociological ideas. Later, we will bring out important differences between Giddens's and Parsons's projects, not least in terms of how the projects are brought off and the success with which they bridge the gap between abstract theory and substantive analysis. First, however, we consider the main lines of Giddens's theory.

Structuration theory

Giddens called his project *structuration theory*, after its key concept of *structuration*. His theory seeks to link together and reconcile the central dichotomy around which sociological approaches are divided: that between *action* and *structure*.

In Giddens's view, sociological theorising falls into two broad types.

Action and structure

On the one hand are theories which emphasise the individual actor as the creator of society; actors possess consciousness and therefore have agency, the capacity to plan and reflect upon their conduct. They give meaning to their circumstances and act towards one another on the basis of these meanings. The outcome of these actions is the formation of relationships and patterns of action which ultimately make up what we refer to as a society. Action theories thus take a bottom-up view of social life; they do not deny that it is structured but regard structures as products of action and interaction. Structural theories, on the other hand, take a top-down view. In Durkheimian fashion, they characterise society in terms of patterns and forms which (1) are independent of individual actors and their intentions and (2) constrain the possibilities of action.

For Giddens, both viewpoints express a partial truth. Giddens aims to show that these two broad perspectives are not incommensurable but complementary and mutually interdependent; we misunderstand the nature of social life if we imagine that one must be correct and the other one wrong. To say that they are two sides of a coin is a bad analogy, since we can only see one side of a coin at a time. It is better to say that they are connected in the manner of the axes which define a two-dimensional geometric space. Of course, if we insist on looking in a one-dimensional way – if we turn the social object into a one-dimensional figure by, say, only looking along its length – then the other dimension disappears and society seems to be purely action or purely structure. Giddens's task, then, is to show how we can see both dimensions at once without going cross-eyed.

Giddens refers to this two-dimensionality of social life as *duality of structure*.

Duality of structure

Social structures seem to have a fixed, object-like character only as long as we observe them from a point of view which leaves aside the dynamic processes of action in and through which structures are continuously sustained and recreated.

These processes are what Giddens refers to by the term 'structuration'.

Structuration

This is a generic term for the many processes of action and interaction involved in the production and reproduction of structure. However, the relationship between the action dimension and the structure dimension is not one-way but two-way.

It is not simply that actions generate structures through structuration, or that actors simply choose to produce actions of a given kind, ones that will sustain structures. That it is possible and necessary for actors to engage in structurating action is to do with the ways structures both *enable* and *constrain* actions. Traditionally, sociology has tended to emphasise the constraining relationship between structure and action, the ways actions are shaped and predetermined by their structural context. Giddens points out, at least as important as constraint is the enabling relationship. Structures make it possible for actions to be performed, since those actions are not free-standing but are actions within a structure, i.e. it is their structural context which makes them possible and intelligible in the first place. Corresponding to the dual constraining/enabling relationship, which characterises structuration, are two general kinds of linkage between the structure and action dimensions: *rules* and *resources*.

In his discussion of rules Giddens draws heavily on the linguistic turn in sociology, which we have commented upon extensively in earlier chapters. For example, from the writings of Winch (see Chapter 6) he draws the point that actions are rule-following; recognising some piece of behaviour as a kind of action involves seeing it in terms of a rule or set of rules.

Rules

Rules are constitutive as well as normative, i.e. rules make actions recognisable as the actions they are as well as defining what should and should not be done in a given set of circumstances.

From the structuralist/semiological tradition of Saussure, Giddens draws the idea that rules form systems which pre-exist any particular instantiation they have in a given item of behaviour (speech). But whereas in Saussure the distinction is drawn between speech (*parole*) and language (*langue*), Giddens distinguishes between *action* and *practices*. Practices are the organised forms of action to which sets of rules apply and which they define. Thus practices mediate between the two dimensions of action and structure; practices are the organised forms or contexts of action (i.e. what Wittgenstein referred to as 'games') and the patterned components of social systems.

Giddens defines resources as follows:

Resources

These are 'the structured properties of social systems, drawn upon and reproduced by knowledgeable agents in the course of interaction' (Giddens 1984: 15). Thus resources refers to anything which provides the actor with power, i.e. with some means for realising his or her ends.

They may take a variety of forms, including material resources (wealth, property, etc.), symbolic resources (personal prestige, the trappings of office, etc.) and biological and cognitive resources (physical strength, skill, knowledge, etc.). In performing any action, the actor draws upon and utilises some of these resources; an action uses up some resources, though Giddens is quick to emphasise that one must not assume a zero-sum conception of resources, i.e. that a resource is necessarily finite and therefore is limited in its distribution and diminished in its use. While this may be true of some kinds of resources in some uses (as when someone uses up their prestige by making improper requests, thereby imposing upon another's deference or goodwill), it is by no means always true. For example, my knowledge is not diminished in its use, nor does my knowledge about something preclude your knowing it also. In fact, the zero-sum situation is the exception rather than the rule in social life, contrary to much sociological theorising about power.

Giddens asserts that 'one of the main propositions of structuration theory is that the rules and resources drawn upon in the production and reproduction of social action are at the same time the means of system reproduction' (1984: 19). Again, this is the idea of duality of structure.

Structure, rules and resources

Structure consists in the organised pattern of rules and resources which actors utilise and in using reproduce. A further feature of structure, therefore, is that it persists in time and space.

Giddens claims that sociological theory has tended to neglect the significance of temporality and spaciality in analysing social life. Rules and resources are structural precisely because they transcend the particular temporal and spatial location tied to any given occasion of their use. Therefore, what crucially is reproduced in action and interaction is this temporal and spatial transcendence. Of course, the form that such reproduction takes is a matter for empirical investigation.

A further element in Giddens's analysis of structuration involves identifying three *modalities* of structure.

Modalities of structure

These are three general forms which structure can take and which are produced and reproduced in action and interaction. These three forms are referred to as *signification*, *domination* and *legitimation*.

By *signification*, Giddens means language and other symbolic orders, i.e. all those ways for human beings to express themselves and communicate with others. The organised forms of communication both make possible particular communicative acts and, at the same time, also reproduce the system of rules, the codes. Members of society share these codes, which makes it possible for them to understand one another.

By *domination*, he refers to all the organised ways in which humans are related to one another in structures of hierarchy and control. Once again, at the same time these structures make possible certain kinds of actions and interactions between persons and also reinforce and reproduce the hierarchies which these actions presuppose.

By *legitimation*, he means the normative aspect of social systems, the sets of moral beliefs which are shared by some or all of a society's members. All actions are subject to normative appraisal, to judgement about whether they are proper, acceptable, desirable and so on. Giddens emphasises that, while such judgements are informed by socially shared assumptions, it may not be the case that all members of society accept the same moral standpoints. Indeed, in the kind of complex and differentiated society we live in such consensus is highly unlikely.

Clearly, these structural modalities are abstractly conceived, but each constitutes a locus around which the various concrete institutions of a society cluster. Thus, again, Giddens's idea has something in common with Parsons's notion of the functional prerequisites of society (i.e. the AGIL framework: see Chapter 5). This is somewhat strange since, as we have indicated, Giddens is highly critical, not to say dismissive, of functionalist thinking in sociology: in fact, Giddens refers to structuration theory as a 'nonfunctionalist manifesto' (1979: 7).

Giddens's synthesis

Much of the controversy surrounding Giddens's structuration theory has centred on what kind of theory it is and whether it successfully synthesises the action–structure dualism. A common criticism is that it fails to do so, merely reproducing and confirming dualism by favouring one side of the dichotomy over the other. Which side the theory of structuration favours seems to depend on where the critic is coming from: critics from the structuralist side (e.g. Sica 1991; Craib 1992) accuse Giddens of attempting to reduce structure to action, and of failing to give sufficient weight to the determining social forces which constrain actors' choices. Conversely, interpretative sociologists (e.g. Thrift 1985) have tended to view structuration theory as an ultimately self-defeating exercise in building an interpretative dimension into what is essentially a structuralist, systematising framework.

What these criticisms are really raising is the question of whether Giddens actually succeeds in synthesising the duality of structure and action. Is the theory of structuration a genuine synthesis or merely an eclectic collection of ideas which are conceptually and methodologically distinct? Giddens draws on such a wide range of sources that it is hard to resist the sense that the main purpose of structuration theory is to find a place for just about every sociological idea, regardless of the compatibility of the assumptions that inform them. The problem, of course, is that detaching ideas from their intellectual origins carries the risk of destroying their intellectual integrity and rendering them sociologically toothless. The most damaging criticism that can be levelled against Giddens is that structuration theory has no real bite; it is bland, contributing no truly distinctive solution to any significant sociological problem. Thus the question of what difference structuration theory might make to the studies that sociologists conduct is more significant than the kind of positioning critique referred to above, i.e. interactionist or structuralist. If the point of the theory is to make possible studies which can grasp the duality of structure that supposedly constitutes social life, how does structuration theory translate into such studies?

Two things are notable here. First, Giddens's own substantive work does little to develop and apply structuration theory, unlike Parsons, whose substantive writings were exemplary in applying his theoretical approach to the analysis of empirical issues. Second, in arguing for the empirical relevance of structuration theory, Giddens frequently cites as studies exemplifying its approach work which was not actually informed by it. For example, Paul Willis's well-known study *Learning to Labour* (1977) is discussed extensively by Giddens (1984) and judged to be exemplary in its theoretical approach, for showing how structural constraint and actors' consciousness are to be reconciled and the reproduction of structure empirically described. But Willis was inspired by quite other ideas; his work was written without any reliance on the main concepts of Giddens's theory, such as structuration and duality of structure. If the empirical insights to be derived from structuration theory turn out to be nothing more than new labels for familiar forms of sociological analysis, what does Giddens's achievement amount to?

Bourdieu: reconciling objectivity and subjectivity

Another notable contemporary synthesist is Pierre Bourdieu. Like Giddens, Bourdieu is centrally concerned with the reconciling of sociological dualisms. Perhaps because of his early background in philosophy, the dualism which occupies centre stage in Bourdieu's thought is the classic epistemological one between objectivism and subjectivism.

Objectivism and subjectivism

Put at its most simple, the question is whether knowledge is independent of the situation of the knower or a product of it.

Bourdieu holds to what is often referred to – though he does not use the term himself – as a social constructionist view of knowledge. He holds that all knowledge is the product of social conditions and therefore is socially determined. A classic criticism of this view – one we have encountered before (see Chapter 7) – is that if applied universally, it raises a problem about the status of sociological knowledge and thus about itself as a claim about the world. If all claims to knowledge are social constructions, why should we accept sociology's claims as anything more than yet another social construction? At the heart of Bourdieu's sociology is an attempt to resolve this problem.

Bourdieu does not believe that what we have called the social constructionist argument means that knowledge is unattached to the world. In particular, the knowledge which sociology itself creates is more than just a product of the professional ideology of sociologists; it is genuine knowledge which tells us something about the world. In other words, Bourdieu's position is that both subjectivism and objectivism express partial truths. Bourdieu advocates a resolution of this dualism which involves building a reflexive sociology – in a particular sense of that nowadays overused term.

To understand what the notion of reflexivity means to Bourdieu, we need to consider his account of the contrast between the subjective and the objective points of view, which are associated with the actor, on the one hand, and the scientist on the other. We have come across this dualism before in earlier chapters, and Bourdieu's version resembles other versions we have encountered. The distinction is between how the social world appears to those acting within it, and thus the kind of knowledge they can possibly have of it, and how it appears to those who seek to study it from the standpoint of science. The subjective point of view is characterised by two features:

1   It is a partial point of view in the sense that the location of the actor within society means that only certain things are available to him or her; only a certain amount of the whole can be seen or comprehended.
2   It is also an interested viewpoint; the actor sees things from a stance shaped by his or her practical concerns, which change over time, sometimes from moment to moment.

The objective point of view, by contrast, is distinguished by comprehensiveness and permanence. The scientist sees things – or attempts to do so – from a 'God's-eye' position above the level of practical involvement and the fleeting impressions of momentary change.

In Bourdieu's view, this dualism gives rise to a paradox which sociology has never adequately resolved. Since the task of the social scientist is to understand, from the standpoint of science, events which are constituted by they way social actors perceive and respond to their experience, it is not sufficient for the social scientist simply to adopt the objective stance and ignore the subjective one. Yet, on the other hand, embracing the subjective point of view would seem to make scientific objectivity untenable. As with Giddens's contrast between action and structure, but perhaps even more sharply, one is faced with the problem of the reconciling of opposites. Needless to say, like Giddens, Bourdieu has what he believes to be a solution.

Bourdieu and phenomenology

The solution involves taking a further step back.

> ## A step back
>
> For Bourdieu, it is not that the sociologist is too far removed from lived social life to study it, but that in a certain sense he or she is not removed far enough. To understand sociology itself and its relation to what it studies, the sociologist needs to take another step back. Just as the sociologist initially distances himself or herself from the social actors under study, so the possibility of reflecting on the doing of sociology means recognising that the sociologist also takes up a stance which is also socially constructed.

The sociologist creates the social world as an objective reality, objectifies it. To understand how the sociologist's process of objectivisation works, it is necessary to objectivise that in its turn, to stand back from it. In Bourdieu's own words, the goal is 'to uncover all the presuppositions inherent in the *theoretical* posture as an external, remote, distant or, quite simply, non-practical, non-committed, non-involved vision' (1990: 60).

Thus Bourdieu sought to apply to the doing of sociology the same perspective as sociology applied to those it studied. It is only from the scientific, objectivist standpoint that the partiality, the subjectivity, of the actors' viewpoint becomes visible. To actors themselves, their experiences are real and solid, their world is fixed and permanent. Stepping back from that world enables the sociologist to see its arbitrary, constructed, incomplete character. But equally, stepping back from the sociological analyst's world of scientific objectivity enables Bourdieu to see that this world, in its turn, is arbitrary and socially constructed.

This process of stepping back is strongly reminiscent of phenomenology. It comes as little surprise, then, to find that Bourdieu cites Husserl (see Chapter 6) and, especially, Merleau-Ponty (a French phenomenologist) as among his main influences. In the world of French social thought of the 1950s and 1960s, the objectivist stance was associated with the structuralism of Lévi-Strauss (see Chapter 9). Structuralism sought to represent social life as the outcome of the workings of sets of objective rules, which work behind the backs of actors. According to his own account of his intellectual development, after an initial flirtation with structuralism, Bourdieu's reading of Husserl and Merleau-Ponty led him to reject it as insufficiently reflexive and unable to theorise actors' intentionality i.e. purposive consciousness: (see Bourdieu 1990). However, though strongly influenced by phenomenology, Bourdieu never fully embraced it. He regarded it as falling into the opposite trap to objectivism, namely excessive subjectivism, which makes it the goal of analysis to recapture the subjectivity of experience. Since every experience is made rather than given, any such attempt to recapture the taste of the soup, as might be said, is doomed to failure.

Bourdieu's three key concepts

The trio of key concepts Bourdieu employs to resolve the dichotomy of objectivism and subjectivism are *habitus*, *practice* and *field*. The world as it is seen from the point of view of the social actor appears objective and solid, as out there and independent of herself or himself. That it does so is due to the actor's habitus.

Habitus

The habitus is a structure of dispositions of thought and action which the actor acquires as a member of a social group or class. It is something like a mental and behavioural set (as pyschologists would say), which the actor takes for granted and which structures her or his experience of things.

The habitus is socially acquired and socially shared, and the actor does not question it – is not even aware of it – since it seems to her or him, and to those around her or him, as just the way things are, the normal way to think about and act towards the world.

The actual forms of activity which are grounded in the habitus and to which it gives rise Bourdieu refers to as practices.

Practices

These are not to be thought of in terms of means–ends rationality, i.e. as the most efficient or effective means for attaining some goal, since each practice has its own endogenous (i.e. intrinsic or built-in) logic. Each social group therefore has a body of practices which are simply 'what one does'.

While each habitus is self-sustaining and provides for the common experience which members of a group share, it is grounded in the social position which defines the group and gives it its identity. This shared situation is what Bourdieu refers to as the field.

Fields

These are social environments inhabited by one, or more usually by several, groups. A group is constituted as such by virtue of its location within the field, which typically involves competitive relations with other groups in the same field.

Clearly, there is a strongly Weberian element in Bourdieu's thought; like Weber (see Chapter 3), he sees society as made up of struggles between various kinds of social groups (classes, status groups) for dominance within this or that field.

While not always utilising these concepts explicitly, Bourdieu's substantive writings present analyses which are consistent with their general thrust. In line with his central concern with the nature and role of knowledge in society, Bourdieu's substantive work centres on the analysis of superstructural phenomena such as education, art and literature. The use of the Marxist term is rather appropriate here, since Bourdieu's substantive analyses owe much to Marxist ideas of ideology and capital. But whereas in Marx ideology is distinct from capital, the one consisting in sets of ideas and the other in material phenomena, Bourdieu puts these two notions together and comes up with the idea of *cultural capital*.

Cultural capital

In each of the fields of education, art and literature, there are some dominant sets of ideas which define what is culturally valued and desirable. These definitions are often held right across society and regarded as objective realities. On closer inspection, each set of ideas is associated with specific social groups or classes and particular historical periods, but they transcend these origins and stand as societally legitimate definitions of what is educationally or artistically worthwhile.

The practices which constitute educational or artistic activity serve to reproduce these definitions and therefore also the relations of dominance and subordination, by reproducing the cultural capital on which these relations depend. Subordinated groups may or may not challenge these relations. Frequently they do not, sometimes because their alternative values possess little cultural capital, and sometimes because their habitus involves assumptions which serve to legitimate the status quo, leading them to take for granted as natural, objective realities situations which place them systematically at a disadvantage in the struggle for dominance. In Bourdieu's own words: 'the different classes and class fractions are engaged in a symbolic struggle properly speaking, one aimed at imposing the definition of the social world that is best suited to their interests (1992: 167).

We hardly need to point out the strongly Marxist shape of these arguments. Indeed, it is not doing them much of an injustice to characterise Bourdieu's analyses as a phenomenologically flavoured Marxism–Weberianism. As with Giddens, there is little doubt that, far from reconciling the objectivity-subjectivity dichotomy and coalescing diverse elements of the various traditions upon which he draws, Bourdieu achieves his theoretical project at the cost of glossing over fundamentally different and opposing assumptions. For example, to speak of classes and interests is at least to describe the world from the point of view of the transcendent, objective sociologist. The point of such descriptions, for Bourdieu just as it was for Marx, is to reveal what is not available to the members of society themselves. People may believe there to be objective standards of educational or artistic merit, but the sociologist will show these beliefs to be ideological constructions. How can such an objectivist, metatheoretical stance be squared with a view of sociology as social action and a concern to respect the subjectivity of the actor as a phenomenon in its own right? In the view of his critics (e.g. Dreyfus and Rabinow 1993), Bourdieu never seriously engages with this issue. The objectivity–subjectivity dualism is not solved but incorporated within the theory as an unresolved tension.

Habermas as synthesiser

The most influential of these recent, all-encompassing theorists must be Jürgen Habermas. Habermas has sought to construct not only pan-sociological theory, but also pan-disciplinary constructions which draw upon philosophy (especially moral philosophy and philosophy of language), political theory, psychology and linguistics (at least). Starting from the synthesis of Marxist and Weberian concerns achieved by the Frankfurt School (see Chapter 8), Habermas sought to construct an analysis of the structure and dynamics of modern society which would combine the views of society as objective and subjective phenomena. He treats analysis as something requiring a dualistic methodology in order to comprehend society as both the subjective understandings of its members and also a system of functionally co-ordinating mechanisms which operate outside the individual's awareness. Society is therefore treated as a complex structure which operates at both a macro and a micro level, being a combination of what Habermas calls, respectively, system and lifeworld (see below). It also involves both voluntarism and determinism in so far as people are capable, under appropriate circumstances, of both acting freely and also being controlled, i.e. their actions are determined by the functional needs of the system. In terms of sociological positions, Marxist and Weberian elements (see Chapters 2 and 3) are complemented by Parsonian and interactionist contributions (see Chapters 5 and 6).

Habermas and the Frankfurt School

Jürgen Habermas sought to renew the optimistic element in the programme of Critical Theory. Beginning as a graduate student in the Frankfurt School in the 1950s, he sought to discover the possibility of realising the emancipatory elements of the Enlightenment project within advanced industrial societies, and has become, latterly, a leading defender of the value of reason, rationality and the Enlightenment against their poststructuralist critics.

Both Marx and the Frankfurt School had preceded Habermas in raising and pursuing the possibility of emancipation, but something was obviously wrong with their conceptions in so far as they had resulted in resignation and despair. Habermas took up their cause, but saw it as needing a radical rethinking of the foundations upon which a more profound understanding of human rationality could reside.

Marx and the Frankfurt School had both taken too narrow a view of reason, recognising only two forms of it, the instrumental kind, associated with domination, and the emancipatory kind, associated with liberation. The Frankfurt School, seeing the emancipatory kind annexed by the instrumental, had naturally drawn their pessimistic conclusion.

Habermas proposed a third kind of human interest, in addition to those of producing well-being (instrumental) and freedom (emancipatory). This interest was in people interrelating with one another, requiring them to be able to communicate with and to understand one another, centrally involving language. Around this hitherto neglected element he developed the two main stages of his work.

Communication and reason

The emphasis on communication changes the idea of reason and rationality into something which is intersubjective; it emerges through dialogue and debate among the members of the community and not as a matter of individual thought and reflection, certainly as far as the political organisation of society is concerned. At least, this ideal of bourgeois societies is of a *public sphere* in which free and open discussion, unrestricted by authority and tradition, takes place. This envisaged basis for rational decision-making about the society's organisation was in actuality a cheat, since only the bourgeoisie exercised unrestricted participation in this process.

Habermas was critical of what he called 'systematically distorted communication', which was the prevailing condition for many in capitalist society, where domination inhibits free expression and where ideological control inhibits not only what people can say but what they can actually think. Moreover, the progress of capitalist society had further corrupted the idea of rational political decision being achieved through free and equal debate in the public sphere. In line with Weber and the Frankfurt School's ideas, Habermas argued that decision-making was increasingly being handed over to large organisations, i.e. the state itself and business organisations, and to their technically trained staffs, who were also becoming much more sophisticated in manipulating the formation of 'public opinion'.

Habermas argued that the fact that the growth of scientific and technical knowledge had allowed the rationalisation of society (to borrow Weber's term) to proceed to an extensive degree did not mean that things were stabilised, for such rationalisation was somewhat counter-productive, inducing a *legitimation crisis*.

Legitimation crisis

Ever-expanding state intervention extends control into more areas of social life, but it also raises expectations which it cannot satisfy. In addition, and at the same time, state intervention also disrupts and dissolves the bases on which the state's legitimacy has traditionally rested.

Habermas initially rooted much of his critique of modern society in terms of the discrepancy between the ideals and the actualities of the society, e.g. the ideal of free and equal discussion was blocked by the actual inequities of the system. In the second and major part of his career, he made the emphasis he had placed on communication the basis for a much more comprehensive account, in which the potential for emancipation was rooted in the nature of communication itself. The systematic distortion of communication was described no longer in terms of the ideals of a particular kind of society, but rather in terms of the requirements for rationality built into the nature of communication itself. Like so many other theorists in the post-war period, Habermas had taken a linguistic turn and the topics of language and communication came to the fore in his thought, as shown in the two large volumes of *The Theory of Communicative Action* (1984, 1986).

Habermas opposed the deeply entrenched idea that instrumental action is the most basic form of action, maintaining instead that it is actually *communicative action* which is basic. The idea that instrumental action is the basic form is, of course, appealing since it follows from, for just one example, Marx's idea that we must first survive in order to do anything else, and that we must therefore have ways of meeting our practical needs, must have an effective instrumental relationship to our environment. Habermas objects to this view because it suggests that all our actions are directed towards making things in our environment serve our needs and purposes, so that our actions are primarily oriented to dominating (i.e. controlling) things in our environment, including our fellow human beings.

> ## Communicative action
>
> Communication with our fellow human beings, however, is basically for its own sake; we want to relate to and understand our fellow creatures and there is therefore no built-in element of domination. If communicative action is taken as the most basic form, then, it opens up the possibility of a society in which social relations are conducted on the basis of mutual recognition of each other as free and independent beings.

To make this case, Habermas must here traffic in counter-factual considerations, for in modern society it certainly appears that instrumental reason is predominant. Marx had argued that history was an expression of human nature, but only a distorted one. Hence one could not extrapolate what human beings are essentially like from their present conditions, but only by understanding what human beings would be like if they were able to live under conditions of freedom. Similarly, Habermas cannot argue that the conditions of emancipation are being met in activities as they are currently organised for, of course, were these conditions being met, then there would be emancipation. Thus he must argue that the conditions of emancipation are built into the nature of human communication in these counter-factual terms; these conditions would apply if people were able to relate to one another under certain conditions, which he sometimes calls an 'ideal speech situation'. This approach gives Habermas the leverage which a critical theory needs: existing circumstances fall short of what they could be, and the recognition of the ideal speech situation gives us something towards which we can aspire as an alternative to the existing state of things. In other words, it gives us a basis for saying what is wrong with the existing state of affairs.

For Habermas as for Hegel, then, the idea of the discussion or debate as a way of arriving at truth is a generally influential model. Hegel, of course, in forming the idea of dialectical logic generalised the model to the whole of history, while Habermas makes it basic to his conception of how emancipation is possible in modern society.

The universality of reason

One idea under severe threat in the thinking of the poststructuralists and postmodernists is the universal character of the results of reason. Habermas is insistent (we are tempted to say, dogmatically) upon the capacity of reason to arrive at universally valid conclusions in respect both of empirical knowledge and of morality, but, of course, it is not to be expected that these conclusions have yet been reached. The ideal, which one accepts in a tacit sense upon entering into an argument, is that a right result will be reached through honest discussion; reason should be the only force involved in the discussion, i.e. the victor in a debate should be the possessor of the better argument. Further, it should not be a matter of the victor imposing the better argument upon the vanquished; instead, an agreement should develop, a consensus be realised, with the 'defeated' party recognising that the winning argument *is* better. Thus the outcome of such a discussion would be a truth which would hold for all the parties to it. The operation of science is, indeed, something akin to this outline.

Borrowing the idea from C.S. Peirce, a turn-of-the-century American philosopher, Habermas assumes that truth in science equates with arrival at general agreement. We do not have it in science now, but the guiding ideal there is that if all scientists freely participate in the exercise of their reason, in the gigantic discussion which is the community of science, they will eventually arrive at the truth, i.e. that which is generally agreed amongst them.

Universal reason

Habermas's idea is, then, that in entering into discussions in social life we take for granted such ideals; our free, reasoned participation will arrive at conclusions which we can all accept and are universal in this sense.

Of course, while these might be the ideals of argument as a genuine truth-finding device, actual arguments do not necessarily respect these ideals, and they are not necessarily directed at arriving at the truth. Argument is often a vehicle for imposing one person's view on another. The presupposition of a proper discussion is that the parties are entirely equal in respect of everything except the force of reason; but, of course, in modern society people are not equal, and they do not necessarily have the right or power to participate in public discussion. They may not be able to speak, may not have the capacity, or may be afraid to do so. If they do speak, their contributions may not be listened to because they are not socially valued persons. Moreover, if they engage in discussion, it may be on the basis of power and resources which cannot match those of others in the discussion. With such systematic distortions for the conditions for speech, it is not to be expected that discussion can indeed arrive at authentically universal results.

System and lifeworld

The capacity for discussion in modern society is restricted. As part of his theory of communicative action, Habermas takes over the Parsonian notion of system, but puts it to critical-theory use. He makes a contrast between *system* and *lifeworld*, which is the major element in his analysis of the dynamics of modern society.

System

The notion of system is the point at which Habermas appropriates Parsonian conceptions, which he treats as giving a *partial* description of society. It is true that modern society is an increasingly complex system, much of which is differentiated into specialised spheres, and articulated by generalised media.

However, this invocation of Parsons is not entirely complimentary, since he is treated as having provided a description only of arrangements which engender pathologies and oppressions in modern society.

Lifeworld

Alternatively, the lifeworld is the repository of (at least the possibilities of) person-to-person relationships; in such relationships people are concerned to communicate, to achieve mutual understanding, to co-ordinate their reciprocal actions – in short, simply to associate with one another.

Communicative action involves these three dimensions of reciprocal relationship; the concern is with people's responses to one another and not with using people for some ends of action. Habermas does not want to say that such orientation is absent from the lifeworld. In his scheme, though communicative action is the essential and basic form of action, people in the lifeworld are also concerned to get other people to do things which are useful for them, involving what Habermas terms *strategic action*.

Strategic action

This involves people in trying to influence one another, and the mention of influence does indeed involve a direct allusion to Parsons's notion of generalised media. Influence is one such medium; power and money will shortly make their appearance.

In summary, the lifeworld is a site where people engage, through communicative action, in those activities which are vital to the reproduction of social life, i.e. those cultural and behavioural patterns for sharing and transmitting their understandings. People are endowed with the taken-for-granted understandings which form the basis for their day-to-day conduct. The lifeworld fulfils the functions of perpetuating cultural knowledge and equipping people to co-ordinate their actions, thereby both to further social integration and solidarity, and also to develop the personal identities of individuals.

The relationship of system and lifeworld

Habermas views this relationship from the point of view of the perpetuation ('reproduction' is the term nowadays more commonly used) of society and assumes that, for a modern, complex society, only part of the perpetuation can be effected through the lifeworld.

Here, he attempts to conjoin the often counterposed elements of structure and agency. Alternative and often closely parallel designations are 'society as seen through the eyes of its members' and 'society as seen by an objective, external observer'.

Both these dimensions are necessary to a comprehensive understanding. Society is, after all, a meaningful phenomenon and works through symbolic communication between its members. Therefore, essential to understanding how it works is what Weber would have termed 'explanation at the level of meaning'. Such explanation alone, however, is not enough, since the activities which reproduce the cultural patterns of the society do not thereby provide for the reproduction of the society as a whole. People's actions in the life-world are directed towards, and carried out in terms of, their effects upon one another, not towards the organisation and perpetuation of the society itself. Thus the ways of perpetuating the whole society cannot simply be understood as a product of people's conscious purposes and intentions; rather, they must be effected through the consequences of what people do, the ways the actions themselves fit together in patterns that none of the participating individuals intended.

Kinds of integration

Accordingly, Habermas differentiates between *social* and *functional* integration.

Social and functional integration

The former is the kind achieved within the lifeworld, on the basis of the conscious awareness of the participants, while the latter is outside of and beyond their awareness; it is an upshot of, rather than any purpose of, their activities.

333

The issue of functional integration is to be comprehended by the theorist in terms of the idea of the boundary-maintaining system. In Durkheimian/ Parsonian style, Habermas adopts a broadly evolutionary concept of society, involving the differentiation of functions over time, and a corresponding development of institutional specialisation. First, the analysis parallels Durkheim's of the evolution from mechanic to organic solidarity (see Chapter 4), emphasising the extent to which, in the earlier case, commonly held sentiments, sanctified by their sacred aura, provide the basis and justification of individual actions, while in the later organic period, with its more advanced division of labour, these common sentiments and their traditionally sacred aura evaporate. The consequence is that individuals increasingly have to work out their mutual understandings and their justifications for their actions and positions, i.e. in not being able to take shared suppositions so much for granted, they make for a progressive rationalisation in the lifeworld. As the extent to which people's actions are decided for them diminishes, they must increasingly choose what to do on the basis of reflective, reasoned consideration. Of course, there is then a greater possibility that individuals will be unable to see eye to eye.

In the simple, undifferentiated society, social and system (or functional) integration must be interwoven, for all transactions are organised around the axes of sex, age and kinship, but the developing complexity of the division of labour leads to their separation. There develop institutions which specialise in the management of the increasingly complex tasks of resourcing and administering all the system's activities. For example, the economy and the political system (especially the state) develop as prominent subsystems of the whole society; they become increasingly independent of the lifeworld with its ways of conducting person-to-person relations. Within both the economy and the bureaucracy, the alternative ideas of instrumental reason hold sway.

Rationalisation, in the more usual Weberian sense (see Chapter 3), continues apace. The two forms of rationalisation are somewhat different, and do not necessarily develop in parallel. Habermas argues that the system elements tend increasingly to develop autonomously, to become progressively detached from the lifeworld. He terms this process a *decoupling* of system and lifeworld.

Decoupling

The two are not simply disconnected; rather, the system elements seek to reshape the lifeworld in their terms. They seek to pursue the rationalisation (in terms of instrumental reason) of all social organisation.

The colonisation of the lifeworld

This process is what Habermas means by talk of the *colonisation* of the lifeworld.

Colonisation and its effects

The intervention of the system in the lifeworld, and the attempt to subject it to rationalisation, will bring pathological consequences.

The disruption of the processes of communicative action will mean that at least some of the requirements of social integration will not be fulfilled, and the kinds of consequences that Parsons – and Merton (see Chapter 5) – attributed to inadequate socialisation and anomie will result on a significant scale: people's sense of the rightness of the social order will be eroded; aspects of social life will become meaningless to them, or will cease to appear as legitimate; people will lose what sense of common purpose they have and become disaffected, losing commitment to their obligations. Conflict and deviance in social relations and psychic strain – even mental illness – in individuals will occur. Further, the impact of the systems of money and power upon the lifeworld will be such as to create crises, the consequences of which will be borne by people in their capacities as workers and as citizens. These crises *could* result in growing class conflict, but have not done so because the workers/citizens have been bought off through social welfare and services, which have also substituted for real citizenship participation in the state. In other words, rather than relating to the system as citizens, people are, instead, put in the position of clients (of the administrative/state structure), or of consumers (through the 'bribes' of the economic sector).

Further still, system integration leads to increasing consolidation of learning and culture in the hands of experts. Their increasing remoteness from the wider public means that specialised spheres do not contribute to or feed back into the general culture. The development of modern society has reduced the possibility of the formation of political ideologies around which dissent could grow. People are highly specialised and individualised in their outlooks, making for a fragmentation of consciousness, rather than the development of a common one.

The increasing development of the colonisation of the lifeworld has led to the legitimation crisis mentioned above, and to the development of mechanisms which attempt to counter the progressive colonisation of the lifeworld. Here Habermas refers to the rise of *new social movements*.

New social movements

These are the various forms of protest, paradigmatically exemplified by opposition to nuclear weapons, which now form around many libertarian and environmental issues.

These movements arise outside the established state structures of power and are much more concerned to be democratic in the sense of being participatory movements, in which discussion rather than power or money is the basis for policy formation. They do not have economic/material objectives, but consider the quality of life, often conceived as protecting and restoring ways of life under threat. For Habermas, the need is to restrict the influence of the system and to reassert the needs of the lifeworld. In a complex modern society, it obviously cannot be a matter of abolishing the system, for our lives are too massively dependent upon it. Instead, the system has to be put back in its proper place, and counter-institutions set up to represent the lifeworld, and to contain and inhibit the system's colonisation efforts. There is a limit to the extent the system can colonise, in so far as the reproduction of the lifeworld simply cannot be done except, to a significant degree, through communicative action. Indeed, this conflict between the system's mode of rationalisation and the nature of communicative action produces the pathological distortions of the lifeworld.

Habermas's attempt to integrate and thereby overcome the persistent dichotomies of social thought is by far the most impressive example of synthesis theorising. His poststructuralist critics have pointed out that his reconceptualisation of reason as a communicative phenomenon, from individual and mental to intersubjective and linguistically based, does not fundamentally alter the role that reason is held to play in human affairs as the final arbiter of truth and deliverer of liberation. In this sense, Habermas's thought remains firmly rooted within the Western Enlightenment tradition; for all his intellectual distance from Descartes (see Chapter 6) they are fellow travellers on the same pilgrimage.

Conclusion

The theorists outlined in this chapter have attempted to respond to the views of poststructuralist and postmodernist thinkers. They question the possibility of a general theoretical account of the totality of society and attempt to dispel disciplinary demarcations, whereas the 'synthesists' reassert the claims of sociological theory as more traditionally understood. None the less, all of them have also assumed that if sociological theory is not to be dissolved, then it must be reconstructed in order to remove the tensions, if not outright inconsistencies, which have been persistent sources of dissent and fundamental dispute within sociology. Their attempts at reconstruction have been made not through radical innovations in foundational assumptions but, instead, largely by the recombination of existing elements into purportedly more inclusive schemes. Whether their strategy has been successful is, like everything else in sociology, a matter for argument, and these various reconstructive proposals have both their enthusiasts and their critics. The latter, as we have indicated, are apt to see these reconstructions as preserving within themselves the very oppositions which they aim to transcend, attempting to cover over rather than fundamentally confront the problematic issues, and leaving unanswered the questions that the Continental social theorists have raised.

Questions

1 'Marxism is just another form of functionalism.' Argue the case for and against this statement.

2 What do you understand by 'neo-functionalism'? Does it constitute a viable approach to constructing sociological theory? Illustrate your answer with detailed references to at least one theorist.

3 What is duality of structure?

4 Why does Habermas need a theory of communicative action?

5 What is the relationship between system and lifeworld?

6 Do the notions of habitus, practice and field help overcome the opposition of objective and subjective?

7 What is the importance of cultural capital in Bourdieu's thought?

8 Do any of the sociological theorists discussed in this chapter effectively meet the challenge to the possibility of general theory made in the work of Foucault, Derrida and Lyotard?

Further reading

Bourdieu, P., 1977, *Outline of a Theory of Practice*. Cambridge University Press. A major statement of his theory.
—— 1984, *Distinction: A Social Critique of the Judgement of Taste*. Routledge. Another major work.
Bryant, C. and Jary, D. (eds), 1991, *Giddens' Theory of Structuration: Critical Assessments*. Routledge. A collection of critical essays.
Calhoun, C. (ed.), 1993, *Bourdieu: Critical Perspectives*. Polity Press. A useful collection.
Colomy, P. (ed.), 190, *Neofunctionalist Sociology*. Edward Elgar. A large selection of neo-functionalist writings.
Craib, I., 1992, *Anthony Giddens*. Routledge. A commentary.
Crews, F., 1986, *Skeptical Engagements*. Oxford University Press. Gives a formulation of theoreticism in the essay 'The grand academy of theory'.
Geuss, R., 1981, *The Idea of Critical Theory: Habermas and the Frankfurt School*. Cambridge University Press. A lucid examination of the concept of a critical theory of society.
Giddens, A., 1984, *The Constitution of Society: Outline of the Theory of Structuration*. Polity Press. The major statement of structuration theory.
Jenkins, R., 1992, *Pierre Bourdieu*. Routledge. An excellent short introduction.
McCarthy, T., 1978, *The Critical Theory of Jürgen Habermas*. MIT Press. A major study, though it does not cover his recent work.

May, Tim, 1996, *Situating Social Theory*. Open University Press. Has useful chapters on Giddens and Bourdieu.

Rasmussen, D.M., 1990, *Reading Habermas*. Blackwell.

Roderick, R., 1986, *Habermas and the Foundations of Critical Theory*. Macmillan. A good introduction to Habermas's thought.

White, S., 1989, *The Recent Work of Jürgen Habermas: Reason, Justice and Modernity*. Cambridge University Press. Covers more recent writing.

■　　■　　■

Chapter 14

Conclusion

We assume that you, the reader, have hung on in there and been buffeted by the countervailing and conflicting theories in this book. In this case, you have not quickly skipped from introduction to conclusion to see – to paraphrase the opening words in one of the immortal Harvey Sacks's lectures – if entry is worth the price of admission. Therefore, you might well now be asking 'where's it all going?'[1]

Our answer to this question begins by recalling where we have come from. In the first two editions of *Perspectives in Sociology*, we made some play with the nature of sociology as a bunch of perspectives which – *pace* those sociologists with synthesising tendencies – apparently cannot be reconciled. In them, we proposed that there was no way of determining a sure path for arriving at sociological knowledge; there was unlikely to be, just over the horizon, a new approach, paradigm or perspective to rescue us from the intellectual difficulties involved in a sociological theorising which can give us a better understanding of our social world. This sober message might have seemed bad enough, yet, as all of us over about the age of two know, things can always be worse. And there, in the third edition, perspicuous readers might have discerned 'a cloud no bigger than a man's hand'. This 'cloud' took the form of critical theory and poststructuralism. In these, we had our first intimations that discussions of hard (positivist) or soft science, e.g. symbolic interactionism and ethnomethodology, might all be parcelled up into one bag and unceremoniously dumped. For, to change the metaphor, the mice were nibbling

away at the foundations of all the perspectives, indeed at the whole enterprise of sociological theory. These foundations are reason and logic. By re-reading some of the bastions of sociological theory – especially Marx – and drawing on Freud and, particularly, Nietzsche, old thinking was deconstructed and the history of thought was re-invented. A major outcome was to reject the reality of a world out there, resulting in a view that we have all become prisoners of language. From this point of view, the pursuit of social science, hard or soft, increasingly seemed to be an absurd undertaking.

Hitherto, we used the notion of sociological perspectives as a way of presenting different and more or less overlapping ways of studying society. In so doing, we suggested that one might pursue one or other of them as a matter of choice. Preferences would be a matter of taste; conviction of whatever perspective[s] seemed most fruitful largely would depend on one's inclinations, background and interests. In the third edition this 'relative autonomy' (cf. Althusser) of each perspective was severely challenged by the presentation of the key ideas of most of the later structuralists, critical theorists and post-structuralists, who appear more fully in the current fourth edition, namely Lévi-Strauss, Lukács, Gramsci, the Frankfurt School, Habermas, Foucault and Derrida. Moreover, in the third edition Freud and Nietzsche joined Marx under the soubriquet 'masters of suspicion', i.e. those seminal thinkers who draw attention to the way our actions are controlled by forces of which we are not conscious. In the third edition, we even referred to 'the Enlightenment project', the eighteenth-century belief in the power of reason, and noted how these thinkers attacked the very idea that reason ultimately could solve all social problems and produce a just and emancipated society. Nevertheless, in the context of the whole book, these references constituted only a cloud on the horizon, about a sixth of the writing. What is more, in that context it was possible to read us as presenting these ideas as just another, or other, additional perspectives, some alternative paradigms.

The present fourth edition clearly changes all that. Now we have made the Enlightenment project a unifying theme. We show how the Frankfurt School attacked the project and how the poststructuralists claim to demolish it. Further, whereas we earlier talked of the idea of perspectives as under attack, doing justice to recent developments means that it has now been abandoned; apart, that is, from our own genuflection to history (with a small 'h') in that we use them as a 'continuer' in our book title. The sheer weight and volume of critical work in social theory effectively has deconstructed the perspectives. In the current edition, Marx, Weber and Durkheim are no longer hidden under comprehensive labels: 'structuralism', 'consensus', 'conflict'. Since they have been re-read – 'reinvented', in the contemporary idiom – and cannibalised by thinkers in many different ways, we needed a more explicit and more comprehensive exposition of the range of their work. With this initial foundation work done, we could more securely yield to the sheer pressures of the problems of presentation, which have obliged us to preserve general labels, e.g. 'symbolic interaction', 'structuralism', 'poststructuralism' and so on. But now such labels are looser in that we stress even more the range and variety of thinking that they embrace and the convenience rather than the accuracy of the label. For example, Barthes appears under two of these headings – structuralism and post-structuralism – while Foucault not only has a whole chapter to himself, but is also presented as holding different, sometimes opposing views at different periods (and sometimes at the same time), as well as appearing as an example of both structuralism and poststructuralism.

In Chapter 1, we briefly sketched the major historical and intellectual forces making for these considerable changes in sociology – and in many other academic disciplines. We also indicated that this edition was organised in the form of a 'story'. Thus in intellectual terms, what these changes mean for sociology can be – very crudely – summarised. Once upon a time, people (subjects) studied objects scientifically. Then they realised that some of these objects were people, who, unlike merely physical objects, could talk back, so science had to be redefined. Sociology consisted in subjects talking to and about other subjects, intersubjectively. Some argued, however, that both subject and object were 'constructs', 'inventions'; they were products of language systems. So do not look for reality out there, but study 'the text', the very ways of speaking themselves. So we have moved from studying objects, to subjects, to language systems. Even here, however, there is no resting place for the weary hunter seeking secure knowledge of the social world. For in pursuing the theme of 'the unruly sign', Derrida shows that even language systems are unstable. So we have a shift in focus from object to subject to, language system to . . . what? Where will the story end? Derrida and Barthes suggest that the only point is the enjoyment, the 'jouissance', derived from the act of studying.

Yet despite these sea changes in social thought, when we review the nature of sociological theorising since World War II, there have been important continuities. Just as the whole of Western philosophy is said to be a series of footnotes to Plato, perhaps sociological theorising still can be fairly said to have most of its roots in the thinking of the founding fathers: Marx, Weber and Durkheim. Time and again, we have encountered some of their basic ideas in what appeared to be the cutting edge of novel arguments. For example, Foucault seems to rely heavily on Weber's notions about the rationalisation and dis-enchantment of society in his analysis of people shifting from subject to object, and on Durkheim's distinction of 'individual' and 'society' in his arguments about decentring individuals.

Here we might attempt to distinguish those thinkers who stand on the shoulders of giants in order to see further from those who merely talk to and about them. In other words, it is legitimate to expect thinkers to take up and to continue classical arguments and to give us fresh insights, ways of looking at the social world from slightly – or greatly – different angles. Doing so is rather different from simply expressing established ideas in different words. Such reformulations present readers with the unenviable chore of translating the new terms back into the original without offering the reward of new insights. Some attempts to synthesise may offer no more than such a word game, a tendency which, at its worst, we have dubbed 'theoreticism'. It is the theorising of the wordsmith who, apparently, wishes to hang on to everything, refusing to discard anything. Paradoxically, such work is self-defeating, for somehow the problems are ironed out – on paper anyway!

The greatest thinkers, however, present us with dilemmas; they push analysis to logical conclusions that we may not like to face. And there are all sorts of loose ends, mind-crushing problem areas. It is much easier to see where thinking has come from than where it is going. Of course, at any given point in time, it is difficult to foresee which thinkers will represent deep-seated trends in future sociological theorising and which will retrospectively come to be seen as reporters of mere fads and fashions that have a current vogue and a negligible future. So, 'where is it all going?' is an open question.

Hence, despite the demise of the idea of perspectives, we are regrettably – and inevitably – left with choices. Are we creatures of reason and logic? Or are we better characterised as the victims of unconscious drives, forces and emotions? What does a 'compromise' position look like? Can the social world be studied using the methods of the natural sciences? Can we add in meanings, and must doing so change the whole methodology of studying the social world? Or must we recognise that talking about 'the social world' falsely implies a world out there and that what we are actually doing is playing a language game? If so, are we really prisoners of language? And as such, must we recognise that even language games have chaotic as well as rule-governed elements? At the end of the day, is sociological theorising just another game? What knowledge does it – can it – possibly give us? And does it matter anyway, as long as we experience some fun? Is this what the long march of sociological inquiry comes to?

Dear reader, we offer no answers to these questions, that task is down to you.

Note

1   The reference is to Lecture 1, Spring 1970, in Sacks (1992: vol. 2, p. 215). The actual quotation is:

> Usually I start the course by doing what I do in the course, without any programmatic statements, without any indication of why it should be of any interest to anybody. But – and this may be unfair – the course will turn out to be more severely technical than most people could possibly be interested in, and some good percentage will drop out, and usually that has the consequence that they get nothing out of the class if they last one time. So I decided to spend the first time telling people something that I take it could hardly *not* be of interest to them. Then, when they drop out, they'd at least have gotten what I figure would be the price of the course. And I guess I should say if *this* isn't absorbing, you could hardly imagine how unabsorbing the rest will be.

We quote these remarks since they seem nicely to capture the spirit of our project in writing this book.

Bibliography

Adorno, Theodor, 1973, *Negative Dialectics*. Routledge.
—— and Horkheimer, Max, 1979, *The Dialectic of Enlightenment*. Verso.
——, Frenkel-Brunswick, E., Levinson, D.J. and Sandford, R.N. 1950, *The Authoritarian Personality*. Harper and Row.
Alexander, Jeffrey, 1982a, *Theoretical Logic in Sociology. Vol. 1: Positivism, Presuppositions and Current Controversies*. University of California Press.
—— 1982b, *Theoretical Logic in Sociology. Vol. 2: The Antinomies of Classical Social Thought: Marx and Durkheim*. University of California Press.
—— 1984, *Theoretical Logic in Sociology. Vol. 4. The Modern Reconstruction of Classical Thought: Talcott Parsons*. Routledge.
—— (ed.), 1985, *Neo-Functionalism*. Sage.
—— 1987, *Sociological Theory since 1945*. Hutchinson.
—— (ed.), 1988, *Durkheimian Sociology: Cultural Studies*. Cambridge University Press.
—— and Colomy, Paul, 1991, 'Neo-functionalism today: reconstructing a theoretical tradition', in G. Ritzer (ed.), *Frontiers of Social Theory*. Columbia University Press, pp. 00–00.
Althusser, Louis, 1969, *For Marx*. Allen Lane.
—— 1971, *Lenin and Philosophy*. New Left Books.
—— and Balibar, Etienne 1970, *Reading Capital*. New Left Books.
Anderson, Perry, 1976, *Considerations on Western Marxism*, New Left Books.
Badcock, Christopher, 1975, *Lévi-Strauss, Structuralism and Social Theory*. Hutchinson.

Baldwin, John, 1986, *G.H. Mead: A Unifying Theory for Sociology*. Sage.

Barthes, Roland, 1967, *Elements of Semiology*. Cape.

—— 1973, *Mythologies*. Granada.

—— 1975a, *S/Z*. Cape.

—— 1975b, *The Pleasures of the Text*. Hill and Wang.

—— 1977a, *Image, Music, Text*. Fontana.

—— 1977b, *Roland Barthes by Roland Barthes*. Macmillan.

—— 1978, *A Lover's Discourse*. Hill and Wang.

—— 1982, *A Barthes Reader*. Cape.

—— 1985, *The Fashion System*. Cape.

—— 1991, *The Grain of the Voice: Interviews 1962–81*. University of California Press.

Baudrillard, Jean, 1980, *For a Critique of the Political Economy of the Sign*. Telos Press.

—— 1988, *Selected Writings*. Polity.

—— 1990, *Revenge of the Crystal: A Baudrillard Reader*. Pluto Press.

—— 1994, *The Illusion of the End*. Polity Press.

—— 1995a, *The Gulf War Did Not Take Place*. Power Press.

—— 1995b, *Symbolic Exchange and Death*. Sage.

—— 1996a, *The System of Objects*. Verso.

—— 1996b, *The Perfect Crime*. Verso.

Bauman, Zigmunt, 1987, *Legislators and Interpreters: On Modernity, Postmodernity and the Intellectuals*. Polity Press.

—— 1992, *Intimations of Postmodernity*. Routledge.

Becker, Howard S., 1964, *Outsiders: Studies in the Sociology of Deviance*. Free Press.

—— 1967, 'Whose side are we on?', *Social Problems*, 14: 239–47.

—— 1970, *Sociological Work: Method and Substance*. Allen Lane.

Bendix, Reinhard, 1960, *Max Weber: An Intellectual Portrait*. Heinemann.

Benjamin, Andrew (ed.), 1991, *The Problems of Modernity: Adorno and Benjamin*. Routledge.

Benjamin, Walter, 1970, *Illuminations*. Cape.

Bennington, Geoffrey, 1988, *Lyotard: Writing the Event*. Manchester University Press.

—— and Derrida, Jacques, 1993, *Jacques Derrida*. University of Chicago Press.

Benton, Ted, 1984, *The Rise and Fall of Structural Marxism*. Macmillan.

Berger, Peter and Luckmann, Thomas, 1967, *The Social Construction of Reality*. Allen Lane.

Berlinsky, David, 1968, *On Systems Theory*. MIT Press.

Bernstein, Richard J., 1985, *Habermas and Modernity*. Polity Press.

Bittner, Egon, 1973, 'Objectivity and realism in sociology', in G. Psathas (ed.), *Phenomenonological Sociology*. Wiley, pp. 109–25.

Blumberg, Abraham, 1969, 'The practice of law as a confidence game', in V. Aubert (ed.), *The Sociology of Law*, Penguin, pp. 221–31.

Blumer, Herbert, 1969, *Symbolic Interactionism*. Prentice Hall.

Boden, Diedre and Zimmerman, Don. H. (eds), 1991, *Talk and Social Structure: Studies in Ethnomethodology and Conversation Analysis*. Polity Press.

Bottomore, Tom, 1984, *The Frankfurt School*. Tavistock.

—— and Nisbet, Robert (eds), 1978, *A History of Sociological Analysis*. Heinemann.

—— and Rubel, Maximillian, 1965, *Karl Marx: Selected Writings in Sociology and Social Philosophy*. Penguin.

Bourdieu, Pierre, 1977, *Outline of a Theory of Practice*. Cambridge University Press.

—— 1984, *Distinction: A Social Critique of the Judgement of Taste*. Routledge.

—— 1990, *In Other Words: Essays Towards a Reflexive Sociology*. Polity Press.

—— 1992, *Language and Symbolic Power*. Polity Press.

—— 1993, *The Field of Cultural Production: Essays on Art and Literature*. Polity Press.

—— 1995, *The Rules of Art: Genesis and Structure of the Literary Field*. Polity Press.

—— and Wacquant, Loic, 1992, *An Invitation to Reflexive Sociology*. Polity Press.

Boyne, Roy, 1991, 'Power–knowledge and social theory: the systematic misrepresentation of contemporary French social theory in the work of Anthony Giddens', in C. Bryant and D. Jary (eds), *Giddens' Theory of Structuration: A Critical Appreciation*. Routledge.

—— 1994, *Foucault and Derrida: The Other Side of Reason*. Routledge.

Brand, Arie, 1990, *The Force of Reason: An Introduction to Habermas' 'Theory of Communicative Action'*. Allen and Unwin.

Bronner, Stephen and Kellner, Douglas (eds), 1989, *Critical Theory and Society: A Reader*. Routledge.

Brubaker, Rogers, 1984, *The Limits of Rationality: An Essay on the Social and Moral Thought of Max Weber*. Allen and Unwin.

Bryant, Christopher and Jary, David (eds), 1991, *Giddens' Theory of Structuration: Critical Assessments*. Routledge.

Button, Graham (ed.), 1991, *Ethnomethodology and the Human Sciences*. Cambridge University Press.

Calhoun, C. (ed.), 1993, *Bourdieu: Critical Perspectives*. Polity Press.

——, LiPuma, L. and Postone, M. (eds), 1993, *Bourdieu: Critical Perspectives*. Polity Press.

Callinicos, Alex, 1976, *Althusser's Marxism*. Pluto Press.

—— 1989, *Against Postmodernism: A Marxist Critique*. Polity Press.

Carver, Terrel, 1980, *Marxist Social Theory*. Oxford University Press.

Clarke, Simon, 1981, *The Foundations of Structuralism*. Harvester.

Cohen, G.A., 1978, *Karl Marx's Theory of History: A Defence*. Oxford University Press.

Collins, Randall, 1975, *Conflict Sociology: Towards Explanatory Science*. Academic Press.

—— 1981, 'On the microfoundations of macrosociology', *American Journal of Sociology*, 186: 984–1014.

—— 1986a, *Weberian Social Theory*. Cambridge University Press.

—— 1986b, *Max Weber: A Skeleton Key*. Sage.

Colomy, Paul (ed.), 1990, *Neofunctionalist Sociology*, Edward Elgar.

Connerton, Paul (ed.), 1976, *Critical Sociology: Selected Readings*. Penguin.

Cooke, Maeve, 1994, *Language and Reason: A Study of Habermas's Pragmatics*. MIT Press.

Coulter, Jeff (ed.), 1991, *Ethnomethodological Sociology*. Edward Elgar.

Craib, Ian, 1992, *Anthony Giddens*. Routledge.

Crews, Frederick, 1986, *Skeptical Engagements*. Oxford University Press.

Crompton, Rosemary, 1993, *Class and Stratification*. Polity Press.

Crook, Stephen, 1991, *Modernist Radicalism and its Aftermath: Foundationalism and Anti-Foundationalism in Radical Social Theory*. Routledge.

Culler, Jonathon, 1976, *Saussure*. Fontana.

—— 1982, *On Deconstruction*. Routledge.

—— 1990, *Barthes*. Fontana.

Dahrendorf, Ralf, 1958, 'Out of utopia: toward a reorientation of sociological analysis', *American Journal of Sociology*, 64: 115–27.

Dawkins, Richard, 1976, *The Selfish Gene*. Oxford University Press.

Denzin, Norman K., 1992, *Symbolic Interactionism and Cultural Studies: The Politics of Interpretation*. Blackwell.

Derrida, Jacques, 1967, *Of Grammatology*. Johns Hopkins University Press.

—— 1978, *Writing and Difference*. University of Chicago Press.

—— 1984, *Margins of Philosophy*. University of Chicago Press.

—— 1986, *Glas*, University of Nebraska Press.

—— 1988, *Limited Inc*. Northwestern University Press.

—— 1991, *A Derrida Reader: Between the Blinds*. Wheatsheaf.

Dews, Peter, 1987, *Logics of Disintegration: Post-Structuralist Thought and the Claims of Theory*. Verso.

Docherty, Thomas (ed.), 1993, *Postmodernism: A Reader*. Harvester Wheatsheaf.

Douglas, Jack, 1967, *The Social Meanings of Suicide*. Princeton University Press.

Drew, Paul and Wooton, Anthony (eds), 1988, *Erving Goffman: Exploring the Interaction Order*. Polity Press.

Dreyfus, H. and Rabinow, P., 1993, 'Can there be a science of existential structure and social meaning?', in C. Calhoun, E. LiPuma and M. Postone (eds), *Bourdieu: Critical Perspectives*. Polity Press, pp. 35–44.

Drury, Shadia, 1994, *Alexandre Kojeve, the Roots of Postmodern Politics*. Macmillan.

Durkheim, Emile, 1951, *Suicide*. Routledge.

—— 1961, *Moral Education*, Collier Macmillan.

—— 1966, *The Rules of Sociological Method*. Free Press.

—— 1976, *The Elementary Forms of the Religious Life*. Allen and Unwin.

—— 1984, The Division of Labour in Society. Macmillan.

—— and Mauss, Marcel 1973, *Primitive Classification*. University of Chicago Press.

Eldridge, John, 1972, *Max Weber: The Interpretation of Social Reality*. Nelson.

Elliott, Gregory, 1987, *Althusser: The Detour of Theory*. Verso.

Elster, Jon, 1985, *Making Sense of Marx*. Cambridge University Press.

Evans-Pritchard, E., 1937, *Witchcraft Oracles and Magic Among the Azande*. Oxford University Press.

Fillingham, Lydia Alix, 1993, *Foucault for Beginners*. Writers and Readers.

Foucault, Michel, 1967, *Madness and Civilisation: A History of Insanity in the Age of Reason*. Tavistock.

—— 1970, *The Order of Things: An Archaelogy of the Human Sciences*. Tavistock.

—— 1972, *The Archaeology of Knowledge*. Tavistock.

—— 1973, *The Birth of the Clinic*. Tavistock.

—— 1977, *Discipline and Punish: The Birth of the Prison*. Tavistock.

—— 1979, *The History of Sexuality*. Allen Lane.

—— 1980, *Power/Knowledge, Selected Interviews and Other Writings*. Harvester.

Frank, Manfred, 1989, *What is Neo-Structuralism?* University of Minnesota Press.

Freud, Sigmund, 1971, *Introductory Lectures on Psycho-Analysis*. Penguin.

—— 1986, *The Essentials of Psycho-Analysis*. Penguin.

Gane, Mike, 1991a, *Baudrillard: Critical and Fatal Theory*. Routledge.

—— 1991b, *Baudrillard's Bestiary: Baudrillard and Culture*. Routledge.

Garfinkel, Harold, 1967, *Studies in Ethnomethodology*. Prentice Hall.

Gasché, Rodolphe, 1986, *The Tain of the Mirror: Derrida and the Philosophy of Reflection*. Harvard University Press.

Geertz, Clifford, 1983, *Local Knowledge*. Basic Books.

Gellner, Ernest, 1985, *Relativism and the Social Sciences*. Cambridge University Press.

Gerth, Hans H. and Mills, C.W., 1948, *From Max Weber: Essays in Sociology*. Routledge.

Geuss, Raymond, 1981, *The Idea of a Critical Theory: Habermas and the Frankfurt School*. Cambridge University Press.

Giddens, Anthony, 1976, *New Rules of Sociological Method: A Positive Critique of Interpretivist Sociologies*. Hutchinson.

—— 1978, *Durkheim*. Fontana.

—— 1979, *Central Problems in Social Theory*. Macmillan.

—— 1984, *The Constitution of Society: Outline of the Theory of Structuration*. Polity Press.

—— 1987, *Social Theory and Modern Society*. Polity Press.

—— 1993, *The Giddens Reader* (ed. P. Cassell). Macmillan.

—— and Held, David (eds), *Classes, Power and Conflict: Classical and Contemporary Debates*. Macmillan.

Glaser, Barney and Strauss, Anselm, 1967, *The Discovery of Grounded Theory*. Aldine.

—— 1968, *Time for Dying*. Aldine.

Glucksmann, Miriam, 1974, *Structural Analysis in Contemporary Thought*. Routledge.

Goffman, Erving, 1959, *The Presentation of Self in Everyday Life*. Doubleday.

—— 1968, *Asylums: Essays on the Social Situation of Mental Patients and Other Inmates*. Penguin.

—— 1971, *Relations in Public: Microstudies of the Public Order*. Penguin.

—— 1983, 'The interaction order', *American Sociological Review*, 48: 1–17.

Gouldner, Alvin, 1968, 'The sociologist as partisan: sociology and the welfare state', *American Sociologist*, 3: 103–16.

Gramsci, Antonio, 1971, *Selections from the Prison Notebooks of Antonio Gramsci*. International Publishers.

Grathoff, R. (ed.), 1978, *The Theory of Social Action: The Correspondence of Alfred Schutz and Talcott Parsons*. Indiana University Press.

Gutting, Garry, 1989, *Foucault's Archeology of Scientific Reason*. Cambridge University Press.

Habermas, Jürgen, 1976, *Legitimation Crisis*. Heinemann.

—— 1984, *The Theory of Communicative Action. Vol. 1: Reason and the Rationalisation of Action*. Polity Press.

—— 1986, *The Theory of Communicative Action. Vol. 2: System and Lifeworld: A Critique of Functionalist Reason*. Polity Press.

—— 1988, *On the Logic of the Social Sciences*. Polity Press.

Hamilton, Peter, 1983, *Talcott Parsons*. Tavistock.

—— 1985, *Readings from Talcott Parsons*. Tavistock.

Hammersley, Martin, 1989, *The Dilemma of Qualitative Sociology: Herbert Blumer and the Chicago Tradition*. Routledge.

Harland, Richard, 1987, *Superstructuralism*, Methuen.

Harris, Roy, 1987, *Reading Saussure: A Commentary on the Cours de Linguistique Génerale*, Duckworth.

Hegel, G.W.F., 1967, *The Phenomenology of Mind*. Harper and Row.

—— 1977, *Phenomenology of Spirit*. Oxford University Press.

—— 1991, *Elements of the Philosophy of Right*. Cambridge University Press.

Held, David, 1990, *Introduction to Critical Theory: Horkheimer to Habermas*. Hutchinson.

Heritage, John, 1984, *Garfinkel and Ethnomethodology*. Polity Press.

Hester, Stephen and Eglin, Peter, 1992, *A Sociology of Crime*. Routledge.

Hobbes, Thomas, 1994, *Leviathan*. Dent.

Hollis, Martin and Lukes, Stephen (eds), 1982, *Rationality and Relativism*. Blackwell.

Holmwood, John and Stewart, Alexander, 1991, *Explanation and Social Theory*. Macmillan.

Holton, Robert and Turner, Bryan, 1986, *Talcott Parsons on Economy and Society*. Routledge.

Honneth, A. and Joas, H. (eds), 1991, *Communicative Action*. Polity Press.

Horkheimer, Max and Adorno, Theodor, 1972, *Dialectic of Enlightenment*. Seabury Press.

Hughes, Everett C., 1971, *The Sociological Eye*. Aldine.

Hughes, John. A., Martin, Peter and Sharrock, W.W., 1995, *Understanding Classical Sociology*. Sage.

Husserl, Edmund, 1970, *The Crisis of European Sciences and Transcendental Phenomenology*. Northwestern University Press.

Jameson, Fredric, 1972, *The Prison of Language*. Princeton University Press.

—— 1991, *Postmodernism, or the Cultural Logic of Late Capitalism*. Verso.

Jay, Martin, 1973, *The Dialectical Imagination: A History of the Frankfurt School and the Institute for Social Research, 1923–1950*. Heinemann.

—— 1984a, *Marxism and Totality*. Polity Press.

—— 1984b, *Adorno*. Fontana.

Jencks, Christopher, 1986, *What is Postmodernism?*. Academy Editions.

Jenkins, Alan, 1979, *The Social Theory of Claude Lévi-Strauss*. Macmillan.

Jenkins, Richard, 1992, *Pierre Bourdieu*. Routledge.

Johnson, B.S., 1969, *The Unfortunate*. Panther.

Kellner, Douglas, 1989, *Jean Baudrillard: From Marxism to Postmodernism and Beyond*. Stanford University Press.

Kelly, Michael, 1994, *Critique and Power: Recasting the Foucault/Habermas Debate*. MIT Press.

Kitching, G., 1988, *Karl Marx and the Philosophy of Praxis*. Routledge.

Knorr-Cetina, Karin and Cicourel, Aaron (eds), 1981, *Advances in Social Theory and Methodology: Towards an Integration of Micro- and Macro-Sociologies*. Routledge.

Kolakowski, L., 1981a, *Main Currents in Marxism. Vol. 1: The Founders*. Oxford University Press.

—— 1981b, *Main Currents in Marxism. Vol. 2: The Golden Age*. Oxford University Press.

—— 1981c, *Main Currents in Marxism. Vol. 3: The Breakdown*. Oxford University Press.

Lavers, Annette, 1982, *Roland Barthes: Structuralism and After*. Harvard University Press.

Leach, Edmund, 1974, *Lévi-Strauss*. Fontana.

Lemert, Edwin, 1967, *Human Deviance, Social Problems and Social Control*. Prentice Hall.

Lenin, V.I., 1963, *What is to be Done?*. Oxford University Press.

Letkeman, Peter, 1973, *Crime as Work*. Prentice Hall.

Levin, Charles, 1996, *Jean Baudrillard: A Study in Cultural Metaphysics*. Harvester.

Lévi-Strauss, Claude, 1963, *Structural Anthropology*. Basic Books
—— 1962, *Totemism*. Pelican.
—— 1970, *The Raw and the Cooked*. Cape.
—— 1972, *The Savage Mind*. Weidenfeld and Nicolson.
—— 1973, *From Honey to Ashes*. Cape.
—— 1978a, *The Origin of Table Manners*. Cape.
—— 1978b, *Myth and Meaning*. Schocken Books.
—— 1981, *The Naked Man*. Cape.
—— 1987, *Anthropology and Myth: Lectures, 1951–82*. Blackwell.
—— 1988, *The Jealous Potter*. University of Chicago Press.
—— 1995, *The Story of Lynx,*. University of Chicago Press.
Lichtheim, George, 1970, *Lukács*. Fontana.
Livingston, Eric, 1987, *Making Sense of Ethnomethodology*. Routledge.
Lombardo, Patrizia, 1989, *The Three Paradoxes of Roland Barthes*. University of Georgia
    Press.
Louch, A.R., 1966, *Explanation and Human Action*. Blackwell.
Luckmann, Thomas (ed.), 1978, *Phenomenology and Sociology*. Penguin.
Lukács, Georg, 1971, *History and Class Consciousness*. Merlin Press.
Lukes, Stephen, 1975, *Emile Durkheim: His Life and Work*. Penguin.
—— 1982, 'Relativism in its place', in S. Lukes and M. Hollis (eds), *Rationality and
    Relativism*. Blackwell, pp. 261–305.
Lynch, Michael, 1985, *Art and Artefact in Laboratory Science*. Routledge.
—— 1994, *Scientific Practice and Ordinary Action: Ethnomethodology and Social Studies of
    Science*. Cambridge University Press.
Lyotard, Jean-François, 1984, *The Postmodern Condition: A Report on Knowledge*.
    Manchester University Press.
—— 1992, *The Postmodern Explained to Children*. Turnaround Books.
McCarthy, Thomas A., 1978, *The Critical Theory of Jürgen Habermas*. MIT Press.
McCarthy, Timothy, 1978, *Marx and the Proletariat*. Greenwood Press.
McHoul, Alec and Grace, Wendy, 1993, *A Foucault Primer*. Melbourne University
    Press.
McIntyre, Alistair, 1970, *Marcuse*. Fontana.
McLellan, David (ed.), 1977, *Karl Marx: Selected Writings*. Oxford University Press.
McNay, Lois, 1994, *Foucault: A Critical Introduction*. Polity Press.
Macey, David, 1989, *The Lives of Michel Foucault*. Hutchinson.
Manning, Philip, 1992, *Erving Goffman and Modern Sociology*. Polity Press.
Marcuse, Herbert, 1955, *Reason and Revolution*, 2nd edn. Routledge.
—— 1964, *One Dimensional Man*. Routledge.
—— 1968, *Negations*. Allen Lane.
Marshall, Gordon, 1982, *In Search of the Spirit of Capitalism*. Hutchinson.
Marx, Karl, 1955, *The Poverty of Philosophy*. Progress Publishers.
—— 1959, *Economic and Philosophical Manuscripts of 1844*. Progress Publishers.
—— 1970, *A Critique of Hegel's Philosophy of Right* (ed. J. O'Malley). Cambridge
    University Press.
—— 1973, *Grundrisse: Foundations of a Critique of Political Economy*. Penguin.
—— 1976, *Capital: A Critique of Political Economy. Vol. 1*. Penguin.

Marx, K. and Engels, F., 1959, *Basic Writings on Politics and Philosophy* (ed. L. Feuer). Doubleday Anchor.
—— 1967, *The Communist Manifesto*. Penguin.
—— 1977, *The German Ideology*. Lawrence and Wishart.
May, Tim, 1996, *Situating Social Theory*. Open University Press.
May, Todd, 1994, *The Political Philosophy of Poststructuralist Anarchism*. Pennsylvania State University Press.
Mead, George Herbert, 1934, *Mind, Self and Society*. University of Chicago Press.
Megill, Alan, 1985, *Prophets of Extremity*. University of California Press.
Merquior, J.G., 1986, *Western Marxism*. Paladin.
—— 1991, *Michel Foucault*. 2nd edn. Fontana.
Merton, Robert, 1957, 'Social structure and anomie', in R. Merton, *Social Theory and Social Structure*. Free Press, pp. 131–60.
Miller, David L., 1973, *George Herbert Mead: Self, Language and the World*. University of Chicago Press.
Morrison, Ken, 1995, *Marx, Durkheim, Weber: Formations of Modern Social Thought*. Sage.
Mouzelis, Nicos P., 1990, *Back to Sociological Theory*. Macmillan.
—— 1995, *Sociological Theory: What Went Wrong*. Routledge.
Nietzsche, Friedrich, 1967, *The Birth of Tragedy*. Random House.
—— 1968, *The Will to Power*. Random House.
Norris, Christopher, 1983, *The Deconstructive Turn: Essays in the Rhetoric of Philosophy*. Methuen.
—— 1987, *Derrida*. Fontana.
—— 1990, *What's Wrong With Postmodernism?*. Harvester Wheatsheaf.
—— (ed.), 1991, *Deconstruction: Theory and Practice*. Routledge.
—— 1992, *Uncritical Theory: Postmodernism, Intellectuals and the Gulf War*. Lawrence and Wishart.
—— 1996, *Reclaiming Truth: Contributions to a Critique of Cultural Relativism*. Lawrence and Wishart.
Pace, David, 1983, *Claude Lévi-Strauss: Bearer of Ashes*. Routledge.
Paglia, Camille, 1993 *Sex, Art and American Culture*. Viking.
Parkin, Frank, 1982, *Max Weber*. Tavistock.
Parkinson, G.H.R. (ed.), 1970, *Georg Lukács: The Man, his Work and his Ideas*. Random House/Vintage Books.
Parsons, Talcott, 1937, *The Structure of Social Action*. McGraw-Hill.
—— 1940, 'An analytical approach to the theory of social stratification', *American Journal of Sociology*, 45: 841–62.
—— 1951, *The Social System*. Free Press.
—— 1953, 'A revised analytical approach to the theory of social stratification', in R. Bendix and S. Lipset (eds), *Class Status and Power*. Free Press, pp. 92–129.
—— 1966, *Societies: Evolutionary and Comparative Perspectives*. Prentice Hall.
—— 1969, *Political and Social Structure*. Collier Macmillan.
—— 1971, *The System of Modern Societies*. Prentice Hall.
—— 1978, *Action Theory and the Human Condition*. Free Press.
—— and Shils, Edward (eds), 1951, *Toward a General Theory of Action*. Harvard University Press.

——, Bales, Robert and Shils, Edward, 1953, *Working Papers in the Theory of Action*. Free Press.

Payne, Michael, 1994, *Reading Theory*. Routledge.

Pefanis, Julian, 1991, *Heterology and the Postmodern: Bataille, Baudrillard and Lyotard*. Duke University Press.

Plummer, Ken (ed.), 1991a, *Symbolic Interactionism. Vol. 1: Foundations and History*. Edward Elgar.

—— 1991b, *Symbolic Interactionism. Vol. 2: Contemporary Issues*. Edward Elgar.

Poetzl, Pamela Major, 1983, *Michel Foucault's Archeology of Western Reason*. Harvester.

Rabinow, Paul (ed.), 1986, *The Foucault Reader*. Penguin.

—— and Dreyfus, Hubert, 1983, *Michel Foucault: Beyond Structuralism and Hermeneutics*. Harvester.

Rasmussen, David M., 1990, *Reading Habermas*. Blackwell.

Rock, Paul, 1979, *The Making of Symbolic Interactionism*. Macmillan.

Roderick, Rick, 1986, *Habermas and the Foundations of Critical Theory*. Macmillan.

Sacks, Harvey, 1992, *Lectures on Conversation*. 2 vols. Blackwell.

Saussure, Ferdinand de, 1983, *Course in General Linguistics*. Duckworth.

Savage, Stephen, 1981, *The Theories of Talcott Parsons: The Social Relations of Action*. Macmillan.

Schrift, Alan D., 1990, *Nietzsche and the Question of Interpretation: Between Hermeneutics and Deconstruction*. Routledge.

Schutz, Alfred, 1962, *Collected Papers. Vol. 1: The Problem of Social Reality*. Martinus Nijhoff.

—— 1964, *Collected Papers. Vol. 2: Studies in Social Theory*. Martinus Nijhoff.

—— 1966, *Collected Papers. Vol. 3: Studies in Phenomenological Philosophy*. Martinus Nijhoff.

—— 1970, *On Phenomenology and Social Relations: Selected Writings*. (ed. H. Wagner). University of Chicago Press.

—— 1972, *The Phenomenology of the Social World*. Heinemann.

—— and Luckmann, Thomas, 1973, *The Structures of the Life-World*. Northwestern University Press.

Seidman, Steven and Wagner, David (eds), 1992, *Postmodernism and Social Theory: The Debate Over General Theory*. Blackwell.

Sharrock, Wes and Anderson, Robert, 1986, *The Ethnomethodologists*. Tavistock.

Sheridan, Alan, 1990, *The Will to Truth*. Routledge.

Shils, Edward, 1978, 'Centre and periphery', reprinted in P. Worsley (ed.), *Modern Sociology*. Penguin, pp. 566–78.

Sica, Alan, 1991, 'The California–Massachusetts strain in structuration theory', in C. Bryant and D. Jary (eds), *Giddens' Theory of Structuration: A Critical Appreciation*. Routledge, pp. 32–51.

Singer, Peter, 1980, *Marx*. Oxford University Press.

—— 1983, *Hegel*. Oxford University Press.

Skinner, Quentin (ed.), 1985, *The Return of Grand Theory in the Human Sciences*. Cambridge University Press.

Skolnick, Jerome H., 1966, *Justice Without Trial*. John Wiley.

Smart, Barry, 1988, *Michel Foucault*. Routledge.

Smelser, Neil J., 1959, *Social Change in the Industrial Revolution*. Routledge.

—— 1962, *Theory of Collective Behaviour*. Routledge.

Smith, Steven, 1984, *Reading Althusser*. Cornell University Press.

Stern, J.P., 1978, *Nietzsche*. Fontana.

Strauss, Anselm, Schatzman, Leonard, Bucher, Rue, Ehrlich, Danuta and Sabskin, Melvin, 1964, *Psychiatric Institutions and Ideologies*. Free Press.

Sutherland, Edwin, 1961, *The Professional Thief*. Holt, Rinehart, Winston.

Tallis, Raymond, 1988, *In Defence of Realism*. Edward Arnold.

—— 1995, *Not Saussure: A Critique of Post-Saussurean Literary Theory*. Macmillan.

Taylor, C., 1979, *Hegel and Modern Society*. Cambridge University Press.

—— 1989, *Sources of the Self*. Cambridge University Press.

Thomas, Keith, 1973, *Religion and the Decline of Magic*. Penguin.

Thompson, E.P., 1968, *The Making of the English Working Class*. Penguin.

Thompson, John B., 1981, *Critical Hermeneutics*. Cambridge University Press.

—— and Held, David, 1982, *Habermas: Critical Debates*, Macmillan.

Thrift, Nigel, 1985, 'Bear and mouse or bear and tree: Anthony Giddens' reconstruction of social theory', *Sociology*, 19: 609–23.

Touraine, Alain, 1995, *Critique of Modernity*. Blackwell.

Turner, Jonathan H. and Maryanski, Alexandra, 1979, *Functionalism*. Benjamin/Cummings.

Turner, Roy (ed.), 1974, *Ethnomethodology*. Penguin.

Wagner, Helmut, 1983, *Alfred Schutz: An Intellectual Biography*. University of Chicago Press.

Weber, Max, 1923, *General Economic History*. Allen and Unwin.

—— 1947, *The Theory of Social and Economic Organisation*. Free Press.

—— 1949, *The Methodology of the Social Sciences*. Free Press.

—— 1965, *The Sociology of Religion*. Methuen.

—— 1978, *Economy and Society*. University of California Press.

—— 1985, *The Protestant Ethic and the Spirit of Capitalism*. Unwin.

White, Stephen, 1989, *The Recent Work of Jürgen Habermas: Reason, Justice and Modernity*. Cambridge University Press.

Willis, Paul, 1977, *Learning to Labour*. Saxon House.

Winch, Peter, 1964, 'Understanding a primitive society', reprinted in B. Wilson (ed.), 1970, *Rationality*. Blackwell, pp. 307–24.

—— 1990, *The Idea of a Social Science*. 2nd edn. Routledge.

Wollheim, Richard, 1991, *Freud*. 2nd edn. Fontana.

Wolpert, Lewis, 1992, *The Unnatural Nature of Science*. Faber.

Worsley, Peter (ed.), 1970, *Modern Sociology: Introductory Readings*. Penguin.

Name index

Subject index